FEMINIST INTERPRETATIONS OF EMMA GOLDMAN

NANCY TUANA, GENERAL EDITOR

This series consists of edited collections of essays, some original and some previously published, offering feminist re-interpretations of the writings of major figures in the Western philosophical tradition. Devoted to the work of a single philosopher, each volume contains essays covering the full range of the philosopher's thought and representing the diversity of approaches now being used by feminist critics.

Already published:

Nancy Tuana, ed., *Feminist Interpretations of Plato* (1994)

Margaret Simons, ed., *Feminist Interpretations of Simone de Beauvoir* (1995)

Bonnie Honig, ed., *Feminist Interpretations of Hannah Arendt* (1995)

Patricia Jagentowicz Mills, ed., *Feminist Interpretations of G. W. F. Hegel* (1996)

Maria J. Falco, ed., *Feminist Interpretations of Mary Wollstonecraft* (1996)

Susan J. Hekman, ed., *Feminist Interpretations of Michel Foucault* (1996)

Nancy J. Holland, ed., *Feminist Interpretations of Jacques Derrida* (1997)

Robin May Schott, ed., *Feminist Interpretations of Immanuel Kant* (1997)

Celeine Leon and Sylvia Walsh, eds., *Feminist Interpretations of Søren Kierkegaard* (1997)

Cynthia Freeland, ed., *Feminist Interpretations of Aristotle* (1998)

Kelly Oliver and Marilyn Pearsall, eds., *Feminist Interpretations of Friedrich Nietzsche* (1998)

Mimi Reisel Gladstein and Chris Matthew Sciabarra, eds., *Feminist Interpretations of Ayn Rand* (1999)

Susan Bordo, ed., *Feminist Interpretations of René Descartes* (1999)

Julien S. Murphy, ed., *Feminist Interpretations of Jean-Paul Sartre* (1999)

Anne Jaap Jacobson, ed., *Feminist Interpretations of David Hume* (2000)

Sarah Lucia Hoagland and Marilyn Frye, eds., *Feminist Interpretations of Mary Daly* (2000)

Tina Chanter, ed., *Feminist Interpretations of Emmanuel Levinas* (2001)

Nancy J. Holland and Patricia Huntington, eds., *Feminist Interpretations of Martin Heidegger* (2001)

Charlene Haddock Seigfried, ed., *Feminist Interpretations of John Dewey* (2001)

Naomi Scheman and Peg O'Connor, eds., *Feminist Interpretations of Ludwig Wittgenstein* (2002)

Lynda Lange, ed., *Feminist Interpretations of Jean-Jacques Rousseau* (2002)

Lorraine Code, ed., *Feminist Interpretations of Hans-Georg Gadamer* (2002)

Lynn Hankinson Nelson and Jack Nelson, eds., *Feminist Interpretations of W. V. Quine* (2003)

Maria J. Falco, ed., *Feminist Interpretations of Niccolò Machiavelli* (2004)

Renée J. Heberle, ed., *Feminist Interpretations of Theodor Adorno* (2006)

Dorothea Olkowski and Gail Weiss, eds., *Feminist Interpretations of Maurice Merleau-Ponty* (2006)

Nancy J. Hirschmann and Kirstie M. McClure, eds., *Feminist Interpretations of John Locke* (2006)

FEMINIST INTERPRETATIONS OF EMMA GOLDMAN

EDITED BY
PENNY A. WEISS
AND
LORETTA KENSINGER

THE PENNSYLVANIA STATE UNIVERSITY PRESS
UNIVERSITY PARK, PENNSYLVANIA

Library of Congress Cataloging-in-Publication Data

Feminist interpretations of Emma Goldman /
edited by Penny A. Weiss and Loretta Kensinger.
    p.   cm.—(Re-reading the canon)
Includes bibliographical references and index.
ISBN 978-0-271-02975-7 (cloth : alk. paper)
ISBN 978-0-271-02976-4 (pbk. : alk. paper)
1. Goldman, Emma, 1869–1940.
2. Anarchists—United States—Biography.
3. Anarchism.
4. Feminist theory.
I. Weiss, Penny A.
II. Kensinger, Loretta.

HX843.7.G65F56   2007
335′.83092—dc22
2007000235

Dedicated to continuing
Emma Goldman's efforts for a more
just and joyful world

Contents

Preface

Nancy Tuana

Take into your hands any history of philosophy text. You will find compiled therein the "classics" of modern philosophy. Since these texts are often designed for use in undergraduate classes, the editor is likely to offer an introduction in which the reader is informed that these selections represent the perennial questions of philosophy. The student is to assume that she or he is about to explore the timeless wisdom of the greatest minds of Western philosophy. No one calls attention to the fact that the philosophers are all men.

Though women are omitted from the canons of philosophy, these texts inscribe the nature of woman. Sometimes the philosopher speaks directly about woman, delineating her proper role, her abilities and inabilities, her desires. Other times the message is indirect—a passing remark hinting at women's emotionality, irrationality, unreliability.

This process of definition occurs in far more subtle ways when the central concepts of philosophy—reason and justice, those characteristics that are taken to define us as human—are associated with traits historically identified with masculinity. If the "man" of reason must learn to control or overcome traits identified as feminine—the body, the emotions, the passions—then the realm of rationality will be one reserved primarily for men,[1] with grudging entrance to those few women who are capable of transcending their femininity.

Feminist philosophers have begun to look critically at the canonized texts of philosophy and have concluded that the discourses of philosophy are not gender-neutral. Philosophical narratives do not offer a universal perspective, but rather privilege some experiences and beliefs over others. These experiences and beliefs permeate all philosophical theories whether they be aesthetic or epistemological, moral or metaphysical. Yet this fact has often been neglected by those studying the traditions of philosophy. Given the history of canon formation in Western philosophy, the perspective most likely to be privileged is that of upper-class white males. Thus, to be fully aware of the impact of gender biases, it is imperative that we re-read the canon with attention to the ways in which philosophers' assumptions concerning gender are embedded within their theories.

This new series, *Re-Reading the Canon*, is designed to foster this process of reevaluation. Each volume will offer feminist analyses of the theories of a selected philosopher. Since feminist philosophy is not monolithic in method or content, the essays are also selected to illustrate the variety of perspectives within feminist criticism and highlight some of the controversies within feminist scholarship.

In this series, feminist lenses will be focused on the canonical texts of Western philosophy, both those authors who have been part of the traditional canon, and those philosophers whose writings have more recently gained attention within the philosophical community. A glance at the list of volumes in the series will reveal an immediate gender bias of the canon: Arendt, Aristotle, Beauvoir, Derrida, Descartes, Foucault, Hegel, Hume, Kant, Locke, Marx, Mill, Nietzsche, Plato, Rousseau, Wittgenstein, Wollstonecraft. There are all too few women included, and those few who do appear have been added only recently. In creating this series, it is not my intention to rectify the current canon of philosophical thought. What is and is not included within the canon during a particular historical period is a result of many factors. Although no canonization of texts will include all philosophers, no canonization of texts that excludes all but a few women can offer an accurate representation of the history of the discipline, as women have been philosophers since the ancient period.[2]

I share with many feminist philosophers and other philosophers writing from the margins of philosophy the concern that the current canonization of philosophy be transformed. Although I do not accept the position that the current canon has been formed exclusively by power relations, I do believe that this canon represents only a selective history of the tradition. I share the view of Michael Bérubé that "canons are at once the location, the index, and the record of the struggle for cultural representation; like any other hegemonic formation, they must be continually reproduced anew and are continually contested."[3]

The process of canon transformation will require the recovery of "lost" texts and a careful examination of the reasons such voices have been silenced. Along with the process of uncovering women's philosophical history, we must also begin to analyze the impact of gender ideologies upon the process of canonization. This process of recovery and examination must occur in conjunction with careful attention to the concept of a canon of authorized texts. Are we to dispense with the notion of a tradition of excellence embodied in a canon of authorized texts? Or, rather than abandon the whole idea of a canon, do we instead encourage a reconstruction of a canon of those texts that inform a common culture?

This series is designed to contribute to this process of canon transformation by offering a re-reading of the current philosophical canon. Such a re-reading shifts our attention to the ways in which woman and the role of the feminine are constructed within the texts of philosophy. A question we must keep in front of us during this process of re-reading is whether a philosopher's socially inherited prejudices concerning woman's nature and role are independent of her or his larger philosophical framework. In asking this question attention must be paid to the ways in which the definitions of central philosophical concepts implicitly include or exclude gendered traits.

This type of reading strategy is not limited to the canon, but can be applied to all texts. It is my desire that this series reveal the importance of this type of critical reading. Paying attention to the workings of gender within the texts of philosophy will make visible the complexities of the inscription of gender ideologies.

Notes

1. More properly, it is a realm reserved for a group of privileged males, since the texts also inscribe race and class biases that thereby omit certain males from participation.

2. Mary Ellen Waithe's multivolume series, *A History of Women Philosophers* (Boston: M. Nijoff, 1987), attests to this presence of women.

3. Michael Bérubé, *Marginal Forces/Cultural Centers: Tolson, Pynchon, and the Politics of the Canon* (Ithaca: Cornell University Press, 1992), 4–5.

Acknowledgments

Loretta's:

My path to this volume began nearly two decades ago in my first feminist theory course, taught by Dr. Penny Weiss. I immediately fell in love with feminist theory and also became fascinated with Emma Goldman's ideas. We read Goldman's "Love and Marriage" in this course and I was amazed at the clear separation of the two issues named in the title that were drawn in this work. Who would have guessed that so many years later Penny and I would still be discussing feminism, revolution, and Emma Goldman? I thank first and foremost Penny for her incredible inspiration as a teacher, for her insights as a friend, and for the pleasure of joining her on this journey.

The effort in time, energy, and scholarship that was spent in creating this volume is a tribute to Goldman's power to continue to inspire and organize people. Early stages of thought were nourished by feedback from participants at panels held during the National Women's Studies Association annual conference in June 2002 and the American Political Science Association preconference special session "Women and Politics" in August 2001. The staff at the Emma Goldman Papers Project was incredibly helpful at key moments and provided vital resources to my work and this volume. Our fabulous contributors, the wonderful staff at the Pennsylvania State University Press—particularly Series Editor Nancy Tuana; Director Sanford G. Thatcher; copyeditor Romaine Perin; and our fine critical peer reviewer, Claudia Card (Emma Goldman Professor of Philosophy!)—made arriving at this destination a worthy adventure. There is both irony and justice in all their conviction that there is a canon on Goldman's thought to re-read.

In 1909–10 Fresno was the site of one of the International Workers of the World's free-speech fights; this place I'm proud to call home remains a place where many daily carry on the struggle for speech, for liberty, and for justice. I am grateful to many in Fresno for nourishing my mind and spirit as I worked on this volume. I am indebted to my colleagues and students in the women's studies program at California State University, Fresno. Their continued dedication to building a vibrant academic community welcoming of all its diversity gives my love of feminism daily invigoration and renewal. Along the way Lynn Jacobsson lent me her kitchen table and ear, Jill Fields her encouragement and editorial eye, and Meta Schettler her love of the writing craft; each in her own way encouraged my commitment to this work. A sabbatical and two Affirmative Action Faculty Development Program Awards granted by California State University, Fresno, allowed me time and travel funds to develop early drafts or research, provided aid in editorial tasks, and enabled me to present work at conferences. Finally, my writing and life have been enriched by those intrepid heroines in Wonder Women Writers. My heart and this work are full of the courage of creativity caught by the magic lasso of loving support provided by Mary Coomes and Theresia Rogerson.

My life owes so much to the unsung heroes of history—all those who have dared to stand up, speak out, and dream of a world where liberty nurtures creativity and feeds human community. In these too-dark hours of this already bloody new century, this volume stands firmly in honor of Goldman and the hundreds of millions of unnamed masses who remain committed to the possibility that "out of the chaos the future emerges in harmony and beauty."

Penny's:

Odd how these things work out. I taught the class that Loretta mentioned in my first year out of graduate school, and was I nervous. Given my own training, or lack thereof, many readings on the syllabus were new to me as well as the students. I remember well Loretta's exuberance reading Goldman. I asked her later what it was that captivated her so—I didn't want to miss it!

Part of the power of Goldman's writings is their ability to move very dissimilar readers in quite different ways. I have used her work in the classroom repeatedly, and am always eager to see students' varying responses, which include anger and excitement, activism and continued study, skepticism and understanding. Whatever their reaction, it is clear from their feedback that it is rare for them to feel more challenged by anything else we read all semester. I find that remarkable testimony.

I love Goldman. Every time I read her I am clearer about her ideas and about my own. I am always moved (to reexamine my daily practices) by the integrity of her life, inspired (to get off my butt) by the political risks she took, tested (to confront her ideas head on) by the intellectual arguments she put forth, and challenged by her honesty as a writer (to also be forthright).

I thank my kids, all teenagers now (though not for long), who have thrived in the many forms of anarchy that always embrace our lives. Years of conversing with them about their ideas, questions, complaints, and reports, as well as about mine, informs my work and touches my soul in ways impossible to trace. Linden, Brennin, and Avian, you are my heart.

Thanks are due to special friends who sustain me: Mary Ann, Pat, and Stephanie. I cherish the ease of our connections, the trust in our conversations. Berenice and Loretta are inspirations. As with Goldman, I find in them extraordinary integrity. Nancy Tuana, thanks for saying "Yes!" the first time I suggested this volume; and Sandy Thatcher, thanks for backing this remarkable series.

I thank Bob, who supports me in so many ways. He will get some extra time for his own work in appreciation for making it easier to find space for this project. He has long been a good sport about living with my anarchy. I dedicate this book to him.

Credits

Special thanks are owed to the following authors, editors, and publishers for reprints found in this volume: Candace Falk and the Emma Goldman Papers for providing the photo of Goldman's grave site, taken by the late Merlin Bowen; Heather M. Wagner, Archivist, and the Hoover Institution on War, Revolution and Peace at Stanford University for the copy of the photograph of Emma Goldman found in their American Pictorial Collection; Jason Wehling, for the reprint of "Anarchy in Interpretation: The Life of Emma" from Goldman.dwardmac.pitzer.edu/Anarchist_Archives/goldman/emmabio.html; Sage Publications for permission to reprint Lori Jo Marso's "A Feminist Search for Love: Emma Goldman on the Politics of Marriage, Love, Sexuality, and the Feminine," originally published in 2003 in *Feminist Theory* 4 (3): 305–20; Texas A&M University Press, for permission to reprint Lynne Adrian's "Emma Goldman and the Spirit of Artful Living: Philosophy and Politics in the Classical American Period," originally published in *Frontiers in American Philosophy*, vol. 1, edited by R. W. Burch and Herman J. Sattkamp; Feminist Studies, Incorporated, for permission to reprint Alice Wexler's "Emma Goldman on Wollstonecraft," originally published in *Feminist Studies* 7 (1): 113–33; *Socialist Review* for permission to reprint Alix Kates Shulman's "Dancing in the Revolution: Emma Goldman's Feminism," 10 (March–April 1982): 31–44; The Feminist Press for the permission to reprint Martha A. Ackelsberg and Kathryn Pyne Addelson's "Anarchist Alternatives to Competition," originally published in *Competition: A Feminist Taboo?* in 1987; Black Rose Books (www.web.net/blackrosebooks) for permission to reprint Marsha Hewitt's "Emma Goldman: The Case for Anarcho-Feminism," from *The Anarchist Papers*, edited by Dimitrios I. Roussopoulos; and finally, Karen Kubby, Director of the amazing Emma Goldman Clinic, for permission to use pages from the Clinic's Web site, at http://www.emmagoldman.com.

Introductory Essays

Digging for Gold(man)

What We Found

Penny A. Weiss and Loretta Kensinger
(with Berenice A. Carroll)

"We know relatively little about the meaning, sources, impact, tensions, development over time, applicability, interconnections, and significance of her thought. This strikes us as a rather astonishing phenomenon, and a fate that Goldman, in all her richness, does not deserve."

In this essay we explain the origin of this book by exploring the gap between our readings of Goldman and the treatment of her in secondary literature. We also document how this underestimation of Goldman is part of a pattern in which the work of women thinkers is typically misread, dismissed, and marginalized. Finally, we explain how the chapters in this book begin to rectify the situation.—*The Editors*

Pick up the essays that have been published on Emma Goldman (1869–1940), and several things will strike you: first, that they are so very few in number; second, that the majority are largely biographical; third, that almost none take seriously her contributions to political theory and feminist theory or attempt to synthesize her thought; and finally, that the handful of essays that are not biographical exist in isolation even from one another, leaving an absence of real debate in the secondary literature on the interpretation of her ideas. Within popular movements Goldman's ideas are most often reduced to slogans, buttons, and bumper stickers. Even then, one of the most popular phrases attributed to Goldman—"If I can't dance I don't want to be part of your revolution"—is not actually a direct quote but an "extrapolation from text to familiar paraphrase" (Shulman 1991, 2). Consequently, we know relatively little about the

The editors thank Berenice Carroll for her insights and contribution of the following several pages, situating Goldman in the historical pattern of dismissing women thinkers. See further Carroll 1990, esp. 140–45.

meaning, sources, impact, tensions, development over time, applicability, interconnections, and significance of her thought. This strikes us as a rather astonishing phenomenon, and a fate that Goldman, in all her richness, does not deserve. Neglect and depreciation of women's work is of course common in most fields of endeavor, but it has been particularly egregious in political and social philosophy and theory.

It is important to recognize that many of the judgments that are expressed concerning Goldman's work are actually of a rote character, sometimes even identical in wording with the judgments rendered on many other women theorists. For example, among the various techniques of depreciation and dismissal of the work of women as intellectuals and scholars is the denial of its "originality." Thus, Daniel Levine, in *Jane Addams and the Liberal Tradition*, declared: "Jane Addams was not an original thinker of major importance. One can find predecessors for almost every one of her ideas. . . . Her importance was not as a manufacturer of ideas, but as their retailer" (1971, xviii). The judgments of scholars on Goldman's intellectual contributions are consistent with this general pattern.

Richard Drinnon, in his 1961 biography of Goldman, *Rebel in Paradise*, perhaps set the tone for the crowd of depreciators, dismissing Goldman as "by no means a seminal social or political thinker" (314). It was, however, Martha Solomon, in her 1987 study of Goldman, who provided the definitive statement of Goldman's alleged lack of intellectual originality. Although she remarked that since Goldman "does not claim to be an innovative theorist, it is superfluous to charge her with a lack of originality" (59), Solomon nonetheless did so, in these familiar terms: "She was not, however, an original theorist. . . . Goldman's works primarily synthesize and adapt the views of other, more original thinkers, as her frequent references to Proudhon, Bakunin, Stirner, and Kropotkin reveal. Her greatest achievements were as an interpreter and as a propagandist of anarchism" (38). The recurrence of such judgments has so tainted the assessment of Goldman's work that it is necessary to address them.

It is certainly true that Goldman's ideas were influenced by many other theorists; in fact, contributors to this collection explore such connections with renewed interest and greater breadth. But the fact that one can "find predecessors for almost every one of [Emma Goldman's] ideas" (in the phrase applied previously to Jane Addams) is irrelevant to whether she was "an original thinker of major importance," unless indeed there are no "original thinkers," since there are none for whom one could not make the same statement.

In his classic study *The Great Chain of Being*, Arthur O. Lovejoy wrote: "Most philosophic systems are original or distinctive rather in their patterns than in their components. . . . The seeming novelty of many a system is due solely to the novelty of the application or arrangement of the old elements which enter into it" (1936, 3–4). Similarly, Pitirim Sorokin argued, concerning the sociological theories of Karl Marx and Friedrich Engels: "The facts are that practically all the sociological ideas of Marx in an identical or even a more accurate form were published by other authors either before or simultaneously with the publication of his *Communist Manifesto* [and other works]" (1956, 521). Sorokin cited a long history of predecessors, extending back to ancient times, in particular for the economic or materialist interpretation of history (521–22). Those familiar with the work of women as social theorists might add to Sorokin's all-male list a number of women whose ideas anticipated or influenced Marx, including Germaine de Staël (on the sociology of knowledge), Mary Wollstonecraft (on the class character of English ideas of "liberty"), and Flora Tristan (on class struggle, working-class solidarity, and an international worker's union—later narrowed by Marx to an International Workingmen's Association).

Richard Drinnon, in his introduction to Goldman's widely published *Anarchism and Other Essays*, acknowledges that Goldman "had a theory, one with imaginative possibilities that still remain to be explored," yet he still somehow concludes that "she was not a theoretician" (Goldman 1969, xiii). Alice Wexler, in *Emma Goldman in Exile*, claims that "from the start, [Goldman] was an unorthodox figure," yet Wexler oddly concludes that "she was never an original thinker" (1989, 10–11). Oz Frankel, in his extensive review of the reception of Goldman's life and work over several decades, credits her with having written "what was probably the first damning account" of the Bolshevik regime in Russia, but he devotes only one sentence (in a forty-page article) to *My Disillusionment in Russia*, with no mention of its theoretical content (Frankel 1996, 906). Upon close examination, terms such as *original, innovative, creative, derivative*, and so forth are found to be as slippery and insubstantial as are the more generalized stamps of approval such as *excellent, brilliant, superior*, or *first rate*. All are essentially barren of substantive meaning and are used with a political rather than an intellectual purpose.

There are encouraging and exciting indications of rapidly growing and

broader interest in Emma Goldman. Her writings and speeches have become increasingly available for popular and scholarly consumption in
edited volumes and on Web sites. In 2001 Peter Glassgold's edited volume
Anarchy! was published, bringing together a collection drawn from the
"over 5,000 pages of printed materials" in Goldman's monthly magazine
Mother Earth (xi). The Emma Goldman Papers Project has published two
of the proposed four volumes of *Emma Goldman: The American Years, a
Documentary Edition,* an astonishing accomplishment and resource.
Academic panels have been organized on her work, including two at
American Political Science Association meetings (2001 and 2002), and
another at the National Women's Studies Association conference
(2002). International interest was seen in the Emma Goldman Collo-
quium, organized jointly by the Universities of Berkeley and of Paris,
which regrettably was canceled in the aftermath of the September 11
crisis. Two books, one as a whole and one in part have finally begun to
deal with Goldman's ideas rather than her life (Haaland 1993; Brown
2003). At least one other book is in the pipeline (Ferguson), and at least
one dissertation focusing largely on Goldman's political philosophy has
recently been completed (Day 2004), the authors of which we are pleased
to include in this volume. What an especially auspicious time to produce
an anthology on Goldman, both collecting published essays that focus on
her social and political thought and adding to them with as much previously unpublished work, creating a compilation that can serve as a tool
for future scholars.

There is an obvious saliency of the issues about which Goldman wrote
and spoke to recent feminist scholarship, to contemporary politics, and
to the history of political theory. The essays in this volume and elsewhere
reveal that this saliency is both personal and global. On a personal level,
many of us learned from Goldman as we, like Goldman herself, discovered feminism, labored against internal tyrants, and worked for social
change in hostile times. Globally, issues central to Goldman's work continue to be at the center of political debate: patriotism and political violence, birth control and governmental control, artistic expression and
freedom of speech, personal relationships and revolution, corporate greed
and global imperialism, rights and liberation. In this volume we move
away from Goldman's life, so well documented in her autobiography as
well as in the numerous biographies of her, and look instead at her contributions to social and political theory. Bringing together for the first time
the writing that takes as its focus Goldman's political ideas, this volume

will hopefully build with others that follow to reach the point where her ideas are at least as well known as her life story.

After the introductory essays, the book is divided into three sections: "Specific Themes and Central Concerns," "Historical Roots and Current Connections," and "Political Change: Theory and Practice." The sections are described below by numerous threads that run through the essays they contain; brief individualized introductions are located in the text before each piece. The sections are linked into a coherent whole through their contributions to the same goal: a fuller understanding and appreciation of the ideas of Emma Goldman.

Goldman's place in political history has certainly received some recognition. She not only has been dubbed "one of the most radical feminists of her era" (see Shulman, reprinted in this volume) and cited as "a leading figure in the international anarchist movement between 1889 and 1940" (see Wexler, reprinted in this volume) but also has even been referred to as someone who "has become an almost mythical figure, the archetypal woman activist" (Glassgold 2001, xi). Most unfortunately, however, Goldman's recognition as an activist has eclipsed any attention to her as a theorist; and turning her into a mythical figure, an icon, involves a process of "heroification" that tends to sanitize, decontextualize, and deradicalize her (Loewen 1995; Frankel 1996).

Specific Themes and Central Concerns

To write about one specific idea in a political theorist's work is to make several assumptions: most especially, that the author speaks to core ideas in political philosophy worthy of attention and that his or her work is an integrated enough whole that one topic can be traced throughout it. To make such assumptions about Emma Goldman is somewhat novel, given the popular claim that she placed little importance on theory. Yet each essay in this section successfully draws from a wide range of Goldman's writing as it tracks, synthesizes, and frames what she says on a single theme. These are thoughtful explorations of Goldman's political theory, and they pay off wonderfully.

The Emma Goldman that emerges from these essays is, first, a more theoretically unified one. In her study of individuality in Goldman's thought, Janet Day writes, "Understanding Goldman's anarchist theory from the standpoint of her conception of the ideal state of being lends coherence to her specific prescriptions for social and economic relations and unifies her ideas." Penny Weiss demonstrates that Goldman "uses the same principles to reveal and to judge what children do and what is done to children as she uses with adults." Lori Marso is able to see the continuities between Goldman's ideas about love and the loves in her life and "the interactions of her thought with the social and political climate in which she lived."

In addition, the authors of these thematic essays rediscover in Goldman an intellectual rigor that is integral to the spirit and method of her anarchism. In her study of religion and spirituality, Kathy Ferguson shows that in addition to the "closed-ended rhetorical practices" (including "irritating absolutes") found in Goldman's writings, "there is her consistent plea for open-endedness, for mobility in identities and ideas, . . . active doubting and rethinking, her refusal to ignore or dismiss that which did not fit." Berenice Carroll demonstrates that Goldman's "intention . . . was not only to provide an analysis of what the Bolsheviks had done wrong, but even more, to rethink the conception of 'the Revolution' that she, Berkman, and others had accepted until then, and to attempt a new, comprehensive, and constructive vision of how a revolution should be made." Candace Falk traces a complex and rich commitment to a vision of free speech embedded in American history and ideals. Once Goldman's work is considered as a coherent whole, once her essays are read not in isolation but as parts of a larger body of writing, we begin to see her thoughtfulness (the fullness of her thought), her breadth and depth, the way she develops her ideas over time, and the experimentation she engaged in as that body of thought matured. Several of these essays focus on ideas that have received very little attention—children, spirituality, and personality, for example. They force us even to rethink what is central in Goldman's philosophy.

We can also see in these thematic essays some aspects of the nature of Goldman's contribution to political theory. Weiss writes that "Goldman provides a model for the kinds of questions political theorists should be asking about children," applauding the fact that "her anarchist feminism and her concern about children's lack of liberty are integrated and integral parts of her political theory." Carroll finds in Goldman's work on revolution "a new valuation of collective action and social construction." Marso shows that Goldman "helps us to think about the connections and tensions between sexuality, love, and feminist politics" and can teach us "about the relationships between theory and practice, one's life and one's beliefs, desires as they conflict with prevailing norms, and how to carry on in the face of disillusionment and despair." Ferguson concludes that Goldman's discursive strategies render "Goldman's political thinking more interesting, more open, and more useful to contemporary feminists who want to both sustain and question our commitments" because "she infuse[s] her radical politics with a spirituality that resists fundamentalism." Falk claims that "Goldman melded her ideas into the American political landscape, providing a counterpoint to the myth of anarchism as a purely European political construct." We can conclude from the essays in this section that we have in Goldman a social theorist who can contribute to the analysis of specific, well-recognized political concepts and practices; who can, in addition, turn the spotlight to more neglected actors and actions; and whose methodologies are noteworthy, legitimate, valuable, and varied.

In exploring Goldman's political theory, these authors have not erased her passion, despite the fact that her passion has been used to dismiss her intellect. When applied to women's intellectual work, and specifically that of Goldman, references to "fervor" and "commitment" have been used to dismiss and depreciate. Thus Solomon wrote: "In reading Goldman's philosophical and political essays, we are struck above all by her fervor and commitment. But her ideological sincerity does not obscure the weaknesses in her presentation of her ideas" (1987, 59). Feminists who would challenge the dichotomous conceptualization of emotion and thought might argue that Goldman's feelings inform, enrich, and illuminate her thought, and vice versa. In fact, Carroll, in this volume, argues that "Goldman herself rejected the opposition of feeling and mind implied" in such criticisms of her. This theoretical stance permeates Goldman's work. Thus, recognized by Day is the adamancy with which Goldman prioritized individual freedom, the depth of her belief that freedom gives meaning to life, and the persistence with which she adhered to it, whether considering work, marriage, or education. Brought to light by Weiss is Goldman's outrage over child-rearing practices and educational schemes that destroy childhood; the strength of Goldman's advocacy for children's freedom and dignity; and the determined way in which Goldman never loses sight of children, whatever her main subject might be. As Ferguson summarizes, "Goldman's reflections do not suggest a dry and brittle doctrine, but an impassioned engagement with a problematic set of issues."

The essays in this first section also display some fascinating overlap, intersections that have not been explored previously because of the dearth of secondary literature on Goldman. How often sexuality appears in these pieces—not just in Marso's essay, with *sexuality* in the title, but also in Weiss's work on children and in Day's study of individual self-expression. It seems to be not only a central concern but also a broadly understood one. Similarly, Falk's study of free speech makes note of violence almost as often as does Carroll's piece on revolution; disillusionment enters the discussion not only of political upheaval but also of love relationships; and the "individual" Day establishes as core to Goldman's thought reappears in every other essay. As it should, Section I as a whole invites readers to make connections and gain insight into Goldman that go beyond even the significant contribution of each individually important essay.

Historical Roots and Current Connections

To take someone seriously as a political thinker requires that they be connected with other political theorists and schools of thought. Feminists know perhaps as well as anyone that making of a theorist an anomaly—as if he or she came from nowhere and touched no one—is often a philosophical kiss of death. Links show one's participation in the conversation that is the history of political philosophy, as a student influenced by it, a colleague helping to develop it, and a teacher influencing it. Further, such links lead to comparisons through which the contribution of a thinker can be seen, understood, and evaluated afresh, hopefully without being swallowed up by or having to fit into the philosophical perspective of another scholar. Moreover, connections offer a fuller sense of a thinker by enabling us to look at him or her anew in each different setting. In this collection, for example, we see diverse aspects of Goldman when analyzing her alongside Peter Kropotkin versus Mary Wollstonecraft, and different elements are highlighted reading her through the lenses of Ralph Waldo Emerson versus bell hooks. It is only in coming to terms with all that these various associations have to offer that we see Goldman most comprehensively.

The essays in Section II provide wonderful models for exploring Goldman's place among political thinkers. All take the links beyond the biographical and into the philosophical. The arrows of influence revealed in these writings are multidirectional and, further, touch figures in anarchism, feminism, socialism, education, literature, and aesthetics, to name the most obvious. The combined effect of them is a sense of Emma Goldman as well read and well connected philosophically, as possessing a powerful mind that synthesized and reshaped the diverse ideas she encountered, and as embodying what Gail Stenstad calls anarchic thinking, or wild thinking—that which is "both subversive and creative [is] . . . wild thinking: thinking which goes beyond conventional boundaries, deviates from expected goals and methods, and is not accounted for or predicted by any theory" (1988, 87).

This second set of essays overlaps most interestingly in terms of the contexts in which Goldman is studied, beginning a new conversation about her in the secondary literature. For example, Alice Wexler, using a historical approach, studies how Goldman, like many nineteenth- and twentieth-century feminists, was inspired by and painted a self-revealing picture of that supposedly quintessentially liberal feminist—the eighteenth century's Mary Wollstonecraft. Alix Kates Shulman continues to look to the history of feminism to read Goldman, but she also compares contemporary feminism to the strands of feminism evident during Goldman's life, concluding that she was "an indisputable radical feminist." Loretta Kensinger turns to more recent feminist frameworks, looking to Charlotte Bunch and bell hooks in order to make visible in a quite different way the feminism at the heart of Goldman's political theory. The three together not only broaden the conversation but also deepen it. Section II both grounds Goldman's thought in the unique constellation of ideas circulating in the period in which she lived and connects her theoretical contributions to conversations current in the world in which we live.

To say of someone that he or she has the ability to synthesize enormous amounts of information is to offer faint intellectual praise. But as the essays here show, the intellectual processes of critical reading, synthesizing, and creating are interwoven for Goldman. Through her consideration of the theories of others she does more than create a patchwork quilt of ideas. She sifts through them, she seizes on some and takes them to new places, she builds bridges where only chasms were previously seen, she transforms. And in so doing, she works with an impressive range of material. As Lynn Adrian claims, "One of the most striking features of Emma Goldman's writing is the extent of her knowledge. She quoted diverse sources, from the Bible to Marx, Whitman to Goethe, Kropotkin to Jefferson, and all with equal fluency."

That Goldman does more than simply adopt the ideas of others comes through repeatedly in the essays in Section II. Jonathan McKenzie and Craig Stalbaum point out ways in which Goldman departs from her anarchist "mentor," Peter Kropotkin. Shulman's Goldman was "an early organizer [of] the women's trade union movement," yet in her understanding of women's interest and freedom she departed from this and other strains of feminism, leading some to call her an antifeminist. Adrian shows another way in which Goldman both used the ideas of others and made them her own. Adrian demonstrates, for example, an important difference between Goldman's idea of "social unity and harmony" and the idea of organic unity found in Emerson and Thoreau, as well as between Goldman's idea of artful living and the Transcendentalists' concept of "*beautiful* living in harmony with nature." And a somewhat similar phenomenon is seen as Wexler explores Goldman's use of Mary Wollstonecraft. Despite the parallels between Goldman and Wollstonecraft, from their personal rebellions against social restrictions on women to their emphasis on independence, Goldman uses Wollstonecraft to show her own understanding of the tragic elements of modern emancipated womanhood and the women who embodied them. Goldman uses those who inspire her not as authors of blueprints that she is obliged to follow, but as suggestive, motivating, influential agents whose ideas are reshaped, combined with others, and reanimated by her.

The connections explored here between Goldman and various other political theorists and schools of thought, from liberalism to transcendentalism, allow and invite us to take her more seriously as a political thinker. In them we can glimpse Goldman's distinctive blend of ideas, the permutations and creations that constitute her political philosophy. We can put together in fascinating, important ways the Goldman revealed in each separate essay and get a fuller and more complicated, richer and more nuanced understanding of her as a political theorist. Hopefully, the analyses can inspire us to make additional connections and ask ever more challenging questions of Goldman and of political philosophy.

Inspiring Political Change: Theory and Practice

Goldman's anarchism was theory deeply intertwined with practice, in numerous senses. First, her motivation was the practical beauty of anarchist possibilities, found in its commitment to individual freedom of action, self-development, and experimentation. Second, this was an ideal she both fervently believed in and worked relentlessly to realize. Third, she was motivated by the very real gap between that anarchist vision and the injustices she witnessed. Finally, both as a means to change and as an end, the way one lives one's life was thought by her to matter enormously. In the final section of this volume, authors touch on ways to act on anarchist feminist principles. They are linked by the fact that all find some degree of inspiration in the political ideas and practices of Goldman; all hope to find ways to make anarchism more realizable, as Goldman claimed it was; and all share her commitment to theory and practice informing each other.

Digging for evidence of how Emma Goldman has been used by others working for causes similar to hers, we found an astonishing range and amount of material. Several plays have been written with her as a central character, including Michael Bettencourt's *Dancing at the Revolution,* Larry Loebell's *Emma Goldman Imagines the Millennium,* Howard Zinn's *Emma,* and Jessica Litwak's *Emma Goldman: Love, Anarchy, and Other Affairs.* There was a band called Songs for Emma, who "wrote songs with her beliefs and big heart in mind." There is an Emma Center in Nashville, Tennessee, that describes itself as an "integrative center for creativity, learning, and community" providing "collective space in which anyone can teach and anyone can learn." Seattle is home to the Emma Goldman Finishing School, an intentional community "based on the principles of societal change, egalitarianism, non-violence, ecology, simplicity, [and] community living," while *In These Times* published an "advice" column called "Ask Emma Goldman." There are, finally, a number of songs inspired by Goldman, including "Modern Day Emma Goldman," by Pretty Girls Make Graves, and "The Night That Goldman Spoke at Union Square," by Flaherty and Ahrens. It is certainly worth wondering whether any other political thinker and activist has inspired such experiments, made room for such creativity, and passed on such principles to later generations.

Goldman wrote: "If I had my life to live over again . . . I should work for Anarchism with the same devotion and confidence in its ultimate triumph" (Shulman 1972, 397–98). The authors in Section III raise questions about *how* to direct such devotion—about effective political action. Marsha Hewitt, for example, argues that "the [feminist] separatist option is a mistake, on the level of both theory and praxis. A sectarian politics based on gender, or on *anything else* . . . stands in danger of being marginalized and irrelevant." Voltairine de Cleyre explains why she both disagreed with and supported Goldman's advocacy of "stealing bread," and why she herself preferred taking power.

The kinds of efforts documented in these essays are quite broad in scope, as were Goldman's own. Martha Ackelsberg and Kathryn Addelson note that the Vancouver Collective not only worked to be an alternative organization internally, but also "work[ed] for broader political change," while the Emma Goldman Clinic advocates "for women's health care needs from the exam room to Capitol Hill." Hewitt reminds us of Goldman's point that change is necessary both internally and externally, in thought, language, morality, culture, art, literature, and economic and social institutions.

Like Goldman, the authors here find a large part of their motivation in the injustices that surround them. Goldman wrote, "Existing institutions prove inadequate to the needs of man. . . . [T]hey serve merely to enslave, rob, and oppress. . . . The history of the American kings of capital and authority is the history of repeated crimes, injustice, oppression, outrage, and abuse, all aiming at the suppression of individual liberties and the exploitation of the people" (2003, 450). The mission statement of the Emma Goldman Clinic declares the clinic's commitment "to end all forms of oppression based on ableism, ageism, body size, classism, ethnic origin, racism, religion, sexism, sexual identity, [and] national origin." Ackelsberg and Addelson point us to the "unequal distribution of social resources," and especially the ways that such inequalities are justified. Anarchist theory and practice provide rich material with which to detect and counter such lies, "noble" or ignoble, and to challenge the structures built upon them. De Cleyre makes reference both to the unjust situation of Goldman the protester—she was at that moment one of the "lonely prisoners in the cells of Blackwell's Island"—and to the injustices that Goldman was protesting, especially hunger.

Perhaps as important as anything to Goldman, the vision of anarchist possibilities also inspires the writers found in Section III. Goldman wrote: "The belief in freedom assumes that human beings can co-operate. They do it even now to a surprising extent, or organized society would be impossible. If the devices by which men can harm one another, such as private property, are removed and if the worship of authority can be discarded, co-operation will be spontaneous and inevitable, and the individual will find it his highest calling to contribute to the enrichment of social well-being" (Shulman 1972, 396). Ackelsberg and Addelson touch diverse possible alternatives to the destructiveness of liberal and capitalist competition—issues close to Goldman's heart. They pay welcome attention to the idea that "anarchism does not mean *lack* of but, rather, *different* structure. . . . Freedom and community are compatible, but communities need to be structured in particular ways to support that freedom." The practices of the Emma Goldman Clinic are informed by the ideal that "women must have self-decision over their own bodies, and all matters concerning contraception and childbirth are to be decided upon by women themselves." This practice is consistent with what Ackelsberg and Addelson describe as anarchist organization: "Freely organized groups, set up by people to meet their own needs, should replace centralized, hierarchical means of coordination." Anarchists try "to effect change by *creating new realities*, on however small a scale." Hewitt speaks of "think[ing] and act[ing] according to the *necessarily* utopian ideal . . . of living creatively."

It is also obvious from the authors here that Goldman's emphasis on living our lives at present with a sort of anarchist integrity and dedication to free expression continues to be of great import. Ackelsberg and Addelson discuss how "the process of revolution takes place in and through structures that reflect the sorts of relationships in which people aim to live. Anarchism implies a concept of revolutionary practice which consists in creating new forms of communal-social existence, new ways to meet people's needs, forms through which people can struggle to overcome their own subordination." Groups and organizations like the Emma Goldman Clinic continue to work on issues central to Goldman's life, such as women's health. Their strategies for change include community education, study groups, and direct action and their organizing principles are grassroots, cooperative, and participatory. All that, and singing and dancing, too. Goldman would be pleased, we think, to be counted as a source of inspiration.

Concluding Thought

The contributors to this collection frequently disagree with one another and use quite different strategies to analyze Goldman. That is as it should be. But it is also the case that each writer approaches her as a serious political thinker, and all evaluate at least some aspects of her work quite positively. That, too, perhaps surprisingly, is arguably as it should be. Most other literature on Goldman primarily emphasizes a litany of weaknesses, tensions, contradictions, omissions, biases, or unresolved problems in her work. Commentators repeatedly refer to Goldman's ideas in pejorative terms, such as "confused," "untheoretical" and "vague." Critics have found ways to tear Goldman down that sit easily with popular impressions of her, but rest less well with what careful study of her work reveals. We cannot rightly destroy (or applaud, for that matter) a body of work that we have yet to dissect carefully, analyze thoughtfully, read imaginatively, and contextualize religiously. Such a corrective scholarly process is needed, and it indisputably receives its largest influx of energy to date in this anthology. The volume is filled with the excitement of intellectual discovery, the recognition of rich political potential, the hope of continued critical examination to come, and shrewd awareness of the human value of what Emma Goldman has to offer. And that is the stage we are at as this volume goes to press. This book provides a vital opening to serious consideration of the rich complexity found in Goldman's theories.

Nancy Tuana, series editor, said in an early review of this work on Goldman that the "volume re-reads the canon by reading her back into it." Unlike most others in the series, this collection is not reconsidering a canonical figure from feminist perspectives. Goldman is most obviously not part of the Western canon; she is often not even included in discussions of anarchist theory (because she is a feminist) or of feminist theory (because she is an anarchist)! It is not even the case that there is a canon *on* Goldman's ideas to reread, if by that we mean an authoritative or dominant scholarly interpretation, though there most certainly are fixed cultural images of her, a fairly set story of her life, and fixed ways of justifying *not* treating her as a theorist. Yes, this series gives feminist theorists a welcome, key opportunity to continue rethinking the canonical thinkers and, more, to reconsider which individuals are in the canon. But making this volume part of the series gives voice to the idea that when we take someone like Goldman seriously, the canon itself shifts a bit. Maybe just a bit, but, as in a gym, the movement of one restless fan causes varying degrees of adjustment down the line. Hopefully work on Goldman will continue with the same determined open-mindedness and generosity of interpretive spirit found here and that every body of theoretical work requires. We look forward to the next stage of Goldman interpretation.

References

Bettencourt, Michael. 1998. *Dancing at the Revolution*. Full and sample scripts available at http://www.m-bettencourt.com/ (accessed January 2006).

Brown, L. Susan. 2003. *The Politics of Individualism: Liberalism, Liberal Feminism, and Anarchism*. Montreal: Black Rose Books.

Carroll, Berenice A. 1990. "The Politics of 'Originality': Women and the Class System of the Intellect." *Journal of Women's History* 2 (Fall): 136–63.

Day, Janet. 2004. "Models of Individuality in Emma Goldman's and Ayn Rand's Theories of Civil Society." Ph.D. diss., Purdue University.

Drinnon, Richard. 1961. *Rebel in Paradise: A Biography of Emma Goldman*. Boston: Beacon.

Emma Center. Information listed on the Nashville Peace and Justice Center member organizations page at http://www.nashvillepeace.org/about (accessed May 2004).

Emma Goldman Finishing School. http://egfs.org (accessed January 2006).

Falk, Candace, Barry Pateman, and Jessica Moran, eds. 2003. *Emma Goldman: A Documentary History of the American Years, Volume 1: Made for America, 1890–1901*. Berkeley and Los Angeles: University of California Press.

Falk, Candace, Barry Pateman, and Jessica Moran, eds. 2005. *Emma Goldman: A Documentary History of the American Years, Volume 2, Making Speech Free, 1902–1909*, 2005. Berkeley and Los Angeles: University of California Press.

Flaherty, Stephan (music), and Lynn Ahrens (lyrics). 1996. "The Night That Goldman Spoke at Union Square." In *Ragtime*. Based on the novel by E. L. Doctorow. http://www.ahrensandflherty.com/ragtime.html (accessed January 2006).

Frankel, Oz. 1996. "Whatever Happened to 'Red Emma'? Emma Goldman, from Alien Rebel to American Icon." *Journal of American History* 83, no. 3:903–52.

Goldman, Emma. 1969. *Anarchism and Other Essays*. With a new introduction by Richard Drinnon. New York: Dover. (Org. pub. 1910.)

———. 2003. "A New Declaration of Independence." Reprinted in *Emma Goldman: A Documentary History of the American Years, Volume 2, Making Speech Free, 1902–1909*. Edited by Candace Falk, Barry Pateman, and Jessica Moran. Berkeley and Los Angeles: University of California Press. (Orig. pub. 1909.)

Glassgold, Peter. 2001. *Anarchy! An Anthology of Emma Goldman's "Mother Earth" (1906–1918)*. Washington, D.C.: Counterpoint.

Haaland, Bonnie. 1993. *Emma Goldman: Sexuality and the Impurity of the State*. Montreal: Black Rose Books.

Levine, Daniel. 1971. *Jane Addams and the Liberal Tradition*. Madison: State Historical Society of Wisconsin.

Loebell, Larry. 2000. *Emma Goldman Imagines the Millennium*. Produced for InterAct Theatre Company. Sample scene at http://www.loebell.com/plays/emma.html (accessed January 2006).

Loewen, James. 1995. *Lies My Teacher Told Me: Everything Your American History Textbook Got Wrong*. New York: New Press.

Lovejoy, Arthur O. 1936. *The Great Chain of Being: A Study of the History of an Idea*. Cambridge, Mass.: Harvard University Press.

Pretty Girls Make Graves. "Modern Day Emma Goldman." Lyrics available at http://www.prettygirlsmakegraves.com/lyrics.asp# (accessed January 2006).

Shulman, Alix Kates. 1972. *Red Emma Speaks: Selected Writings and Speeches by Emma Goldman*. New York: Vintage.

———. 1991. Dances with Feminists. *Women's Review of Books* 9, no. 3. Available: http://sunsite3.berkeley.edu/Goldman/Features/dances_shulman.html (accessed September 5, 2005).

Solomon, Martha. 1987. *Emma Goldman*. Boston: Twayne.

Songs for Emma. http://www.brokenrekids.com/SongsForEmma/info.html (accessed January 2006).

Sorokin, Pitirim. 1956. *Contemporary Sociological Theories*. New York: Harper & Bros. (Orig. pub. 1928.)

Stenstad, Gail. 1988, "Anarchic Thinking." *Hypatia: The Journal of Feminist Philosophy* 3, no. 2:87–100.

Wexler, Alice. 1989. *Emma Goldman in Exile: From the Russian Revolution to the Spanish Civil War*. Boston: Beacon Press.

Zinn, Howard. 2002. *Emma: A Play in Two Acts About Emma Goldman, American Anarchist*. Cambridge: South End Press. (Orig. pub. 1986.)

Anarchy in Interpretation:

The Life of Emma Goldman

Jason Wehling

*"Because the biographies, taken as a whole, are very sympathetic to Emma Goldman, contro-
versy has not been easily forthcoming. . . . Yet in her contemporary setting, Emma was viewed
by an overwhelming majority as worse than the devil. Anyone who later set out to malign her
would have a tough go at it to outdo those who had smeared her when she was alive, through the
yellow journalism that helped to create the myth of Emma the dirty bomb-thrower."*

Some version of the story of Goldman's life is familiar to most who know anything at all
about her. Indeed, her life has overshadowed her ideas; for this reason alone we were
somewhat reluctant to repeat the admittedly fascinating tales. Our problem was solved
when we came upon Jason Wehling's essay. Instead of offering a biography of Goldman,
he provides a study of her biographies. This enables us to see some of the politics of
biography, as well as to take note of the areas of Goldman's life over which there exists
broad agreement and considerable discord, substantial neglect, and significant attention.
—*The Editors*

Emma Goldman was many things—a feminist, a writer, and a riveting
public speaker—but first and foremost, she was an anarchist. Not coinci-
dentally, her life in many ways parallels the life of anarchism as a movement. Anarchism, although its roots are dated much earlier, was born
just two years after Emma's birth. Mikhail Bakunin, a Russian revolutionary, as Emma was to become, split the international Communist movement in two, creating anarchists, who followed Bakunin, and
Communists, who saw Karl Marx as their teacher. Emma lived through
the era of anarchist terror that rained upon the rulers of the world and
experienced the aftermath of the Russian Revolution. Ironically, George
Woodcock, writing in 1962 about the history of the anarchist movement,
declared anarchism dead as of 1939, with its untimely demise in Spain
(Woodcock 1962, 443); Emma died a mere year and a half after this
defeat at the hands of Franco's fascists.

Interestingly, with the rebirth of anarchism in the 1960s, in parallel with the emergence of the New Left's emphasis on decentralization and opposition to hierarchy and at its height in the explosive Paris General Strike of 1968, Emma was reborn as well. Beginning in 1961, with the appearance of Richard Drinnon's *Rebel in Paradise*, many biographers have turned their attention to Goldman and published works on her life: Candace Falk, in 1984; Alice Wexler, in the same year; Martha Solomon, in 1989; John Chalberg, in 1991; and Marian Morton, in 1992. Wexler, Solomon, and Falk all agree that the resurgence in the interest of Emma in the late 1960s and early 1970s is a reflection of a renewed interest in feminism and anarchism. "In part, this fascination with Goldman reflects a general upsurge of interest in anarchism since the sixties" (Wexler 1984, 2).

Emma was exceedingly controversial during her own lifetime. President Teddy Roosevelt called her a "madwoman . . . a mental as well as a moral pervert"; according to the *New York Times*, she was a "mischievous foreigner . . . apart from the mass of humanity." The *San Francisco Call* opined that she was a "despicable creature . . . [a] snake . . . unfit to live in a civilized country." The government labeled her the "ablest and most dangerous" anarchist in the country.

By contrast, Kate Richards O'Hare, a socialist who occupied a neighboring jail cell to that of Goldman, declared, "The Emma Goldman that I know is not the Propagandist. It is Emma, the tender, cosmic mother, the wise understanding woman, the faithful sister, the loyal comrade. . . . Emma don't believe in Jesus, yet she is the one who makes it possible for me to grasp the spirit of Jesus" (Drinnon 1961, 251). William Marion Reedy of the *St. Louis Mirror* said this: "There is nothing wrong with Miss Goldman's gospel that I can see except this: SHE IS ABOUT EIGHT THOUSAND YEARS AHEAD OF HER AGE!" (Drinnon 1961, title page). It is hard to believe that these contradictory quotes could possibly describe the same person.

Emma was even controversial within the radical movement itself. She was one of the first radicals to address the issue of homosexuality, and she opposed women's suffrage and touted the virtues of "free love." To her counterparts who placed their faith in the cure-all solution of class warfare, such ideals were bourgeois inspired at best. Her ideological mentors included Walt Whitman, Henry David Thoreau, Peter Kropotkin, Bakunin, and Mary Wollstonecraft. Among her acquaintances were Wobbly organizers "Big" Bill Haywood and Elizabeth Gurley Flynn, writers Eugene O'Neil and Jack London, and socialists John Reed and Eugene Debs. She had an enormous influence on Margaret Sanger and Roger Baldwin, the founders of two of the most important institutions of contemporary American liberalism, Planned Parenthood and the American Civil Liberties Union (ACLU), respectively.

But to mainstream Americans Emma was known as a demonic, "dynamite-eating anarchist." Goldman was hounded for much of her life by two of the most notorious law enforcement officials in American history: Anthony Comstock and J. Edgar Hoover. As a result of the reputation she acquired, she was jailed in 1893, 1901, 1916, 1918, 1919, and 1921—the charges ranging from inciting to riot to advocating the use of birth control to opposition to World War I. She was exiled by the United States, Soviet Russia, Holland, and France and was denied entry into many more nations.

A Life in Context

All this started with her birth on June 27, 1869, in Kovno, Lithuania. By 1886, Emma and her sister Helene emigrated to Rochester, New York. That same year, in Chicago, following the foundation of the May Day workers holiday, the Haymarket affair transpired. This event enthralled young Emma, who was devastated when the anarchists accused of involvement in the incident were executed the following year. Goldman credited this event for her divorce from her husband of less than a year. In 1889, Emma moved to New York City, where she joined the Yiddish anarchist movement and met her lifelong companion, Alexander Berkman.

This friendship proved to be a decisive occurrence in her life; in 1892, she conspired with Berkman in his failed attempt to assassinate Henry Clay Frick in retaliation for Frick's role in the attack on strikers at Homestead. Berkman eventually served fourteen years in Western Penitentiary for his crime; Goldman's guilt over Berkman's accepting sole responsibility for a crime in which they had both participated remained a major influence for the rest of her life. Following the failed assassination of Frick, Emma not only gained national renown, but also became prominent in the anarchist movement. In 1895 she traveled to Vienna to study medicine, attending lectures by Freud, and to London, where she met

Kropotkin. She returned to the United States a year later, then over the following few years made frequent cross-country speaking tours.

Her anarchist agitation was interrupted in 1901 when Leon Czolgosz, a self-proclaimed anarchist, assassinated President William McKinley. Emma was blamed for Czolgosz's action and was forced into hiding by a massive wave of antianarchist hysteria. In 1906, the same year in which Berkman was released from prison, Emma began publishing *Mother Earth*. A few years later, Emma met Ben Reitman, who would remain her lover until her arrest in 1917. She was jailed as a result of her work in the No-Conscription League and for her antiwar stand toward World War I, which caused *Mother Earth* to be shut down by the government.

After serving out their two-year sentences, Emma and Berkman were deported in 1919 to Soviet Russia. At first, Emma was excited to see firsthand the revolution she had fought to bring about all her life. But it did not take long for her to realize that the Bolsheviks were no anarchists and that the massive dictatorship created by Vladimir Lenin was crushing the "spontaneity of the masses." In 1921, Libertarian sailors revolted at Kronstadt against the Bolshevik government. The suppression of Kronstadt by the Communists was too much for Emma and Berkman and, in a state of disillusionment, they made the decision to finally leave Russia. For the following few years, traveling from country to country—those that would permit her entry—she wrote a long series of articles and two books about her experience in the Soviet Union and the ideological contradictions that she perceived within that state.

After living in the United Kingdom for many years, she eventually married James Colton, in 1926, for the convenience that, through the marriage, British citizenship offered, allowing her to travel to Canada. Later, she lived in seclusion in France for a number of years, writing her autobiography, which was published in 1931. During her long period of exile, Emma constantly desired to return to the United States, her chosen home. But the notorious anarchist was, well, still notorious and was denied entry except for a brief, ninety-day visit in 1934.

The year 1936 was the highest of the highs and the lowest of the lows for Goldman. Her cerebral second half, Alexander Berkman, committed suicide, after prolonged agony caused by an aggravated case of prostate cancer. Just a week later, an anarchist-inspired revolution erupted in Spain. For the following three years, Emma committed herself to the support of the anarchosyndicalists and their fight against Communists,

Republicans, and especially fascists—all of whom refused to accept the revolution in Spain.

This long, astonishing life finally came to an end in 1940. While attempting to save an Italian anarchist from deportation to Fascist Italy, where he faced certain death, Emma died from a stroke in Toronto. Only after her death was she admitted back into the United States, where she found her eternal resting place at Waldheim Cemetery in Chicago, near the Haymarket martyrs, who unwittingly helped to shape her life.

Reasons Behind Biography

Needless to say, the life of Emma Goldman, infamous and full of contention, has been interpreted many different ways. The first attempt to create a biography of Goldman was made by one of her lovers, Hippolyte Havel, a fellow anarchist. This "sketch"—it is a mere forty pages in length—was written as an introduction to a collection of essays by Emma that was published in 1910. Because it was written more that thirty years before her death and given its relatively early publication and obviously preferential view, it is limited in its ability to portray Goldman's life accurately. The intention of the piece was not necessarily to glorify Goldman, but it was written at a time when she was personified as a walking she-devil by a sensationalizing press and a belligerent government. The text was mainly a response to this disparaging view of anarchists in general. In fact, the last section of this short biography is wholly devoted to a defense of anarchism against the gross misrepresentation it was receiving at the time.

It was not until thirty years after her death that a more solid attempt at biography was attempted by Richard Drinnon. His *Rebel in Paradise* is considered by most of the biographers who have followed Drinnon to be the standard chronicle of the life of Emma Goldman. This biography is largely devoted to a revision of the distorted view left by the media of Goldman's day and, therefore, focuses primarily on historical events of her life. Drinnon devotes an entire chapter to the conspiracy by the federal government, mainly at the behest of a young and ambitious J. Edgar Hoover, to deny Emma American citizenship in order to eventually deport her. In his introduction, Drinnon is very frank about his bias, stating that just choosing someone like Goldman to write about is in itself subjective. "No doubt my basic sympathy for the radical style in politics helped shape this empathy and understanding" (Drinnon 1961, vii). But unlike Havel's earlier work, Drinnon wrote, "this book is, first and foremost, a critical biography of the woman" (viii). Drinnon comes off as sympathetic yet avoids any partisanship.

Candace Falk relates in her introduction how she and her dog, which she had named Red Emma, stumbled on a box of letters written by Emma to her lover, Ben Reitman, in the early 1970s. Naming a dog after your subject would indicate empathy, and Falk is, like Drinnon and Havel, empathetic toward Goldman. But unlike her predecessors, Falk is not interested in Emma as an anarchist; rather, she sees Goldman as a lover, a woman, and a human being. Using previously undiscovered letters, Falk investigates Emma's private sexual life, focusing primarily on her relationship with Reitman.

Falk wrote *Love, Anarchy, and Emma Goldman* because "no single source could answer my questions about Emma. There was a path-breaking biography by Richard Drinnon, *Rebel in Paradise*, but it did not delve deeply into the relationship between Emma and Ben" (Falk 1984, xiii). She does not try to compete with past material or try to rewrite Emma's public life in light of the new information Falk has gained from the letters. "Rather than chronicle her public life in parallel detail, I chose to write a companion piece to her own account in the autobiography and to the Drinnon biography" (xiii). Because of this focus, in her biography Falk emphasizes the decade of the relationship between Goldman and Reitman (1908–17), while purposely neglecting much of the rest of Goldman's life.

Alice Wexler's biography of Goldman ran to two volumes, the first of which, subtitled *An Intimate Life*, arrived in 1984, the same year as the Falk book. In this first volume, Wexler follows Emma up to her deportation from the United States; in the second volume, *Emma Goldman in Exile*, she completes Emma's life. Wexler's intent is to investigate Emma's inner, or personal, life. She notes: "While the historical Emma Goldman was more problematic, more contradictory, and less romantic in certain ways than the ebullient figure of legend, the reality of her life was no less heroic and in many ways more interesting and moving" (Wexler 1984, xviii). Again, Wexler is not antagonistic to Emma; in fact, Wexler may herself be partial to anarchism, for she writes for anarchist journals such as *Our Generation*.

Wexler's biography not only treats the previously unexplored territory of Emma's personal life (excluding her relationship with Reitman, of course); Wexler also places Goldman in the proper context of the anarchist movement, of which Emma was an integral part. Each figure in Emma's life, often described only in passing in other biographies, is detailed and oriented properly in the context of his or her impact on Emma Goldman. The reader gets to know Berkman, Kropotkin, Mary and Abe Isaaks, and Johann Most in a way that other authors do not allow. But at the same time, Wexler states that she is attempting to demystify Emma's life in its two manifestations—the demon, created by the government; and the angel, by Emma herself in her autobiography.

Martha Solomon, whose book *Emma Goldman* was published in 1987, admits that biographers who had preceded her had adequately chronicled the life of Goldman. "This work will not attempt to compete" with the earlier works—those by Goldman, Drinnon, Falk, and Wexler—"but will try, instead, to focus on Goldman as a writer and rhetorician" (Solomon 1987, preface). Solomon's goal is to analyze Goldman the writer. Emma did write a great deal—six books and hundreds of pamphlets and articles, not to mention the myriad speeches she gave throughout her life. Solomon's biography of Goldman is contained in the first chapter; the rest of the book is devoted to an analysis of Goldman's writings, placing them in the context of her life. Solomon's goal "is to evaluate [Goldman] in a spirit she would have preferred: appreciating her creative contributions and acknowledging her limitations" (Solomon 1987, 149). But, like her predecessors, Solomon is sympathetic: "Goldman, who lived this remarkable life, is the key to any interest [this book] contains. The flaws are my own" (Solomon 1987, acknowledgments).

In a contrast to the works that have been discussed here, Marian Morton's *Emma Goldman and the American Left*, could be said to be unsympathetic; it is, however, by no means belligerent. As the title implies, this life focuses on Emma as a member of the Left. "This is therefore a political biography and a story of the American Left" (Morton 1992, x). Much of the book details the histories of radical organizations such as the Socialist Party of America and the Communist Party of the United States. Because of Goldman's unusual role in the Left as an anarchist, Morton has a rough time relating Emma to her leftist contemporaries. Usually Morton falls into a pattern of explaining what Emma was doing at a particular time and then detailing the accomplishments of other leftists—often without making any connection.

Not surprisingly, when the reader arrives at the book's conclusion, there is a feeling that Emma's life ended in failure. One may perhaps surmise that Morton is some variety of socialist and found Goldman's anarchism annoying, or at least unrealistic. Unfortunately, Morton does not reveal her personal politics. Beyond this, the book is poor especially when compared with Wexler's work, which details the American Left in much better detail (for example, Wexler mentions the Seattle General Strike of 1919, whereas Morton does not).

John Chalberg's biography was written as a volume in a series of "great" American biographies. The author is obviously not an anarchist or even a radical and therefore his work may be most prone to criticism, but the biography comes off as being clear and relatively sympathetic. Instead of there being the usual bias that a biographer inserts into a subject's life, it seems that in Chalberg's case the tables were turned and the subject influenced the biographer: "As a white male, a native Minnesotan, a reticent Scandinavian, a husband and a father of more children than the national average, and a suburbanite with the inevitable two-car garage and obligatory mortgage, I can testify that living with Goldman has not been reassuring or comforting. But it has been interesting" (Chalberg 1991, ix). Chalberg's biography adds little in regard to new historical interpretations and can be seen as a briefer version of the one sketched by Drinnon thirty years earlier.

Conformity over a Nonconformist

As mentioned above, the biographies of Emma Goldman, taken as a whole, are rather sympathetic in tone; as a result of this and of a number of other factors, they have much in common. First, their dates of publication are relatively recent and are clustered in a very narrow period of time—most of these works were written within a span of two decades. In her day, Emma was viewed by an overwhelming majority of the public as akin to the devil. Anyone who later set out to malign her would have a tough go at it to outdo those who had smeared her when she was alive, through the yellow journalism that had helped to create the myth of Emma the dirty bomb-thrower.

Second, and perhaps more important, and as Drinnon suggests in his introduction, the act itself of choosing Goldman as a subject for a biography reflects back on the author. Interestingly, all her biographers found

Emma inspirational but at the same time annoying. Drinnon remarks, "When I began research on her life, I began skeptically, for her autobiography and the other accounts of her career seemed to make her too extraordinary a woman to be taken seriously. And along with everyone else, I regarded her anarchism as a particularly bizarre form of political lunacy. Months of research passed before I learned that my skepticism was pseudo-sophistication and my condescension was only conventional ignorance. Emma Goldman was in truth a remarkable woman" (1961, vii). Echoing these sentiments, Wexler relates that "when I first learned about Emma Goldman I found her both admirable and irritating. As I studied her memoirs and vast correspondence, I was often dismayed by her self-deceptions and vanities, her frequent scorn for other radicals and feminists. Gradually, however, I found my vexation changing to empathy" (1984, xix). Such opinions of Goldman were not new, as Wexler documents; Agnes Ingis, a contemporary of Emma, felt the same way: "Emma was an irritant and an inspiration to many. I cannot think of her as beloved, but surely as an inspirer to courage" (Wexler 1984, 184).

A third factor contributing to the conformity of the biographies is the fact that they all rely, to varying degrees, on *Living My Life*, in which "Emma Goldman set out to write a great American female epic, an anarchist odyssey, showing how, after she committed herself to anarchism at the age of twenty, she remained true to her 'ideal' through the vicissitudes of a long, adventurous life" (Wexler 1989, 141). Solomon agrees with Drinnon that Goldman's "autobiography was a work of art primarily because her life was as well" (Solomon 1987, 130). Chalberg believes that "Goldman did not always tell her story accurately or well, but she did tell it at great length and with great passion" (1991, 181); he drew from her account the anecdotes with which he animates Emma in the pages of his book. Morton admits to a dependence on Goldman's autobiography; in the preface to her 1992 work, she notes that she "relied heavily" on *Living My Life*. Drinnon acknowledges his extensive use of the autobiography in his discussion of Goldman's early years. In fact, without Emma's testimony, the details of such events as her meetings with Lenin and Kropotkin would be unknown.

This is not to say that the biographers took Emma at her word. All agree that *Living My Life* is prone to bias for obvious reasons. Wexler argues that Goldman underrepresented Reitman's contribution to the anarchist movement, focusing only on her problems with him (Wexler 1989, 149). Further, she charges Emma with an unfair attack on Johann

Most, who disassociated himself from Goldman and Berkman after the failed assassination on Frick. Wexler maintains that Most repudiated the "propaganda of deed" years before Berkman's *attentat* in 1892 (Wexler 1984, 150). While Wexler takes Emma to task for fudging anarchist facts, Solomon primarily criticizes Goldman's literary style. Summing up, Solomon says, "Ironically, [Goldman's] autobiography remains interesting not as a history of anarchism (which she envisioned to be its value) but as a chronicle of a personal struggle to live a free life as a woman" (Solomon 1987, 154).

Despite acknowledging their dependence on *Living My Life*, the work seems to have influenced the biographers more than many would like to admit. With the exception of Wexler, the writers place most of their emphasis on the periods covered in Goldman's autobiography. Much attention is paid to the span of time leading up to her deportation, but after that point, time passes quickly, with few details offered. This problem is most pronounced in the Chalberg book; Emma departs from Russia at page 160, leaving a scant nineteen pages on which to recount the rest of her life.

An Anarchist Even Among Believers in Anarchism

Where the biographies really diverge most profoundly is over Emma's particular brand of anarchism. Havel described Emma as "an Anarchist pure and simple" (1910, 44), but it seems that this assertion is not so simple. Chalberg makes a bizarre statement that "Emma considered herself an anarchist for many years but did not establish a formal party affiliation" (1991, vii). He does not seem to understand that anarchism is inherently antagonistic to the rigid and institutional nature of a party apparatus. Nearly all the biographers devote at least a couple of pages to a description of what anarchism stands for, but the way in which each writer comprehends anarchism has a strong effect on how he or she portrays Emma's life.

Drinnon admits his disdain for anarchism in his introduction, yet he makes a noble attempt at a clear definition of it, advising that "a forest of confusion may be bypassed by realizing that Emma was simply an extreme federalist-democrat" (1961, 132). For Falk, anarchism is not an important component in the focus of her work; this is not true of Morton. Falk and

Morton, however, express similar opinions of anarchism. Falk states at one point that Emma's depression was the result of "the inevitable effect of an unattainable political philosophy" (1984, xiii). Morton seems to agree: "Because it cut its adherents loose from institutional restraints, anarchism was a lonely philosophy. The exhilarating freedom from country, creed and sometimes family was often accompanied by the frightening realization of solitude. . . . An anarchist is supposed to be at home nowhere" (1992, ix–x).

Solomon grapples with the problem of anarchism clumsily. She quotes Emma: "The function of anarchism in a revolutionary period is to minimize the violence of the revolution and replace it by constructive efforts" (Solomon 1987, 62). From this Solomon concludes that "in essence, Goldman was forced to acknowledge that the theory she cherished was too avant-garde to be useful in correcting immediate problems" (62). Solomon's analysis is not congruent with Emma's statement. Solomon accuses Goldman's explanation of anarchism as being "too vague and unconvincing" (62). Yet later on, when Emma defends the syndicalism of the Spanish CNT (Confederación nacional del trabajo [National Confederation of Labor]), Solomon praises Emma for being specific, seemingly without understanding the difference between syndicalism and anarchism (Solomon 1987, 49).

Throughout her biography, Solomon remains convinced that Goldman's ideology is contradictory. "Like a wide-angle lens on a camera, her anarchism widens her field of view but distorts her vision" (Solomon 1987, 86). She says that Goldman's "theories are better as a model for the life of a rebel than as a foundation for a new society" (60). But in the end Solomon seems to give a little: "Regardless of our attitude towards her theories, we must respect her personal integrity and her commitment to an ideal" (155).

Not surprisingly, Goldman's biographers, without exception, agree on the causes of Emma's decision to embrace anarchism. They put forward a number of inspirations for her choice. According to Drinnon, "Emma soaked in the ideas of Chernyshevshy as rain is soaked in by the desert sands" (Drinnon 1961, 29). Nikolai Chernyshevshy, in his work *What Is To Be Done?* (1863), had a great influence on the Russia intelligentsia and on Goldman. Along with that of Chernyshevshy, a further stimulus on Emma's ideological growth was Edward Bellamy's *Looking Backwards*, but it was the pivotal event of the Haymarket affair that definitively pushed Emma into the world of radical anarchists. Havel claims: "The

Haymarket tragedy developed her inherent Anarchist tendencies: the reading of the *Freiheit* made her a conscious Anarchist" (1910, 18). This agreement among Emma's biographers regarding the causes of her political inclinations is, again, a result of their grounding their texts in *Living My Life*. Goldman was very clear, for example, about the importance of the Haymarket tragedy in fostering her radicalism.

So what constituted Emma's anarchism? Emma herself offered an answer, explaining that Kropotkin "was a prominent figure in the realm of learning, recognized as such by the foremost men of the world. But to us he meant more than that. We saw in him the father of modern anarchism" (Avrich 1988, 81). As Drinnon puts it, "Quite understandably, Peter Kropotkin became Emma Goldman's true teacher and inspiration" (1961, 41). But Wexler disagrees, arguing that while Kropotkin exerted a strong influence on Emma, she was able to move beyond his theories. This is especially true in her commitment to sexual liberation (Wexler 1984, 48). Going further, Wexler asserts that Emma's anarchism was much more sophisticated than many realize, in that Emma (who might have argued with the assertion) actually created her own moral code (97).

Indeed, among the biographers, some, such as Solomon, point to the differences between Kropotkin and Goldman. A common quote that is used comes from Kropotkin, who says that "the [Free Society] is doing splendid work, but it would do more if it would not waste so much space discussing sex." Most end the quote there, but the "quarrel" continues in *Living My Life*. Emma relates her reply to Kropotkin: "All right, dear comrade, when I have reached your age [she was thirty, Kropotkin fifty-seven], the sex question may no longer be of importance to me. But it is now, and it is a tremendous factor for thousands, millions even, of young people." Emma relates the reaction to her comment: "Peter stopped short, an amused smile lighting up his kindly face. 'Fancy, I didn't think of that,' he replied. 'Perhaps you are right after all.' He beamed affectionately upon me, with a humorous twinkle in his eye" (Goldman 1982, 253).

A theme developed by all the biographers is the tension between Emma's individualism and her collectivism. All state that such a tension exists, but disagreement arises when some place more importance on one side over the other. Chalberg believes Goldman to be closer to collectivism than to individualists such as Benjamin Tucker (Chalberg 1991, 29–30) and that Bakunin and Kropotkin are her teachers. While he may be right, his earlier statement on anarchism, noted above, throws his knowledge of that political movement into question.

Taking up the argument from the other side is Solomon, who argues fiercely that Emma was an "individualistic anarchist" whose "anarchism was essentially libertarianism" (1987, 52, 46). "The clearest conflict," she claims, "in Goldman's thinking was that between the elitism implicit in her commitment to individualism and the egalitarianism intrinsic to anarchism" (59). Interestingly, Wexler agrees with Solomon to a degree, arguing that Emma sided more with the individualism of Max Stirner than with Kropotkin's Communism (Wexler 1984, 137). But Wexler adds that the "spirit of revolt" is perhaps the most important aspect of Emma's thinking (92).

Of the two, Wexler's position is the more credible. A number of Solomon's statements suggest that she may never have even read Kropotkin, undermining her argument. Havel situates Goldman in a class with Josiah Warren, Pierre-Joseph Proudhon, Mikhail Bakunin, Kropotkin, and Leo Tolstoy, while making no mention of Max Stirner or Friedrich Nietzsche, as Solomon does. Morton, the political biographer, states that Emma was a Communist of the Bakunin and Kropotkin variety while leaning "towards the individualism of American Anarchists" (1992, ix). Interestingly, Emma herself places herself in the company of Thomas Jefferson, Patrick Henry, William Lloyd Garrison, John Brown, and Henry David Thoreau (Chalberg 1991, 136).

Much of this disagreement may be in part the result of what many biographers see as Emma's disdain for the masses—a sort of intellectual elitism. Again, it is Solomon who goes out on a limb, saying that "she increasingly perceived the masses as impediments to social change" (1987, 54). Wexler maintains that "Goldman always insisted that this pessimism grew directly out of her experience in Russia" (1989, 79). Obviously one who champions the masses, drawing directly from Kropotkin, cannot at the same time maintain that the masses are inherently reactionary—Emma at times is guilty of just this contradiction.

Another theme that fuels the divergence of opinion vis-à-vis Emma's anarchism is what Wexler describes as Goldman's "anti-Communism," wherein Emma may have confused her disdain of the Bolsheviks with a rejection of collectivism. To a degree, Wexler blames Emma's anti-Communism on Goldman's isolation and loneliness in exile, remarking, "Emma Goldman experienced her two years in Russia as a personal defeat" (Wexler 1989, 57, 110).

The controversial deviation in Emma's ideology has led to a historical disagreement over when this shift occurred. Once again, Solomon takes the extreme position, stating, "Not only [did] Goldman defend the internal and external policies of the Bolsheviks, but she cavalierly dismisses the opposition of many revolutionaries, like her theoretical mentor Peter Kropotkin, to Bolshevik policies" (1987, 56). Solomon maintains that Goldman made a sudden break after the Kronstadt uprising. In fact, if one read only what Emma wrote, this would be a logical conclusion. But Emma was much more complicated. Chalberg is correct in pointing out that she may have been confused by Lenin's *The State and the Revolution*, for in this pamphlet Lenin argues, as would an anarchist, that freedom cannot coexist with the continuation of the state. Chalberg agrees that Emma's public break did occur after Kronstadt, but privately Emma was questioning the Russian Revolution much earlier.

Wexler asserts that Emma may have become disillusioned with Bolshevism while still in prison in the United States (1984, 258). By May 1920, Emma was definitely disillusioned with authoritarian Communism; John Clayton of the *Chicago Tribune* quotes Emma as saying the Bolsheviks were "rotten" and tyrannical (in Wexler 1989, 35). Wexler describes Emma's agony in trying to decide whether to attack the Bolsheviks in "pro-capitalistic" papers such as the *New York World*—a dilemma in which she found herself in a period that was after Kronstadt. It seems that even this was hard for Emma to decide on.

Emma's Anarcho-Feminism

Another area of disagreement has arisen over Emma's feminism, of which, as with everything, she had her own particular brand. This time the extreme position is taken by Morton, who finds Emma bordering on antifeminism. Morton quotes Emma: "Woman, essentially a purist, is naturally bigoted and relentless in her effort to make others as good as she thinks they ought to be," then admits that this is in fact a reference to women who were trying to make prostitution illegal in states where women could vote (Morton 1992, 65). A controversy regarding Goldman's stance on women can be expected, for Goldman took the highly contentious position of opposing the movement toward women's suffrage. Solomon takes Emma to task: "Her attacks on woman's suffrage," she claims, "[overlook] the symbolic importance of that measure" (Solomon 1987, 85).

Wexler, who seems best at analyzing Emma's ideology, argues that Goldman was a strong feminist, perhaps stronger than middle-class women who demanded the vote but did not devote their energies to the abysmal conditions that lower-class women had to endure. Solomon was right; voting is symbolic—Emma was more interested in putting bread in the mouths of poor women, and to hell with symbolism. While Wexler defends Goldman, she does not address the charge of antifeminism, perhaps because her book predates those by Solomon and Morton that made the charge.

Emerging from this debate on feminism is the question of who came first to the issue of birth control, Goldman or Margaret Sanger. Interestingly, Morton advocates for Emma's position as the innovator; Sanger, however, maintains in her autobiography that the issue was always hers—Goldman had little to do with popularizing birth control. In fact, Sanger is widely acknowledged as coining the term *birth control*. Morton backs her assertion by pointing out that the first person to be arrested for birth control was an anarchist, Ezra Heywood (Morton 1992, 75). Sanger did work for Emma's publication, *Mother Earth*, before the former began her crusade for birth control—that is not disputed. Despite this, Chalberg gives Sanger the credit for introducing the issue of reproductive rights (Chalberg 1991, 119, 121). Drinnon leaves the issue open, but he quotes a student of the movement (whom he does not name): "Margaret Sanger borrowed much from Emma Goldman and the anarchists in the terminology and theory of reform which characterized 'The Woman Rebel'" (Drinnon 1967, 210). Either way, it is undisputed that Sanger was to become more involved in this crusade than was Emma, the former eventually making birth control her only issue.

The Influence of Berkman and Czolgosz

"Despite her stature in the anarchist movement," Morton writes of Goldman, "she was subordinate to powerful male leaders" (1992, 62). There is no denying that the anarchist movement was largely made up of men—Emma along with Voltairine de Cleyre were the exceptions. Emma was deeply influenced by the men in her life, particularly by Leon Czolgosz, publicly, and Alexander Berkman, personally.

In embarking on a biography of Goldman, one discovers quite quickly that such a project requires a sub-biography of Berkman, because the lives of these two figures are inseparable, from the point at which they, together, enter the anarchist movement. Chalberg attempted to write a Goldman biography without including an extensive treatment of Berkman, but this proved to be problematic and was not attempted by other authors. Wexler emphasizes the importance to Emma of Berkman, while exposing the conflict between them, reporting that Emma "lived her life partly as a performance for [Berkman's] benefit, as a rivalry with him, and an attempt to win his love and approval" (Wexler 1984, 152). Further, Wexler maintains that Emma waited as long as she did to break openly with the Bolsheviks because she was waiting for Berkman's disillusionment, as support for her own feelings (1989, 49); "Emma would turn loyalty to Berkman almost into a religion" (1984, 70).

Many took Emma's love for Berkman as a rationale for her staunch defense of Leon Czolgosz after he assassinated President McKinley. Even though Berkman repudiated the act as misguided, many biographers, Chalberg among them, speculate that Goldman, in defending Czolgosz, was fighting for Berkman (Chalberg 1991, 79). In other words, Emma saw Czolgosz's act as not unlike Berkman's attempted assassination of Frick, of which plan she was an integral part. Havel, writing in defense of Emma, also takes this position. Wexler, by contrast, asserts that Goldman's defense of Czolgosz resulted from Goldman's feeling responsible, at least in some small way, for inciting his act (Wexler 1984, 110).

Subjective Sources and Interpretations of Revolution

Much of the degree of emphasis that biographers place on the anarchist movement can be analyzed through their sources. Solomon uses some standard anarchism survey texts, such as Irving Horowitz's *The Anarchists*, Paul Avrich's *The Haymarket Tragedy*, and George Woodcock's *Anarchism: A History of Libertarian Ideas and Movements*. Wexler's much stronger emphasis is seen in her inclusion of many specific histories of anarchism, such as Paul Avrich's *Kronstadt*, Voline's *The Unknown Revolution*, Peter Arshinov's *History of the Makhnovist Movement*, G. Maximov's *The Guillotine at Work*, Gerald Brenan's *The Spanish Labyrinth*, George Orwell's *Homage to Catalonia*, Burnett Bolloten's *The Spanish Revolution*, and Jos Peirats's *Anarchists in the Spanish Revolution*. In addition to these, Wexler cites works by more contemporary theoreticians on the subject of anarchy, Noam Chomsky, Murray Bookchin, and Sam Dolgoff, reference to which none of the other biographers deem necessary.

Interestingly, Chalberg, who offers the most mainstream view of Emma, refers to a large assortment of histories from the anarchist perspective. He lists an assortment of histories of the Spanish Civil War/Revolution, rivaling the list Wexler produces, yet one questions whether he in fact has made use of them, for none of the information ends up in his biography. Solomon's and Falk's emphases, on Emma's writing and on her relationship with Reitman, respectively, do not require copious detail of Emma's experience in the anarchist movement. Morton, whose focus is the American Left, devotes a dismal four pages to the Spanish conflict; this is surprising because the Spanish Civil War was important not only to Emma's life, but equally to the Left, not just in the United States—this paucity of information may be a result of Morton's sparse source material. Drinnon's biography was written before many of these anarchist histories were written (or at least translated into English), yet he proves to be sympathetic and does a remarkable job in detailing the events from Emma's perspective. In fact, Drinnon cites *The Spanish Cockpit*, Franz Borkenau's eyewitness account of anarchist Spain, which the other authors neglect.

The chapter titles chosen by the Goldman biographers that pertain to the last period in Emma's life often expose the authors' point of view: "Nowhere at Home: Nowhere the Revolution" (Morton), "Against an Avalanche" (Falk), "Spain: The Very Top of the Mountain" (Drinnon), "Spain and the World" (Wexler), "At Home, but Never at Peace" (Chalberg). Morton's "Nowhere the Revolution" portrays a bleak picture. Morton chose subjects important to the "mainstream" Left; but was not the Spanish Republic an important rallying cause for the American Left in the 1930s? Falk's title gives a similar impression. Wexler's title is unremarkable, but is the most sympathetic to the notion that Emma was inspired by events in Spain. Drinnon's title is perhaps the most accurate, for Spain was the closest Emma ever got to seeing the realization of what had she fought for all of her life. As was alluded to earlier, the later part of Emma's life was neglected by many of her biographers, which may explain wide disparity in these chapter titles. Of all the authors, Wexler devotes the most attention to this period, giving more than thirty-seven pages to the Spanish Civil War; Drinnon is close behind, with twenty-three pages. Falk, however, gives only seven pages, Morton four, and Chalberg a scant three.

It is interesting that these biographers produced such thin coverage of these important years. Wexler remarks on the fact that greater attention is paid to Goldman's career in the United States before 1920, but adds, "In some respects the most dramatic years of her life were yet to come" (1989, 2). She goes on to comment that "it is one of the many ironies of Emma Goldman's life that the historical record of her career in America is so thin while her quieter years in exile are documented by mountains of letters" (4). In other words, there is no good reason why this period has been neglected by other biographers. Falk, who relied heavily on Emma's letters, quotes her as saying, "I must say I find it infinitely easier to express myself in letters than in books" (Falk 1984, xvii). In fact, Emma wrote so many letters that they have been published in two separate volumes: *Nowhere at Home: Letters from Exile of Emma Goldman and Alexander Berkman*, edited by Richard and Anna Marie Drinnon, and *Vision on Fire: Emma Goldman on the Spanish Revolution*, edited by David Porter.

Final Assessments of an Anarchist Life

Both Drinnon and Wexler end their works on Goldman with quotations assessing her life. Drinnon quotes from a letter to Goldman from Evelyn Scott of February 14, 1936: "You were the only one there, I often feel, who had a third attitude and the power of personality to carry it into activities not representable in art. But you to me are the future they will, paradoxically, hark back to in time" (Drinnon 1961, 412).

Wexler uses a quote from Emma herself, who was at the time describing Mary Wollstonecraft, but Wexler felt it appropriate for Emma's life as well. "In conflict, with every institution of their time since they will not compromise, it is inevitable that the advance guards should become aliens to the very ones they wish to serve; that they should be isolated, shunned, and repudiated by the nearest and dearest of kin. Yet the tragedy every pioneer must experience is not the lack of understanding—it arises from the fact that having seen new possibilities for human advancement, the pioneers can not take root in the old, and with the new still so far off they become outcast roamers of the earth, restless seekers for the things they will never find" (Wexler 1989, 245).

References

Avrich, Paul. 1988. *Anarchist Portraits*. Princeton: Princeton University Press.

Chalberg, John. 1991. *Emma Goldman: American Individualist*. New York: HarperCollins.

Drinnon, Richard. 1961. *Rebel in Paradise: A Biography of Emma Goldman*. Chicago: University of Chicago Press.

Drinnon, Richard, and Anna Marie Drinnon, eds. 1975. *Nowhere at Home: Letters from Exile of Emma Goldman and Alexander Berkman*. New York: Schocken Books.

Falk, Candace Serena. 1990. *Love, Anarchy, and Emma Goldman*. New Brunswick: Rutgers University Press. (Orig. pub. 1984.)

Goldman, Emma. 1982. *Living My Life*. Salt Lake City, Utah: Gibbs M. Smith.

Havel, Hippolyte. 1910. "Biographical Sketch." In *Anarchism and Other Essays*, by Emma Goldman. New York: Mother Earth.

Morton, Marian J. 1992. *Emma Goldman and the American Left: Nowhere at Home*. New York: Twayne.

Porter, David, ed. 2006. *Vision on Fire: Emma Goldman on the Spanish Revolution*. Edinburgh: AK Press.

Solomon, Martha. 1987. *Emma Goldman*. Boston: Twayne.

Wexler, Alice. 1984. *Emma Goldman: An Intimate Life*. New York: Pantheon Books.

———. 1989. *Emma Goldman in Exile: From the Russian Revolution to the Spanish Civil War*. Boston: Beacon Press.

Woodcock, George. *Anarchism: A History of Libertarian Ideas and Movements*. Harmondsworth, U.K.: Penguin Books, 1962.

Part One

Specific Themes and
Central Concerns

1

Let Icons Be Bygones!

Emma Goldman: The Grand Expositor

Candace Falk

"[Her] words—especially those tinged with hints of violence—were banished as guilty provoca-teurs, capable of toppling the social order, by those who disregarded the longing for justice they represent. To trust in the belief that the unconditional freedom—beginning with the exercise of free speech . . . serves, rather than threatens, the public good requires that we reinterrogate the provocative and enduring legacy of Emma Goldman as a champion of free speech."

Free expression is a vital concern in Goldman's writing, and a cause to which she dedi-cated herself. Given Goldman's stand on political violence, Falk is sensitive to the com-plexity posed by Goldman's unequivocal demands for freedom of speech. Combining historical analysis and theoretical reflection, this essay highlights the power of words to galvanize, to motivate action, and to strike fear.—*The Editors*

Dancing in the Dark

The almost irresistible signature phrase of the 1970s—"If I can't dance it's not my revolution"—captured Emma Goldman's joyous approach to social change.[1] It sparked the imagination of generations of free spirits. These words dispelled the fear of an austere, authoritarian revolution, demanding joy instead as integral to the process of creating a world of new possibilities. Goldman's name and face, even to those who knew relatively little about her, became synonymous with the spirit of a count-erculture that valued equally personal liberation and political change. Emma Goldman was the embodiment of an irrepressible, fun-loving rebel, ready and willing to fight injustice.

There was an undeniable synergy of the resurgent women's movement, the anti–Vietnam War movement, and the almost omnipresent cultural revolution of the 1960s and 1970s—movements sparked by the civil rights movement and by "the old Left" just years before. Emma Goldman's ideas about women's freedom and sexuality and her bold critique of marriage resonated strongly with a generation set on countering cultural norms associated with domination and oppression. Her celebration of freedom and of beauty, and her positive spirit of rebellion against the forces of oppression, seemed a perfect fit. When her essays and memoir were brought back into print, the books elicited a loyal following of kindred spirits.[2]

The reissue of her 1931 autobiography bridged personal and political concerns and offered a model of political activism born of passion. Images of Goldman's face, her head crowned by her floppy turn-of-the-century hat, adorned T-shirts and political posters; her name, in displays of veneration, was given to children and even pets. Just as many women and cultural radicals at the turn of the twentieth century were drawn to Goldman's lectures as part of the fascination with avant-garde ideas and the current of interest in the New Woman, my contemporaries and I in the "make love, not war" era of the 1970s devoured Goldman's *Living My Life*—as if it were written for us.

Goldman's own contemporaries, however, who lived in the turbulent eye of America's stormy Gilded Age or Progressive Era or in Russia in the 1920s or Spain in the 1930s, might have recognized the characterization of Emma as one who encouraged people to kick up their heels and cast off their old tired restrictive morality, but most likely also associated her name with less exuberant methods of changing the balance of power, including a harder-edged message about the necessity to resist force with force.[3]

Even with her acceptance of violence as an inevitable part of social transformation, and her willingness to risk anything for her "beautiful Ideal," those who feared anarchism's inherent violence and mocked its utopianism as impractical, and those who in 1919 deemed Goldman herself dangerous enough to deport, could not deny her remarkable eloquence in the face of injustice.[4] Emma Goldman—"the daredevil, the one who . . . defied laws and convention" more than a hundred years ago—continues to embody a spirit of rebellion against systemic greed, to represent a vision of a world of possibility grounded in unrestrained freedom and mutual respect and a social order fused with cooperation and desire rather than the force of law and rigid societal mores.[5]

Many young anarchists of our day, once dubbed the "postfeminist era," still see Emma Goldman as an iconic figure and regard her in a manner more consistent with the ways in which she was perceived in her own time.[6] Influenced by the sexual revolution and by the feminist revival of her works, often not by name or parameters of interest, present-day anarchists (like those who lived in the era of the second wave but did not identify with its dominant interpretation and focus) have expanded on definitions of sexuality—incorporating a continuum of sexual preference and gender identity issues, transnationality, race, and ethnicity—and introduced critical theory into the mix in new ways. They do not restrict themselves to attaining equal opportunity in a man's world but, like the affinity groups of the nonhierarchical second wave women's movement, also believe in transforming the whole. Most visible, however, are those activists who are drawn to the resonances that arise between Goldman as an internationalist and as a critic of capitalism as it has evolved into an advanced worldwide economic system. A new generation sees itself reflected in the mirror of Goldman's spirited rebellion—in this iteration against global greed and exploitation—and thus, the feisty-edgy Emma Goldman lives on.

This continuity rests in part on the breadth of Goldman's definition of anarchism, the overarching philosophical base for her political work. She included under its rubric universal justice unconfined by natural boundaries, seeing this as integral to her battles for free speech, women's independence, sexual freedom, birth control (for which she went to jail), worker's rights, and education to foster critical thinking, all interrelated and essential components of change. With this broad range of commitments, it is easy to see how Goldman gradually emerged as an icon for all seasons, a spokesperson cum Rorschach for a panoply of pressing concerns. A futurist and visionary, described in 1908 as "8,000 years ahead of her time," she had an uncanny prescience that continues to propel the Goldman legacy.[7] And yet the question of what drives the attraction to a seductive yet one-dimensional symbol begs for analysis—not only in order to evaluate the ways in which the spotlight that is shined on Goldman has obscured her shadow side, but also to question the powerful impulse to distill the life and work of a prominent historical figure into an emblem of an idea.

If the wave metaphor (popularized through the description of "the second wave" women's movement) still holds water, it is clear that, even with the ebbs and flows, Goldman's tide continues to roll in. Awareness of Goldman and her ideas peaked in the United States from 1890 to 1920, a period now considered part of the first wave of the women's movement. Goldman clearly returned to prominence in the second wave of the

1960s and 1970s, and her forceful presence continues to surge through tributaries of the third (1990s–2000s). Such tributaries (both past and present) will continue to emerge as scholars and activists begin to explore the discoveries of the past twenty-six years (1980–2006 and counting!) of the Emma Goldman Papers Project's work of assembling, preserving, and contextualizing her written legacy—and as well as the works of others for whom Goldman's life and legacy have been an important source of inspiration and contemplation. Our present knowledge of Goldman is informed by masses of documentation from her life. These documents offer insight into the woman, the times, and the movement from which she (and interest in her) emerged.

As we enter the twenty-first century, let us reassess popular assumptions about one of the twentieth century's greatest women, reframe and expand existing scholarship, create a historiography of Goldman research and of the waxing and waning of public interest in various elements of her life and work—and rethink the pros and cons of searching for heroines and heroes to spur the process of extraordinary change. Goldman herself spurned those who tried to ascribe to her superhuman powers, assuring them that she may be "a fool" but she certainly was not "a prophet."[8]

"A womanly looking woman, with masculine mind and courage"

In an era in which few women mounted a speaker's platform, Goldman was bound to elicit curiosity and fascination. In 1897, she was described by a reporter as "in every sense a womanly looking woman, with masculine mind and courage."[9] Although this baffling gender-bending template of the attitudes of her times may have constituted an enticing mix for a woman in the public eye—and a great boost for newspaper circulation—it was a combination that evoked uneasiness and even fear as quickly as it did adoration. Characterizations in the mainstream press of "the High Priestess of Anarchism" ranged from Goldman as the "ultrafem," intelligent, charming spokeswoman for liberty to Goldman as the she-devil who inspired the assassination of President William McKinley.[10] Goldman may have been a victim of the public gaze—labeled, caricatured, demonized—but she also knew how to manipulate her outer image to her advantage. Adept at connecting to an audience and reaching beyond the ordinary definition of politics, this Russian Jewish immigrant had the remarkable capacity to break down barriers of class, gender, race, and ethnic divides in the audiences she addressed by identifying a collective desire for liberation. Titillating her listeners with challenging ideas they did not dare give voice to, Goldman set the bar for freedom high.

Her lectures, which generally appealed to audiences across class and ethnic lines, and to liberals and radicals alike (and still do in our own time), featured provocative ideas about sexuality and a genuine concern for women's freedom. Her promotion of women's independence, especially from the bonds of marriage, along with her advocacy of sexual liberation, often were experienced as more threatening to the upholders of the status quo than were her anarchist ideas about retaliatory violence. Militant pronouncements, reports, and opinions speckled the pages of Goldman's magazine, *Mother Earth*, throughout its long stretch of consistent publishing from 1906 to 1917 (when it was barred for its anticonscription stance), but the only issue ever held up, briefly, at the post office under the Comstock Law, with its vague, broad definition of obscenity, contained Goldman's essay on prostitution, "The White Slave Traffic."[11] Rather than accept the commonplace view of prostitutes as perpetrators of a sinful crime, she defended them as victims of a system of economic exploitation and exclusion of women from the workforce; as a consequence, she herself was accused in print of a crime. Cultural mores became the focus of reactive fear, perhaps because the revolution in the role of women within the family seemed more imminent, inevitable, and widely accepted than the prospect of a violent revolutionary transformation of the entire industrial capitalist economy. Even with Comstock's authority and priorities as a representative of the forces of conservatism, repressive practices never completely succeeded in turning back the tide of social change. However, if Goldman could have had her way, the striking transformations taking place on issues of sexuality, and women's equality and independence, would have extended also to economic justice.

Goldman was never a believer in the idea that the vote for women promised their equality and independence, but she was happy to ride the wave of interest in women's political participation. She set herself firmly against the powerful thrust of activism for suffrage with the pronouncement that true emancipation entailed a complex unraveling of the bonds of outer and inner constraints; it was a process that could never be achieved in a voting booth alone. Instead she addressed the social and economic conditions that held women back, and in so doing, positioned herself against those who sanctified the trappings of traditional family life.[12] She hoped to inspire women to expand their horizons beyond a preoccupation with children, husbands, and immediate social circles: to encourage them to disrupt the cycle of economic dependence and tap into their own desires.

Rather than join with the splinter groups within the suffrage movement that shared her broader vision but opted for a more pragmatic stand, Goldman enjoyed her role as a gadfly prodding them all further to the left. Acknowledging the acerbity of her comments, she admitted, "Yes, I may be considered an enemy of woman; but if I can help her see the light, I shall not complain."[13] In her lecture and essay "The Tragedy of Women's Emancipation," Goldman poked fun at the New Woman and the gathering force of the suffragists. Publishing the essay in the very first issue of her journal, *Mother Earth*, in March 1906, she hoped to shatter illusions about the dramatic changes that would accompany women's enfranchisement, writing disparagingly about the false assumption that freedom and equality could be achieved through legislation. In the same vein, she rejected the suffrage movement's underlying essentialism, debunking the myth that women were pillars of morality, incorruptible by economic or political influence. She especially criticized this single-issue group's growing separatism, seeing it as counter to any possible realization of universal freedom. What she ultimately hoped for was an abandonment of "the absurd notion of the dualism of the sexes, or that man and woman represent two antagonistic worlds"; she approached the issue of freedom philosophically, positing that "peace and harmony between the sexes and individuals does not necessarily depend on a superficial equalization of human beings . . . [but rather] . . . how . . . in oneness with others [one can] . . . still retain one's own innate qualities." Then, she counseled each suffragist to broaden her battlefield and confront "the necessity of emancipating herself from emancipation," always cognizant that all individuals must free themselves from internal as well as external constraints.

Convinced that anarchism's inclusive philosophy of life would benefit both women and men across social strata, Goldman widened her reach by emphasizing that issues of women's inequality and oppression were also an opportunity to transcend entrenched class conflicts. She criticized the supposed progress of a society in which women neither "[are] met with the same confidence . . . [nor] receive the same remuneration[,] . . . [exchanging] the narrowness and lack of freedom of the home . . . for the narrowness and lack of freedom of the factory, sweat-shop, department store, or office. . . . [such] independence is . . . but a slow process of dulling and stifling women's nature, her love instinct and her mother instinct . . . [and turning them into] professional automatons"; such "artificial stiffness and its narrow respectabilities . . . produce an emptiness in woman's soul that will not let her drink from the fountain of life." For Goldman, "true emancipation begins neither at the polls nor in the courts. It begins in [a] woman's soul."[14]

On the one hand, Goldman was a staunch critic of the suffragists and even of the New Woman's faux freedom in the workplace. But on the other hand, she saw the potential of women as a force for change; she looked especially to those who were not hungry and worn down by the grind of daily existence, who were educated about a world of possibility, and who had the energy to dream—all necessary springboards for a movement for real change. Her attitude about the revolutionary potential of this class of women mirrored her experience and understanding of the Russian women who fought against the czar—and she searched for glimmers of their spirit in the United States. She asserted in the pages of *Mother Earth* that "in America, women and not men, will prove to be the most ardent workers for social reconstruction. Already we find in all radical movements women as the most zealous workers."[15]

Still, Goldman could not help but judge middle-class suffragists as too puritanical, humorless, and limited in life experience—mocking them as people who mistakenly "banished man as a disturber . . . except perhaps as the father of a child." She was by inference also critiquing what she called the general phenomenon of "the hypocrisy of Puritanism."[16] The core of her argument against those who believed that women were superior and incorruptible (which she would repeat in many forms thereafter) was her belief that "woman's freedom is closely allied to man's freedom." Then, shifting the focus away from particular reforms, including suffrage, she delved inward to what she believed were more universal necessities and advocated "the most vital right . . . to love and be loved"— sentiments that ultimately gained her the support of many who longed for intimacy and community and who might otherwise have dismissed the totality of her anarchist ideas as frightening, impractical, and having little to do with ordinary life.

(Auto)biography and Its Discontents

In the 1970s, interest in Goldman spiked with the reissue of her autobiography, *Living My Life*, copies of which were passed from woman to woman, the tattered condition of their soft covers a tribute to the fascination and perceived relevance of this work to the women's movement. In Goldman's own time, the book was a popular success, but its two-volume hardcover format was too expensive for the public she hoped to reach. Still, it set her life in bold relief for posterity—her story unmediated by others who she feared might have misunderstood the earnestness of her quest or the intensity of her plight, and shielded from those who might not understand why she deemed it necessary to distort and omit key events in her life. She hoped the book would secure her a place in the historical record and ensure that the memory of her movement, its victories and defeats, could never be cast out, as she herself had been. In the short run, however, she banked on the book's provoking the kind of buzz that would help create popular support for a speedy return to her adopted home. In fact, Eleanor Roosevelt read the book, and loved it, which might very well have contributed to the issuance of Goldman's ninety-day visa in 1934, whereby she was able to return to the United States after twenty-five years of exile.

In one of the most notable memoirs of the twentieth century, and among the few written so eloquently about a woman's experience in the political realm, Goldman recounted the passionate intensity of a life lived in tireless pursuit of a singular ideal: "My life—I had lived in its heights and its depths, in bitter sorrow and ecstatic joy, in black despair and in fervent hope. I had drunk the cup to the last drop. I had lived my life. Would I had the gift to paint the life I had lived!"[17] In her self-portrait, she chose to foreground her inner drama and to interweave the specifics of her varied political activity as reactions to the forces of history around her. By couching her intermittent despair and militant political engagement in tales of love and stylized optimism told with novelistic detail, Goldman actively created an enduring dramatic and heroic impression of her own life. A tremendous literary accomplishment, the autobiography was intended to sweep the reader into history, rather than to document its precise detail.

Living My Life was Goldman's attempt to etch her story, in her own words, into the historical record. It is difficult to assess whether the extent of her omissions and expositions of contradictory stances in her memoir were intended to protect her and others from being misunderstood or even retroactively censured by the law, or whether the book reflects an unconscious unease toward aspects of her intimate life and militant political engagement, especially in the United States. Not surprisingly, she projected a uniformly positive image of her plight as a deported but always principled anarchist. Shrewdly, however, she acknowledged (though did not overwhelm her story with details of) the shadowy aspects of her life— while being careful not to expose the edgy intrigue of her militant involvements or the extent of the torment that wracked her intimate life.

Love, Anarchy, and Emma Goldman

In spite of her triumphant self-representation as one who transcended her own personal despair, and her feisty crowd-attracting lectures—with such titles as "Free Love," "Jealousy—Its Cause and Possible Cure," and "Variety or Monogamy, Which?"—a sadder image has emerged of a woman beset by her inability to practice the convictions she espoused, especially in love.[18] Daily, she struggled to exorcise ordinary feelings of jealousy, an emotion she counseled others to cast off, and, despondent, felt "condemned before the bar of [her] own reason."[19] She provided glimpses of this inner struggle in her autobiography, although she still felt too vulnerable to write anything that might detract from her intention to inspire others to engage in the exalted life of political activism. *Love, Anarchy, and Emma Goldman,* the book I wrote after discovering Goldman's love letters, began as the story of her steamy relationship to Ben Reitman (Goldman's hobo lover and manager who, titillatingly also was a doctor specializing in gynecology). The book became a broader rumination on Goldman's multilayered conflicts: between her desire for complete independence and for the security of a binding relationship, between her belief in free love and her inability to vanquish jealousy, between her present circumstances and an ideal imagined future. In the 1980s, this portrait of the conflicted Goldman (especially in relation to men) was difficult to absorb for those who sought triumphant women heroines. Over time, her complexity of character deepened and humanized Goldman, for whom love and politics were completely intertwined— and eventually was incorporated into "the feminist canon."[20]

Undercurrents

Although Goldman often underplayed her political militancy, her auto-biography revealed many long-held secrets—confessions about involvements that might have landed her in jail had they been disclosed when they first occurred. The most dramatic example of such involvements was her part in plotting Alexander Berkman's attempt to assassinate the steel magnate Henry Clay Frick in retaliation for Frick's assigning Pinkerton guards to the Carnegie steel plant; these guards viciously shot and killed striking workers. In fact, she asserted during the time when she was writing her book, her relationship with Berkman, her closest friend and comrade, was "the pivot around which my story was written" and that "my connection with Berkman's act and our relationship is the leitmotif of my 40 years of life."[21] Goldman's liberal contemporaries struggled to reconcile themselves to the cloak-and-dagger impression of her political work, while her memoir revealed her own belief that her youthful engagement with the violent edge of the revolutionary anarchist movement was an integral part of her understanding of the process of change.

Emma Goldman was an anarchist. Echoing admirers of Goldman before them, many feminists of the second wave did not see a connection between her vision of a harmonious, radiant world and the tactics of using force against force. For Goldman, an immigrant from the Russia of the slain czar, her involvement (even peripheral) in "revolutionary violence" was consistent with the role she played as a public intellectual—luminary of women's freedom and of free expression in the United States—honoring the gradual changes of attitude that were also necessary in the transformation of ingrained prejudices and reactionary values. That she believed in self-defense, including assassination, and especially in avenging violent attacks on strikers and to combat the impoverished economic conditions that were often reinforced by the rule of law and by corrupt politicians, was relatively clear in her autobiography; some, however, including myself, chose not to see the extent to which those beliefs permeated her life. What we focused on instead was Goldman's strong advocacy of women's independence; we held her as a model of a truly liberated woman devoted to freedom for all—and to peace.

The evidence is mounting that the Goldman who was remembered with such admiration by feminists of the 1970s not only may have carried a book to lectures lest she spend a long night in jail, but (metaphorically or perhaps actually) also may have hidden a pistol under one of her many stylish capes. Off the dance floor, we find Goldman plotting in back rooms with comrades and offering material and political support to those who felt that there was no other option but to fight fire with fire, to strike back against a system of injustice. Goldman brought the audiences of her time along with her, making challenging ideas (not only about violence, but also about sexuality) intelligible. New evidence of the extent of her dangerous liaisons, and of the vicious conditions that bred the violence that occurred, challenge us to find the comprehensible center from which to reframe our understanding of Goldman as she is unmasked.

Integrating the Findings of the Emma Goldman Papers

Goldman wrote her autobiography relying solely on her memory and on a small amount of material available to her. Historical research, scholarly publications, and an avalanche of original documents collected over the past twenty-five years, however, have stimulated many new syntheses and reframings of Goldman's actions and thoughts and of the period and the movement that were informed by her eloquence and determination.[22] The process of poring over her papers and revisiting each text has revealed disquieting nuances that suggest the need to reconsider the Goldman "canon."[23] Again, explicit evidence of her association with militants ready to "take action"—to fight force with force—challenges previous assumptions, held especially by members of the second-wave women's movement (and encouraged in the pages of Goldman's autobiography), that she had cast off the involvement with violence of her youthful years.[24] If we read backward, with this awareness, shadowy nuances are seen to be discreetly woven through the text of her memoir and can be decoded. Although Goldman's weapons of choice were the spoken and written word, her role as interlocutor between those who participated in militant acts of retaliation and those who sought to understand them suggest her knowledge of and acquiescence to the logic of violence.[25]

For example, in her autobiography, she wrote an enthusiastic account of her visit with the Russian representative of the Socialist Revolutionaries, Catherine Breshkovskaya, who inspired Goldman to work for the revolution in Russia by helping with propaganda, fund-raising—and "smuggling ammunition" into that country. The trusted Eric B. Morton,

the San Francisco anarchist (code-named "Ibsen" in the Goldman-Berkman prison correspondence) who, with others, attempted to dig Berkman out of his cell and into freedom, was designated by Goldman to "carry out" Breshkovskaya's request to transport the guns across the seas. In a related passage in the autobiography, Goldman's entrepreneurial foray into setting up her own scalp and facial massage parlor, often interpreted as demonstrating the range of her talents and ingenuity, takes on a new meaning. There she mentions that "a massage parlor would well serve . . . as a cover for the Russian work we were to go with"—a likely, though obscure, reference to the act of running guns.[26]

As she reconstructed her past through correspondence with those who shared her early days in the movement, her letters, written in the process of composing her autobiography, revealed, among other things, that there was a wider circle involved in planning the shooting of Frick by Berkman. Looking back, she wrote: "It was just thirty five years ago to day that your act robbed you of your youth. I remember as if it was yesterday how I felt when together with [Claus] Timmerman I was up all night hanging around Park Row to get the papers telling of your act."[27] However, the part played by Timmerman, the editor of the militant anarchist journal *Der Anarchist* is omitted from the autobiography, giving a more spontaneous and less conspiratorial impression of the manner in which the act of violence was conceived.

Among the Emma Goldman Papers remarkable discoveries, not so incidentally, is revealing a reference to a letter written by Timmerman the name, long held secret, of the man who threw the Haymarket rally bomb and who was never convicted or even identified. From piecing together the available evidence, which is admittedly inconclusive, it appears that Timmerman answered a query from Carl Nold (also directly involved in the Frick assassination plans) and named a German shoemaker, Georg Schwab, as the man one of the old German comrades alluded to in a letter stating that "the old timers are mostly dead including the bomb thrower, who died in 1924 in the Poor-hospital in Blackwell's Island."[28]

Evidence of such links to the most militant of the anarchists confirms the suspicion that the act against Frick, like many events before it, was neither spontaneous nor orchestrated solely by Berkman, Goldman, and "Fedya" (comrades and roommates in a ménage a trois who had pledged to give their lives to the anarchist cause) as recounted so dramatically in Goldman's autobiography and in Berkman's prison memoir.[29] Letters written years later show that there was a complex and sophisticated web of people involved—including Fedya, who was set to finish the job should Berkman miss (as he did) but who was foiled by a police spy. And then there was Robert Reitzel, the editor of *Der arme Teufel*, whose Detroit apartment was the first hideout for their accomplice and friend Fedya for a trip planned and paid for by Goldman.[30] During Berkman's incarceration Goldman traveled around the United States and, from 1897 on, even to England, feigning to be collecting funds for his legal fees. From reading around the documents, it is clear that at least one phase of the fundraising was a cover for collecting money to buy the material necessary to dig a tunnel to effect Berkman's release.

The documents also suggest that Goldman and Berkman played different but not exclusive roles. Later recounting these days, Goldman spoke directly to the press, explaining that it was Berkman who undertook to shoot Frick because Goldman would be better able to explain the reasons for the deed. In her writings on a number of occasions Goldman used the phrase "the psychologic moment," an expression that could easily be interpreted as marking a turning point in Goldman's realization of political truths about injustice, but that is actually a code for the moment of readiness to undertake violent action.

When in 1916 Jean Crones, a chef at Chicago's University Club, poisoned the soup at a banquet held at the club for Archbishop Mundelein, it was Goldman's lover Ben Reitman who initially hid Crones and then shepherded him to his escape.[31] Goldman's articulation of her support of such acts was often veiled, especially when she responded to questions by reporters, not because she was self-protective in the face of potential censorship but to erect a shield for the anarchists involved. To her comrades, she defended the ambiguity of her public statements in the mainstream press: "I have never opposed force or propaganda by deed, either publicly or privately . . . and I have and always will stand on the side of the one who has been courageous enough to give his own life in taking or attempting to take the life of a tyrant, whether industrial or political. I am on the side of every rebel, whether his has been beneficial or detrimental to our cause; for I do not judge an act by its result, but by its cause . . . and the cause of each and every rebellious act has been organized despotism, robbery and exploitation on the part of society, and the innate sense of justice and a rebellious spirit on the part of the individual." She repeated the refrain labeling intolerable conditions as the root cause of violence (not only in the United States but also in such countries as Russia) and insisted that anarchism was in fact "the direct foe of violence," proclaiming her certainty that the destruction of a violent society inevitably would spark the evolution of a more equitable social order.[32]

She explained that, contrary to popular opinion, not all anarchists were engaged in such activities, but most who committed symbolic acts of retaliation targeted individuals who were perceived to be the culpable agents of institutionalized aggression. Many who may have opposed such tactics still upheld the universal right to a fair trial and often contributed to the legal defense of perpetrators.[33] Given her own history, and lifelong association with Berkman, it is not surprising that Goldman rarely condemned anarchists who resorted to violence, no matter how strongly she disagreed with the tactic or the timing of the act—they were the soldiers of the social war raging around her who risked themselves for their cause.

Thus, the presumption of a mere youthful foray on the part of Goldman, or her lack of knowledge about the whereabouts and plans of perpetrators of violence, can no longer be part of the Goldman mythology. And yet nor can the harassment and arrests she endured simply for expressing ideas, for offering her political critique, ever be considered conscionable. Suspecting foul play, though lacking direct evidence, law enforcement officers often suppressed lectures by Goldman on issues completely unrelated to such tactics to wear her down, mute her influence, and attach a personal cost to her political acclaim. The relationship between Goldman's vision and methods—the long trajectory from her link to public education and to clandestine force—calls for a reframing of her legacy.

Goldman's writings, particularly in her magazine, *Mother Earth* (1906–1917), display her agile political balancing act. Her correspondence, ranging from love letters to requests for funds for political trials, to letters written in code to evade the gaze of prison and post office censors, now decoded, reveal the extent of her links to clandestine activities.[34] *Emma Goldman: A Documentary History of the American Years, 1890–1919*, the four-volume selected edition produced by the Emma Goldman Papers Project, includes, among other texts, political tracts documenting differences between individuals and groups of anarchists with regard to tactics as well as philosophy, and displays the changing inflections of Goldman's voice as she began to reach out to liberals on the left who were sympathetic to free speech issues. But there is an obvious slippery slope between the expression of a point of view and the advocacy of violence in a country founded by a revolution and guided by a constitution framed by individuals who asserted a need to remain vigilant against tyranny.

A Club Instead of a Torch

Free expression—an ideal encoded in the Constitution, and symbolized by the American flag waved across the seas—lured political exiles and anchored citizens of the United States with the dignity of its exalted promise. And yet within the country's own borders, a constant battle raged to safeguard free speech from the danger of becoming a meaningless mantle protecting only the most conformist political and cultural views. Goldman mocked the illusory symbol of freedom on America's shore, declaring "If we as a nation were not such unspeakable hypocrites, we should long since have placed a club instead of a torch in the hand of the Goddess of Liberty."[35] A small cluster within the "huddled masses yearning to breathe free" fled political repression at the turn of the twentieth century and sailed toward the welcoming facade of the Statue of Liberty, but would soon be barred for harboring controversial ideas.[36]

Impelled by a view of anarchism as a threat infiltrating the country from afar, and responsible for the assassination of President McKinley in 1901 (although the perpetrator was an American born of Polish immigrants), Congress passed a rash of acts aimed at exclusion and targeting foreign anarchists, the most powerful of these laws being the 1903 Immigration Act.[37] For the first time in the history of the United States, many immigrant hopefuls would be denied entry on the basis of their political ideology. Emma Goldman's success in defusing the force of antianarchist legislation in 1903 stands among her lesser-known accomplishments and as a testament both to the blossoming of her political talents and to her pioneering role in extending the principles of free speech beyond national boundaries. In what appears to have been a fabricated test case, she effectively organized a coalition ranging from anarchists to liberals, to protest the law's enforcement.[38] The mobilizing event was the judicial appeal of John Turner, an English anarchist-syndicalist who was charged with intention to lecture on anarchism and labor, jailed, and ordered to be deported. Although he technically lost his legal appeal, the public's opposition temporarily stemmed a wave of repression, especially against anarchists.[39] But even Goldman's Herculean efforts could not change the exclusionary current of the history of U.S. immigration, in which advocating for the rights of those who were not citizens (and who continue to constitute an under-underclass) has never been an easy call.

Just as the government's tightening of the reins on personal liberty in response to national crises was a recurring historical phenomenon, so too were Goldman's attempts part of a long established tradition of building coalitions between groups whose primary and sometimes exclusive concern was the right of free speech and radicals with more varied and, on the surface, more ideologically based agendas. This coalition between liberals and anarchists frayed with the advent of World War I, in part because of these groups' conflicting positions on the war and in part because of the escalating consequences for voicing opposition. Still, a pattern of resistance was repeated again and again, and then propelled by the inconsistent consequences of dissent.

Despite the attractive universal constitutional guarantee of free speech, in Goldman's time such speech was considered a privilege, was regulated by the state, and was only minimally protected under federal law. In an era of unpredictable extremes, when the right to organize labor had not yet been won, in many areas political tolerance was often calibrated to the government's changing perception of what constituted danger to national security and to capitalism. The 1880s through the 1910s saw an escalating culture of violence, with a rash of fatal attacks by company guards, private detectives, and state militia against striking workers. Goldman was harassed, plagued by death threats, always on edge.[40] At a time when the memory of Chicago's Haymarket anarchists, executed in 1887 without conclusive evidence of guilt, still haunted her, it took tremendous courage to challenge the existing order. Anarchists, who on the whole never trusted government to be a fair arbiter of grievances and who regularly egged progressives to resist entrenchment in the system, inadvertently became champions of the same right to free expression upon which liberal democracy in the United States staked its superiority in the world.

Goldman and other radicals who spoke out against antilabor tactics, against laws limiting immigration on the basis of political beliefs, against restrictions on the dissemination of birth control information, and against the criminalization of anarchism were, in the process, protecting and broadening the parameters of free speech. Although anarchists believed that speech was not something the government had the authority to grant, and many even worried that free speech fights could divert attention from the ongoing battles between labor and capital, an argument can be made for the significant role of the anarchists as sacrificial guardians of the First Amendment.[41]

Goldman melded her ideas into the American political landscape, providing a counterpoint to the myth of anarchism as a purely European political construct and a portent of chaos and violence. Within a few years of her arrival in the United States, and in the wake of the Haymarket affair, she discovered anarchism. The country seemed predisposed to anarchism, with its undercurrent of resistance to big government and its belief in individual freedom, represented by Henry David Thoreau's writings on civil disobedience and Ralph Waldo Emerson's on individualism.[42] Goldman was often portrayed by the press and the government as a political outsider, a feared though exotic "other," but she actually felt more closely identified with America than was evident to those who could not see beyond her persona as an immigrant, an anarchist, a woman, and a Jew. And yet when in 1907 her entitlement to participate in domestic political debates was challenged, she asserted: "I was in this country ten years before I ever appeared in public. I have been here 22 years now. I know conditions here as they are, and I would like to know if I have not a right to talk to my fellow Americans."[43]

In Goldman's lexicon, anarchism was a harbinger of freedom in concert with the spirit of America, a belief she shared with the Haymarket anarchists who preceded her and with many of her closest comrades and political mentors. She felt confident that she could bring the American public closer to her movement by dispelling their wariness of even the use of the word *anarchism;*[44] she informed Americans that "the first tendency of anarchism is to make good the dignity of the individual human being by freeing him from every kind of arbitrary restraint—economic, political, social."[45] Despite the fact that most laws were established to maintain order and to counteract the fear of uncontrolled "anarchy," Goldman believed that "individual instinct, standing for self-expression . . . [and] the social instinct, which inspires collective and social life[,] . . . in their latent condition are never antagonistic to each other." And yet she counseled "every person endowed with even a certain amount of sensitivity and independence . . . [to] rebel against the meanness and narrow-mindedness surrounding him, against the lie and the restrictions of . . . individual freedom," warning that "with no opportunity to show his opposition to the present situation . . . hatred, scorn, resentment and despair will build up in his breast until it threatens to smother him." Although she knew that many people conflated anarchism with violence, she contended that at its root, "anarchism is the only philosophy of peace, the only theory of a social relationship that values human life above all else."[46]

Nonetheless, the political tactics of Emma Goldman and many others in her circle encompassed both the violent and the peaceful, with no sense of inherent contradiction. She defended her militant comrades with the assertion that "it is the terrible economic inequality and great political injustice that prompt such acts [of violence], not anarchism." She linked her support for those who were willing to fight and die as martyrs for freedom, in what she regarded as a vicious social war, to the morality of violence by American patriots defending their freedom against British colonization. "The history of progress," she proclaimed, "is written in the blood of men and women who have dared to espouse an unpopular cause," for instance, "the black man's right to his body, or woman's right to her soul. If, then, from time immemorial, the New has met with opposition and condemnation, why should my beliefs be exempt from a crown of thorns?"[47] She linked heroic stories of her youth about Russian revolutionaries and the assassins of the czar to the American revolutionary and to Thomas Jefferson's assertion "The tree of liberty must be refreshed from time to time with the blood of patriots and tyrants." And yet she claimed that while such ideas were fine for the nation's founding fathers, they branded Goldman "fit for the stake."[48] Anthony Comstock—the post office official whose selective enforcement of "obscenity" law restrictions conflated advocacy of sexual freedom with political opposition to the institutions of religion, the family, and the state—shared this negative projection of Goldman and her circle, whom he intermittently harassed through his attempts to stop the flow of their ideas through the mail system.[49]

Goldman's pronouncements frightened authorities who correctly understood that the anarchist fight for free speech was rarely devoid of angry charges against the government or against big business in its exploitation of labor. Again, in her efforts to draw people to her cause, at times Goldman deemed it politically expedient to equivocate, rather than reveal the extent of anarchists' involvement with violence. And yet, in her essay "Self-Defense for Labor" (written while Matthew Schmidt, one of the men accused in the bombing of the Los Angeles Times building, with at least twenty deaths, was in hiding from the police at her apartment and with her friends), she documented the outrageous violence against workers in 1914 and urged them in the name of "their own self-respect and dignity to no longer submit meekly to the indignity, injustice and crimes heaped upon them."[50] Although she suggested that workers find a more effective means than the general strike, she chose not to elaborate on the particulars. While she never completely denied her consistent support for those who found retaliatory violence an effective palliative for injustice, the details of her supporting role in covert activities were usually too dangerous to record on paper. Through the corroboration of reminiscences and innuendo, however, much of Goldman's "unwritten" history is now recorded.

Making Speech Free

Goldman wrote a speech, as early as 1893, arguing that "the men who shed their blood for the independence of this land, and who offered up their lives to secure the liberty and rights of the American people, must have had a very different understanding of the right of free speech." She focused on the contrast between the principle and practice of the first amendment to the Bill of Rights when she wrote: "The Constitution of the United States declares that Congress shall make no laws abridging the freedom of speech; but what has that to do with the police of the United States? They have 'evolved' their own laws, laws to suit their own purposes, and the most interesting thing about their laws is that they are almost always sustained in the courts, by the press, and public opinion."[51] And yet, aware of the likelihood that her lecture would be banned, she chose not to deliver it.[52]

In fact, for Goldman, averting the harassment of the police seemed to be part of life on the lecture trail. In 1909, after witnessing the Anarchist Squad of the local police force breaking up Goldman's New York Sunday drama series presumably because she had strayed from the designated topic, Alden Freeman, the radical outcast of the Standard Oil family, joined the campaign for free speech. Mischievously, he invited Goldman to a luncheon at the exclusive Mayflower Society, without revealing to other members of this club whom he would be bringing as his guest; he was convinced that if they would simply meet her, their fears of his notorious friend would be dispelled. Instead, the outraged members felt duped and proposed that Freeman be expelled or forced to resign from the club. Undeterred, he increased his efforts by bringing Goldman to his hometown of Orange, New Jersey, where he found, to his surprise, that she, once again, was barred from speaking. As a last resort, this time backed by the sanctity of private property, Freeman, who knew that the police would have no authority to intrude upon his home, opened his sprawling

lawn and large barn to all who wanted to hear Goldman without interruption. Newspapers picked up the story of a millionaire's bridging the
gulf between rich and poor (Freeman's relationship with Goldman would
end, however, in 1914 when Freeman learned that the Ferrer Modern
School in New York, to which he had contributed, doubled as a meeting
place for planning a bombing). The papers reported Freeman's pride at
having offered East Orange "this chance to observe that Miss Goldman
has neither hoofs nor horns and does not ride on a broomstick."[53] Then
in Philadelphia, "the City of the Liberty Bell," just a few months after
the East Orange, New Jersey, event, she was met with the dramatic and
imposing sight of four hundred policemen lining her lecture hall. Un-
daunted, she ridiculed them as "an iron wall of physical power and ignorance worn with age," while casting herself as the representative of "a
truth and a never-to-be destroyed longing for liberty." Goldman, strongly
influenced by the Enlightenment, had faith in progress and rationality
even as she endured constant police harassment; she proclaimed that
although "the club may be a mighty weapon . . . it sinks into insignifi-
cance before human reason and human integrity." In response, the police
attempted to silence her, but their intentions were circumvented by Voltairine de Cleyre, the Philadelphia anarchist, who read aloud a transcript
of Goldman's lecture, which was then published in newspapers, thereby
spreading her ideas far beyond the audience for which it was initially
intended.[54] Goldman spoke wherever she detected signs of openness to
her ideas and even welcomed such spectacles of blatant censorship as
opportunities to galvanize public awareness of the importance of freedom
of speech, freedom of assembly, and freedom of the press.

At a time when the public lecture was one of the most effective and
compelling forms of transmitting challenging ideas, Goldman, whose
ideas fell clearly outside the political mainstream, was considered among
the worlds' most accomplished speakers. Her ability to stir audience
awareness of the outrageous economic and social inequities sparked not
only the radical activism of anarchists, but also the engagement of a wide
range of advocates of liberal reform. Her versatility as a lecturer on a
variety of topics—all premised on the concept of the constructive potential of unlimited freedom—attracted a significant progressive following
and drew huge crowds to her talks. Newspapers began to print stories of
interest to her growing following in an effort to increase readership; as
early as 1908, when she was "one of the most talked about women in the
world," the *New York World* offered Goldman a forum from which to

explain her ideas, in a onetime Sunday feature titled "What I Believe."[55] Although she was a staunch critic of gradualism, and of liberal electoral politics, the fact that she worked so remarkably well with single-issue advocates of civil liberties, workers' rights, and women's freedom, often even successfully prodding them just a bit further to the left, was among her most appealing popular draws.

With the aid of the new material brought to light by the Emma Goldman Papers Project, rethinking Emma Goldman—her life and work, and especially her words—offers us all an opportunity to reassess this historical crossroad; and if we still need a moniker for this complex historical figure, let it be, perhaps, "the Grand Expositor," and let us take on the challenge of her wars of words and actions.

Grand Expositor of the Twentieth Century

Emma Goldman believed that free expression was the greatest safeguard of a sane society. "Free speech," she wrote, "means either the unlimited right of expression or nothing at all. The moment any man or set of men can limit speech, it is no longer free."[56] Offering her "beautiful Ideal" of anarchism as a harbinger of freedom and a curative counterpoint to societal ills and the greed endemic to burgeoning capitalism, she spoke out about the exploitation of labor, the hypocrisy of American politics, the excessive limitations on sexual freedom, and the dangers of the erosion of free speech.[57] The force of her words lives on in the written fragments of her extraordinary life, as a reminder—and as a warning.

In part because she dared to go against the grain, to speak her truth to the powerful and to articulate the longings of the "victims of capital," she was branded by government officials as a "pernicious" disturber of the peace and was feared as a woman so alienated from the rule of law that she even regarded women's suffrage as a futile effort.[58] In spite of the efforts to discredit her, there was a steady flow of socially active liberals and radicals for whom Goldman's vision was a template for the peace and harmony to which they aspired. Many who identified with neither conservatives nor radicals nevertheless acknowledged that their civil liberties rested on the courage of the Emma Goldmans of the world who—in the face of harassment, imprisonment, and even deportation—held steadfast to the quest for universal freedom.

Government authorities feared Goldman's eloquence and barred her when they could, viewing her speeches as defiant actions, dangerously persuasive weapons employed in turbulent times against the social and political order. It was not uncommon for local police to lock the door of a hall slated for a Goldman lecture, or to carry her off the stage the moment she began to speak.[59] Sometimes, to dramatize the relentless suppression of her talks, Goldman would sit on the speaker's platform with a handkerchief tied across her mouth—the anarchist queen upon her throne, gagged—to the laughter of the audience, faced with the spectacle of the notorious Goldman silenced.

Such playfulness, however, was eclipsed by the United States' entry into World War I. Government agents stalked Goldman; her utterances against the draft were considered treasonous, and the police regularly used her speeches as bait for arresting those protesting conscription and the war. In deference to the many young men who found themselves rounded up at her antiwar lectures upon their inability to show a draft card, Goldman would set limits on her own speech by suspending the mass meetings at which such incidences occurred. Eventually she too would be arrested and held in prison for speech construed as a "clear and present danger" to a country on the verge of war.[60] On trial, with provocative eloquence and in her own defense, Goldman countered President Woodrow Wilson's declaration of war abroad in defense of democracy at home, affirming her brand of patriotism: "We love America. . . . But that must not make us blind to the social faults of America. That cannot make us deaf to the discords of America. *That cannot compel us to be inarticulate to the terrible wrongs committed in the name of patriotism and in the name of the country.* We simply insist, regardless of all protests to the contrary, that this war is not a war for democracy. If it were a war for the purpose of making democracy safe for the world, we would say that democracy must first be safe for America before it can be safe for the world [emphasis added]."[61]

Goldman's address to the jury at her trial paralleled the style of her lectures and writings, inviting critical thinking and protest against "terrible wrongs" and appealing to audiences and readers across class, cultural, and even political divides and inspiring them to take action against injustice. For U.S. Attorney Francis Caffey, her oratorical skill constituted a threat; in a 1917 intergovernmental memo he warned, "Emma Goldman is a woman of great ability and of personal magnetism, and her persuasive powers are such to make her an exceedingly dangerous woman."

Testing the Limits of Free Expression

Avid First Amendment absolutists, who may have cringed at the refusal by anarchists to disavow violence, were confronted with an implicit obligation to protect anarchists' right to free speech as part of the complex challenge of and commitment to the independent exercise of free speech for all, and are still compelled to remain vigilant.[62] They too, with the courage of an Emma Goldman, must fight the winds, trust in the power of the people to serve the public good, and believe in the possibility of freedom. Ultimately, the right to express dangerous ideas has proved to be the strongest guarantor of the right to free expression.

As it affected Goldman and her circle, the right to free speech was neither static nor secure, and contradictions existed. On the one hand, the barrage of antianarchist legislation enacted after the McKinley assassination threatened to drive the American anarchist movement underground.[63] On the other hand, the absence of a systematically enforced body of laws or a national surveillance agency to restrict dissenters actually allowed Goldman and others in the anarchist movement considerable freedom. They continued to publish their radical periodicals, even after the Comstock Act had been expanded in 1908 to force anarchism within the strictures governing obscenity standards (with the intention of barring anarchist publications from the mails). At a time when the courts regarded the First Amendment as applying only to acts of the federal government, state and local authorities were free to provide as much or as little protection as they chose. For Goldman and the militants she defended, the vitality of America's ideal of the right of free speech was best expressed in open debates, lectures, and written works, and in acts against restrictive laws and practices. In spite of intermittent harassment and intermittent arrests, Goldman continued to publish her magazine without interruption from 1906 to 1917, when the specter of the United States' entry into World War I began to loom; her stance against military conscription, as noted earlier, was deemed a clear and present danger to national security. Although Goldman's words reached thousands of people each year, as she spread her ideas about the promise of anarchism, she could not hold back the torrent of reactionary conservatism that overtook the country.

For Goldman, the defiant female newcomer who barges into town after town, the inconsistent suppression of the spoken and printed word created an air of the Wild West in regard to American law enforcement, a toned-down version of a shoot-'em-up scenario involving the anarchist lecturer and local authorities, each party eager to defeat the other in a decisive showdown. Perhaps Goldman's deportation was the government's final shot.[64] Goldman's defeats presaged her victories; her victories, however, often unraveled in defeat.

A Complex Legacy

Censorship, an attempt to erect a gate around the mind of the anonymous other, an effort to eradicate unsettling thoughts, cast negative projections of the chaos of an imagined world without restraint. Goldman's words—especially those tinged with hints of violence—were banished as guilty provocateurs, capable of toppling the social order, by those who disregarded the longing for justice they represent. To trust in the belief that unconditional freedom—beginning with the exercise of free speech, which may include defense of and empathy with those who commit acts of violence—serves, rather than threatens, the public good requires that we reinterrogate the provocative and enduring legacy of Emma Goldman as a champion of free speech.

Each generation reads history through its unique lens of experience and inherited memory. The force of Goldman's personal magnetism and persuasive powers lives on in her written works. When she wrote her autobiography, she filtered her experience through memory, using few sources. The American women's movement relied primarily on her memoir and selected essays, embracing those parts of Goldman's writings that meshed with their ideas and tactics, especially on sexuality. The constituency of those interested in Goldman has since changed from feminists to anarchists and global activists. This new generation has brought Emma back into the chiaroscuro of our era. Whether Goldman's standing will grow or diminish with time and the new material that has been unearthed by the Emma Goldman Papers Project is yet to be seen.

With the documents collected in the Goldman Papers now amassed and assembled, an enormous body of primary sources are presently available for research, permitting a deeper exploration than previously of a wide terrain of individual and social history. Without negating the strong insights and foresight that exist in earlier works in the field, and the remarkable array of thinking inspired by Goldman on feminism, the current challenge for Goldman scholars—especially in the United States—is, as alluded to earlier, to reframe and incorporate revelations about Goldman's intimate association with violence and to acknowledge the absolute centrality of anarchism to her political and social message.

Emma Goldman remains an important figure. The light and shadows of her ideas and actions have not muted the strength of the sharp portrait of her complex life etched into historical memory. She lived in an era permeated by violence, which erupted not only in the government's use of force to suppress dissent and labor unrest, but also in efforts by militant radicals to destroy a corrupt old order, set on clearing the way for a more equitable order to emerge. Could she have found more peaceful ways to counter injustice and heal the wounds of a social war between the rich and poor, or did the brutality surrounding her limit her strategies for change? Remnants of these troubling dilemmas lingered on for Goldman—and continue to plague our world today. Haunting contemporary parallels suggest that we, too, must find ways to transcend ingrained patterns of conflict if we are ever to break the accelerating cycle of violence.

Emma Goldman believed that the most violent element in society was ignorance. She spoke her truth not only to the powerful, who censored her, but also to the powerless, who longed for the more equitable world she articulated with such legendary eloquence.

Notes

1. The quotation is from Alix Kates Shulman, "Dancing in the Revolution: Emma Goldman's Feminism," *Women's Review of Books* 9, no. 3 (1991) (reprinted in the present volume). Shulman captured the essence of the passage in Goldman's autobiography, in which Goldman recounted castigating a young man who berated her for dancing with "too much abandon." He believed that such behavior was undignified for one who was about to become a force in the anarchist movement. Goldman asserted that the movement should not become a cloister, nor should she be expected to become a nun. She wanted "freedom, the right to self-expression, everybody's right to beautiful, radiant things." Emma Goldman, *Living My Life* (New York: Alfred A. Knopf, 1931; New York: Dover, 1970), 56. Page numbers are from the 1970 edition. All works cited are by Emma Goldman, unless indicated otherwise.

2. *Anarchism and Other Essays* (New York: Mother Earth, 1910; reprint of 3d ed., rev. [1917], New York: Dover, 1969); *Living My Life*.

3. For example, Goldman was close to the anarchist revolutionary women's group of the Confederación national del trabajo–Federación anarquista ibérica (National Confederation of Labor–Anarchist Federation of Iberia [CNT-FAI]) in Spain, the Mujeres Libres, for whom women's solidarity and freedom were integral to their militant efforts to transform Catalonia and other parts of Spain

during the Spanish Civil War and beyond. The primary focus of this essay is Goldman's American years; the reader interested in her experiences and ideas during her time in Russia and in Spain, as well as her general European interchanges, should consult the Emma Goldman Papers Project microfilm and book editions. See *Emma Goldman Papers: A Microfilm Edition,* ed. Candace Falk, Ronald J. Zboray, et al., 69 reels (Alexandria, Va.: Chadwyck-Healey, 1991–93), available through ProQuest (http://proquest.com); microfilm compendium: *Emma Goldman: A Guide to Her Life and Documentary Sources,* ed. Candace Falk, Stephen Cole, et al. (Alexandria, Va.: Chadwyck-Healey, 1995). Also available on Emma Goldman Papers website, http://sunsite.berkeley.edu/Goldman.

4. See article in the *Chicago Daily Journal,* March 17, 1908, in *Emma Goldman: A Documentary History of the American Years,* vol. 2, *Making Speech Free (1902–1909),* ed. Candace Falk, Barry Pateman, and Jessica Moran (Berkeley and Los Angeles: University of California Press, 2005), 290–94, later published as a pamphlet, *A Beautiful Ideal,* Chicago: JC Hart, 1908, in *EGP,* microfilm reel 47, and reworked as "Anarchism, What It Really Stands For," published in Goldman's *Anarchism and Other Essays,* 47–67.

5. Quotation from a letter from Emma Goldman to Ben Reitman, July 29 [1911], Ben Reitman Collection, Archives of the University of Illinois, Chicago; and in *The Emma Goldman Papers,* microfilm, Alexandria, Va.: Chadwyck-Healey, 1991–93, with compendium book, *Emma Goldman: A Guide to Her Life and Documentary Sources,* 1995; and *EGP,* vol. 3, *Light and Shadows (1910–1916),* forthcoming. See also Falk, *Love, Anarchy, and Emma Goldman.*

6. See Sean Carswell, "Searching for Emma Goldman," *RazorCake,* no. 10 (October/November 2002); reprinted as "Destroying Mothers," in a later issue of *Clamor,* no. 19 (March/April 2003): 51–53.

7. William Marion Reedy, "Daughter of a Dream," *St. Louis Mirror,* November 5, 1908.

8. "Emma Goldman, Anarchist," interview, *San Francisco Call,* April 27, 1898, 16, in *Emma Goldman: A Documentary History of the American Years,* vol. 1, *Made for America, 1890–1901,* ed. Candace Falk, Barry Pateman, and Jessica Moran (Berkeley and Los Angeles: University of California Press, 2003), 333.

9. "What Is There in Anarchy for Woman?" *St. Louis Post-Dispatch,* October 24, 1897, in "Forging Her Place: An Introduction," 42–45; and in *Made for America,* 289–92.

10. "Emma Goldman, High Priestess of Anarchy, Whose Speeches Inspired Czolgosz to His Crime," *Chicago Tribune,* September 8, 1901, reprinted in *Made for America,* 460–63.

11. A number of militant statements appeared in issues of Goldman's magazine that escaped being barred from the mails: "Speaking of rulers . . . they really should welcome every bomb-thrower as an omen that their divine right has reached an end" ("Observations and Comments," *Mother Earth* 1, no. 5 [July 1906], 4); "M. A. Schmidt is no 'common criminal' but a fighter for social justice and freedom" ("Notes and Observations" section, June 1916; Matthew Schmidt was a member of a group responsible for bombing the antilabor *Los Angeles Times,* causing twenty deaths). "The White Slave Traffic" appeared in *Mother Earth* 4, no. 11 (January 1910): 344–51.

12. The theme of the inadequacy of women's suffrage emerged in Goldman's writings: "The Tragedy of Women's Emancipation" appeared in *Mother Earth* in 1906 and was published as "Woman Suffrage" as well as "The Tragedy of Women's Emancipation" in Goldman's first book, *Anarchism and Other Essays.* She developed these ideas and incorporated a critique of suffragists who voted for war, in "The Women's Suffrage Chameleon," published in *Mother Earth* 12, no. 3 (May 1917).

13. "Woman Suffrage," in *Anarchism and Other Essays.*

14. "The Tragedy of Women's Emancipation," *Mother Earth* 1, no. 1 (March 1906): 9–18.

15. "The End of the Odyssey," *Mother Earth* 5, no. 5 (July 1910): 159–63.

16. "The Hypocrisy of Puritanism," in *Anarchism and Other Essays,* 167–76.

17. *Living My Life,* 993.

18. For Goldman's speeches, see, for example, her lecture series in Portland, Oregon, in 1915. See illustrations in *Light and Shadows,* and Web site exhibition (http://sunsite.berkeley.edu/Goldman).

19. See Candace Falk, *Love, Anarchy, and Emma Goldman* (New York: Holt, 1984; revised and condensed, New Brunswick: Rutgers University Press, 1990, 1999), 4; Emma Goldman to Ben Reitman, June 1908, University of Illinois at Chicago Manuscripts and Archives, *EGP*, microfilm reel 1 (UI-C).

20. Feminists of the second wave were adding their ideas and research to the already existing Goldman canon of the prefeminist era. See note 22, below.

21. Emma Goldman to Arthur Leonard Ross, January 13, 1929, *EGP*, reel 20.

22. The Emma Goldman Papers Project was launched in 1980 at the University of California, Berkeley, with the support of the National Historical Publications and Records Commission of the National Archives of the United States in response to the groundswell of interest in Emma Goldman, who by then had been designated a "founding mother" of the movement for women's liberation and for the right to free speech. Initiated to prevent the loss of the memory of her efforts and impact, the project's mission was to collect, organize, and publish the letters, records of government surveillance, trial transcripts, unpublished manuscripts, and newspaper clippings to reconstruct the written remnants of Goldman's life and work for the permanent historical record.

Over the past twenty-six years, with the help of hundreds of scholars, students, archivists, and librarians, we have amassed more than thirty thousand documents by or about Emma Goldman, much of which are now published in microfilm and in the first two volumes of a planned four-volume selected edition. We devoted the early years of the Emma Goldman Papers Project to filling gaps in the historical record.

The multivolume series *Emma Goldman: A Documentary History of the American Years*, covering the years 1890–1919, is a selection from these and other documents—letters to and from Emma Goldman, government surveillance and trial transcripts, newspaper clippings, lecture notes, political essays, meeting announcement placards, graphics and photographs, and oral and written personal recollections. Included annotations and glossaries of key people, publications, and organizations ensure that readers will understand references to individuals and events. The analytical introductions are born of years of study of the context and political ideas that underlie each volume. It is from this base and the reading of the works of other scholars in the field that—among the many insights into and discoveries about a variety of concerns from the era that were revealed through the work—a more violent perception of Goldman's ideas and associations came to light than was previously imagined by the women's movement attuned most closely to her feminism.

The present chapter was written primarily with the insights of the first two published volumes as its foundation; with the publication of the third volume, *Light and Shadows, 1910–1916*, covering the period of Goldman's greatest publishing productivity and extensive outreach, the elements of her thinking on women's and sexual freedom will be developed more fully. In part because this period is the best known, I have chosen to share that which has been discovered in the course of the research and writing of the first two volumes.

23. Among the works that have built upon Goldman's life, and are included in the canon before her reemergence as a critical figure to 1970s feminists, are Charles Madison, "Emma Goldman, Anarchist Rebel," in *Critics and Crusaders* (New York: Holt, 1947); Eunice Schuster, *Native American Anarchism: A Study of Left-Wing American Individualism* (Northampton, Mass.: Smith College, 1932); Richard Drinnon, *Rebel in Paradise* (Chicago: University of Chicago Press, 1961).

24. See Emma Goldman to Ben Reitman, September 25, 1914, re: 1914 Lexington Avenue; Emma Goldman's "Telegram" in *Mother Earth* 9, no 5 (July 1914): 154.

25. See, for example, "Psychology of Political Violence," in *Anarchism and Other Essays*.

26. *Living My Life*, 364–65; see also Lucy Parsons Lang, *Tomorrow Is Beautiful* (New York: Mac Millan, 1948), 41.

27. Letter from Emma Goldman to Alexander Berkman, July 22, 1927, *The Emma Goldman Papers*, microfilm, Alexandria, Va.: Chadwyck-Healey.

28. Letters from Carl Nold to Agnes Inglis, January 12, 1933; February 6, 1933; March 1, 1933, Labadie Collection, University of Michigan, Ann Arbor; see also note 30, and note 37, below.

29. *Living My Life*, 62; Alexander Berkman, *Prison Memoirs of an Anarchist* (New York: Mother Earth, 1912), 1.

30. According to Paul Avrich, Reitzel also devised a plan for the Haymarket anarchist's escape; see Avrich, *The Haymarket Tragedy* (Princeton: Princeton University Press, 1984), 384–85.

31. Jean Crones is a pseudonym for Nestor Dondoglio, an Italian anarchist-communist. Paul Avrich, *Sacco and Vanzetti* (Princeton: Princeton University Press), 98.

32. Quotation from "An Open Letter," essay in *Free Society*, February 17, 1901, reprinted in *Made for America*, 434–37.

33. See, for example, "Emma Goldman Blames Police," *Chicago Tribune*, March 29, 1908.

34. See Alexander Berkman to Emma Goldman, December 20, 1901, in Berkman, *Prison Memoirs of an Anarchist*, 412–17 and *Made for America*, 484–88.

35. "Police Brutality," *Mother Earth* 1, no. 9 (November 1906): 2–3.

36. Quotation from Emma Lazarus, "The New Colossus," poem inscribed at the foot of the Statue of Liberty, Liberty Island (formerly Bedlow's Island), in New York City's south harbor.

37. The 1886 Haymarket bombing at a labor demonstration in Chicago in which several of those killed or injured were policemen and the subsequent 1887 hanging of the anarchists associated with the event (some of whom were wrongfully accused) initiated a cycle of fear and a correlation between anarchism, foreigners, and violence that would take years to unravel. Much of the antianarchist legislation that followed the assassination of President William McKinley in 1901 had been conceptualized and framed during the decade before in response to the Haymarket affair.

38. See Candace Falk, "Raising Her Voices: An Introduction," in *Emma Goldman: A Documentary History of the American Years, 1902–1909*, vol. 2, *Making Speech Free*, ed. Candace Falk, Barry Pateman, and Jessica Moran (Berkeley and Los Angeles: University of California Press, 2005), 20–24.

39. See "Raising Her Voices," 19–2. For the aftermath and impact of the Turner case, see *Making Speech Free*, 111–39.

40. See *Living My Life*, 301.

41. See Emma Goldman to Abe Isaak, December 4, 1903, Collection of Dr. William A. Peltz, De Paul University, Chicago, c/o Potsdam Archives, Germany (original letter in Staatsarchive, Potsdam); Peter Kropotkin to Emma Goldman, December 16, 1903, Tamiment Library; reproduced in *Making Speech Free*, 124–25, 127–28.

42. See Falk, "Forging Her Place: An Introduction," in *Made For America*, 67–68.

43. "High Priestess of Anarchy Here," *Ohio State Journal* March 8, 1907, reprinted in *Making Speech Free*, 209–12.

44. Emma Goldman to Peter Kropotkin, May 31, 1907, State Archive of the Russian Federation, formerly TSGAOR, Central State Archive of the October Revolution, Moscow; reproduced in *Making Speech Free*, 225–29.

45. "Reds Leader Flays Police," *Chicago Daily Journal*, March 17, 1908; reprinted in *Making Speech Free*, 290, 294.

46. See "What I Believe," essay, *New York World*, July 19, 1908, reprinted in *Making Speech Free*, 339–48.

47. "What I Believe," echoing the sentiments of a "founding father" of the United States, Thomas Jefferson.

48. *Living My Life*, 301.

49. For Comstock's definitions of *obscenity* to encompass radical publications and journals about sexuality, see *Making Speech Free*, 20–21, 557–58. Ezra Heywood, an editor of *The Word*, was arrested in May 1890 for publishing articles about sexual education and challenging Comstock's judgment and was sentenced to two years of hard labor. Moses Harmon, the seventy-five-year-old editor of *Lucifer*, was found guilty of publishing letters about sex education, the health rights of married women, and free speech and was sentenced to a year of hard labor; see *Making Speech Free*, 194n1.

50. See "Donald Vose," *Mother Earth*, January 1916. Quotation from "Self-Defense for Labor," *Mother Earth* 8 (January 1914): 328–31.

51. "Our Friends, the Enemy," report, *Mother Earth* 4, no. 4 (June 1909): 110–11; reprinted in *Making Speech Free*, 443–45.

52. See "The Law's Limit," *New York World*, October 17, 1893; reprinted in *Made for America*, 177–82.

53. See "Miss Goldman Talks in Freeman's Barn," *New York Times*, June 9, 1909; reprinted in *Making Speech Free*, 446–48.

54. See "To the Editor of *Public Ledger*," letter, *Philadelphia Public Ledger*, October 3, 1909; reprinted in *Making Speech Free*, 454–56.

55. Grace Potter, who had contributed to *Mother Earth*, was the go-between for the July 19, 1908, *New York World* article by Goldman, "What I Believe."

56. Emma Goldman, To the Readers of *Mother Earth*, "En Route," April 30, 1908, 111, no. 2.

57. See "What I Believe" and note 4, above.

58. Quotation from police affidavit, August 25, 1893; reproduced in *Made for America*, 149.

59. In 1909, she was carried off the stage upon her saying the word *Ibsen*. See interview in the *New York Times*, May 30, 1909, in *Making Speech Free*, 431–43.

60. The "clear and present danger" test of whether the criminalization of speech violates the first amendment was first articulated by Justice Oliver Wendell Holmes in the majority opinion affirming the conviction in Schenck vs. United States, 249 U.S. 47 (1919). Later, Justices Holmes, Brandeis, and Cardozo would invoke this test in dissenting from majority opinions that affirmed convictions for radical speech and pamphleteering.

61. "The Trial and Conviction of Emma Goldman and Alexander Berkman," from Goldman's "Speech to the Court," "Address to the Jury, 9 July 1917," *Mother Earth* 12, no. 5 (July 1917): 1.

62. Among such First Amendment proponents was Theodore Schroeder (1864–1953), civil libertarian lawyer and secretary and driving force of the Free Speech League. See *Making Speech Free*, 557–58.

63. On April 3, 1902, the Criminal Anarchy Act passed in Albany, New York; later that month, on April 30, it passed in Trenton, New Jersey; on March 3, 1903, the federal Immigration Act (known as the anarchist exclusion act) was passed.

64. For a full, annotated account of Goldman's deportation proceedings, including trial and imprisonment, and deportation, see *Emma Goldman: A Documentary History of the American Years*, vol. 4, *The War Years, 1917–1919*, ed. Candace Falk and Barry Pateman (Berkeley and Los Angeles: University of California Press, forthcoming).

2

A Feminist Search for Love

Emma Goldman on the Politics of Marriage, Love, Sexuality, and the Feminine

Lori Jo Marso

"What might we learn from Goldman's experience about the relationships between theory and practice, one's life and one's beliefs, desires as they conflict with prevailing norms, and how to carry on in the face of disillusionment and despair? . . . Seeking to articulate a vision of 'true freedom,' Goldman offered her own life as an example to others. . . . She hoped to live a model of a philosophical and political ideal that could make women's lives free as well as emotionally satisfying."

While there has been a long-standing interest in Goldman's personal life and political activity, Marso's essay is distinctive for linking them with Goldman's theoretical writing and for applying the insights from those intersections to feminist politics today. Whether viewed by her or by us as relative successes or failures, Goldman's experiential and theoretical wrestling with such things as jealousy and femininity continue to prove insightful and instructive.—*The Editors*

Emma Goldman is far better known for her dramatic life and for her anarchism than for any contribution to political and feminist theory. An anarchist activist who constantly challenged the political and social *status quo*, Goldman was a rousing orator and a prolific pamphleteer, as well as founder and editor of the anarchist journal *Mother Earth*. She was jailed many times (once for two years) for her political activity, which included support for the labour movement and striking workers, opposition to the World War I draft, advocating free speech and free love, work on the birth control campaign, and opposition to state and government power. In late 1919, Goldman was deported from the USA to the Soviet Union along with several hundred other immigrant radicals including her long-time colleague, friend, and early lover, Alexander Berkman.[1] Hoping to find some of their ideals enacted in the Soviet Revolution,[2]

Goldman and Berkman were severely disappointed by the concentration of state power and the suppression of dissidents in their country of birth.[3]

Goldman famously chronicled her anarchist activities in her two-volume autobiography, *Living My Life* (1970a, 1970b). Her presentation is fascinating for its historical context as well as for details of the sacrifices and commitments such an intense political life required. I will argue here, however, that it is not solely Goldman's political life that makes her important for us to study today. Rather, it is in the intersection of her life with her thought, specifically her intimate and sexual life as studied in conjunction with her essays on marriage, sex, love, women's emancipation, and femininity, where a study of Goldman contributes important insights to contemporary feminist debates. Most importantly, she helps us to think about the connections and tensions between sexuality, love, and feminist politics. Chronicled in Goldman's many public speeches and political writings, we witness her philosophical commitment to an anarchist feminism that rejects marriage and the conventional nuclear family. In conjunction with this philosophy, Goldman lived a life of free and open sexual expression, engaging in direct action on behalf of campaigns for birth control, free speech, and the complete acceptance of unconventional sexual practices. At the same time, she neither rejects nor condemns romantic love; she places intimate connections with others as central to her life and her politics; and she suggests that the basis for women's emancipation should spring from the full and complete expression of what she calls the 'feminine instinct'.

Rather than turn to the 'state' to deliver women's emancipation (as her sister suffragists were doing), Goldman desired women to free themselves by unleashing their 'instincts'. She even called for the freedom of 'feminine desire' to permit the 'deep emotion of the true woman' (1969a, 217). This language sounds suspiciously conservative and even echoed some of the language of the anti-suffragists. Despite her early and open defense of homosexuality,[4] for example, some of her rhetoric evoking notions of femininity and true womanhood could today be suspected of harbouring heterosexist norms and gender essentialism.

I will argue, however, that Goldman's assumptions about women's 'difference' as well as her vision of sexual freedom and revolutionary love offer a radical critique of intimacy that can contribute to contemporary feminist debates. Since Goldman had to constantly butt up against conventional norms, she was unable to express feminine desire fully in the way that she thought would be most freeing. In short, for a variety of reasons, Goldman was not always able to live out her beliefs and commitments in the ways she had hoped. Feminists have expressed disappointment over this apparent 'failure' to live up to her ideals, but I will take a different approach. An appreciation of Goldman's thought, as well as the interactions of her thought with the social and political climate in which she lived, engender multiple historical insights into our own concerns.[5]

Understanding the complexities of Goldman's theory of love and sexuality in conjunction with the dilemmas of desire she experienced in her own life helps us to appreciate both Goldman's life and work, and the context in which it developed. What may we learn from Goldman's experience about the relationships between theory and practice, one's life and one's beliefs, and one's desires as they conflict with prevailing norms, and how to carry on in the face of disillusionment and despair? I am particularly interested in thinking through Goldman's life and work, as she experienced and understood it, as an example of how even the most radical and forward-thinking women can get trapped by the contemporary patriarchal norms under which they live, often even unconsciously internalizing these norms.

Although Emma Goldman consistently and fundamentally challenged the political *status quo*, gender roles, and normative sexuality, she remained ambivalent about the meanings attached to femininity. At the same time, Goldman's vision of intimacy and eroticism has plenty to teach us about shortcomings in our contemporary understandings of intimacy, both in what is possible and what is hoped for. I explore Goldman's views on these matters, as well as her writings on her personal experiences, in order to illuminate the continuing paradoxes feminists face in regard to definitions and experiences of femininity.

Goldman's Writings on Marriage, Love, Sexuality

Goldman defines anarchism in the following way:

> [Anarchism] stands for the liberation of the human mind from the dominion of religion; the liberation of the human body from the dominion of property; liberation from the shackles and restraint of government. Anarchism stands for a social order based on the free grouping of individuals for the purpose of producing

real social wealth; an order that will guarantee to every human being free access to the earth and full enjoyment of the necessities of life, according to individual desires, tastes, and inclinations. (1969b, 62)

Goldman's 'beautiful vision' necessitated the emancipation of women. Although many anarchist writers acknowledged the importance of women in the movement, none of the principal (male) theoreticians gave sustained attention to questions of feminism (Ackelsberg, 1991, 17). Like socialist feminist Alexandra Kollantai (1972), Goldman had to fight her political colleagues on the question of which issues were to be labeled 'digressions' and which were central to the revolutionary movement. Goldman recalls a conversation with Peter Kropotkin, for example, in which he complains that the anarchist paper, *Free Society*, would do better were it not to 'waste so much space discussing sex' (1970a, 253). And even where there *was* agreement on the political importance of sexuality, there was, as Ackelsberg puts it, 'more than one way to apply an anti-authoritarian analysis to sexual and familial relations" (1991, 26).

Could free sexual expression exist between equals and how would woman's reproductive role influence her social and political contributions? Goldman was certain about at least one thing. Her life experience had made it clear that no true freedom for women could exist without a fundamental revolution at the intimate level between human beings in their relationships of love and sexuality. She insisted on bringing to light the inequality that is manifested in our most intimate relationships, such as marriage and the nuclear family. Debating the role of women in the 1935 Spanish anarchist movement, Goldman berates a colleague for claiming that it is the 'innermost wish' of Spanish women to have 'broods of children'. Goldman retorts:

All your assurance not withstanding, I wish to say that I have yet to meet the woman who wants to have many children. That doesn't mean that I ever for a moment denied the fact that most women want to have a *child*, though that, too, has been exaggerated by the male. I have seen too many tragedies in the relations between the sexes; I have seen too many broken bodies and maimed spirits from the sex slavery of woman not to feel the matter deeply or to express my indignation against the attitude of most of you gentlemen. (1975, 186)

Goldman recognized sexual and reproductive freedoms as the cornerstone to basic human rights, seeing the curtailment of these freedoms in the most common and accepted practices mandated and promulgated by and through the state. Marriage, for example, condemns women to 'life-long dependency, to parasitism, to complete uselessness, individual as well as social' (1969c, 228). It compounds the degrading effects of capitalism, annihilating woman's 'social consciousness, paralyz[ing] her imagination, and then impos[ing] its gracious protection, which is in reality a snare, a travesty on human character' (1969c, 235). The home, 'though not so large a prison as the factory, has more solid doors and bars' (1969c, 233).

Ironically and tragically, these prison bars of marriage rarely fail to tantalize young women. The bars appear 'golden', their shininess 'blind[-ing] woman to the price she would have to pay as wife, mother, and housekeeper' (1969a, 224). In spite of her oppression, 'woman clings tenaciously to the home, to the power that holds her in bondage' (1969d, 197). Goldman seizes on the heart of the problem: what women are taught to desire is that which also denies them their freedom. The very substance of what makes a woman feminine is what holds her in bondage. Being a mother, a wife, a lover, as defined by Goldman's historical moment, was to be financially, emotionally, socially, and politically dependent. Studying sexuality in nineteenth-century feminist thought, feminist historians Ellen Du Bois and Linda Gordon note the contradictions women lived: 'what was conceived as women's greatest virtue, their passionate and self-sacrificing commitment to their children, their capacity for love itself, was a leading factor in their victimization' (1983, 12).

But the options for women were very limited. A woman may even be aware of her potential slavery within marriage and walk into it open-eyed having surveyed other, even less desirable, alternatives. "We find many emancipated women who prefer marriage, with all its deficiencies, to the narrowness of an unmarried life, narrow and unendurable because of the chains of moral and social prejudice that cramp and bind her nature' (Goldman, 1969a, 221).

What were the alternatives beyond marriage? If a woman were to remain unmarried, she might have been labeled a spinster, a 'loose' woman, or a whore. Partially in response to these limited alternatives, the late nineteenth century witnessed the rise of the feminist movement. Women activists of many political persuasions advanced new visions of gender relations, women's social role, and even, of course, women's potential role in politics. Some feminist historians have called the late nineteenth century a 'golden age for single women' noting opportunities for gainful employment and even new fashions—confining corsets and hoop skirts were replaced by dark skirts and simple blouses (Ware 2002, 3).

Yet, even the more progressive options had their drawbacks. Emma Goldman claimed at the time, that taking on the role of the 'new woman' was to accept the notion that women must make themselves professional (even male) in order to be taken seriously. She found that the American suffragists, for example, bought into the idea that if woman was to be emancipated, she must give up on her femininity, her sexuality, everything that makes her a woman. Echoing conservative anti-suffragists, but from a profoundly different political perspective, Goldman argued that the suffrage model taught women that they needed to relinquish any claims to femininity in order to be free.

Susan B. Anthony, as the most famous example, seemed to embody this sacrifice of femininity for the cause of being openly critical of the time and effort that 'baby-making' stole from the women's rights movement (Wheeler 1995, 49). Goldman argued that the suffrage model made it appear that gaining freedom as a woman could only be purchased at the price of losing one's femininity.

And as suffrage became married to the Progressive Movement, the emphasis on female morality repulsed Goldman.

Yet, while she ridiculed the claim that women were morally superior to men and especially the suffrage claim that 'women's nature suited them to the new social responsibilities of the state' (Evans 1997, 154), she also emphasized that women should be allowed and encouraged to express freely their 'true' femininity. What Goldman calls partial or external emancipation makes modern woman an 'artificial being', a woman who must be confronted 'with the necessity of emancipating herself from emancipation' (Goldman 1969a, 214, 215). This woman is a 'compulsory vestal, before whom life, with its great clarifying sorrows and its deep, entrancing joys, rolls on without touching or gripping her soul' (1969a, 217). This woman is not 'brave enough to acknowledge that the voice of love is calling, wildly beating against [her] breast, demanding to be heard, to be satisfied' (Goldman 1969a, 222). 'Emancipation, as understood by the majority of its adherents and exponents, is of too narrow a scope to permit the boundless love and ecstasy contained in the deep emotion of the true woman, sweetheart, mother in freedom' (Goldman 1969a, 217).

In short, Goldman disagreed with her suffragist sisters on almost everything. Goldman argued that the fight for and even the winning of, the vote was bound to ensnare woman in new chains.[6] The kind of freedom gained through the law would constitute only a partial freedom, an empty promise. Goldman repeatedly insisted that the vote would never and could never fundamentally transform women's lives: a woman may think herself free, but in reality, only be trapped within new confines (Goldman 1969a, 224).

The alternatives, then, as Goldman assessed them, were severely limited. Why would any woman willingly choose to live an unconventional life? Were there even any models a woman could choose to follow if she desired something more than a conventional life or partial emancipation? Seeking to articulate a vision of 'true freedom', Goldman offered her own life as an example to others. It is in her life as example that she attempts to most clearly distinguish her politics from the suffragists as well as the moralists inside and outside the suffrage movement. In her two-volume autobiography, *Living My Life* (1970a, 1970b), Goldman speaks candidly about her early and varied sexual experiences, her longings and desires, and her many passionate love affairs, often with younger men.

Throughout her essays on sexuality, love, and marriage, Goldman maintains a distinction between marriage and 'real love', forced motherhood and the 'mother instinct', false or partial and 'true' emancipation. 'Marriage and love have nothing in common', she writes (Goldman, 1969c, 227). A 'healthy, grown woman, full of life and passion', must be 'free and big enough to learn the mystery of sex without the sanction of State or Church', rather than 'subdue her most intense craving, undermine her health and break her spirit', in the battle to abstain from 'the sex experience until a "good" man comes along to take her unto himself as a wife' (Goldman 1969c, 231). Marriage sanctions a motherhood 'conceived in hatred, in compulsion' (Goldman 1969c, 236): 'Yet, if motherhood be of free choice, of love, of ecstasy, of defiant passion', it would be a 'free motherhood' (Goldman, 1969c, 236, 237).

Real or true freedom, in Goldman's definition, does not spring from externally granted laws or rights, but rather from 'woman's soul'. If woman is to be truly free, not only in law but in terms of personal liberation, 'her development, her freedom, her independence, must come from and through herself (Goldman 1969d, 211). By refusing to be a 'sex commodity', refusing to 'bear children, unless she wants them', refusing to be 'a servant to God, the State, society, the husband, the family', woman will make herself a force for 'real love, for peace, for harmony' (Goldman 1969d, 211).

But the choice of true freedom involves difficult sacrifices and brings on complicated dilemmas. Can 'sexual varietism' satisfy a person's emotional desires, one's need to have an intimate confidante and committed lover? Does one have to completely give up on emotional commitment and/or mutual dependency in order to be truly free? Goldman's wish was to live her life as a free woman while simultaneously living within community and mutually supportive bonds. She hoped to live in accordance with her philosophical and political ideals, demonstrating that women's lives could be free *as well as* emotionally satisfying. She proclaims: 'if partial emancipation is to become a complete and true emancipation of woman, it will have to do away with the ridiculous notion that to be loved, to be sweetheart and mother, is synonymous with being slave and subordinate' (Goldman 1969a, 224).

In an effort to realize the goal of 'free motherhood' and work towards true emancipation for women, Goldman employed various political methods. She worked tirelessly on the birth control campaign for over ten years. Advocating knowledge of and access to birth control for all women fruitfully combined Goldman's philosophy of anarchist freedom with concrete measures towards political and social change.

At the same time, however, the philosophical problem that the reality of children and lovers posed remained a thorny one for anarchist feminists like Goldman. Even if motherhood and mutual love were freely chosen, could a woman be fully free as an individual when her life was emotionally intertwined with another, or as in motherhood, if she were completely or even partially responsible for another human life? Questions of mutual dependency and reciprocity remained nagging ones for Goldman in her philosophy and in her life.

Living Within the Confines of Femininity

Finding few contemporary women who shared her ideals, Goldman sought role models and companions in history. Reading the work of Mary Wollstonecraft, Emma Goldman finds a model of a heroine's life that, according to Alice Wexler (1981), was both inspiring and terrifying at the same time. In a speech written in 1911 as a tribute to Mary Wollstonecraft's life and work, Emma Goldman focuses on the contradictions between the reputation of Wollstonecraft as author of A *Vindication of the*

Rights of Woman and the private life of the woman who needed, as Goldman contends, "love, unreserved, passionate love" (1981, 119).

This unreserved need for love is revealed in private letters from Wollstonecraft to her American lover, Gilbert Imlay. Wollstonecraft met Imlay during the heady days of the French Revolution. Believing that with Imlay she might experiment with more democratic forms of domesticity, she fell in love, gave birth to a daughter outside marriage, and was soon abandoned by her lover.

Wollstonecraft's voice in letters to her unreceptive former lover is that of a melancholy, lonely, desperate woman struggling to raise a child by herself in a decidedly unfriendly environment for single mothers. Engulfed with grief at the failure of French Revolutionary goals as well as the failure of her experiment with revolutionary forms of conjugality, Wollstonecraft admits in one letter that 'when I am thus sad, I lament that my little darling, fondly as I doat on her, is a girl—I am sorry to have a tie to a world that for me is ever sown with thorns' (1979, 273). These aspects of Wollstonecraft's life fit uncomfortably with her reputation as author of the most important feminist writing of the eighteenth century, a canonical woman thinker who advocated a vision of women as strong, independent, and potentially rights-bearing individuals. In conjunction with this claim to feminist authority, the fact that Wollstonecraft was sometimes a dependent, needy, and despondent woman did not surprise and, in fact, attracted Emma Goldman.

Goldman's reading of Wollstonecraft's life points to the ways in which she was thinking about the dilemmas within her own life and the feminist politics of her time. Building her case against the suffragists, Goldman points to Wollstonecraft's life to prove the 'inadequacy of mere external gain as a means of freeing their [our] sex' (1981, 116). Goldman notes: 'Mary's own tragic life proves that economic and social rights for women alone are not enough to fill her life, nor yet enough to fill any deep life, man or woman. It is not true that the deep and fine man—I do not mean the mere male—differs very largely from the deep and fine woman. He too seeks for beauty and love, for harmony and understanding. Mary realized that, because she did not limit herself to her own sex, she demanded freedom for the whole human race' (1981, 116). Referring repeatedly to beauty, love, deep emotion, and affection in this essay on Wollstonecraft, Goldman emphasizes the importance of the transformation needed in intimate relations for the revolutionary movement. Goldman identifies Wollstonecraft as a kindred spirit, a woman with deep and unwavering commitment to intellectual life and the revolutionary movement, but also a woman who longed for true love. As Goldman puts it, 'Life without love for a character like Mary is inconceivable, and it was her search and yearning for love which hurled her against the rock of inconsistency and despair' (Goldman, 1981, 119).

The dilemma of the political and feminist woman in love, the relationship between feminine desire and anarchist feminist authority increasingly occupied Goldman's thoughts as she ended one failing or unsatisfying relationship after another. Goldman's autobiography makes clear her frustration in trying to live in intimacy with someone while maintaining her political activities and identity. Her constant desire was to find a partner with whom she could combine politics with intimacy.

Ed Brady, for example, an anarchist colleague with whom Goldman shared her life, work, and bed for almost five years, initially was someone on whom Goldman pinned her 'dream of love and true companionship' (Goldman 1970a, 151). 'Surely it must be possible', she hoped, 'for a man and a woman to have a beautiful love-life and yet be devoted to a great cause' (Goldman 1970a, 154). The tug of war between the emotional and the political was a constant dynamic in Goldman's life' 'To the end of my days I should be torn between the yearning for a personal life and the need to giving all to my ideal' (Goldman 1970a, 153). Though Goldman claimed that her 'giving to humanity' only increased her own need, making her 'love and want Ed [Brady] more' (Goldman 1970a, 193), Brady felt, in contrast, that Goldman's 'interest in the movement' was nothing but 'vanity, nothing but craving for applause and glory and the limelight' (Goldman 1970a, 183).

Examining her work in conjunction with her life, it is clear that Goldman was trying to reconcile sexual and individual freedom with the demands of love and reciprocity. One of Goldman's feminist biographers, Candice Falk, has argued that the tension between a desire for love and the commitment to anarchist principles remained a primary one throughout Goldman's life. In reading Goldman's enormous volume of correspondence, Falk has identified a 'tone of desperation, even of resignation' (Falk 1990, xii) that is not associated with Emma, the freedom fighter. When Goldman 'was vulnerable to political repression, she responded with daring and defiance, but when she was vulnerable in a love relationship it triggered feelings of abandonment and desperation' (Falk 1990, xiv).

Goldman's dream of an ongoing political partnership and intimacy was realized only for moments at a time. When she met another of her lovers, Ben Reitman, Goldman hoped it might signal the start of a 'new chapter in [her] life' with someone 'who was lover, companion, and manager' (1970a, 425). Reitman was Goldman's love during her most tumultuous years on the birth control campaign. Goldman writes of the 'great hunger for someone who would love the woman in me and yet who would also be able to share my work' (1970a, 433). In *Living My Life* (1970a, 1970b), Goldman intentionally denies her intense passion for Ben Reitman and the ways in which she was beholden to her desire to make the relationship work.[7] In a 1909 letter to Reitman, Goldman expresses the contradictions she feels in her life. She desperately fears losing Reitman's love and companionship, while still desiring to be a model of freedom and independence for others:

> Meetings, free speech, are nothing to me now, if my love, my life, my peace, my very soul is to be mutilated. Work with you, so long as I had faith in your love, meant the greatest sweetest joy in life. That may account for my utter abandonment, my utter dissolution to my love for you. That may also account, why I the woman who has been treated with respect by friend and foe, could crouch on her knees and beg and plead with you . . . I have no right to bring a message to people when there is no message in my soul. I have no right to speak of freedom when I myself have become abject slave in my love. (2001, 98)

Goldman despised her dependency—on Brady, on Reitman, on her own longing for intimacy and affection from another human being. Living outside the boundaries of conventional society and defying all expectations for women made it nearly impossible for Goldman to achieve the kind of emotional fulfilment she so desperately hoped for. This was certainly not an unusual situation for feminists of the period, particularly for anarchist feminists as they chose to reject so radically social norms. Feminist theorist Ann Ferguson reminds us, 'our fragmented subjectivities require support by a number of oppositional communities that provide alternative meanings and material support' (1995, 373). While Goldman was the centre of multiple anarchist communities and alternative forms of 'family', she continued to long for a special intimacy with one individual. Redefining models of family and ways of intimacy was a particularly difficult challenge for women of Goldman's historical moment. Others, too, were struggling with these same questions, yet lacking the material and

psychological resources it would take to redefine so radically ways of loving, each individual felt they were struggline alone. Documenting 'modern love' in Greenwich Village in the early twentieth century, Ellen Kay
Trimberger argues, 'women might give each other private support, but
there was not at this time a women's movement that publicly discussed
changes in personal life, marriage, and sex, nor one that helped women
articulate what changes were in their interests' (Trimberger 1983, 143).

Goldman's contemporary, feminist Voltairine de Cleyre, also struggled
alone with questions of self-definition. In a study of anarchist women,
Margaret Marsh argues that de Cleyre's correspondence reveals 'that
grinding poverty drove her to contemplate marriage for economic security, that she suffered periods of acute despondency because she considered
her life a failure, and that on one occasion her depression nearly resulted
in suicide' (Marsh 1981, 135). In a letter written in 1925, Emma Goldman confides to Berkman:

> We all need love and affection and understanding, and woman
> needs a damn sight more of that when she grows older. I am sure
> that is the main cause of my misery since I left America. For since
> then I have had no one, or met anyone who gave a fig for what I
> do and what becomes of me. Of course, you dear, I am not speaking
> of our friendship; that is a thing apart. But I mean exactly what
> you mean, someone intimate, someone personal who would take
> some interest, show affection, and really care . . . I am consumed
> by longing for love and affection for some human being of my own.
> I know the agony of loneliness and yearning. (1975, 128)

Telling Berkman that she longs to express 'love and affection for some
human being of [her] own', Goldman suggests a break with the philosophy of anarchist feminists who argue that sexual freedom necessarily implies a rejection of emotional possession. Putting sexual freedom and the
critique of domesticity at the centre of her analyses, Voltairine de Cleyre
felt that to conquer jealousy and to reject any claims or hold over any
other individual was central to a revolutionary strategy. To be jealous or
possessive was to make a claim to private property.[8] While Goldman
makes similar claims against jealousy, seeing it as the 'most prevalent
evil of our mutilated love-life' (Goldman 1998, 215), she tempers her
condemnation by acknowledging that the 'two worlds' of 'two human
beings, of different temperament, feelings, and emotions', must meet in

'freedom and equality' if they are to conquer the 'green-eyed monster' (Goldman 1998, 221, 216).

As Goldman fluctuated between desires for political and personal fulfilment, times of political disappointment became for her the moments when she felt most powerfully that something was lacking in her life as a woman. Writing to Berkman in 1925 of an anarchist friend and colleague, Goldman describes the 'tragedy of all us modern women':

> It is a fact that we are removed only by a very short period from our traditions, the traditions of being loved, cared for, protected, secured, and above all, the time when women could look forward to an old age of children, a home and someone to brighten their lives. Being away from all that by a mere fraction of time, most modern women, especially when they see age growing upon them, and if they have given out of themselves so abundantly, begin to feel the utter emptiness of their existence, the lack of the *man*, whom they love and who loves them, the comradeship and companionship that grows out of such a relation, the home, a child. And above all the economic security either through the man or their own definite independent efforts. Nearly every modern woman I have known and have read about has come to [this] condition. (Goldman 1975, 131)

This is a condition Goldman knows well. Despite the fact that she has struggled to free herself from the confines of traditional marriage and motherhood, despite the fact that she has lived a life of sexual freedom and political activity, in private correspondence Goldman says that she suffers from having failed to achieve a long-term relationship that would satisfy her 'feminine' desire.

Goldman's 'Beautiful Ideal'

How may we understand the meanings and contradictions of what Goldman refers to as 'feminine' desire? When Emma Goldman makes reference to 'femininity', the 'mother instinct', and 'woman's soul', she articulates a very basic difference between men and women, failing to specify whether that difference is based in biology, psychology, social/

political hierarchies, psycholinguistic/symbolic organization, or some combination of these factors. Golman's appeals to difference are often used rhetorically, but reflect her own observations about her life and the lives of other women she knows. Goldman's radical life and practical activities put her in contact and solidarity with huge numbers of women of all classes and types. In her lectures and campaigns for birth control and women's sexual freedom, she reached out to women of the middle classes; at the same time, working for the rights of prostitutes and homosexuals, Goldman appealed to both lower and middle classes, radical and liberal audiences. In addition, her years working as a midwife for impoverished women who could not afford doctors, healthcare, or a back-alley abortion put Goldman in intimate contact with the destitution of the poorest and most desperate women.

Yet, in spite of Goldman's knowledge of the ways in which women are divided, she still often grouped women together in a category without any subtle or even obvious distinctions. As a propagandist, Goldman tended to exaggerate many of her claims, speaking of women in an uncomplicated, even essentialist, way. While fully aware of the differences between and among women, Goldman still found it appropriate to speak of women as differentiated as a group within a structure of gender inequity. And she continued to speak of feminine desire.

In challenging the notion of a rational and unitary subject, psychoanalytic theory has been helpful in attempting to explain some of the more seemingly irrational and contradictory aspects of our personalities, especially sexual desire. In labeling her desire 'feminine' and in valuing romantic love, Goldman is at odds with her more 'rational' or 'political' self that would choose to remake these aspects of conventional femininity. In Goldman's life we witness a philosophical and political commitment to a complete break with traditional norms of femininity combined with what appears as personal sadness over her failure to achieve and maintain what may be considered conventional kinds of feminine/gendered bonds (that is, within a monogamous love affair, or with a child). Here, a psychoanalytic explanation of desire as yearning for unattainable fulfillment (as in Lacanian analysis) may offer a way of understanding Goldman's lament for an unattainable intimacy that she calls feminine.

Yet, Goldman herself questioned the way the 'feminine' has been shaped by social, historical, and economic constraints and never accepts the idea of the feminine as an unshaped or unchanging essence. Goldman never specified what women may do with a newfound freedom or with the possibility of expressing an authentic feminine desire. She found it more important to make her audiences understand that gender inequity structures the world to limit women's freedom severely than to specify what women may do or what women may want, once they have the opportunities. Goldman consistently emphasized the importance of the theatrical and the performative in appealing to audiences, sparking their untapped radicalism and jolting their political consciousness.

In her work to move people to action, Goldman stressed the importance of the utopian dimension of her thought. She was certain that to rouse social discontent with current conditions, an appeal must be launched to 'both mind and heart' (Goldman 1969e, 17). Goldman counted herself among the 'real revolutionist[s], the dreamer[s], the creative artist[s], the iconoclast[s] in whatever line' (Goldman 1987, 51–52). Her searing critique of current political/economic/social conditions promised a new vision; what she called a 'beautiful idea' of a new society where the human spirit would be free of oppression and restored to dignity and worth. Her vision was that of a feminist anarchist future where all would be free in love and work to develop themselves as fully human and creative beings.

Goldman would agree with feminist theorists such as Stevi Jackson who reminds us, 'our subjectivities, including that aspect of them we call emotions, are shaped by the social and cultural milieu we inhabit, through processes which involve our active engagement with sets of meaning available in our culture' (Jackson 2001, 260). Lauren Berlant, too, has emphasized the material, cultural, and historical context which structures how our most intimate relationships get played out. She notes the mix of fantasy and materiality in stressing the importance of understanding 'how to articulate the ways the utopian, optimism-sustaining versions of intimacy meet the normative practices, fantasies, institutions, and ideologies that organize people's worlds' (Berlant 2000, 2).

Goldman's life and theory serve as a case study of the ways her desire for a new kind of intimacy and longing for the 'beautiful dream' of her anarchist vision were to butt up against the harsh reality of the lack of community, material and psychological support needed for her vision to transpire. At the same time that Goldman delivers an anarchist dream of woman's desire to be free from oppressive social conditions and expectations, she can only hint at how this revolution may create a space for new forms of intimacy and specifically how a newly liberated feminine desire may be articulated within these changes.

Central to this though, as I have argued throughout, was Goldman's commitment to the free expression of sexuality. She was as disillusioned with normative conceptions of desire and femininity as she was with the elusive quest for equality. Although Goldman portrayed her own sexuality as heterosexual, and, longing for commitment and constancy, her ideal makes space for people to express themselves sexually in whatever way they may desire. Once freed from the grip of normative heterosexuality with its accompanying claims about the conventional family, traditional motherhood, the duties of men and women, and so on, Goldman was convinced that people would invent new and freer ways of expressing themselves in their most intimate relations. Goldman herself flirted with the idea of having a lesbian love affair (and she may have even done so) with anarchist colleague Almeda Sperry who clearly adored her (Katz 1992, 523–29). Reframing the struggle for women's (and indeed, for human) emancipation in terms that spoke to our needs for freedom, Goldman was able to put forward the absolute necessity of freeing women on their own terms, without having to sacrifice love or varieties of sexual expression and without reference to male-defined and state-centred notions of equality as the measure by which to judge progress.

Familiarity with Goldman's experience, however, reminds us of the constraints that patriarchy imposes on the lives of even the freest-thinking women. Having witnessed the failure to achieve her political ideal in the USA and having become completely disillusioned by the revolution in the Soviet Union, near the end of her life, Goldman was particularly bereft of ideals on which to pin her hopes. In a letter to Berkman written in early 1929, Goldman relates the difficulty of writing her autobiography; having to relive and remember her passions in light of their demise: "It is not only the writing, it is living through what now lies in ashes and being made aware that I have nothing left in the way of personal relations from all who have been in my life and have torn my heart . . . I should have known that it would be torture to revive the past. I am now paying for it' (Goldman 1975, 145). Must the inspirational be accompanied by the terrifying, as Goldman witnessed in the life of Wollstonecraft and was fulfilled almost as prophecy in Goldman's? Surely the fact that these two women were able to talk so frankly in letters about dilemmas they experienced as women trying to recreate models of love and sexuality speaks to the necessity of studying the personal alongside the philosophical/political. Goldman remarks that, 'Had Mary Wollstonecraft not written a line, her life would have furnished food for thought . . . but she has given us both, she therefore stands among the world's greatest, a life so deep, so rich, so exquisitely beautiful in her complete humanity' (Goldman 1981, 121).

From studying Goldman's life as it intersects with her philosophy of love, freedom, and sexual expression, we are reminded of the contradictions of feminine desire under conditions of patriarchy as well as the necessity of changing consciousness to embrace new forms of intimacy in our most personal relationships. One important contribution that Goldman makes is her theorization of feminine desire as distinct from male models of femininity. Important, too, is the fact that Goldman's theory of individual freedom and the centrality of sexual expression and desire for this freedom does not exist as an abstract concept untethered by social/political change. Her utopian vision of a feminist future, though unrealized in her own historical moment, is one that may inspire us to move forward.

Drucilla Cornell has asked: 'Why is it so difficult to feminism to sustain itself as a movement and transmit its lessons to the next generation so that we can build on what we have achieved in the past rather than be fated to engage in the same battles over and over again?' (Cornell 1998, 48). Engaging in the work of feminist genealogy is to learn from the experience, disappointments, and theoretical inspiration of women who have come before us. This represents one step towards breaking the cycle of endless repetition of the same battles. Goldman's life represents the difficulty, as well as the necessity, of believing in a utopian aesthetic that can inspire new visions of freedom.

Acknowledgments

For helpful comments on an earlier draft of this article, thanks to Martha Ackelsberg and Andrea Foroughi. I also thank Marla Brettschneider, Tom Lobe, and Patricia Moynagh for their comments on this article and even more important, for engaging in long conversations about Goldman's life and politics.

Notes

1. Goldman was deported, along with 248 other immigrants in September 1919, after serving two years in prison for opposing the World War I draft. She lost her citizenship on a technicality. The government denaturalized her former husband and by law, at that time, a woman's citizenship followed her husband's.

2. Since the 1917 Revolution, Goldman and Berkman had thought about going back to their home country but their political work in the USA (as well as a genuine commitment to the USA on Goldman's part) precluded their making the move.

3. Upon deportation to Soviet Russia, Goldman and Berkman refused to toe the Communist Party line on the Soviet Union's potential for human emancipation. Though they had fully supported the Revolution from abroad, witnessing the Soviet repression of political dissidents sobered their early enthusiasm. Goldman's exposé of Soviet brutality in *My Disillusionment with Russia*, published in 1923, incurred the wrath of radicals around the world.

4. Goldman called homosexuality the 'problem most tabooed in polite society' (1970b, 555). Over the objections of many of her anarchist comrades, Goldman often spoke on the theme of prejudice against homosexuality on her lecture tours. Blanche Wiesen Cook argues that though Goldman felt 'a profound ambivalence about lesbianism as a lifestyle' she was 'the only woman in America who defended homosexuality . . . and was absolute about a person's right to sexual choice' (1977, 56). Jonathan Ned Katz includes excerpts from fascinating letters from Almeda Sperry, an anarchist colleague, to Emma Goldman. He argues that it is 'difficult to know exactly what occurred between Sperry and Goldman' (Katz 1992, 523), but the letters from Sperry leave no doubt as to her romantic and sexual feelings for Goldman. If Goldman had a lesbian affair with Sperry, she did not acknowledge this in her own autobiography nor theorize its importance in terms of her own divergence from heterosexual norms. Goldman did, however, openly support homosexual desire and the free expression of sexuality.

5. Without a history, political movements like ours swing back and forth endlessly, reacting to earlier mistakes and overreacting in compensation, unable to incorporate previous insights and transcend previous limitations' (Du Bois and Gordon 1983, 8). For an historical perspective on the debates surrounding sexuality in Emma Goldman's time, see Du Bois and Gordon.

6. Women in the American suffrage movement exhibited a wide range of political perspectives on the singular importance of the vote over the seventy-five years they struggled to achieve their goal. Even Susan B. Anthony and Elizabeth Cody Stanton, the early pioneers, differed regarding women's rights beyond suffrage. For a fascinating discussion regarding how personal circumstances and family backgrounds may have affected these women's political perspectives, see Rossi 1995.

7. This was more acute since many of the anarchist colleagues whom Goldman most respected, Berkman included, did not feel that Reitman was politically committed to the cause and treated him as peripheral, merely Emma's lover.

8. Margaret S. Marsh notes that Voltairine de Cleyre, an anarchist feminist and friend of Emma Goldman's, ended an important relationship because she felt unable to conquer her possessiveness (Marsh 1981, 172).

References

Ackelsberg, M. 1991. *Free Women of Spain: Anarchism and the Struggle for the Emancipation of Women*. Bloomington: Indiana University Press.

Berlant, L. 2000. 'Intimacy: A Special Issue'. In L. Berlant, *Intimacy*. Chicago: University of Chicago Press.

Cook, B. Weisen. 1977. 'Female Support Networks and Political Activism: Lillian Wald, Crystal Eastman, Emma Goldman'. *Chrysalis* 3:43–61.

Cornell, D. 1998. *At the Heart of Freedom: Feminism, Sex, and Equality*. Princeton: Princeton University Press.

Du Bois, E., and L. Gordon. 1983. 'Danger and Pleasure in Nineteenth Century Feminist Sexual Thought'. *Feminist Studies* 9, no. 1

Evans, S. 1997. *Born for Liberty: A History of Women in America*. New York: Free Press.

Falk, C. 1990. *Love, Anarchy, and Emma Goldman: A Biography*. New Brunswick: Rutgers University Press.

Ferguson, A. 1995. 'Feminist Communities and Moral Revolution'. In P. Weiss, ed., *Feminism and Community*. Philadelphia: Temple University Press.

Goldman, E. 1970. (1923]). *My Disillusionment in Russia*. New York: Thomas Crowell.

———. 1969a. 'The Tragedy of Women's Emancipation'. In E. Goldman, *Anarchism and Other Essays*. New York: Dover.

———. 1969b. 'Anarchism: What It Really Stands For'. In E. Goldman, *Anarchism and Other Essays*. New York: Dover.

———. 1969c. 'Marriage and Love'. In E. Goldman, *Anarchism and Other Essays*. New York: Dover.

———. 1969d. 'Woman Suffrage'. In E. Goldman, *Anarchism and Other Essays*. New York: Dover.

———. 1969e. 'The Drama: A Powerful Disseminator of Radical Thought.' In E. Goldman, *Anarchism and Other Essays*. New York: Dover.

———. 1970a. *Living My Life*. Vol. 1. *New York: Dover*.

———. 1970b. *Living My Life*. Vol. 2. New York: Dover.

———. 1975. In R. and A. Drinnon, eds., *Nowhere at Home: Letters from Exile of Emma Goldman and Alexander Berkman*. New York: Schocken Books.

———. 1981. 'Mary Wollstonecraft, Her Tragic Life and Her Passionate Struggle for Freedom'. *Feminist Studies* 7, no. 1: 112–33.

———. 1987. *The Social Significance of Modern Drama*. London: Applause Theatre Books.

———. 1998. 'Jealousy: Causes and a Possible Cure'. In A. Kates Shulman, ed., *Red Emma Speaks: An Emma Goldman Reader*. Amherst, Mass.: Humanity Books.

———. 2001. 'Letters to Ben Reitman, 1909–1919'. In S. Ostrov Weisser, ed., *Women and Romance: A Reader*. New York: New York University Press.

Jackson, S. 2001. 'Love and Romance as Objects of Feminist Knowledge'. In S. Ostrov Weisser, ed., *Women and Romance: A Reader*. New York: New York University Press.

Katz, J. 1992. 'Almeda Sperry to Emma Goldman: Letters'. In J. Katz, *Gay American History: Lesbians and Gay Men in the USA*. New York: Penguin.

Kollantai, A. 1972. 'Sexual Relations and the Class Struggle' and 'Love and the New Morality'. Trans. and intro. Alix Holt Montpelier. Bristol: Falling Wall Press.

Marsh, M. 1981. *Anarchist Women, 1870–1920*. Philadelphia: Temple University Press.

Rossi, A. 1995. 'A Feminist Friendship: Elizabeth Cady Stanton and Susan B. Anthony'. In M. S. Wheeler, ed., *One Woman, One Vote*. Troutdale, Ore.: NewSage Press.

Trimberger, E. 1983. 'Feminism, Men, and Modern Love: Greenwich Village 1900–1925'. In A. Snitow, C. Stansell, and S. Thompson, eds., *Powers of Desire: The Politics of Sexuality*. New York: Monthly Review Press.

Ware, S. 2002. *Modern American Women: A Documentary History of New York*. New York: McGraw-Hill.

Wexler, A. 1981. 'Afterword'. *Feminist Studies* 7, no. 1.

Wheeler, M., ed. 1995. *One Woman, One Vote: Rediscovering the Woman Suffrage Movement*. Troutdale, Oreg.: NewSage Press.

Wollstonecraft, M. 1979. 'Letter to Gilbert Imlay, December 1794. In R. Wardle, ed., *Collected Letters of Mary Wollstonecraft*. Ithaca: Cornell University Press.

3

Religion, Faith, and Politics

Reading Goldman Through Nietzsche

Kathy E. Ferguson

"The manner in which Goldman engaged religion is intriguing. Sometimes she used frontal assault, applying a compressed combination of arguments from Durkheim, Marx, and Nietzsche. . . . Sometimes she used humor. . . . On other occasions she met religious figures with respect. . . . In all these constructions her atheism is not the simple opposite of religion, but a complex rejection of and engagement with her opponent."

Religion is one of many subjects on which Goldman's stance has been oversimplified and, as a consequence, easily dismissed. In showing the rich complexity of Goldman's atheism, Ferguson accomplishes two larger goals: she highlights Goldman's willingness—even determination—to engage in "active rethinking" on a wide range of difficult ideas and practices, and she explores the value of this approach for radical politics today.—*The Editors*

Emma Goldman was enthusiastic about the "new ideas" of Nietzsche as she encountered them in Vienna during her studies there in 1895. Yet Goldman's Nietzsche bears little resemblance to the Nietzsche inherited by many later readers: her Nietzsche is not the antifoundationalist thinker whose counterhistories paved the way for Foucault's genealogies; nor is he the grim nihilist blamed for enabling Nazism with his desperate embrace of the "overman." Goldman instead glimpsed a different Nietzsche, a joyous Nietzsche. It was "the magic of his language, the beauty of his vision" that enchanted her, not his epistemological insights into regimes of truth (Goldman 1970, 172). She was far less concerned about the will to power over truth than she was about the need for ideals: "The Ideal is the spark that fires the imagination and hearts of men. Some idea is needed to rouse man out of the inertia and humdrum of his existence and turn the abject slave into an heroic figure" (Shulman 1972, 99). Similarly, she was scornful of those who read Nietzsche as "the perpetrator of national hatred and machine gun destruction," finding "only bad readers and bad pupils interpret him so" (168–69). Goldman's Nietzsche scorned fixed ideas and encouraged the noble sentiments over the base in everywoman and everyman.

I am intrigued by the role that Nietzsche played in Goldman's political imaginary, both the yawning silences and the enthusiastic endorsements. Her encounters with religion and her reflections/actions concerning faith are useful grounds upon which to explore the Goldman-Nietzsche encounter, because that terrain hosts vigorous and contestable connections between Goldman's anarchism and Nietzsche's exuberant anti-pieties. In the Goldman-Nietzsche link I am looking not so much for insight into religion per se, but for guidance on ways to conceptualize radical political values and to inhabit political commitments. Cognizant of Nietzsche's warnings concerning the potential violence in any affirmations, and equally determined to seek political change, how do feminists and our fellow travelers go about "affirming the (inevitably imperfect) positive while at the same time refusing closure"? (Hirschmann and Di Stefano 1996, 21). Reading Goldman's Nietzsche, as well as reading Goldman through Nietzsche, offers strategies for political affirmations and insights useful to contemporary feminist projects of democratization and pluralization.

"Bad" Religion and "Good" Faith— What's the Difference?

Questions concerning religion and faith were central to Goldman's thinking and activism. While she had unmitigated contempt for organized religion, she referred to her own anarchist vision as a "beautiful ideal." Richard Drinnon notes her "attempted spiritualization of politics," her invocation of a revolutionary sensibility, which always accompanied her critiques of established institutions (Shulman 1972, 32). The word *spirit* comes from the Latin *spiritus*, meaning "breath, courage, vigor, the soul, life" (*Webster's New Twentieth Dictionary of the English Language*, 2d ed.). While Goldman dispensed with the deity who is said to bestow it, she continually invoked the "animating vapor infused by the breath," the "life principle" as both the grounds and the vehicle of her politics (*Webster's*, 2d ed.). Her spiritualization of politics included valorization, on the individual level, of a spirited disposition, an enthusiastic, vigorous temperament, and on the collective level of an animating principle or inspiration (*Webster's*, 2d ed.). "The new social order," she declared, "rests, of course, on the materialistic basis of life; but while all Anarchists agree that the main evil today is an economic one, they maintain that the solution of that evil can be brought about only through the consideration of every phase of life—individual as well as the collective; the internal, as well as the external phases" (Shulman 1972, 50).

Radical thinkers, as Jane Bennett has explained, challenge the established ideals of their societies "by way of contrast with other, younger, and more amorphous constellations" (Bennett 1994, 666). Counter-ideals are best expressed not as blueprints but as imagined political spaces capable of hosting radically different ways of life. The pervasive hostility of the hegemonic social order to Goldman's imaginings necessitated a vigorous idealization on her part. "It is through idealization," Bennett continues, "that a kind of life is given to proto-selves and embryonic aspirations that can't catch their breath in the current ethical and political atmosphere" (666). Never apologetic for her utopian commitments, Goldman sketched her vision over and over for the American public: "Anarchism, then, really stands for the liberation of the human mind from the dominion of religion; the liberation of the human body from the dominion of property; liberation from the shackles and restraint of government. Anarchism stands for a social order based on the free grouping of individuals for the purpose of producing real social wealth, an order that will guarantee to every human being free access to the earth and full enjoyment of the necessities of life, according to individual desires, tastes, and inclinations" (Shulman 1972, 59).

In response to accusations that her Ideal was impractical, she turned to Oscar Wilde:

> A practical scheme, says Oscar Wilde, is either one already in existence, or a scheme that could be carried out under the existing conditions; but it is exactly the existing conditions that one objects to, and any scheme that could accept these conditions is wrong and foolish. The true criterion of the practical, therefore, is not whether the latter can keep intact the wrong or foolish: rather it is whether the scheme has vitality enough to leave the stagnant waters of the old, and build, as well as sustain, new life. In light of this conception, Anarchism is indeed practical. More than any other idea, it is helping to do away with the wrong and

foolish; more than any other idea, it is building and sustaining new life. (Shulman 1972, 49).

But what kind of idealization does Goldman practice (Bennett 1994, 665)? Does she reinstitute an anarchist version of the dogmatic orthodoxies she otherwise critiques, or does she infuse her radical politics with a spirituality that resists fundamentalism? Does Goldman give us, in Zarathustra's language, an old tablet or a new one? Zarathustra imagines the difference as follows:

> When the water is spanned by planks, when bridges and railings leap over the river, verily those are not believed who say, "Everything is in flux." Even the blockheads contradict them. "How now?" say the blockheads. "Everything should be in flux? After all, planks and railings are *over* the river. Whatever is *over* the river is firm; all the values of things, the bridges, the concepts, all "good" and "evil"—all that is *firm*.
>
> But when the hard winter comes, the river—animal tamer, then even the most quickwitted learn mistrust; then verily, not only the blockheads then say, "Does not everything *stand still?*"
>
> "At bottom everything stands still"—that is truly a winter doctrine, a good thing for sterile times, a fine comfort for hibernators and hearth-squatters.
>
> "At bottom everything stands still"—*against* this the thawing wind preaches. The thawing wind, a bull that is no plowing bull, a raging bull, a destroyer who breaks the ice with wrathful horns. Ice, however, *breaks bridges!*
>
> O my brothers is not everything in flux *now?* Have not all railings and bridges fallen into the water? Who could still cling to "good" and "evil"?
>
> "Woe to us! Hail to us! The thawing wind blows!"—thus preach in every street, my brothers. (Nietzsche 1954, 201)

Several intertwining themes animate Zarathustra's words. He sketches a profound mobility at the heart of things, eroding the winter thoughts that repeatedly reinstate their claims to find both a firm bridge above the flux and a solid bottom underneath it. These seductive reinstatements require strategies of exclusion and erasure to maintain their appearance of solidity, to account for the troubles at hand by displacing and disguising their cruelties: suffering readily fosters "the singular hegemony of winter doctrines" (Connolly 1999, 53). Zarathustra paradoxically reaches toward an account of the fundamentals of things, while throwing doubt on every effort to make things fixed and permanent. He presents truth both as an effort (indispensable but always incomplete) to freeze our accounts of things, and as the always mobile flux that continues to haunt those accounts, "the surplus and noise that circulate through every solid formation and create possibilities for new becomings" (Connolly 1999, 54). Zarathustra expresses gratitude for the thawing wind that destroys the ice, the ice that breaks the bridges. The thawing wind opens up the rich abundance and excess of life, "as if a full apple offered itself to my hand, a ripe golden apple with cool, soft, velvet skin, thus the world offered itself to me today; not riddle enough to frighten away human love, not solution enough to put to sleep human wisdom, a humanly good thing the world was to me today, though one speaks so much evil of it" (Nietzsche 1954, 187).

While Zarathustra looks upon this apple in a dream, he carries this encounter to his battles with the waking world, cherishing its quiet fullness, "not inquisitively, not acquisitively, not afraid, not begging" (Nietzsche 1954, 187). In Connolly's insightful reading of the aphorism of the tablets: "Gratitude for the abundance of life, then, carries acceptance of a contestable conception of being into ethics and politics. But such a temperament is not located beyond the play of identities, understandings, and principles. It is inserted into these media, rendering them more responsive to that which exceeds them, more generous and refined in their engagements with difference. Without the infusion of such gratitude, high sounding principles will be applied in stingy, punitive ways (1999, 54). The ethical sensibility ensuing from the thawing wind is one attuned to generosity and care for the world.

Zarathustra's delight in the indeterminate plenitude of the apple is always mixed with his keen nose for the platitudes of the "omni-satisfied." "Verily, I also do not like those who consider everything good and this world the best" (Nietzsche 1954, 194). Those who "chew and digest everything" are the happy counterparts of the "hibernators and hearth-squatters" (194, 201) residing in winter doctrines of fixity and judgment. Zarathustra relentlessly sniffs out the lurking ressentiment in those who "cling to 'good' and 'evil,'" who insist on a moral economy of redemption and punishment (200). Yet his understanding of the processes of judgment alerts him to the reappearance of our enemies within ourselves:

"*Even in ourselves* the old idol-priest still lives who roasts what is best in us for his feast" (200). Zarathustra's contempt for pity rejects both the search for transcendental reasons for suffering and the demand for revenge against the pain that is written into life. He reserves his compassion for those suffocated by winter doctrines.

Looking for Emma . . .

Keeping in mind Zarathustra's reflections on winter doctrines, and Connolly's politicizations of their ethical and political implications, I return to Goldman's discussions of/encounters with religion and faith. Does Goldman give us a winter doctrine or a thawing wind? More precisely, what aspects of her ideas and actions would freeze feminism into a mirror image of our opponents, and what aspects might move us toward both openness and affirmation?

Goldman's writings on organized religion are straightforwardly critical and dismissive, parallel to her views on the state. "Christianity," she declares, "is the conspiracy of ignorance against reason, of darkness against light, of submission and slavery against independence and freedom; of the denial of strength and beauty, against the affirmation of the joy and glory of life" (Shulman 1972, 194). This statement sets up a familiar pattern of dualisms: reason versus ignorance, dark versus light, knowledge versus ignorance, freedom versus slavery. Here Goldman seems to reject religion by setting up atheism as simply, clearly, and entirely its opposite, so that nothing need be done except expel the bad and retain the good. Such statements support those who read anarchism as a competing orthodoxy, a new religion, the flip side of the old.

Yet Goldman offers other reflections on faith that suggest a more complex perspective. Her defense of atheism is based on her reading of its open-endedness, fluidity, respect for life, in contrast to a "static and fixed" theism (199). She advocates a kind of vitalism, a joyous energy, "the eternal yea to life, purpose, and beauty" (202). Her affirmations of anarchism are tied to this open-endedness, to her resistance to being "bound by fixities" (199).

These affirmations flow into her political activism as well. Famous for the alleged remark "If I can't dance, I don't want to be a part of your revolution," Goldman, in her public presence in the United States, combined fierce condemnation of state power with robust cultural inquiry.[1] She brought Ibsen, Shaw, and Strindberg to United States working-class and middle-class audiences, along with birth control, free speech, and union organizing. Her affirmations are, at times, woven into recognition of their incompleteness, her ideology informed by a mischievous joie de vivre. In these moments her combination of political critique with aesthetic enjoyment offers substantial food for thought for political thinkers struggling to articulate positive values while recognizing the dangers of foundational claims.

Goldman's own articulation of her commitments often supports the first, more conventional reading of her anarchism as a reinstitution of the religions she abhorred. Goldman's coming-to-anarchism is a conversion narrative par excellence. Her earliest political explorations are heavily construed in the language of religious faith; the execution of the "Haymarket martyrs" (five men put to death in Chicago for allegedly causing the Haymarket riots in 1886, and later pardoned by the governor) was the catalyst, she recalled, in her autobiography, "a great ideal, a burning faith, a determination to dedicate myself to the memory of my martyred comrades, to make their cause my own, to make known to the world their beautiful lives and heroic deaths" (Goldman 1970, 10).

Familiar, melodramatic religious tropes dominate her earliest self-accounts: sacrifice, witness, trial, redemption. As a very young woman (Goldman was in her early twenties when she embraced anarchism) she declared, "Nothing personal mattered. Only the Cause mattered" (Goldman 1970, 26). Attracted to the "fervor" of the young and dogmatic Alexander Berkman, she followed "the path of anarchism" (33, 34). She recounts her "worship" for Johann Most, the fiery anarchist speaker of the *Freiheit* circle in New York, and her admiration for his "spiritual awakening" (40, 64). Every new opportunity for activism during those turbulent times was "a call," her response always in the form of a pledge: "I will go" (54). She and her young comrades "made a pact—to dedicate ourselves to the Cause in some supreme deed, to die together if necessary, or to continue to live and work for the ideal for which one of us might have to give his life" (62). Political change is framed as "the reawakening of the masses" (79) for which anarchism provides a "spiritual light" that will "usher in the Dawn" (Shulman 1972, 63). Rebirth metaphors abound: "Fortunately, the Dawn is emerging from the chaos and darkness. Woman is awakening, she is throwing off the nightmare of Morality; she will no longer be bound" (Goldman 1970, 132). While the adolescent ardor of the earliest writings and recollections calms down a bit in Goldman's later accounts, the religious metaphors persist: she referred to her participation in the Spanish revolution as "coming home after a life-time of pilgrimage" and compared her emotions to those her "forbearers must have felt when they entered the holy temple" (Porter 1983, xi).

The conventional religious imagery is reinforced in Goldman's accounts by equally conventional organic metaphors. Organic tropes reassure Goldman and her readers that her political agenda is consistent with, and affirmed by, an alleged underlying nature:

> It is the harmony of organic growth which produces variety of color and form—the complete whole we admire in the flower. Analogously will the organized activity of free human beings endowed with the spirit of solidarity result in the perfection of social harmony—which is Anarchism. Indeed, only Anarchism makes non-authoritarian organization a reality, since it abolishes the existing antagonism between individuals and classes. Anarchism, whose roots, as it were, are part of nature's forces, destroys, not healthful tissue, but parasitic growths that feed on the life's essence of society. It is merely clearing the soil from weeds and sagebrush, that it may eventually bear healthy fruit. (Shulman 1972, 49)

The organic metaphors erase tension; they hide the act of embracing certain political values at the expense of others by folding Goldman's affirmations into an untroubled telos of health: "There is no conflict between the individual and the social instincts, any more than there is between the heart and the lungs: the one, the receptacle of a precious life essence, the other the repository of the element that keeps the essence pure and strong. The individual is the heart of society, conserving the essence of social life; society is the lungs which are distributing the element to keep the life essence—that is, the individual—pure and strong" (Shulman 1972, 51). Oppressive institutions are characterized as "parasites" and "deathly germs" (303). In her address to the jury that convicted her of conspiracy to interfere with conscription, leading to her imprisonment in 1917 and deportation to Russia two years later, Goldman characterized herself as a physician diagnosing illness in a patient—society—in order to effect a cure, that cure being anarchism (317).

The rhetorical counterpart of Goldman's reassuring organic imagery is her threatening mechanical images, notably of the clock: "Real wealth consists in things of utility and beauty, in things that help to create strong, beautiful bodies and surroundings inspiring to live in . . . if we are to continue in machine subservience, our slavery is more complete than was our bondage to the King . . . centralization is not only the death knell of liberty, but also of health and beauty, of art and science, all these being impossible in a clocklike, mechanical atmosphere" (Shulman 1972, 53–54). Mechanical images always represent danger: " [The state's] highest attainment is the reduction of mankind to clockwork" (55). Reflecting not only the antimachine rhetoric popular in her time, but also her own personal experiences, acquired when she was a factory laborer, with Fordism's discipline and surveillance, she equated "mechanization" with "concentrated dullness" (93) and with "uniformity and sameness" (Goldman 1970, 16). Mechanical images denote that which is artificial, controlling, bad; organic images mark the space of the natural, the free, the good.

If Goldman's thinking were exhausted by these closed-ended rhetorical practices, there would be little reason to return to her words. Yet there are other discursive practices at work, other vehicles through which she puts her imagined possibilities into circulation. First, there is her consistent plea for open-endedness, for mobility in identities and ideas, for difference. Second is her intervention into the dichotomy between the religious and the secular; she both refused and engaged religion, often in ingenious ways. Third, there are her own struggles with people and experiences that pushed her to reformulate her categories of analysis, her active doubting and rethinking, her refusal to ignore or dismiss that which did not fit. These strategies of understanding sabotage the fixity and self-assurance at work in the system-sustaining tropes described above, making Goldman's political thinking more interesting, more open, and more useful to contemporary feminists who want to both sustain and question our commitments.

An Emphasis on Process

In a widely read 1908 essay Goldman remarked: "'What I believe' is a process rather than a finality. Finalities are for gods and governments, not for the human intellect. Life is something more than formulas. In the battle for freedom, as Ibsen has so well pointed out, it is the *struggle* for, not so much the attainment of, liberty, that develops all that is strongest, sturdiest and finest in human character" (Shulman 1972, 35). Nearly thirty years later she continued this theme in her essay "Was My Life Worth Living?" published in *Harper's Magazine:* "I have always striven to remain in a state of flux and continued growth, and not to petrify in a niche of self-satisfaction" (Shulman 1972, 397). She shared with Max Stirner a hatred for "fixed ideas," with Emerson the value of "the active soul," with Faust a horror of reducing complex beings to calculations of expediency (114, 51, 110). She was appalled at schools that insist on sameness, that "shape every human being according to one pattern" (108). Goldman participated in founding several "modern schools," determined to create an alternative to the prevailing educational setting: "In fact, our halls of learning, from public school to the university, are but strait-jackets for teachers as well as pupils, simply because a strait-jacket of the mind is the greatest guarantee for a dull, colorless, inert mass moving like a pack of sheep between two high walls" (118).

Calling consistently for more room for and appreciation of creativity, she equated freedom with the ability to act: "Real freedom, true liberty is positive: it is freedom to something, it is the liberty to be, to do, in short, the liberty of actual and active opportunity" (98). She praised Nietzsche and Stirner for their critique of "a pernicious slave morality, the denial of life, the destroyer of all the elements that make for strength and character" (86). Goldman interpreted Nietzsche's master morality as having "nothing to do with the vulgarity of station, caste, or wealth. Rather did it mean the masterful in human possibilities, the masterful in man that would help him to overcome old traditions and worn-out values, so that he may learn to become the creator of new and beautiful things" (187). Horrified by static ideas, she claimed "eternal change, thousandfold variations, continual innovation are the essence of life" (109). Arguing (unsuccessfully) before the jury that convicted and deported her, Goldman spoke against the collapse of complex ideas around a single axis of meaning. She made a plea for difference: "But may there not be different kinds of patriotism as there are different kinds of liberty?" (323). In "The Philosophy of Atheism," she condemned theism for its "absolutism," its "paralyzing effect upon thought and action" (Shulman 1972, 200–201). Her atheism declined the divine in order to affirm the multiple possibilities within the human, which she saw as unknowable under conditions of oppression:

Poor human nature, what horrible crimes have been committed in thy name! Every fool, from king to policeman, from the flat-headed parson to the visionless dabbler in science, presumes to speak authoritatively of human nature. The greater the mental charlatan, the more definite his insistence on the wickedness and weaknesses of human nature. Yet, how can any one speak of it to-day, with every soul in a prison, with every heart fettered, wounded, and maimed? Freedom, expansion, opportunity, and, above all, peace and repose, alone can teach us the real dominant factors of human nature and all its wonderful possibilities. (59)

Yet she did not attribute the possibilities for anarchism solely to the unrealized future; with Peter Kropotkin, she saw the grounds of her political vision in her own society, in its interstices and unpredictable disruptive spaces, as well as in heroic moments of revolutionary opportunity (Goldman 1970, 155).

Debts to Otherness

Goldman's atheism did not lead her to secularism. She did not seek to sequester religion in a separate private realm, but to engage it in political debate. She heaped scorn on European socialists who declared religion to be a "private affair" in their efforts to minimize metaphysical disputes and garner more votes. "For goodness sake," she remarked sarcastically, "let's not offend respectability, let's not hurt the religious feelings of the people" (Shulman 1972, 42).

The manner in which Goldman engaged religion is intriguing. Sometimes she used frontal assault, applying a compressed combination of arguments from Durkheim, Marx, and Nietzsche. Invented by human beings to account for phenomena they did not understand, "the God idea" represents an unnecessary dependence that human beings can outgrow (196–97). As an opiate of the masses, "religion and morality are a much better whip to keep people in submission than even the club and the gun" (128). As a manifestation of slave morality, "the sickroom atmosphere of the Christian faith" acts as "the denial of life, the destroyer of all the elements that make for strength and character" (192, 186). Goldman does not let even early Christianity off the hook, seeing in Christ "the embodiment of submission, of inertia, of the denial of life" (188).

These critiques did not exhaust her repertoire of strategies to engage religion. Sometimes she used humor: "Heaven must be an awfully dull place if the poor in spirit live there" (190). "The Scriptures tell us that God created Man in His own image, which has by no means proven a success" (111). She sometimes satirized religion irreverently, participating in mock religious services and redefining the meaning of religious sacraments (105). On other occasions she met religious figures with respect, making friends with the prison priest at Blackwells Island, requesting the Bible that he refrained from pressing on her, recognizing a fellow traveler: "My own ideal, my faith, was at the opposite pole from his, but I knew he was as ardently sincere as I. Our fervor was our meeting ground" (Goldman 1970, 146). While in most of their public statements referring to Goldman American clergy denounced her, a few religious leaders discerned an uneasy kinship. She was invited to speak from the pulpit of a Detroit minister who was later run out of town in the ensuing scandal. After hearing her speak on atheism to a large assembly of clergymen, a rabbi remarked, "In spite of all Miss Goldman has said about religion, she is the most religious person I know" (Shulman 1972, 106). Goldman's recognition of her partial similarity to that which she ardently opposed sometimes extended to deconstructing the totality she usually treated as "religion," finding significant differences within that broad category. While all religions, in her view, preached submission, she preferred Catholicism because "it is less hypocritical" and "it makes allowance for human frailties and it has a sense of beauty" (Goldman 1970, 143). In all these constructions her atheism is not the simple opposite of religion, but a complex rejection of and engagement with her opponent.

Possibilities for Rethinking

Alex Kates Shulman, in a commentary on Goldman, characterized Goldman's ideas as relatively static: "She was an activist, not a theoretician. The libertarian vision she began with at twenty served for theory, and from it, together with her large emotional resources, flowed her commitment to action" (Shulman 1972, 21). While there is no doubt that Goldman's "large emotional resources" were central to her political career, Goldman's self-understanding did not segregate thinking, feeling, and acting into discrete activities. Her account of her life is woven with episodes of doubt and reconsideration, of events that discomforted her and prompted fresh thinking. While her overall belief in her "beautiful ideal" animated her entire life, the particular meanings of this ideal, its applications to specific questions and circumstances, required continual rethinking. An early example of this rethinking occurred when Goldman's aesthetic inclinations clashed with the demand for political purity within anarchist ranks. Why, she asked, should beauty be only for the ruling class? An employer who dismissed her request for a raise denied that she had any need for "the occasional book or a theatre ticket"; he allowed that "for a factory girl [she] had rather extravagant tastes" (Goldman 1970, 17). Later her male comrades made the same arguments: young Alexander Berkman relentlessly demanded that anarchists must be "consistent," must foreswear all "bourgeois" pleasures and connections: "It is inconsistent for an anarchist to enjoy luxuries when the people live in poverty" (Goldman 1970, 32). Goldman responded by redefining necessity: "But beautiful things are not luxuries," she insisted; "they are necessaries. Life would be unbearable without them" (32). While she continued to admire Berkman for his "singleness of purpose" and "selfless devotion," she refused the charge of "narrow egoism" and "frivolity" because she loved flowers, theater, and dance (76, 56). "I would live my beautiful ideal," she declared, refusing the instrumentalism of "the Cause": "I want freedom, the right to self-expression, everybody's right to beautiful, radiant things" (56).

Throughout her life she mused on the tension between her lifework in the anarchist movement and her desire for a child. Very aware that men could be both fathers and activists because they gave so little time to their children, and equally aware that such an option would not be available to her, she refused the surgery that she believed would have allowed her to conceive. Yet this resolution of the dilemma did not abolish the tension, or eliminate her appreciation of the manyness inhabiting identity and desire: "I was not hewn of one piece, like Sasha or other heroic figures. I had long realized that I was woven of many skeins, conflicting in shade and texture. To the end of my days I should be torn between the yearning for a personal life and the need of giving my all to my ideal" (153).

Another early experience spurred Goldman to rethink the accepted anarchist dichotomy between reform and revolution. During her first speaking tour in upstate New York, when she was still much under the spell of the charismatic Johann Most, Goldman entertained her audience with a sarcastic denunciation of the struggle for the eight-hour day, "scoffing at the stupidity of the workers who fought for such trifles"

(Goldman, 51). At the end of her speech, an older man in the audience made a plea for the immediate significance of "minor" reforms in the concrete and immediate lives of the workers, especially for those workers too old to hope to see more revolutionary change during their life times. In her autobiography she recalls: "The man's earnestness, his clear analysis of the principle involved in the eight-hour struggle, brought home to me the falsity of Most's position. I realized I was committing a crime against myself and the workers by serving as a parrot repeating Most's views. I understood why I had failed to reach my audience. I had taken refuge in cheap jokes and bitter thrusts against the toilers to cover up my own inner lack of conviction" (52–53). Goldman's reflections do not suggest a dry and brittle doctrine, but an impassioned engagement with a problematic set of issues.

Goldman's most well known public revision of her arguments concerned the status of violence and the relations of means to ends. She records early doubts about the ethics of violence, worrying that advocates of her beloved Cause would mimic their oppressors. "Could idealists be cruel? The enemies of life and joy and beauty are cruel. They are relentless, they have killed our great comrades. But must we, too, exterminate?" (44). Continuing doubts about the ethics of endangering others in pursuit of an ideal came to a head in her confrontation with the anarchist *attentat*, the act of political violence that was supposed to serve as a catalyst in stimulating mass revolutionary action. Her painful struggles with this issue eventually produced a complex argument that opposed the *attentat* while insisting that it be understood as a response to systemic institutionalized violence. Given the context of continual violence against labor, and periodic, highly publicized assassinations of public figures by anarchists (including the assassination of President William McKinley, an act that the press and the police tried desperately to pin on Goldman), this was not, as they say, an "academic" topic. It was an explosive political issue. Goldman's early beliefs that the noble ideal of her Cause justified any methods gave way to a more nuanced argument about the interconnection of means to ends. In the afterword to her book describing her disillusionment with the Russian Revolution, Goldman wrote: "There is no greater fallacy than the belief that aims and purposes are one thing, while methods and tactics are another. This conception is a potent menace to social regeneration. All human experience teaches that methods and means cannot be separated from the ultimate aim. The means employed become, through individual habit and social practice, part and parcel of the final purpose; they influence it, modify it, and presently the aims and means become identical" (Shulman 1972, 355–56).

A final example of active rethinking, perhaps the most wrenching of Goldman's political life, occurred through her confrontation with ambiguity and irresolvable contradiction in the dilemmas of the Spanish anarchists during the civil war. Caught between the communists and the fascists, forced to choose between the struggle for anarchism and the struggle against fascism, the Spanish anarchists joined a coalition government that quickly betrayed them. Presenting this situation to radical audiences outside Spain, Goldman found herself in the unusual position of pleading with both sides to understand the tragedy of a no-win situation. She did so by invoking empathy: those "who are far removed from the struggle" are not able to see the situation as are those immersed in it (Shulman 1972, 384). Empathy for others meant more than putting *yourself* in their place; rather, it meant imagining what it is like *for them*, in *their* place. Goldman's practice of empathy is echoed in contemporary feminist ideas of "co-feeling," defined as "the ability *to participate* in another's feelings (in their terms)" (Gilligan and Wiggins, quoted in Hirschmann and Di Stefano 1996, 163). In Goldman's words, "It requires something more than personal experience to gain a philosophy or point of view from any specific event. It is the quality of our response to the event and our capacity to enter into the lives of others that help us to make their lives and experiences our own" (Shulman 1972, 388). She struggled with the ambiguities that faced her and her comrades without abandoning her commitments. "Life is stronger than theory," she reflected in a letter to a friend during the struggles in Spain, continuing to embrace her ideals without denying their limits (Porter 1983, 227).

Are We Frozen or Thawing?

Goldman's prose is often extravagant, bombastic, strident, excessive. She often ridicules some particular authority by appealing to a diffuse authority of "all radical thinkers" and "all the great men of the world"; "all human evolution" confirms her views, as does "every intelligent being" and "the whole history of man" (Shulman 1972, 36, 37, 97, 190, 356). Her sentences are bolstered by a litter of irritating absolutes: *all, none, always, never.* She often appeals, in passing, to the most conventional of distinctions between "truth and falsehood" and "facts [and] fancy," between the "unmasking" of error and the revelation of "the real" (Goldman 1970, 186, 91).

Yet when Goldman reflects more carefully on the concrete events before her, a more complex picture competes with such careless certitudes. While she was passionate in her commitments to her "beautiful ideal," she also sometimes found such passion "painfully disturbing" (114). She was notoriously intolerant of compromise or equivocation, yet the vision that moved her was one of open possibility. Goldman's intriguing essay (unpublished in her lifetime) titled "Jealousy: Causes and a Possible Cure" briefly addresses her own encounters with the critic of winter doctrines:

> "Beyond good and evil means beyond prosecution, beyond judging, beyond killing, etc. *Beyond Good and Evil* opens before our eyes a vista the background of which is individual assertion combined with the understanding of all others who are unlike ourselves, who are different.
>
> By that I do not mean the clumsy attempt of democracy to regulate the complexities of human character by means of external equality. The vision of "beyond good and evil" points to the right to oneself, to one's personality. Such possibilities do not exclude pain over the chaos of life, but they do exclude the puritanic righteousness that sits in judgment on all others except oneself. (Shulman 1972, 168–69)

Here Goldman distinguishes between the existential suffering that is woven into life and the political suffering that accompanies the exercise of winter doctrines. She embraced Nietzsche not only for "the fire of his soul, the rhythm of his song" (Goldman 1970, 172) but also for his skepticism about judgment and his plea for difference. Her scathing critique of oppressive institutions is accompanied by her concern with facilitating the conditions for a vital inner life, for "generous feeling," for the circumstances that make us "big and fine" (Shulman 1972, 170). In other essays Goldman tracked the desire to punish both to a violated sense of possession and to a self-righteous opposition between innocence and guilt. In defiance of the demonization of criminals in her day, she declared that "we all have the rudiments of crime in us, more or less, according to our mental, physical, and social environment" (296).

With Zarathustra, Goldman periodically returned to the fixity of winter thoughts, perhaps for their convenient rhetorical force, perhaps for the comfort they offer against suffering, or perhaps simply for the purchase they provide in the struggle against oppression. Yet Goldman also fostered a fluid and open-ended ethos. We might think of her as exemplifying an ethos that William Connolly calls nontheistic spirituality, embodying vigorous investments in the felt truth of a spiritual realm combined with gratitude for the abundance of existence. With Nietzsche, Goldman would no doubt "consider every day lost in which we have not danced at least once" (Nietzsche 1954, 210).

Note

1. For Alex Kates Shulman's account of the life of this famous but not literally accurate quote, see "Dances with Feminists," The Emma Goldman Papers, http://sunsite3.berkeley.edu/Goldman/Features/dances_shulman.html.

References

Bennett, Jane. 1994. "Kafka, Genealogy, and the Spiritualization of Politics." *Journal of Politics* 56, no. 3:650–70.

Connolly, William. 1999. *Why I Am Not A Secularist*. Minneapolis: University of Minnesota Press.

Goldman, Emma. 1970. *Living My Life*. Vol. 1. New York: Dover. (Orig. pub. New York: Alfred A. Knopf, 1931.)

Hirschmann, Nancy, and Christine Di Stefano, eds. 1996. *Revisioning the Political: Feminist Reconstructions of Traditional Concepts in Western Political Theory*. Boulder, Colo.: Westview Press.

Nietzsche, Friedrich. 1954. *Thus Spoke Zarathustra: A Book for None and All*. Translated by Walter Kaufman. New York: Penguin Books.

Porter, David, ed. 1983. *Vision on Fire: Emma Goldman on the Spanish Revolution*. New Paltz, N.Y.: Commonground Books.

Shulman, Alix Kate, ed. 1972. *Red Emma Speaks: Selected Writings and Speeches by Emma Goldman*. New York: Vintage Books.

———. 1991. "Dances with Feminists." The Emma Goldman Papers. http://sunsite3.berkeley.edu/Goldman/Features/dances_shulman.html.

4

The "Individual" in Goldman's Anarchist Theory

Janet E. Day

"Every prescription she advocates is designed to create an environment in which the individual and his or her inborn nature and latent powers can develop, grow, and achieve their most mature and unhindered expression. The individual comes first in every scheme . . . but the ends are most efficiently achieved through the cooperation of the many individualities in association."

Day's essay illuminates the status of individuality in Goldman's anarchist theory. To understand the meaning of "potential realized," she carefully examines Goldman's related notions of human nature, consciousness, education, and self-expression. Day argues that Goldman's social, political, and economic practices are selected based upon their ability to maximize the individual's freedom.—*The Editors*

Emma Goldman's anarchist theory is best understood from the perspective of the individual and how the various prescriptions for social and economic relations are intended to serve the inner person and his or her growth into a mature consciousness of self. Goldman identifies three distinct perspectives on the individual evident within contemporary society: individuality, individualism, and "mass man." Individualism and mass man, she argues, are corrupted versions of the individual that nature intended and so any social mores or institutions that lead to such a state of being should be rejected. The individual defined through individuality is the only natural state of the individual. Goldman's libertarian anarchist prescriptions are intended to create the social conditions that enable an individual to develop a consciousness of self and mature into a perfect personality. Absolute freedom and individual autonomy are necessary for the realization of the fullest potential of the inner person. Understanding Goldman's anarchist theory from the standpoint of her conception of the ideal state of being lends coherence to her specific prescriptions for social and economic relations and unifies her ideas.

I begin this analysis by identifying the various ways in which Goldman conceives of the individual and by discussing her ideal individual. Then Goldman's social and economic ideas are examined in relation to her conception of the individual, to identify how specific prescriptions address her concern to produce an environment in which the individual is afforded the necessary freedom and autonomy for the discovery and maturation of the inner self. I conclude by investigating an unresolved tension within her thinking and how that might affect her overall concern for producing the optimal environment for individuated growth and development.

The Individual

When Goldman speaks of the individual and individuality, she is speaking of two distinctly different conceptions of identity. The individual is latent potential and individuality is potential realized. Potential realized is an ongoing process of discovery and development of the inner person. Outcomes other than individuality may be realized, such as individualism or mass man. A person's environment is an important determinant of whether latent potential in the individual will ultimately be developed and expressed as individuality.

The individual is born with "latent qualities and [an] innate disposition," which are readily subject to external environmental influences (Goldman 1983, 50). It is the interaction of latent qualities and innate disposition with the individual's personal experience that produces distinct personalities. Goldman summarizes this complex interaction: "The individual is not merely the result of heredity and environment, of cause and effect. He is that and a great deal more, a great deal else" (111).

Goldman identifies various latent qualities universally possessed by individuals: people are born with a "primitive sense of justice and right," an "original sense of judgment" (1925a, 6), a "love of freedom," the "craving for liberty and self-expression," and "that persistent quality of individuality" (135, 439, 118). The tenor of these qualities suggests that she holds a positive opinion of human nature and believes that, under the right circumstances, its natural expression is conducive to positive relations with others. In its broadest contours, this is an accurate characterization of Goldman's position of human nature; however, a closer inspection reveals a more nuanced understanding.

The problem of identifying the true character of human nature, as Goldman sees it, is being able to capture an accurate picture of it through the distorting lens of our ever corrupting social and religious conventions. She taunts critics who object to her faith in the natural and uninhibited expression of human nature: "Poor human nature, what horrible crimes have been committed in thy name! Every fool, from king to policeman, from the flatheaded parson to the visionless dabbler in science, presumes to speak authoritatively of human nature. The greater the mental charlatan, the more definite his insistence on the wickedness and weakness of human nature. Yet, how can any one speak of it to-day, with every soul in prison, with every heart fettered, wounded, and maimed?" (7). If the true essence of human nature cannot be clearly seen through the distortion produced by society's effort "to cramp human emotion and originality of thought in the individual into a strait-jacket from its earliest infancy" and "to shape every human being according to one pattern," then who can say her faith is misplaced? (132). Goldman's upbringing taught her to believe in the Western philosophical and religious dichotomy of good and evil. However, her experience with anarchist theories led her to reevaluate her earlier understanding: "I found that there is no straight and clearly marked line between good and evil. Both are interwoven and overlap each other. Surely neither good or evil can be chosen by one's mere 'free will.' I have found that good and evil are terms for human actions conditioned by various forces outside of man. Their meaning and content are subject to modifications and development in accordance with the changes constantly going on in the social and ethical values at various periods of human life" (1932a, 176). Labeling the impulses of human nature as either good or evil is simply the application of societal judgment and is time bound, as well.

The impulses of human nature are in and of themselves natural and neutral in Goldman's assessment. For example, she says that sex urges are natural. When society adopts a moral code that forbids the expression of natural sex urges except within the confines of marriage, any expression outside this imposed boundary is labeled aberrant behavior. In one context the behavior is natural; in another it is sinful even though the sexual impulse is the same. The problem is not with the impulse but rather with society's attempt to control people through coercive and destructive moral codes.

Goldman's concern is greater than just that of labeling natural in-stincts. If society imposes boundaries on conduct involving the expres-sion of natural impulses, what happens to the character of those urges when so confined? Using the example of a young woman, Goldman an-swers: "When still a young, beautiful flower, she falls in love with a re-spectable young man. But Morality decrees that unless he can marry the girl, she must never know the raptures of love, the ecstasy of passion, which reaches its culminating expression in the sex embrace" (1983, 171). The young man will find an outlet for his sex urges in the embrace of a prostitute, but the young woman, embraced by the straitjacket of familial and societal mores, "has no outlets. She develops headaches, insomnia, hysteria; grows embittered, quarrelsome, and soon becomes a faded, withered, joyless being, a nuisance to herself and everyone else" (171). If she bucks social mores and turns to prostitution, the sex urge becomes a commodity and thus a distortion of its primordial and natural impulse. Goldman concludes that the corruption of the sex urge is not the result of its inherent nature, but of society's imposed moral code.

The example of criminals as evidence of human nature's dichotomy of good and evil loses its force when, Goldman points out, it is taken into account that "ninety percent of all crimes are property crimes, which have their root in our economic iniquities" (52). Again, the greater bur-den of cause and effect lies with society and its embrace of capitalism, which produces inequalities. Under a just economic system, people would not be inclined toward criminal activities. However, Goldman does grant that some crimes are the result of causes related to the inherent nature of the individual. "I do not mean to deny the biologic, physiologic, or psychologic factors in creating crime; but there is hardly an advanced criminologist who will not concede that the social and economic influ-ences are most relentless, the most poisonous germs of crime" (337). The correct societal response toward such afflicted individuals would be a "spirit of a deeper sense of fellowship, kindness and understanding" and the provision of appropriate mental health intervention (52).

The case against human nature's depravity, and the need for society to control its effect on behavior, in Goldman's estimation, is greatly inflated by a distorted and false understanding of cause and effect. It is not the character of human nature that is at fault, but rather mores and the economic system adopted by society that produce attitudes and behaviors within individuals destructive of familial and social bonds. People have both "individual and social instincts—the one a most potent factor for individual endeavor, for growth, aspiration, self-realization; the other an equally potent factor for mutual helpfulness and social well-being" (64). It is only when an individual has a "consciousness of self" that he or she is then able to understand his or her relationship with others (65). Absent the conditions necessary for the healthy development of a self, an individual's attitude and behavior reflects the perversion of human nature produced by society's suppression of natural instincts. If one does not know oneself, how then can one live in harmony with others?

Men and women share equally in the universal qualities that constitute human nature. Several passages in Goldman's writing indicate that she believes that women possess distinct qualities that are inherent in their nature. In one place, she makes reference to woman's nature as including a "mother instinct"; in another, she claims that "motherhood is the highest fulfillment of woman's nature" (161, 211). Corresponding references suggesting that men possess a "fatherhood instinct" are not to be found in her available writings. Haaland points to Goldman's "biologically deterministic views" as being "consistent with those of late Victorian sexologists, whose works she applauded and admired" (1983, 41). Goldman, in her anarchist prescriptions, places particular importance on the expression of this biological instinct. However, she advocates radically different social and political reforms from those of mainstream contemporary feminists. Haaland summarizes the different perspectives: "Goldman's approach was more philosophical and less pragmatic [than those of progressive women reformers], eschewing incremental change in favor of fundamental reform. Reform for the progressive women reformers meant opening up key institutions (e.g., education) to women. Goldman, in contrast, argued for a transformation in women's soul" (1983, 51). Even though Goldman believes that the desire to bear children is instinctual, she does consider it possible for a woman to choose not to heed its beaconing call. Except for the mother-instinct difference, she does not, however, regard women as being different from men. Women are just as subject to "all human follies and mistakes" as are men (193).

A final consideration is an individual's capacity both of spirit and for intellectual reasoning. Goldman considers human nature to be plastic and thus subject to the influence of our ever imposing social, religious, and political conventions. The degree to which a person is influenced by such externals is an individual matter. She marvels at anarchist Peter Kropotkin's ability to rise above his noble birth and the circumstance of his youth to sympathize with the poor and working underclass of his native Russia. Goldman muses: "Those who prate of conditions as the omnipotent factor in determining the character and shaping ideas, will find it very difficult to explain the personality and spirit of Peter Kropotkin" (1929, 1). However, she views people such as Kropotkin as the exception. "I realize that those who have the courage to defy the economic and social whip are among the few, and we have to deal with the many" (1983, 224). Most people do not possess Kropotkin's strength of spirit and thus the necessity for anarchist prescriptions, progressive education, and changes in social practice.

Goldman's statements concerning the capacity of the masses for intellectual reasoning suggest that she believes that many people are merely mediocre. In an interview conducted after a speech and published in *The World*, she states that "it would be unwise to talk to them [the audience members] too seriously or try to explain their situation to them philosophically, as they had not education or reason enough to understand. The only thing to do was to appeal frequently to their sentiments" (1893, 1). In her criticism of the Russian Revolution and Lenin's programs, Goldman bemoans the attitude propagated among the proletariat by many of the revolutionaries that the intelligentsia is to be hated. "Everywhere political demagogues play upon the ignorance of the masses, teach them that education and culture are bourgeois prejudices, that the workers can do without them, and that they alone can rebuild society" (1926, 3). Possessing the stronger spirit and greater capacity of understanding and intelligence, the intelligentsia is to guide those who are less endowed with such capacities. However, every individual does equally possess the capacity for self-discovery and self-development. The maturation of personality, while an individual experience, is nonetheless a cooperative endeavor.

Individuality

The ideal state of a human being, one who has developed in harmony with his or her nature, is individuality. Goldman provides a definition: "Individuality may be described as the consciousness of the individual as to what he is and how he lives. It is inherent in every human being and is a thing of growth. . . . The very essence of individuality is expression; and sense of dignity and independence is the soil wherein it thrives. . . .

The living man cannot be defined; he is the fountainhead of all life and all values; he is not a part of this or of that; he is a whole, an individual whole, a growing, changing, yet always constant whole" (1983, 111, 112). In the interest of critically examining the role of the individual in Goldman's social and political prescriptions, it is necessary to extract the fundamental components of her definition of individuality, to establish the links between the two concerns.

Goldman identifies two types of consciousness: consciousness of self and consciousness of relations with others. Consciousness of self has several components. The first is a consciousness of "being different from others" (439). Recognizing that one is not a carbon copy of the next person and that one possesses attitudes, desires, and needs in a unique combination is the beginning of wanting to explore the essences of the self within. The expression of that distinctive combination is the basis of an individual's personality. Another component of consciousness of self concerns the more universally possessed latent qualities, such as the sex impulse and the need to love and be loved. Goldman's critique blames society and its mores for often masking or distorting the true character of universal and natural feelings. Just because these essences are universally possessed does not necessarily mean that each individual is fully in touch with them and that he or she will mature in a healthy manner. An individual's social environment is critical to whether the particular combination and universally possessed qualities will fully develop and express themselves in a normal and healthy manner.

Consciousness of self precipitates consciousness of one's relation with others. The innate social instinct develops if the individual actively seeks to know him- or herself and then to identify and develop his or her latent qualities and innate disposition. Using the example of child education and the Modern School, Goldman praises the school's mission "to develop the individual through knowledge and the free play of characteristic traits, so that he may become a social being, because he has learned to know himself, to know his relation to his fellow-men, and to realize himself in a harmonious blending with society" (145). Social relations begin with "knowing thy self" and then progress to a realization of the proper relation of the self with others.

People, even though they are born with innate natures, do not necessarily realize the full expression of their latent qualities. It is often the case that their environment from birth imposes upon them a form that is not in harmony with their true nature. Goldman lays the blame on "every institution of our day, the family, the State, our moral codes, [which] sees in every strong, beautiful, uncompromising personality a deadly enemy; therefore every effort is being made to cramp human emotion and originality of thought in the individual into a strait-jacket from its earliest infancy; or to shape every human being according to one pattern; not into a well-rounded individuality, but into a patient work slave, professional automaton, taxpaying citizen, or righteous moralist" (131–32). The prescriptions of anarchism are aimed at creating an environment that is essential to individuated growth.

Goldman firmly believes that "sex emotions and love are among the most intimate, the most intense and sensitive, expressions of our being" (215). These emotions are the product of the whole being of each individual involved in the relation. "They are so deeply related to individual physical and psychic traits as to stamp each love affair an independent love affair, unlike any other love affair. In other words, each love is the result of the impressions and characteristics the two people involved give to it" (215). Such free expression of an individual's inner self could only be realized in an environment free from puritanical mores that govern sexual encounters and love relations.

Individualism

Goldman is careful to make a distinction between individuality and individualism. What she is advocating is individuality, a spiritual state of the inner person. She makes the observation that "corrupt and perverse 'individualism' is the strait-jacket of individuality. It has converted life into a degrading race for externals, for possessions, for social prestige and supremacy" (1983, 112). The foundation of the United States' concern for material values is its embrace of capitalism. She characterizes this state of affairs as "the brute struggle for physical existence" and nothing more (118). The form that economic relations take and the political system under which people live are connected to the values a society adopts. Under capitalism, "rugged individualism" is valued; under anarchism individuality is championed.

Mass Man

The other state of the individual that Goldman criticizes is that of "mass man." Her critique is aimed at the cowardice of the individual who fails to think independently, and who is fearful of others, which leads to the destruction of human relations and social harmony. Goldman complains that the aim of the mass "has always been to make life uniform, gray, and monotonous as the desert. As a mass it will always be the annihilator of individuality, of free initiative, of originality" (1983, 85). If self-consciousness and individuality are censured by the masses, the "consequence is that instead of being a mass of individuals, each one fearlessly blurting out his own conviction, as a nation compared to other nations, we are a mass of cowards. More than any other people we are afraid of each other" (81–82). How individuals relate with one another is distorted because the individual is foreign to him- or herself. As a result of the mass's strictures, not only is the individual harmed, but society as a whole is injured.

The goal, then, for Goldman is to ensure the conditions necessary for individuality to be actuated within each individual. These conditions can only be realized by the prescriptions offered by anarchism, which "are part of nature's forces, [and which] destroy, not healthful tissue, but parasitic growths that feed on life's essence of society" (63). No amount of tinkering with existing social and political institutions would ever fully eliminate the suppression of individuality. The instituting of anarchism would radically alter the basis for social relations by setting the individual as the standard by which all prescriptions are measured and judged. In comparing political theories of her time, Goldman claims that "Anarchism alone steadfastly proclaims that society exists for man, not man for society. The sole legitimate purpose of society is to serve the needs and advance the aspiration of the individual" (123). Given Goldman's definition of the individual, and her desire to promote individuality as the preferred state of the being, the task at hand is to critically examine the link between the individual and anarchism's prescriptions, and the ways in which they produce the sought-after end of promoting the development and expression of individuality.

Social Prescriptions

Individuals do not exist in a vacuum; they necessarily exist in some context with others. How an individual relates with others is contingent on whether he or she has developed a consciousness of self. Arriving at a consciousness of self is a dialectical process in which the individual is born with certain universal and particular latent qualities whose discovery and maturation are often dependent on the environment in which the process takes place. "It must be borne in mind," Goldman advises, "that it is through the channel of the child that the development of the mature man must go" (1983, 132). With an awareness of this wisdom, Goldman's vision of how anarchism addresses the problem of arriving at a consciousness of self from childhood to adulthood provides a natural framework for a critical analysis of her ideas.

The quality of a child's environment, whether it is nurturing and facilitates self-discovery and growth, is a factor of people and institutions. Goldman considers the point at which a woman decides to conceive a child as a crucial factor in whether the child will have a promising beginning in its journey to become a unique personality. Her analysis of motherhood is intricately linked to her critique of marriage. She argues that the moral and cultural underpinnings that justify the institution of marriage degrade the dignity of women and create an environment hostile to the nurturing and maturation of young, developing individualities.

"Motherhood is the highest fulfillment of woman's nature," but motherhood does not require the institution of marriage in order for the mother instinct to find its fulfillment, Goldman argues. Convention has it that before a woman is to conceive a child, she must first be situated in a marriage. Moreover, love and marriage are often linked together when in fact they "have nothing in common; they are as far apart as the poles" (204). The truth of the matter is that "marriage is primarily an economic arrangement, an insurance pact" from the perspective of the woman (205). A woman is expected to fulfill her wifely duties by producing progeny for her husband; he, in turn, will provide her with economic support. The motivation for child bearing is not necessarily based in love, but is an expectation imposed on the woman by family and society. What a "wonderfully inspiring atmosphere for the bearing of life, is it not?" Goldman asks sarcastically. She retorts, "If motherhood is the highest fulfillment of woman's nature, what other protection does it need save love and freedom?" (211).

The crux of the matter concerning child bearing rests both with the climate into which the child is born and the woman's free expression of the mother instinct—the two are intricately linked. If the mother conceives for motivations other than those that are an intimate expression of her inner nature, it is possible that she will resent or even hate her offspring. Goldman brought a particular concern for women's issues to anarchist critique that other anarchists neglected. Writing in support of the legal use and availability of contraception, she reasoned that "surely a [woman] ought to be in a position to decide how many children she should bring into the world, whether they should be brought into the world by the man she loves and because she wants the child, or should be born in hatred and loathing" (2001, 136). The optimal state into which a child is born is one in which love and the free expression of the mother instinct is the motivation for conception. In that case, the child's closest relation will not be imposing upon him or her the baggage of resentment, which would poison the spirit of his or her developing individuality.

Another concern Goldman has is that in marrying, the woman "loses her own individuality, even her name she is not allowed to keep" (1897b, 9). Goldman's internal writing patterns suggest that she considers a person's name an element of his or her identity. When mentioning in her writing those with whom she agrees or toward whom she possesses warm feelings, Goldman almost always refers to them by using their full name in her first reference. In further references, she will often use only the individual's first name. In contrast, she will often refer to those with whom she disagrees by their surname only, or their surname in conjunction with the reference that society uses to indicate marital status. The difference in Goldman's references in her writing suggests that she places particular importance on the relationship between one's name and one's identity.

One possible explanation for Goldman's pattern of name usage may be found in the way she names those with whom she disagrees. Using an individual's last name only, or in conjunction with a reference to educational or marital status, may point to her belief that the person whom she mentions does not exist as an individuality, but rather as a conglomeration of "individuals." An individual's first name distinguishes a particular Smith from all other Smiths. A surname represents a totality of individuals over time, a product of hand-me-down values and traditions. The individuality of the person becomes occluded when only the surname is used in reference to the particular individual, and thus Goldman prefers using a person's first name as a component of identity. Seeing oneself as an individual, a distinct personality, is an important element in creating an environment in which the individual and individuality are afforded elevated importance. For the woman to surrender her last name when she enters into marriage, and from then on be referred to as "Mrs.

Smith," means losing a little of her individuality as well as signaling her acquiescence to social norms that further deny that woman other aspects of her uniqueness. Therefore, the symbolism of names is linked to larger issues of identity and social conventions.

The dignity of the individual is tied up in a person's freedom and ability to think and act independently; social norms discouraged "proper" women from being independent thinkers and economically self-supporting. The married woman, Goldman observes, is expected to become "absorbed" by the man, lose her identity; and so "it incapacitates her for life's struggle, annihilates her social consciousness, paralyzes her imagination, and then imposes its gracious protection, which is in reality a snare, a travesty on human character" (1983, 210). The consequence of the marriage arrangement is that the wife becomes the protectorate of her husband as he is her economic provider, her moral conscience and her supreme advisor. Developing a consciousness of self was not considered a prerequisite for a healthy, loving relationship. Economic dependence and the social sanctions that bind a woman to the marriage institution make a woman foreign to herself and to her child. Furthermore, they create a social environment that is prejudicial toward the child and its opportunity for a free and unencumbered upbringing by sanctioning the practice of denying the dignity of the individual.

Goldman's focus on issues of particular concern to women goes beyond just an interest in the individual woman. In the larger picture, the marriage institution is but a single cog in the larger machinery of social, economic, and political relations that deny the dignity of the individual. The individual is championed either in all types of relations that make up humankind, or in none. It is nearly impossible to segregate a particular attitude for sanction from all others without contaminating the whole lot. The acceptance of the marriage institution, as it is conventionally understood, sanctions the idea that it is permissible for one individual to absorb another's identity, and thus, makes of the woman a parasitic growth, both psychologically and economically. Furthermore, "it is because marriage relations are the foundation of private property, ergo, the foundation of our cruel and inhuman system," that Goldman insists that the institution must be abolished (1897a, 2). She goes on to say, "If we want to accomplish Anarchy, we must first have free women at least, those women who are economically just as independent as their brothers are, and unless we have free women, we cannot have free mothers, and if mothers are not free, we cannot expect the young generation to assist us in the accomplishment of our aim, that is the establishment of an Anar-chist society" (2). The successful upbringing of the child and the even-tual realization of an anarchist society are linked to the social relations of present society. Even before the child is just a glimmer in its mother's eye, the social environment is a crucial factor in whether it will begin life in a climate supportive of the principles of human dignity.

Having discredited the marriage institution, the question is raised about the type of social environment in which the child will be born and raised. In a draft titled "The Passing of the Family," Goldman explains anarchism's vision of familial relations:

> We shall regard other people's children as we regard our own, other people's parents and other people's brothers and sisters as our own. "Home, sweet home" ties may appear beautiful to-day. But as our ideals socialize they will seem narrow, crude, savagely isolated and cold and confining. We shall have to leave the family group to get our breath. We shall need larger distributing centers for our bigger affections. We shall open up our hearts and enter-tain non-relatives with kinsmen, strangers with life-long inti-mates. We shall live easily, affectionately among whomsoever happens to be our neighbors. And we shall feel toward them as the people of old felt toward the clan, as we of to-day feel toward our next of kin. (n.d., 8)

The formalization of familial relations will no longer dominate societal organization. Whether someone is "related" and called by the endearing title of *mother* or *father* or *sister* will not be based on the accident of birth, but will be evidence of deeply felt sentiment, the true measure of relationship. The advantage of such an arrangement is twofold: the individual attains a higher status and dignity, and the bonds of commu-nity are strengthened by real and heartfelt feelings.

Goldman continues her description of social relations by concluding, "What is now provided us in the lesser measure and the lower degree by the little loving home circle we shall then receive in the fuller measure and the loftier degree of the community of many" (8). The loving, rais-ing, and educating of the child in this larger family becomes a social responsibility shared among the many. People are mistaken, Goldman contends, when "they tenaciously cling to the idea that the child is merely part of themselves—an idea as false as it is injurious" (1983, 135).

Raising a child in the image of its parents denies the child the opportunity to develop into a unique and distinct personality. In the larger circle of community envisioned by anarchists the child is situated within an environment conducive to the fullest maturation and expression of its inner being. Moreover, the child's social instinct is stimulated at an early age and thus presages the child's later consciousness of relations with others.

Unencumbered by the cloak of familial identity and expectations, children would be free to develop their own personality in harmony with their nature. In an anarchist society, children would still engage in a formal educational process, but the teaching philosophy would radically differ from traditional methods of discipline, recitation, and conformity. Traditional educational methods aim to produce well-behaved drones for the state, Goldman claims, who will not challenge its legitimacy and authority. She says, "I think it is high time that all advanced people should be clear on this point, that our present system of economic and political dependence is maintained not so much by wealth and courts as it is by the inert mass of humanity, drilled and pounded into absolute uniformity, and that the school today represents the most efficient medium to accomplish that end" (143). She looks to the example of the educational theories of the Modern School in Europe as an example of teaching methods consistent with anarchism's orientation toward self-directed and individuated development leading to a social consciousness.

Goldman explains the mission of the Modern School: "Education is a process of drawing out, not driving in; it aims at the possibility that the child should be left free to develop spontaneously, directing his own efforts and choosing the branches of knowledge which he desires to study" (144). The finished "product" is not predetermined by the teaching goals laid down by a board of education or the state, but by the child and its inner nature working itself out in freedom. This is not to say, however, that the educational process should be devoid of any aim. "The social purpose of the Modern School," Goldman points out, "is to develop the individual through knowledge and the free play of characteristic traits, so that he may become a social being, because he has learned to know himself, to know his relation to his fellow-men, and to realize himself in a harmonious blending with society" (145). It is the needs of the child's inner being that are prioritized, rather than society and its need for automatons to prop up its domestic authority and staff its army so it may wield its power in foreign lands.

Because Goldman has faith in the natural goodness of human nature, she claims it is not necessary to discipline a child. "To discipline the child is invariably to set up a false moral standard, since the child is thereby led to suppose that punishment is something to be imposed upon him from without, by a person more powerful, instead of being a natural and unavoidable reaction and result of his own acts" (145). Determination of "right and wrong" exists as a natural law within the child's inner being, directing the child's thoughts and actions, naturally leading to concordant relations with others. A self-directing individual makes the need for external controls superfluous. Since anarchism, which is against all forms of law, authority, and coercion, needs people to be strong in mind and spirit so they may live in harmony, and for society to be orderly and peaceful, self-directed individuals are a critical component of its success.

Anarchist critiques view all external moral codes as tools of oppression used by the those in power against the weak-spirited masses, the former using such tools to protect their positions of privilege and authority. When moral codes based in religious precepts and social norms are internalized, the individual's behavior is motivated by mechanisms of submission and not by the injunctions of natural law that are situated universally in human nature. Goldman links religion with all other moral codes found in society's institutions in a symbiotic relationship: "Needless to say, society is obsessed by more than one morality. Indeed, every institution of to-day has its own moral standard. Nor could they ever have maintained themselves, were it not for religion, which acts as a shield, and for morality, which acts as the mask. . . . Through the medium of religion they have paralyzed the mind of people, just as morality has enslaved the spirit. In other words, religion and morality are a much better whip to keep people in submission than even the club and the gun" (170). The soil of the individual's soul is contaminated by religion, disarming its victim of the defenses of a robust and self-directing spirit. Poured into the resulting void is an inert will subject to the contrivances of those who desire power and wealth. Religious dogma, and the resulting institutional moral codes, are really acts of violence against nature and the human spirit.

Christianity "preaches the gospel of non-resistance, of slavish acquiescence in the will of others; it is complete disregard of character and self-reliance, and therefore destructive of liberty and well-being" (234). Absent a strong spirit as a defense against the ever forceful promulgation of humanity's inferiority and depravity, the natural law of the inner person is silenced. People, Goldman concludes, confuse "the teachings of Christ with the great struggles for social and economic emancipation" (234). Christ's Sermon on the Mount preaches self-denial and praises those who are weak in spirit as the ones who will inherit the earth. An individual of such character lacks the necessary courage to do battle against the injustices of this world and, instead, places all hope in the next world. Anarchism seeks to build individuals who are strong in spirit and self-directing and who place their hope and expend their energies in creating a just society for today and for all people.

Having clearly rejected most existing social ethics and moral codes, Goldman is not seeking to replace the discredited codes with another system of her own choosing. She warns radical parents away from the temptation to instill their own moral values in their children. As correct and worthy of promulgation as a parent might judge these values to be, the danger lies in the psychological forces that move the spirit of an independent individual. "The child being fed on one-sided, set and fixed ideas, soon grows weary of rehashing the beliefs of its parents, and sets out in quest of new sensations; no matter how inferior and shallow the new experience may be, the human mind cannot endure sameness and monotony" (138). Parents, and those who facilitate the educational process, need to trust that the child will, given the necessary freedom and liberty, develop its own understanding of right and wrong. It is only through the actual experience of trial and error, working things out for oneself, that an individual develops the ability to determine his or her own values and then use them as self-directing guideposts throughout life.

Goldman explicitly links self-directed behavior with the goals of anarchism: "Anarchism repudiates any attempt of a group of men or of any individual to arrange life for another. Anarchism rests on faith in humanity and its potentialities, while all other social philosophies have no faith in humanity whatever. The other philosophies insist that man cannot govern himself and that he must be ruled over. Nowadays most people believe that the stronger the government the greater the success of society will be" (1933, 12). A successful society begins with self-directed individuals who are willing to accord to others the freedom and liberty necessary to determine their own values and their application to each individual's life. The process of discovering one's values and becoming a self-directed individuality begins in childhood.

Directed internally by the prompting of innate human nature, the child will embrace a code of conduct that is consistent with natural law. Goldman defines this natural law as "that factor in man which asserts itself freely and spontaneously without any external force, in harmony with the requirements of nature. For instance, the demand for nutrition, for sex gratification, for light, air, and exercise, is a natural law. But its expression need not be the machinery of government, needs not the club, the gun, the handcuff, or the prison. To obey such laws, if we may call it obedience, requires only spontaneity and free opportunity" (1983, 70). A moral code governing human behavior, despite having a universal quality, is nonetheless the domain of the individual because it is the individual who determines its contours and applies it only to his or her own conduct as an integral part of becoming a self-conscious individuality.

In an anarchist society, all individuals are responsible for creating their own values as directed by the inner process of working out their innate nature. For individuals to exist in social harmony, people must be willing to allow for differences in moral values and refrain from imposing upon others their own understanding. The only limitations on such free expression would be efforts by an individual to deny the human dignity of another person through the enslavement of a that person's spirit, mind, or body.

Another area in which Goldman advocates the free and unhindered expression of a child is the development of its sexual impulse. The educational system should accept the awakening of the sexual feelings in the young child as an integral component of its developing personality:

> Children and adolescent people have their young dreams, their vague forebodings of the sexual urge. The senses open slowly like the petals of a bud, the approaching sex maturity enhances the sensibilities and intensifies the emotions. New vistas, fantastic pictures, colorful adventures follow one another in swift procession before the sex-awakened child. . . . The radiance of youth—alas, of so brief duration—is inseparably bound up in the awakening of eroticism. It is the period when ideas and ideals, aims and motives, begin to fashion themselves in the human breast; that which is mean and ugly in life still remains covered with a fantastic veil, because the age which marks the change from child to youth is indeed the most exquisitely poetic and magical phase in all human existence. (147)

The awakening of the sexual impulse in the child should be embraced as the natural consequence of the child's inherent nature and not condemned as something sinful and, thus, shameful.

Goldman links the awakening sexual impulse to the heightening of the child's emotional sensibilities, creative powers, growing idealism, and zest for life. Puritanical insistence on chastity outside marriage "is but an artificial imposition upon nature" and "expressive of a false shame of the human form," Goldman argues (153). Permitting the natural development and expression of the sexual impulse in the child both assists in the development of the child's personality and orients the child to a proper understanding of human sexuality.

Possessing a proper understanding of human sexuality leads to improved relations between men and women, Goldman reasons. "Most moralists and many pedagogues still adhere to the antiquated notion that man and woman belong to two different species, moving in opposite directions, and hence, must be kept apart" (149). When the coming together of a man and woman is predicated on social duty and economic need, each, of course, has divergent and conflicting interests in the relationship. When the coming together is predicated on love, the man and woman come together as equals.

Goldman extols the benefits of an upbringing free from the usual social and educational constraints of traditional societal mores. The individual child and the development of the child's latent powers and social instinct are prioritized. Allowing the inborn nature of the child to find its natural and uninhibited expression is the central principle for any child-rearing scheme under anarchist theory. For an anarchist society to be successful, every individual must be at liberty to develop a consciousness of self, because it is intricately linked to the awakening of the social instinct. The social instinct is the basis for associational life, in which the use of coercion is rejected in favor of self-directed individuals.

Economic Prescriptions

The educational process prepares the young person to assume a place in society as a productive member of the economic system. Goldman envisions individuals choosing their line of work as an expression of their inner selves. The economic system under anarchism will consist of voluntary productive and distributive associations designed to afford the individual the greatest possible freedom in his or her expression of personality.

An individual's vocational choice is an element of his or her personality. Goldman is particularly interested in the spiritual aspect of an individual's existence and not merely in the material necessity of physical survival. She notes the relationship between the spiritual aspect of an individual's personality and engagement in labor, as experienced by "one to whom the making of a table, the building of a house, or the tilling of the soil is what the painting is to the artist and the discovery to the scientist—the result of inspiration, of intense longing, and deep interest in work as a creative force" (68). All modes of work should be understood from the standpoint of embodying some deeper, more meaningful component of the individual's inner self. Furthermore, the engagement in labor should also stimulate the person's interest in the work and, thus, encourage further the growth and development of consciousness of self.

One's vocation must be freely chosen. Under capitalism, Goldman observes, very few individuals are in a position to make such a free choice. Manual laborers are caught in the trap of their struggle for existence. It would be frivolous of them to attempt to address the needs of their inner being, as they perpetually find themselves at the precipice, in danger of losing the fight for physical survival. The intellectual proletarian, Goldman points out, is also rarely afforded much freedom in vocational choice. "Material considerations and desire for greater social prestige are usually the deciding factors in the vocation of the intellectual. Added to these is the tendency to follow in the footsteps of family tradition, and become doctors, lawyers, teachers, engineers, etc." (119).

Traditional familial structure often encourages choices and behavior in the young person that conform to the family's social and economic status rather than nurture the creative forces of the inner self that makes each individual unique, another reason why anarchists reject traditional familial relations. By simply following family expectations, the individual is never made to engage in the difficult task of developing a consciousness of self.

When the "worth" of a profession is judged on the basis of its value to society as a whole, the individual and his or her spiritual needs have been overlooked; it is this perspective that leads to the "rugged individualism" that Goldman criticizes. Rugged individualism is the result of people's struggle for physical survival and social status. The state of one's existence is judged by the criteria of external, material considerations and not by the degree to which an individual's personality finds expression in a chosen profession. The consequence of this perspective is that individuals are set one against the other in a race for externals, thereby suppressing the social instinct.

The economic system under anarchism, as Goldman envisions it, would nurture the social instinct and cultivate solidarity of interests. "Syndicalism is," she claims, "in essence, the economic expression of anarchism" (91). Goldman's focus on syndicalism in her writing is mainly concerned with its form as a protest movement against European capitalism. My examination is particularly concerned with syndicalism as it would operate in an ideal anarchist society—it is a forward-looking glance. From Goldman's discussion, the principles of future economic relations can be identified and connected with her overriding interest in the individual.

Under anarchism, individuals would not necessarily operate in isolation from one another as independent economic agents. The social instinct would guide economic relations by bringing together individuals who share a common interest: "The ultimate purpose of Syndicalism is to reconstruct society from its present centralized, authoritative and brutal state to one based on the free, federated grouping of the workers along lines of economic and social liberty" (91). These federated groups would exist as small, autonomous organizations unconnected formally to a larger, hierarchical institution. The essential character of the relation between federations would be one of solidarity of interests expressed as a social consciousness on a level that embraces all humanity.

Goldman's vision of society, one that demonstrates a concern for all humanity, and is free from the usual tensions that are often evident between and within organized groups, can be constructed from her observation of the practices of syndicalism in Europe and the United States. One example she offers is the permeability of the separate groups that she witnessed "while at the headquarters of the Confédération" in Europe. She saw "cases of workingmen who came with their union cards from various parts of France, and even other countries of Europe, and were supplied with meals and lodging, and encouraged by every evidence of brotherly spirit, and made to feel at home by their fellow workers of the Confédération" (98). Goldman also points to examples of solidarity that extend beyond membership within trade unions and demonstrate the spirit of cooperation and mutual aid felt among all laborers. "No less in importance than the mutual aid activities of the Syndicalists is the cooperation established by them between the city and the country, the factory worker and the peasant or farmer, the latter providing the workers with food supplies during strikes, or taking care of the strikers' children. This form of practical solidarity has for the first time been tried in this country during the Lawrence strike, with inspiring results" (98). Solidarity exists on two levels: among those with whom a relation exists based on immediate interests, and among all humankind based on the natural sentiments of the social instinct, which identifies each person as a member of the human race. The usual antagonisms of social-class distinctions and the race for externals would be absent in an anarchist society because the prevailing attitude among all individuals would hold that vocation is a matter of the inner person and an expression of his or her personality.

The internal workings, organization, and decision making of these federated groups are somewhat ambiguous in Goldman's writing. Some clues to her thinking can be gathered from the 1907 Amsterdam Anarchist Conference, at which she and Max Baginski presented a paper titled "Anarchism and Organization." Goldman and Baginski support the idea of and necessity for organizations because they believe that these are important in the spiritual development of the individual. Goldman says: "There is a mistaken notion that organization does not foster individual freedom; that, on the contrary, it means the decay of individuality. In reality, however, the true function of organization is to aid the development and growth of the personality" (1907b, 311). The internal workings of an organization, then, must prioritize the individual and function in ways that promote the individuality of the individual.

Such an overriding orientation toward the individual negates the usual use of democratic or parliamentarian decision-making techniques often used in organizations. Prior to leaving for the congress, Baginski wrote: "Anarchists do not believe in 'binding resolutions,' nor in majority decisions. We expect much, however, from voluntary co-operation, and the international exchange of ideas, opinions and experiences. The 'power to resolve' does not depend upon the number of ayes and nays. It springs from the free, rational perception of things" (179).

The problem with majoritarian norms is that they suppress individual initiative and perpetuate a system that condones authoritarian practices. Independence of thought in the individual is suppressed by the psychological force of the "group." Goldman believes that cooperation and assent within a group should come about through a process of rational exchanges, exposing each individual to factual information and well-reasoned arguments. From this process of intellectual give-and-take, the individual is either persuaded and cooperates with the group's aims, or is dissuaded and chooses not to join in the particular activity; in either case, there is no consequence to an individual's standing within the organization. Goldman concludes "that collective activity in no way denies individual action; on the contrary, they complete each other" (313).

The insistence on individual thought and action, even within these federated groups, is consistent with Goldman's concern for the individual. She says, "Of all social theories Anarchism alone steadfastly claims that society exists for man, not man for society. The sole legitimate purpose of society is to serve the needs and advance the aspiration of the individual" (1983, 123). Organizations, when properly construed, assist the individual by encouraging original thought and expression of personality. Within the group, a dialectical process takes place in which the individual contributes "ideas, opinions and experiences" and receives, in turn, "ideas, opinions and experiences" from others. The criterion, in the ideal personality, of what to accept and reject is based on the individual's needs as a self-conscious individuality. An individual's social consciousness would act as a moderator against the pursuit of strictly selfish goals.

Goldman's vision of syndicalism under anarchism differs from the contemporary understanding of unionism. The federated groups would be smaller in size and lack the typical authoritarian hierarchy and bureaucracy, compulsory membership and large coffers. Goldman rejects all forms of authority, as well as bureaucracy, which are the means through which the few can efficiently and completely control the many. "Man's true liberation, individual and collective," Goldman stresses, "lies in his emancipation from authority and from the belief in it" (120). Because individuals exist in a dialectical relationship, membership in a particular, or for that matter any, federation is strictly voluntary. The other distinction she makes concerns large union coffers. The problem for Goldman "consists in the fact that they create class distinctions and jealousies within the ranks of labor, so detrimental to the spirit of solidarity" (92). The main function of federated groups is to address the spiritual needs of the inner person and foster the sentiments of social consciousness and harmony.

In addition to cultivating feelings of social solidarity within their ranks, federated groups would engage in various types of educational and training programs. Goldman's experience with syndicalist practices in

France led her to give high praise to the very practical and enriching kinds of educational programs offered to members.

> And all these Syndicalist activities are permeated with the spirit of educational work, carried on systematically by evening classes on all vital subjects treated from an unbiased, libertarian standpoint—not the adulterated "knowledge" with which the minds are stuffed in our public schools. The scope of the education is truly phenomenal, including sex hygiene, the care of women during pregnancy and confinement, the care of home and children, sanitation and general hygiene; in fact, every branch of human knowledge—science, history, art—receives thorough attention, together with the practical application in the established workingmen's libraries, dispensaries, concerts and festivals in which the greatest artists and littérateurs of Paris consider it an honor to participate. (98)

Some programs stimulate the mind, others inspire the spirit, and still others nurture the body. The focus is the individual and his or her well-being as a whole person, but the ends are reached through the mutual cooperation of the members of the community.

The training programs available to federation members serve several purposes. The first is to develop the skills necessary for individuals to excel in their chosen vocation. For an anarchist society to function well, it is important that individuals possess the necessary skills to act as self-reliant individualities. This requires individuals to achieve a high degree of proficiency in their chosen profession as well as a broad understanding of their particular industry. The second purpose is to educate workers so that eventually all industries will be owned and operated by employees. Syndicalism anticipates this eventuality by using training programs "so that when labor finally takes over production and distribution, the people will be fully prepared to manage successfully their own affairs" (99). Goldman uses the example of the glassblowers' strike in Italy as evidence of the feasibility of employee-owned operations. Goldman boasts, "Their cooperative plan of work and distribution during the strike has proved so satisfactory in every way that the experimental factory has been permanent and a part of the cooperative organization of the workers" (99).

Cooperative employee-owned and -operated factories were much more than theory for Goldman; she saw in syndicalism the potential of human initiative, the capacity for self-reliant individuality, and the possibility of cooperation and solidarity among workers. The key factor in bringing about anarchism's vision of an economic system based on federated groups lies both in the cultivation of a populace of self-conscious individuals and in the maturation of the social instinct. Individuals are at liberty to freely choose their vocation; federated associations are nonauthoritarian and noncompulsory and encourage independence of thought and action; and educational and training programs address the whole person in their breadth of subject and attention to cultivating the inner person. The individual is always the center of every strategy, but the ends are most efficiently achieved through the cooperation of the many individualities in association.

Conclusion

I have tried to present Goldman's social, economic, and political prescriptions and her critical concern for the individual as she has expressed them in her writing and lectures. Although her theories are not always presented systematically or supported with an underlying philosophical analysis of any great depth, it is clear that her concern for the individual is a common thread running through all her prescriptions. In every critique of existing social theories, Goldman expresses her analysis and criticism in the context of the effect of the theory's practical implications on individuals and their inner being. Every prescription she advocates is designed to create an environment in which the individual and his or her inborn nature and latent powers can develop, grow, and achieve their most mature and unhindered expression. The individual comes first in every scheme. It is assumed that if the individual and his or her needs are taken care of first, then the satisfaction of social needs will naturally follow. An enormous faith in the goodness of human nature is required to support such a positive conception of human potentiality and social harmony. Especially since Goldman admits that the true character of human nature is difficult to determine because of the distorting effect of traditional societal mores and institutions, her trust of human nature and the possibility of an anarchist society is all the more extraordinary. Her ideas and attitudes, however, do not exist without certain tensions that are not always resolved in her writings, nor are the practical implications of her prescriptions always clear. These tensions and the vagueness in her prescriptions are worth examining because they speak to the practicality of her ideas.

The vagueness in some of Goldman's writing is not necessarily the intentional avoidance of an issue. The very essence of anarchism is freedom. She says: "Anarchism is not, as some may suppose, a theory of the future to be realized through divine inspiration. It is a living force in the affairs of our life, constantly creating new conditions. The methods of Anarchism therefore do not comprise an iron-clad program to be carried out under all circumstances. Methods must grow out of the economic needs of each place and clime, and of the intellectual and temperamental requirements of the individual" (74). The fact that anarchism is not an "iron-clad program" leaves open vast expanses of uncovered territory.

Goldman is advocating a society in which all bureaucratic, democratic, majoritarian, authoritarian, and coercive means are excluded from all types of relationships. What is missing in her theory is an extended and in-depth analysis of the psychological aspects of group behavior. Voluntary associations, while not compulsory in a formal sense, can nevertheless exhibit coercive types of behavior simply as a result of differences in personalities and emotional needs. Freedom, as Goldman defines it, is not just freedom from external means of coercion and authoritative institutions; it is also freedom in the inner being of an individual—a spiritual disposition of the soul. There is a hidden dialectical tension between her romantic notion of an unfolding individuality and the fact that it involves hard work to cultivate a consciousness of self. Potentially, some individuals will more readily engage in this difficult task than others. The consequence of this difference of engagement could negatively affect how individuals relate to one another and the potential for an anarchist society free from coercion.

Goldman only hints at the possibility that not all individuals equally engage in the difficult task of cultivating a consciousness of self, and she does not deal with the possible consequences that unequal engagement might impose on social relations. She provides a brief version of a "state of nature" story in which she describes a time when there was not a state: "The individual, and later the family, was the unit of social life where each was free and the equal of his neighbor. Human society then was not a State but an association; a voluntary association for mutual protection and benefit. The elders and more experienced members were the guides and advisors of the people. They helped manage the affairs of life, not to rule and dominate the individual" (112, 113). She imagines a time when people lived in a way similar to the that of the type of anarchist society that she advocates. She then goes on to explain the demise of this idyllic society: "Political government and the State were a much later development, growing out of the desire of the stronger to take advantage of the weaker, of the few against the many" (113). She says that it is the desire of the stronger to take advantage of the weaker that leads to the development of the state, but she does not give an account of the source of this desire. Is the desire rooted in human nature? Where did the desire for power come from if it is not found in our nature? Is the desire a product of society and social relations? If so, what sort of fail-safes are needed to guard against this tendency? Possibly the source of this desire for power is the unequal strength of spirit within individuals resulting from differences in the degree to which one person actively engages in self-discovery and development of personality as compared with another.

Psychological coercion does not need the cloak of method and institution to impose its will upon another. Strong personalities have a way of exerting themselves and emotionally needy individuals have a way of gravitating to stronger personalities. It may be a natural step from the unequal development of a consciousness of self within a community to the development of societal mores and institutions which sustain the authority of a few over the many. Given the degree of vagueness in many of her prescriptions, such as those concerning the wage-exchange system, property ownership, personal living arrangements, and situation and responsibility of child rearing, the psychological aspects of group behavior seem a necessary consideration in any analysis having to do with occasions of interactive relations.

It can reasonably be assumed that Goldman is against all forms of psychological coercion, but such an attitude is not sufficient for preventing them. The goal of Goldman's anarchist prescriptions is to produce individuals who are strong in spirit and thus all people would possess equally strong personalities. The problem with this theory lies in the fact that she acknowledges the difficulty, and even the natural reluctance, of engaging in the task of cultivating a strong, healthy spirit. Furthermore, people develop and mature at different rates and so it cannot be assumed that people are actually and always equally matched in temperament. The success of group relations seems dependent on hurdling a very high bar, that of equally possessed strong spiritual dispositions. It is not entirely clear that Goldman believes that all people are really capable of such a great feat. The tension never seems to be fully resolved in Goldman's thinking. The lack of resolution of this tension matters because of the interactive nature of the various relations in which individuals engage and the benefits she believes are derived from cooperative endeavors. If she perceives a certain inequality among individuals in their capacity to engage in the difficult task of developing into a self-conscious individuality, then her lack of attention to the psychological dynamics of group behavior is problematic. Inequality is the source of dominion of one over another, whether it concerns intellectual prowess, property holdings, or strength of spirit. Eliminating societal and institutional barriers may not be enough to guarantee the type of absolute freedom and autonomy that Goldman believes is necessary for the fullest growth and development of the individual.

References

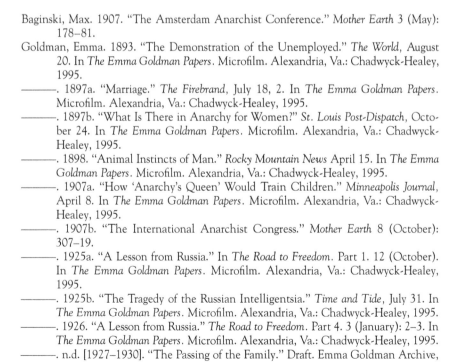

Baginski, Max. 1907. "The Amsterdam Anarchist Conference." *Mother Earth* 3 (May): 178–81.

Goldman, Emma. 1893. "The Demonstration of the Unemployed." *The World*, August 20. In *The Emma Goldman Papers*. Microfilm. Alexandria, Va.: Chadwyck-Healey, 1995.

———. 1897a. "Marriage." *The Firebrand*, July 18, 2. In *The Emma Goldman Papers*. Microfilm. Alexandria, Va.: Chadwyck-Healey, 1995.

———. 1897b. "What Is There in Anarchy for Women?" *St. Louis Post-Dispatch*, October 24. In *The Emma Goldman Papers*. Microfilm. Alexandria, Va.: Chadwyck-Healey, 1995.

———. 1898. "Animal Instincts of Man." *Rocky Mountain News* April 15. In *The Emma Goldman Papers*. Microfilm. Alexandria, Va.: Chadwyck-Healey, 1995.

———. 1907a. "How 'Anarchy's Queen' Would Train Children." *Minneapolis Journal*, April 8. In *The Emma Goldman Papers*. Microfilm. Alexandria, Va.: Chadwyck-Healey, 1995.

———. 1907b. "The International Anarchist Congress." *Mother Earth* 8 (October): 307–19.

———. 1925a. "A Lesson from Russia." In *The Road to Freedom*. Part 1. 12 (October). In *The Emma Goldman Papers*. Microfilm. Alexandria, Va.: Chadwyck-Healey, 1995.

———. 1925b. "The Tragedy of the Russian Intelligentsia." *Time and Tide*, July 31. In *The Emma Goldman Papers*. Microfilm. Alexandria, Va.: Chadwyck-Healey, 1995.

———. 1926. "A Lesson from Russia." *The Road to Freedom*. Part 4. 3 (January): 2–3. In *The Emma Goldman Papers*. Microfilm. Alexandria, Va.: Chadwyck-Healey, 1995.

———. n.d. [1927–1930]. "The Passing of the Family." Draft. Emma Goldman Archive,

International Institute of Social History, Amsterdam. In *The Emma Goldman Papers*. Microfilm. Alexandria, Va.: Chadwyck-Healey, 1995.

———. 1929. "Peter Kropotkin, Humanity's Friend." *The Road to Freedom* 6 (February): 1–2. In *The Emma Goldman Papers*. Microfilm. Alexandria, Va.: Chadwyck-Healey, 1995.

———. 1932a. "America by Comparison." Edited by Peter Neagoe. In *Americans Abroad: An Anthology*. The Hague: Servire Press. Also in *The Emma Goldman Papers*. Microfilm. Alexandria, Va.: Chadwyck-Healey, 1995.

———. 1932b. "Educational Experiments in Germany." Draft. Emma Goldman Archive, International Institute of Social History, Amsterdam. In *The Emma Goldman Papers*. Microfilm. Alexandria, Va.: Chadwyck-Healey, 1995.

———. 1933. "An Anarchist Looks at Life." Speech at Foyle's Twenty-ninth Literary Luncheon, March 1. Emma Goldman Archive, International Institute of Social History, Amsterdam. In *The Emma Goldman Papers*. Microfilm. Alexandria, Va.: Chadwyck-Healey, 1995.

———. 1983. *Red Emma Speaks*. Edited by Alix Kates Shulman. New York: Schocken Books.

———. 2001. *Anarchy! An Anthology of Emma Goldman's* Mother Earth. Edited by Peter Glassgold. Washington, D.C.: Counterpoint.

Haaland, Bonnie. 1983. *Emma Goldman: Sexuality and the Impurity of the State*. Montreal: Black Rose Books.

5

Emma Goldman and the Theory of Revolution

Berenice A. Carroll

"If we are open to a reconstruction of Emma Goldman's theory of revolution . . . it might best be characterized as a set of analytical and prescriptive ideas and principles, evolving over time in her own thought and inviting an ongoing conversation among her readers, in her time and in succeeding generations."

Revolution is central to creating a world built on the principles of Goldman's "beautiful idea." Carroll's analysis shows that Goldman's ideas on revolution changed and deepened throughout her life. While Goldman knew firsthand the costs and dangers of political upheavals, having lived in exile in Russia during its first years of revolution, she nonetheless understood a radical upheaval to be necessary to achieve the anarchist dream. Focusing particular attention on My *Disillusionment in Russia* and My *Further Disillusionment in Russia,* Carroll both places Goldman's ideas within their historical context and distinguishes them from those of her contemporaries.—*The Editors*

It would be an error to assume that the failure of the Revolution was due entirely to the character of the Bolsheviki. . . . Were any other party in control of the government in Russia the result would have been essentially the same. . . . The Russian Revolution reflects on a small scale the century-old struggle of the libertarian principle against the authoritarian. . . . Not mere substitution of one political party for another in the control of the Government, not the masking of autocracy by proletarian slogans, not the dictatorship of a new class over an old one, not political scene shifting of any kind, but the complete reversal of all these authoritarian principles will alone serve the revolution.

But to make the Revolution was not enough. It was necessary for it to advance and broaden, to develop into economic and social reconstruction. That phase of the Revolution necessitated fullest play of personal initiative and collective effort. The development and success of the Revolution depended on the broadest

exercise of the creative genius of the people, on the
cooperation of the intellectual and manual proletariat.
—Emma Goldman, My *Disillusionment in Russia*, 1922

But if the [Spanish Anarchists] should be defeated they
will yet have shown the first example in history how
Revolutions should be made.
—Emma Goldman, to Milly and Rudolf Rocker, August
26, 1936

"To set forth the lessons of the Russian Revolution"

When Emma Goldman began work on her book on the Russian Revolution, she later wrote, "I was overwhelmed with the magnitude of my
subject. The Russian Revolution, greater and more profound than the
French, as Peter [Kropotkin] had rightly said—could I do it justice?"
(1970a, vol. 2, 944). Beset by doubts about her ability to accomplish this
formidable task, living in insecure and difficult personal circumstances in
Berlin on a temporary visa, as a deported exile from the United States
and a political refugee from Bolshevik Russia, assailed and threatened
from both right and left for her ideas and actions since leaving the Soviet
Union or in years long past, it was many weeks before she was able to
begin. One day, in the midst of a storm, "as if by magic the load I had
carried for months lifted. . . . Thunder and lightning, followed by wind
and rain, beat against the windows of my room. I wrote on, oblivious of
everything except the storm in my own soul" (945). At last she was able
to work steadily on the book. Finally, she faced "the hardest part of my
book to do—an Afterword that was to set forth the lessons of the Russian
Revolution which our comrades and the militant masses will have to learn
if future revolutions are not to be failures" (947).

This book, though it was Goldman's most important contribution to
the theory of revolution, is not well known today and has received limited
attention in contemporary Goldman scholarship.[1] Despite the great revival of interest in Emma Goldman as an anarchist leader, a feminist,
and a flamboyant personality, little serious attention has previously been
given to her as an intellectual, and still less to her ideas on revolution as
a significant theoretical contribution. Indeed, she has been accorded
much the same treatment in this regard as is prevalent for other women
theorists, and with as little justice.

In previous writings I have argued that the intellectual work of women in the field of political and social theory has been severely neglected or dismissed and depreciated (Carroll 1990, 2000), and some key points from that argument appear in the introduction to this volume. In this chapter I deal, first, with the particular application of this argument to Goldman's work on the Russian Revolution; second, with the background and circumstances of her experiences in Russia; third, with the publication and reception of her book on those experiences; and finally, with her ideas on revolution as expressed primarily in My *Disillusionment in Russia* and in her writings on the Spanish Revolution.

As we have seen, in the introduction to this volume, Goldman's theoretical contributions were often dismissed as "unoriginal," "derivative," or "emotional," or passed over in silence. In the case of My *Disillusionment in Russia,* Oz Frankel gave it short shrift even while acknowledging that it had chronological priority as "probably the first damning account" of the Bolshevik regime. Alice Wexler, Martha Solomon, and others emphasized the influence on Goldman of Peter Kropotkin, and Marian Morton wrote that "Goldman borrowed much of her analysis of the Russian Revolution from Kropotkin." But Morton added perceptively: "*or from what she had re-created as Kropotkin's*" (1992, 122; emphasis added).

This passing remark, generally overlooked, expresses well an important fact about the process of "influence" of one thinker on another. The apparent dependence of a writer on her sources is often less complete than may be thought. Gerald L. Bruns has argued that exact imitation and copying are actually very difficult: "Scripture is something that is always turning into new versions of itself" (quoted in Carroll 1990, 155–56). In My *Disillusionment in Russia,* Goldman described two meetings with Kropotkin from which she came away without notes, and may well have been inclined to "re-create as Kropotkin's" a number of her own ideas about the revolution.

In this context, we may note Alice Wexler's remark that although Goldman was "attracted early" to Kropotkin's anarchism, "she never shared Kropotkin's unwavering faith in the revolutionary potential of the masses" (Wexler 1989, 10–11). While Wexler's concern was to suggest Goldman's indebtedness to Kropotkin and to argue that Goldman "was never an original thinker," this passage makes clear that on certain points Goldman's views were in serious disagreement with those of Kropotkin. While this would seem to acknowledge that Goldman's ideas were not, after all, entirely "derivative" or "imitative," the language frames the point as a matter of "faith," not intellect, hinting at the familiar charge of "emotionalism," presented more explicitly by Martha Solomon.

Oz Frankel reported a number of remarks to this effect in reviews of *Living My Life*, Goldman's autobiography, such as Freda Kirchwey's comment in the *Nation* that Goldman's "emotion is both intense and universal, her expression of it—in words and actions—unrestrained, her courage completely instinctive. . . . Always she feels first and thinks later—and less." The *New Republic* commented on her "instinctivism" and "eccentric emotionalism," and even a friend, John Haynes Holmes, remarked that parts of her book are "screaming with feeling, sobbing uncontrolled temperament, explosives, eruptions, like from a volcano" (Frankel 1996, 908). Although these comments pertained to Goldman's autobiography rather than her book on the Russian Revolution, they reflect a view of Goldman that explicitly dismisses her intellect: "Always she feels first and thinks later—and less."

Goldman herself rejected the opposition of feeling and mind implied in these remarks, and she argued explicitly in *My Disillusionment in Russia*: "It is the personal reactions of the participants and observers which lend vitality to all history and make it vivid and alive" (1970b, xlii). As one reads what Goldman has to say about revolution and many other issues, it is difficult to conclude that she "thinks less" or that the tone of her analysis is that of "screaming with feeling." Indeed, in reading *My Disillusionment in Russia*, one may well understand Goldman's own fear, as she set out to write it, that she would not be able to "make the story as vivid and moving as its reality" (1970a, 944). As though to repudiate in advance the charges of "emotionalism," Goldman herself had made clear, in her preface to the first volume of the American edition of *My Disillusionment in Russia* (1922), that she had waited for eight months after leaving Russia in December 1921 before beginning the book, so as not to be writing "fresh under the influence of the ghastly experience" (1970b, xlii). And later she felt that the writing was "pale and colorless, without the power she could command when she was 'intensely aroused over something'" (Wexler 1989, 71).

Her aim, she wrote, was to "relate honestly, frankly, and as objectively as humanly possible to me the story of my two years' stay in Russia" (1970b, xlii). But she did not intend, she explained, to "write a history" in the sense of a supposedly "objective" account. Rather, her intent was to provide one of the "human records of the period" such as those from which Peter Kropotkin had drawn his interpretation of the French Revolution, and to produce a document through which future historians might draw connections with other revolutions and thus come to understand better the revolutionary process itself. However, Goldman went beyond the goal of leaving a document for interpretation by future historians, to offer her own theoretical analysis.

My *Disillusionment in Russia*: Background and Context

Goldman was deported from the United States to Russia, together with Alexander Berkman and more than two hundred other political prisoners, in the hysteria of the "Red Scare" of 1919. The deportees returned to "Mother Russia" with mixed feelings of pain and anger at this forcible expulsion from their long-term home in the United States, yet with high hopes and expectations of what they would find in revolutionary Russia. Despite their anarchist ideas and past conflicts with Marxist and Bolshevik politics, they had greeted the revolution with enthusiasm. At the outset, they looked to the Bolshevik regime as a new phase of the mass revolution that had swept the czarist government from power, and they were disposed to support it (see, for example, Goldman 1917). In the 1922 preface to My *Disillusionment in Russia*, Goldman wrote: "From November, 1917, until February, 1918, while out on bail for my attitude against the war, I toured America in defense of the Bolsheviki. . . . I defended them as embodying *in practice* the spirit of the revolution, in spite of their theoretic Marxism" (1970b, xliv; emphasis in the original).

Upon arrival in Russia, Goldman and Berkman even doubted and disbelieved reports from anarchist comrades and others of a brutal repression of political and economic dissent by the Bolshevik government and the Cheka (the secret police), accepting the arguments presented by some that, should they in fact exist, such things were necessary to defend the revolution. But over time, Goldman's direct observations of the appalling conditions of life for the Russian people and mounting evidence of repression led her to accept that "still voice within me which urged me to face the overpowering facts" (1970b, xli). Berkman was slower to accept these realities, and in the end it was the bloody suppression of the Kronstadt sailors' rebellion by the Red Army under the command of Leon

Trotsky, theretofore seen as one of the heroes of the revolution, that completed their disillusionment with Bolshevik rule in Russia. Goldman and Berkman themselves were in danger of becoming victims of the repression, when they received invitations to attend the International Anarchist Congress in Berlin in December 1921 and left Russia for the last time, entering upon the long years of exile in which both ended their lives, Berkman by suicide in France in 1936, Goldman following a stroke during a fund-raising tour of Canada for the Spanish Anarchists in 1940.

Goldman and Berkman: "We have always helped each other in our work"

Richard Drinnon, in *Rebel in Paradise*, accuses Goldman of having exploited Alexander Berkman to edit her writings and especially to provide her with materials from his Russian diary for My *Disillusionment in Russia* (Drinnon 1961, 244–45). Here Drinnon refers primarily to Berkman's letter of October 22, 1922, to Michael Cohn, in which Berkman complained that he was spending all his time editing Goldman's book, which had preempted the interest of his prospective publisher, and that he feared his own would be viewed as merely a repetition of hers, which would appear first (Goldman and Berkman 1975, 27–28.) Berkman need hardly have worried, since, as Drinnon reported, when Berkman's *The Bolshevik Myth* was published, "discerning critics pronounced it superior to Emma's book" (Drinnon 1961, 245). The words "discerning" and "superior" tell us more about Drinnon's attitude toward the work of Berkman and Goldman than about the substantive merits of the two books, but it is difficult to know what to make of Berkman's fears and complaints.

Years later, in a diary entry of May 22, 1930, Berkman claimed that he had written "the entire last chapter"—presumably the "Afterword"—of My *Disillusionment in Russia*. This claim has been little noticed, but it is mentioned by Alice Wexler, who comments only, "If he did, Goldman never acknowledged his contribution" (1989, 262n91). Reporting in this diary entry a long letter from Goldman, Berkman wrote that she felt that he had not helped her enough by giving his opinions while she was writing her autobiography. Moreover, "in writing the book on R[ussia], she says, I also didn't help. . . . She forgets that I gave her [my] Russ[ian] diary for use, though I was myself to write on R[ussia]. And besides I wrote for her the entire last chapter. Seems [to] have forgotten it" (Berkman 1930). One may speculate on the grounds or the motives for Berkman's claim, but there is little if any "evidence" on which to base a judgment of its veracity. Comparisons of various writings by Goldman and Berkman as to content, style and language, and their correspondence relating to differences between them in their views, however, do not appear to support this claim.

Berkman himself, though upset about the potential effect on his own book of his having given Goldman "all the data, material, documents etc. which I had accumulated (and translated)," acknowledged that he had "consented, willingly and cheerfully," to her use of this material and that her writing and his were different not only in style but also in point of view. In the same diary entry of 1930 he defended himself by adding, "But she means more moral help and what could I in that way? When she and I begin to talk on issues, deep differences immediately develop and often lead to personal irritation" (Berkman 1930).

Indeed, a comparison of the content of the two books shows that they are very different. Berkman's book, subtitled *Diary 1920–1922*, is written in that form, primarily anecdotal and framed in conversational dialogue, while Goldman's book is much more discursive and theoretical. Although some of the events recounted, such as a joint visit to Peter Kropotkin, appear in both books, the accounts differ greatly in length and content. Many events and topics are entirely different, reflecting meetings with different individuals and their differing experiences and viewpoints, division of labor among members of a group traveling on tour in the Ukraine, and different substantive concerns.

Further, the correspondence between Goldman and Berkman makes clear that Berkman also relied on Goldman for editorial support and encouragement. He once wrote her that "I need your aid more in my work than you do my help" (undated letter, cited in Drinnon 1961, 267). In 1927, while he was working on the book later published under the title *Now and After: The ABC of Communist Anarchism*, and Goldman was traveling on a lecture tour in Canada, he went through a crisis of inability to write and sent her a long letter appealing for her advice. Although he admonished her not to "act hastily, to drop everything there and to come here," it was evident that he wished for that. "I should like very much to have you here [in Paris] this summer," he wrote. "I could write better when you are about, when I can consult you, and so on" (Goldman and Berkman 1975, 74). Goldman replied as soon as she received the letter, saying that her first impulse was to "to cable you that I will book passage on the first steamer out." But she did not have the money for the return voyage even if she could have abandoned her commitments. She did take time then to write at length advising and comforting him, urging him to take several weeks' break, and expressing confidence that he would be able then to "continue as you have started, which, as I have both cabled and written you, is [a work in] a splendid style and will turn out to be the most valuable ABC work on anarchism in existence and so badly needed" (75–76). On December 7, 1927, he wrote again urging her to return, but by then he had made substantial progress on the book and sent her eight chapters to review. He wrote:

> As to my work, you know how much your opinion helps me. I have often wished you would be somewhere where I could at least reach you within a day or two days, even by mail, so as to consult you on various points. . . . As it is, I have been looking forward anxiously and impatiently for your opinion of the eight chapters I sent you. It is true that we often have entirely different views on many matters; we come to the same conclusions, very often, by entirely different routes, sometimes even by opposite routes. But we have always helped each other in our work, in spite of all that.
>
> In the last analysis, of course, each must do his own thinking and his own writing. I could no more write your book than you could mine. But each can help the other with advice, suggestion, etc. (79).

Ten days later Goldman replied that she had received his manuscript the previous day, had read it that night, and had just sent him a cable saying it was "splendid" (81). She went on to offer further reassurance as well as editorial comments. When she returned to France in February 1928, she and Berkman continued to consult each other about their work. She was having trouble getting started on her autobiography, and on June 25 Berkman sent her a birthday greeting with some brief suggestions, then turned to a set of questions he was dealing with for his own book. On the twenty-ninth she replied that she had started to write, but she told him: "I have made up my mind not to let you see a line until you have finished your book. I simply won't let anything take much of your time or interfere with your writing" (86). She went on to respond at some length to the questions he had posed, offering there and in another letter a few days later a number of remarks on significant theoretical issues, in some cases reflecting certain differences between them, which are considered below.

Those differences were often as intense on a personal level as they were important on an intellectual level. On November 23, 1928, Goldman reminded Berkman of this in vivid terms: "Didn't I see it in Russia, where you fought me tooth and nail because I would not swallow everything as justification of the Revolution? How many times did you throw it into my teeth that I had only been a parlor revolutionist? That the end justifies the means, that the individual is of no account, etc., etc. . . . . Like you I once thought the cause everything. . . . I think, if you will search your heart, you will find that you have simply not entirely outgrown your old beliefs. Neither have I, for that matter, only that you cling to them more (Goldman and Berkman 1975, 95, 96). "Berkman's reply was revealing: "In Russia? . . . Your opposition to the bolsheviks seemed to me too sentimental and womanish. I needed more convincing proofs, and until I had them I could not honestly change my attitude. After all, I think that is the difference of the male and female mentality" (98).

My Disillusionment in Russia: Misadventures and Reception

The book Goldman wrote after her departure from Russia was a detailed exposition of the experiences and observations of her two years there and her analysis of them from the viewpoint of anarchist revolutionary theory. Goldman had simply titled the book My Two Years in Russia, but when it first appeared in 1923, the publisher (Doubleday, Page) changed the title to My Disillusionment in Russia. The change distressed Goldman because she felt it would be wrongly understood to mean she had become disillusioned with the revolution in Russia, which was not her intention. But worse still, by unfortunate circumstance, the last chapters of the book, which Goldman described as "the most vital part" (1970b, li), failed to reach the publisher at that time and were not published until the following year in the United States, under the title My Further Disillusionment in Russia. To confirm her fears, most reviewers failed to recognize that a large part of the text was missing, rendering their judgments on the truncated first version. In 1925 a complete edition was published in

England, but it is likely that significant damage had been done to the potential impact of the book. The appearance of the Apollo paperback edition in 1970, however, brought the work back into circulation, and the appearance of reprint editions in later years is evidence of its enduring interest.

Oz Frankel, in his review of the reception of Goldman's work, devoted only one sentence to My Disillusionment in Russia. To some extent this reflects the slight attention to this work in the general literature on Goldman over the years, yet the book was not entirely neglected when it appeared, and indeed won her praise in some unexpected and unwanted quarters on the political right, as well as vilification from some former allies on the left.

For the most part, My Disillusionment in Russia has been seen by both reviewers and scholars as simply a partisan anarchist diatribe against the Bolsheviks. Goldman is accused of disproportionately magnifying their faults and ignoring or discounting the positive advances of the Bolshevik state, achieved against great odds in a period of foreign intervention and counterrevolutionary civil war.[2] It is true that the book was nearly unrelieved as an indictment of the Bolshevik leadership and their policies, but less so of the Communist rank and file, and never of the Revolution itself, nor of "Soviet Russia," both of which she believed the Bolsheviks had betrayed and destroyed.[3]

Goldman's Indictment of the Bolshevik State

In her account of her visit to Peter Kropotkin in July 1920, Goldman reported that Kropotkin had told her: "You see a small political party which by its false theories, blunders, and inefficiency has demonstrated how revolutions must not be made" (1970b, 98). In the preface to My Disillusionment in Russia, Goldman picked up on this theme, summing up the charges against the Bolshevik State as follows: "In the great uprising the Bolsheviki assumed the voice of the people. They clothed themselves with the agrarian programme of the Social Revolutionists and the industrial tactics of the Anarchists. But after the high tide of revolutionary enthusiasm had carried them into power, the Bolsheviki discarded their false plumes. It was then that began the spiritual separation between the Bolsheviki and the Russian Revolution. With each succeeding day the gap grew wider, their interests more conflicting. Today it is no exaggeration to state that the Bolsheviki stand as the arch enemies of the Russian Revolution" (1970b, xliii–xliv).

Returning to this theme again and again throughout her book, Goldman gave ample grounds for readers to assume that it was her main message. Her indictment of the Bolshevik leadership and the dictatorship it instituted was sweeping and relentless. The methods of the Bolshevik State "were based on *coercion*, which in the course of things necessarily developed into systematic violence, oppression, and terrorism" (1970b, 250; emphasis in the original). The Bolsheviks, operating on the premise that the Communist Party was "the advance guard of the proletariat," maintained openly that they must keep the state power in their own hands.

The centralization of political power in the hands of the Party, Goldman argued, undermined the free development of the revolution. The Bolsheviks proceeded to eliminate all parties and organizations that opposed their policies, including the Anarchists, the Left Social Revolutionaries, the Mensheviks, "and finally everybody who dared aspire to an opinion of his own" (248). Throughout the book she describes examples of the repression, in which the Bolsheviks adopted all the methods of the old regime: mass executions (despite the official abolition of capital punishment); imprisonment and torture; exile to Siberia or elsewhere; spying and harassment by the Cheka; suppression of freedom of speech, press, and protest.

The introduction of Lenin's "new economic policy" (NEP), though "just in time to ward off the disaster which was slowly but surely overtaking the whole Communist edifice," resulted simply in the "accumulation of the wealth of the former bourgeoisie by the new Soviet bureaucracy." Thus the revolutionary process of social expropriation was turned into the mere "transfer of wealth from one set of individuals to another" (245, 247). Moreover, protests against the NEP by even devoted longtime Communists were met with "the clearing of the Party ranks of all 'doubtful' elements" through expulsion and repression, now turned against not only Anarchists and other dissenting groups, but also anyone "suspected of an independent attitude and those who did not accept the new economic policy" (246). To Communists who opposed the NEP, Goldman wrote, Lenin responded: "Only fools can believe that Communism is possible in Russia now" (247). In that, Goldman conceded, Lenin was certainly right. What had been instituted instead was "thirty-three categories of pay, different food rations, privileges to some and indifference to the great mass"—in short, an "all-powerful, centralized Government with State Capitalism as its economic expression" (247–48). To the repressive methods of the old regime, the Bolsheviks added more modern methods: subordination of the main forces that had driven the Revolution forward, through co-optation, intimidation, and diminished status. These forces, as discussed further below, included the Soviets, the trade unions, the cooperatives, the intellectuals, and the cultural associations (248, 253–55).

To Outline "the practical, constructive efforts during revolution"

Despite the detailed attention Goldman gave in My Disillusionment in Russia to the failings and misdeeds of the Bolsheviks, it is necessary to recognize that she did not intend her book to be only, or even primarily, an indictment of the Bolshevik dictatorship, but rather an analysis of the Russian Revolution as a case study or example illustrating broader theoretical principles of revolution. Few readers recognized this, though Richard Drinnon did remark, in his 1961 biography of Goldman, Rebel in Paradise, that her "Afterword" in the book was "an interesting analysis of the forces behind the Russian Revolution and an attempt to outline a general anarchist theory of revolutions" (Drinnon 1961, 246). Unfortunately, Drinnon's two-paragraph summary of the book (246–47) tended to confound it with Berkman's The Bolshevik Myth, emphasizing their shared condemnation of the Bolshevik state while losing sight of Goldman's effort to "outline a general anarchist theory of revolutions."

In Living My Life, Goldman wrote that though she had not wanted her book on Russia "to go out into the world without some definite conclusions," she did not feel it was possible then to deal fully with all "the complex problems of the subject": "I felt that for an adequate treatment of the constructive side of revolution I myself had to get away from the phantom of the Communist State far enough for objective writing" (1970a, 947). Although Alexander Berkman agreed that "in light of the Russian events a thorough revision of the old conception of revolution had become imperative," he advised her that it was not necessary to attempt that in this book. "He or I or both of us might undertake it later," she recalled that he told her. Her friend Rudolf Rocker concurred, and she decided "to jot down a few thoughts, some fragments that might serve as a sketch for a larger work on the vital subject" (947). On January 9, 1925, Goldman wrote in a letter to Harold Laski, "Your contention that the closing chapter of the second volume should have been enlarged is correct. The subject it treats would need a whole volume" (Goldman and Berkman 1975, 40).

Thus Goldman's ideas on the lessons of the Russian Revolution for revolutionary theory and practice were not fully developed in My *Disillusionment in Russia*. Nor did she or Berkman ever write the book they thought they might do later to offer "a thorough revision of the old conception of revolution." Berkman did expand on some of the points Goldman had suggested in her book in his *Now and After: The ABC of Communist Anarchism* (1929), but as discussed below, he and Goldman differed substantially on key issues. Goldman indicated the direction of her thinking in many articles, speeches, and letters, but she never developed them fully in another book.

Nevertheless, it is possible to discern the main points of Goldman's analysis of the Russian Revolution and her conception of "the practical, constructive efforts during revolution" in My *Disillusionment in Russia* and other writings (1970a, 947).

"The myth that the Bolsheviki and the Revolution are synonymous"

The starting point of Goldman's analysis was the need to draw a sharp distinction between "the Revolution" and the Bolshevik dictatorship, and to go beyond the Russian Revolution to consider its implications for revolution in the future.

In both My *Disillusionment in Russia* and *Living My Life*, Goldman recalled that Kropotkin had urged her to make this distinction, and not lose faith in the Revolution itself. Goldman and Berkman had visited Kropotkin twice, in March and July 1920, before his death in February 1921. Kropotkin had declined to write his own critique of the Bolshevik regime, explaining that it would have been useless for him to do so because of the repression, which would not allow his protests to be known, and because he anticipated serious negative consequences if they did become known. To begin with, it would put not only himself but also others in danger, "with the Cheka constantly at one's door." Moreover, "as long as Russia was being attacked by the combined Imperialists, and Russian women and children were dying from the effects of the blockade, he could not join the shrieking chorus of the ex-revolutionists in the cry of 'Crucify!' He preferred silence" (1970b, 36). Kropotkin warned also that "anything said or written against the Bolsheviki was bound to be interpreted by the outside world as an attack upon the Revolution and as alignment with the reactionary forces" (1970a, 770–71).

This was indeed what both Goldman and Berkman found on publication of their articles and books after their departure from Russia.[4] But Goldman was distressed by the poor state of Kropotkin's health and what it might portend. "The thought that Peter Kropotkin might go to his grave and that the world might never know what he thought of the Russian Revolution was appalling" (1970b, 37). Accordingly, she reported at some length on what he had said on those occasions (1970b, 35–37, 98–100; 1970a, 770–71, 863–64).[5]

In the 1922 preface to My Disillusionment in Russia, Goldman wrote that her "final decision to speak out is for the sole reason that the people everywhere may learn to differentiate between the Bolsheviki and the Russian Revolution" (1970b, xlvi). That her concern was for "the people everywhere" she sought to emphasize again, asserting, "Not my concern for the Russian people only has prompted the writing of this volume: it is my interest in the masses everywhere" (1970b, 1).

Thus Goldman's analysis of the nature and dynamics of revolution was not limited only to the revolution in Russia, but was intended as a contribution to revolutionary theory and practice in general. It was not, she contended, the character of the Bolsheviks themselves that determined the negative outcome in Russia, but rather the principles and methods that they adopted, which would have the same outcome anywhere: "It was the authoritarian spirit and principles of the State which stifled the libertarian and liberating aspirations. Were any other political party in control of the government in Russia the result would have been essentially the same" (250).

Goldman's intention, then, was not only to provide an analysis of what the Bolsheviks had done wrong, but even more, to rethink the conception of "the Revolution" that she, Berkman, and others had accepted until then, and to attempt a new, comprehensive, and constructive vision of how a revolution should be made. In that context we may discern, through a careful reading of *My Disillusionment in Russia*, together with other relevant writings, the key elements of that vision.

"Revolution: A fundamental transformation of values"

Foremost among the goals of a revolution, Goldman had come to conclude, was a fundamental transformation of values. She wrote in *My Disillusionment in Russia*: "No revolution can be truly and permanently successful unless it puts its emphatic veto upon all tyranny and centralization, and determinedly strives to make the revolution a real revaluation of all economic, social, and cultural values" (1970b, 252). Goldman also called up a phrase attributable to Friedrich Nietzsche, the "transvaluation of values." She wrote, "The great mission of revolution, of the Social Revolution, is a *fundamental transvaluation of values*. A transvaluation not only of social, but also of human values. The latter are even preëminent, for they are the basis of all social values" (1970b, 258–59; emphasis in the original). In speaking of "human values," she explained, "The ultimate end of all revolutionary social change is to establish the sanctity of human life, the dignity of man, the right of every human being to liberty and well-being" (1970b, 261).

Goldman was more specific in contrasting these broad concepts with her observations and experiences in Russia, particularly in encounters with officials of the Bolshevik State. In the early phases of the Revolution, she maintained, there was an "already awakened conception of the new revolutionary values," which, however, was "systematically destroyed" by the state bureaucracy: "The sense of justice and equality, the love of liberty and of human brotherhood—these fundamentals of the real regeneration of society—the Communist State suppressed to the point of extermination. Man's instinctive sense of equity was branded as weak sentimentality; human dignity and liberty became a bourgeois superstition; the sanctity of life, which is the very essence of social reconstruction, was condemned as un-revolutionary, almost counter-revolutionary" (1970b, 259).

In placing "human values" at the core of "the real regeneration of society" and "the very essence of social reconstruction," Goldman was moving beyond conventional liberal notions of individual human rights. Despite the strong influence of individualist anarchism in her earlier thought and continuing dedication to individual freedom and "the libertarian principle," she was moving toward a new valuation of collective action and social construction.

Goldman's insistence on justice and equality, human dignity and liberty, and the sanctity of life was linked to her condemnation of the State not only on the ground that the State was brutal and oppressive, but also that "the triumph of the State meant the defeat of the Revolution" (1970b, 250). For the Revolution to achieve its central goals of human betterment, it must not be fettered by dictatorial direction and control: "If I were to sum up my whole argument in one sentence, I should say: The inherent tendency of the State is to concentrate, to narrow, and monopolize all social activities; the nature of revolution is, on the contrary, to grow, to broaden, and disseminate itself in ever-wider circles. In other words, the State is institutional and static; revolution is fluent, dynamic" (1970b, 257). In seeking to maintain the power of the State under the will of the Communist Party, "the central authorities attempted to force the activities of the people into forms corresponding with the purposes of the Party," and to "monopolize all economical, political, and social activities—even all cultural manifestations," for the sole purpose of strengthening the State (1970b, 249–50). But in doing so, Goldman argued, they set up a fatal opposition with the Revolution itself: "The Revolution had an entirely different object, and in its very character it was the negation of authority and centralization. It strove to open ever-larger fields for proletarian expression and to multiply the phases of individual and collective effort" (250).

Social Revolution: "The complete social, economic, and industrial re-organization" of Society

Although she had come to hold humanitarian values as the highest priority of revolution, Goldman still saw sweeping social revolution—"the complete social, economic, and industrial re-organization" of society—as a central goal of revolution and one of the foundations necessary to achieve those human values she sought (1970b, 242–43). On the revolutionary action that had taken place in the summer of 1917 (that is, before the accession of the Bolsheviks to power), she wrote, "During that period the peasants possessed themselves of the land, the workers of the factories, thus demonstrating that they knew well the meaning of social revolution" (1970b, xliii). Goldman emphasized repeatedly, however, that the destruction of the old order and the expropriation of the land and factories by the peasants and workers did not yet fully meet the demands of true social revolution: "To make the Revolution was not enough. It was necessary for it to advance and broaden, to develop into social and economic reconstruction" (1970b, 244).

In that regard, Goldman later argued that the Spanish Revolution succeeded far beyond the Russian Revolution, despite the eventual victory of the fascist forces under Franco. Goldman traveled in Spain three times during the period of the revolution and the civil war.[6] In August 1936, she wrote to Milly and Rudolf Rocker in high praise of "the constructive work our comrades in Catalonia are doing," in particular, "the socializing of the land, the organization of the industries" (1983, 55–56). In September 1936 she wrote to her niece, "The most impressive of their achievements so far is the marvelous order that prevails, the work in factories and shops of those I have seen now in the hands of the workers and their organizations" (56).

In correspondence, speeches, and articles, Goldman dwelt in detail on the Spanish anarchist collectives in industry, agriculture, education, culture, and emergency relief for war victims and orphans (60–79). Throughout her accounts, she emphasized the egalitarian and libertarian character of the collectives. Describing a visit to a major established champagne vineyard and plant, she reported, "The plant is now collectivized and run by the workers themselves" (60). On a visit to a wood industry collective, she wrote, "I was especially impressed with the replies to my question as to what actually had the workers gained by collectivization. Would you believe it, the answer always was, first, greater freedom. And only secondly, more wages and less time of work" (62).

Describing a newly established textile workshop in a converted old monastery, Goldman emphasized the voluntary and creative character of the collective, which must have struck her as contrasting sharply with what she had called the "militarization of labor" and egregious working conditions she had witnessed in Russia:

> A group of unemployed workers of the same trade had undertaken the task of creating this new collective. It was all done by voluntary agreement, without one single worker having been coerced into it. While the venture had not yet reached perfection, the

workers connected with it knew exactly what they wanted, and were pressing ahead in spite of all obstacles and imminent danger from bombardments. This collective factory was not merely for the production of things, but planned as a place for the physical and cultural life of those cooperating in the scheme. A dining room was in the midst of building; a dispensary, a lecture hall and reading room and ever so many other plans were already under way. We found a radio installed with connections to the shops where, while the women and girls were working, they could listen to the news, to good music. (62–63)

There were also large-scale enterprises, such as a textile collective with "a membership of thousands." Goldman noted that none of its plant and equipment had been expropriated; the collective was paying rent for its building and "hard cash" for materials. Most of the members were women and girls (63).

That Goldman stated this last point without comment was characteristic of her attention to women in her writings on the Russian and Spanish Revolutions. In these contexts, Goldman does not directly address feminist issues, and frequently uses masculinist language, such as in the word *man* to refer to human beings. However, she often notes the presence, roles, and conditions of women. Thus she reports or comments on the status of women workers, the importance and treatment of individual women leaders, the continuation or reappearance of prostitution in Bolshevik Russia, and other matters affecting women and their participation in society. Although she took special interest in some individual women as revolutionary leaders, it is one of the limitations of her analysis that she does not consider on a theoretical level the roles of women in revolution.

The same or even greater dedication to the constructive work of the revolution that Goldman reported in industry she found also in the Spanish countryside. Writing of the Alba de Cinca community, she expressed her admiration for "the spirit and ability of the peasantry in the villages I had visited to collectivize the land and to bring into being what they called 'Communismo Libertario' [Libertarian Communism]." At Alba de Cinco the members had set up three councils: "a Council of Labor, of Food Supplies and of Defense. The three work in a federated way, of course. Federation is the very essence of the ideas and practice of the CNT-FAI [National Confederation of Labor–Anarchist Federation of Iberia]" (66). In Madrid she visited a center for the Federation of Peasants, encompassing seven hundred syndicates and three hundred collectives, with a membership of one hundred thousand, including both laborers and small landowners. "The Federation has departments of statistics, propaganda, [and] interchange and sections dealing with oil, wine, and all other kinds of provisions. We were taken into the scientific laboratory which [was to engage in] chemical and agricultural experiments and analyses. . . . In connection with this an experimental school for agricultural engineers was organized" (67).

In December 1938, Goldman marveled that despite the terrible events and setbacks of the civil war, "the collectives, such as transport, wood industry, textile and garment workers, milk collectives and many more, continue to be manned by members of the CNT. The same holds good of the collectives on the land" (58–59). And Goldman concluded: "In other words, whatever thrusts the Spanish Revolution has received, and I know better than many other visitors to Spain how deep the wounds are, I must nevertheless insist that collectivization and socialization still represent the most potent revolutionary achievement of the Spanish Anarchists" (59; also Goldman 1972, 377).

"The necessary social consciousness"

The key factor driving a revolution, Goldman held, was the revolutionary consciousness or psychology of the masses. Goldman argued that this was even more important than advanced economic development (1970b, 242).[7] She disputed the view, attributed to Marx, that "a social revolution is possible only in countries with a highly developed industrial system and its attendant social antagonisms." The United States and other countries, she argued, had already reached an advanced level of industrial development, but clearly this was "by no means sufficient to give birth to a new society or to call forth a social revolution" (242). What was missing was "the necessary social consciousness." Without it, there could be no revolution; with it, the revolution could not be held back. Rosa Luxemburg in 1906 had argued that revolution "cannot be called at will" by a political party or leaders.[8] Neither can it be made to wait, wrote Goldman in 1922: "Events in Russia, in 1917, demonstrated that revolution does not await this process of industrialization and—what is most

important—cannot be made to wait. The Russian peasants began to expropriate the landlords and the workers took possession of the factories
without taking cognizance of Marxian dicta" (243).

In the case of Russia, the revolutionary consciousness had developed
rapidly in the early stages of the Revolution despite the fact that Russia
still had an agrarian economy. Goldman traced the revolutionary mass
psychology of the Russian populace to the history of revolutionary struggle in the previous century. She might well have made reference to the
prominent role of revolutionary anarchism (particularly of the Narodnaya
Volya [People's Will]) in that history, but called up, instead, the image of
a broader movement: "That psychology involved the passionate yearning
for liberty nurtured by a century of revolutionary agitation among all
classes of society" (242).

Moreover, the February Revolution prepared the ground for even more
radical action, so that "within a few months the people were ready for
such ultra-revolutionary slogans as 'All power to the Soviets' and 'The
land to the peasants, the factories to the workers,'" slogans that "signified
the complete social, economic and industrial reorganization of Russia"
(243). These were the ideas that animated the popular uprising in the
days of the October–November Revolution, and the Bolsheviks, swept
into power by the events of those days, adopted those slogans as their
own. "For several months following October they suffered the popular
forces to manifest themselves, the people carrying the Revolution into
ever-widening channels" (245). But the revolutionary momentum was
brought to a halt by the policies of the Bolsheviks, designed to centralize
all power in the hands of the Communist Party and the State.

In Spain, however, Goldman saw the revolutionary consciousness of
the masses as deeper, and their preparation for the constructive work of
revolution as stronger, than had been the case in Russia. In Russia, she
acknowledged, even she had shared the false notion that "the principal
thing is to get people to rise against the oppressive institutions and that
everything else will take care of itself" (Goldman and Berkman 1975,
69). The reality was that despite the evident readiness of the masses for
the social revolution in the fall of 1917, they were not fully prepared to
undertake the enormous reconstructive tasks that confronted them or to
resist the Bolshevik assumption of dictatorial powers.

In contrast, Goldman found both kinds of preparation in Spain. The
accomplishments and endurance of the collectives that she described
with such admiration were grounded in the long history of the anarchist

movement in Spain, dating back to at least 1845.[9] Goldman spoke repeatedly of "the libertarian spirit of the Spanish people" (1983, 117) and maintained that the Revolution "rose from the very bowels of the Spanish earth. It was entirely imbued with the collective spirit of the Spanish masses" (38). In August 1938 she reiterated, "It will interest you to know that I found in some villages four generations steeped in Libertarian Communism. To them the idea was not merely on paper or in books, but a living force" (34).

Goldman did not deny that even among anarchists, those who might take on positions of power might "lose their judgment and grit" and follow policies inconsistent with anarchist principles (28). She was in fact deeply troubled by some of the decisions and actions of the Anarchist leadership, which were under severe criticism in the international Anarchist movement (96ff.) But she defended them on grounds of the extraordinary achievements of the Anarchists in the Spanish Revolution and held to the hope that those in the Barcelona leadership would be brought back to their true aim, "the independence and right of the people" (28).

At the same time, drawing a distinction similar to that between the Bolsheviks and the Revolution in Russia, she saw the Spanish Revolution itself as arising from the people, not at the bidding of any charismatic leaders. She wrote in October 1936: "One thing is certain: the Revolution is safe only with the people and peasants, not in Barcelona. . . . [T]heir anarchism is not the result of books. They have received it with their mothers' milk. It is now in their very blood" (27–28). A few months later she wrote that "the Revolution in Spain is absolutely and completely a proletarian Revolution without leadership of any sort" (29). At about the same time, in a letter to Roger Baldwin, she expanded on this point: "One thing I can tell you already: the Revolution is safe with the workers and peasants of Catalonia, Aragón and the Levante. . . . I have travelled through these parts, have visited the collectivized towns and villages and I have seen the spirit of the people. I know they are imbued with the ideal so many of us have [advocated] for a lifetime. . . . The most impressive phase of the Revolution to me is that it has no leaders, no great intellects. It is entirely a mass Revolution risen from the depth of the Spanish soil, the depths of the needs and aspirations of the workers (57).

While Goldman saw "the necessary social consciousness" as the driving force of revolution, she recognized that prior preparation was also essential. The positive achievements of the Anarchists in Spain, she argued, rested not only on their deeply rooted Anarchist tradition, but also on conscious preparation and organization. In an article about the Albalate de Cinca collective, published in March 1937, Goldman wrote that "the superior quality of the Spanish Anarchist movement to those of other countries consists in the constructive preparatory work which our comrades had carried on almost from the inception of the CNT" (64). Several years earlier, she reported, the CNT had surveyed their affiliates and membership to determine their ability to "take charge of the means of production and distribution," and found a surprising level of knowledge and competence among even "the simplest workers and peasants." In addition, "they had been trained ideologically that it was not the creation of a formidable State machine but the capacity to produce for the needs of the whole community which guarantees the life and safety of the Revolution." Thus "the Spanish workers had years of experience and preparation for the supreme moment of a social revolution" (64).

In Russia, conditions of war and hardship became the pretexts for the triumph of dictatorship and oppression, but in Spain, Goldman argued, the prior years of experience and preparation gave the collectives the skills, strength, and commitment necessary to continue their constructive efforts, despite the losses and obstacles of war and internecine political conflict. In these dire circumstances, they "demonstrated in a masterly manner their pre-revolutionary schooling in the economic life of the country. While still fighting almost with bare hands—they at the same time proceeded to expropriate the factories and shops—the entire transport system as well as the land—and they set to work to build a new mode of life" (64–65). Although in the end they too were overwhelmed by the military forces deployed against them, Goldman perceived their unique combination of consciousness and preparation as essential to the success of any future revolution.

"The methods of the Revolution and the State": Ends and Means

Goldman argued that it was not only the "aims and tendencies" of the Revolution and the State that stood diametrically opposed to each other, but also their methods. From her perspective, *direct action* by the masses was the essential method of revolution: "The *actual* Russian Revolution

took place in the summer months of 1917. During that period the peasants possessed themselves of the land, the workers of the factories"
(1970b, xliii; emphasis in the original). To the extent that the peasants
made any major gain from the Revolution, it was not because of the
Bolsheviks, but "through their own direct efforts, set in motion long
before the October change" (xlviii). In this the peasants were ultimately
more successful than the industrial proletariat. "Owing to the circumstance that they form by far the largest part of the population and are
deeply rooted in the soil, they could not as easily be torn away from it as
the workers from their means of production" (xlviii). At the outset, however, "the Russian workers, like the peasants, also employed direct action.
They possessed themselves of the factories, organized their own shop
committees, and were virtually in control of the economic life of Russia"
(xlviii).

But the Bolshevik state could not tolerate the independent and free
development of workers' control. The introduction of the NEP had
brought with it policies of "one-man management" and "militarization
of labor," which Goldman described as "a militarized industrial army . . .
that could be whipped into line only by rigid discipline, it was claimed"
(51). On visits to a number of factories, Goldman found the workers in
most places bitter, fearful, overworked, and hungry. The new measures
were opposed by the workers as imposing intolerable conditions on them
and standing in contradiction with efforts to achieve "the new communist aspirations [which] can be obtained only through the collective efforts of the workers themselves," as Alexandra Kollontai put it in her
pamphlet *The Workers' Opposition* in 1921. But the Workers' Opposition
was suppressed. Goldman, interviewing a bitter worker in a flour mill in
1920, had asked: "Has the Revolution given you nothing?" To which the
worker replied, "Ah! The Revolution! But that is no more. Finished"
(55).

Thus Goldman argued that, beyond the kinds of mass direct action
that were necessary in the early phases of a revolution, popular participation was essential in the ongoing process of social and economic reconstruction: "Only free initiative and popular participation in the affairs of
the revolution can prevent the terrible blunders committed in Russia"
(253). These "terrible blunders" were manifestations of the authoritarian
state, to which free development of new social structures and libertarian
institutions represented neither a goal nor a method but rather a threat
to its control and supremacy. As we have seen, Goldman was to find her

positive vision astonishingly close to realization in the Spanish collectives fifteen years later, but by the time she left Russia in 1921, the popular structures that had emerged in the early phases of the Russian Revolution were essentially crushed.

These included the Soviets, the trade unions, and the cooperatives. Goldman gave special emphasis to the Soviets, which had first appeared in the Revolution of 1905. Revived in 1917, they spread, in Goldman's words, "spontaneously and rapidly" throughout Russia. The Soviets were spontaneous local councils of workers, soldiers, peasants, and others.[10] The Bolsheviks at first supported them (using them indeed as the icon of the new state, the "Union of Socialist Soviet Republics") but soon saw them as a threat to the State, reduced their powers, and moved to subordinate them to the will of the Communist Party.

The trade unions, in Goldman's view, were "still in their childhood," weak in numbers and malleable. The Bolsheviks nurtured them at first, seeing them as "a school for Communism." But to Goldman, who was conscious of issues relating to children and education, it seemed to her "an antiquated school where the spirit of the child is fettered and crushed" (249). She saw the Russian trade unions under Bolshevik rule as more subservient to the State than anywhere else in the world.

As to the cooperatives, she recalled that on both occasions of her visits to Kropotkin, he had described them as "the main medium that could have bridged the interests of the peasants and the workers," the city, and the country (36, 99). The Bolsheviks, Goldman wrote, had "transformed them into cogs of the Government machine and thereby destroyed their usefulness and efficiency" (249).

As Goldman watched these developments, alongside numerous reports of arrests, imprisonment, torture, and executions of anarchists and other dissidents, she wondered at the terrible contradictions they implied in the character of the Communist leadership: "The Communists I had met daily during six months—self-sacrificing, hard-working men and women imbued with a high ideal—were such people capable of the treachery and horrors charged against them? Zinoviev, Radek, Zorin, Ravitch, and many others I had learned to know—could they in the name of an ideal lie, defame, torture, kill?" (68). The explanation she was coming to was that "the Communists believed implicitly in the Jesuitic formula that the end justifies *all* means. In fact, they gloried in that formula. . . . Obsessed by the infallibility of their creed, giving of themselves to the fullest, they could be both heroic and despicable at the same time. They could work twenty hours a day, live on herring and tea, and order the slaughter of innocent men and women" (70; emphasis in the original).[11] What was perhaps even worse, they had lost sight of the value basis of "the end": "Any suggestion of the value of human life, quality of character, the importance of revolutionary integrity as the basis of a new social order, was repudiated as 'bourgeois sentimentality'" (70). In place of such human values as the goal of the Revolution, the Bolsheviks had set the Dictatorship of the Proletariat and the Communist state: "All the succeeding acts of the Bolsheviki, all their following policies, changes of policies, their compromises and retreats, their methods of suppression and persecution, their terrorism and extermination of all other political views—all were but the *means to an end* the retaining of the State power in the hands of the Communist Party" (245; emphasis in the original).

Moreover, this development exemplified, in itself, one of the central principles enunciated by Goldman, namely that "methods and means cannot be separated from the ultimate aim. The means employed become, through individual habit and social practice, part and parcel of the final purpose: they influence it, modify it, and presently the aims and means become identical" (260).

"To eliminate as much as possible the need for violence"

For Goldman, the problem of violence, in particular the use of violence in revolutionary action, was the hardest conundrum of all. In 1892, Goldman had supported Berkman in his (unsuccessful) attempt on the life of the steel magnate Henry Clay Frick, and she went so far as to publicly horsewhip her former mentor, Johann Most, for casting aspersions on Berkman's motives and condemning his act—not to mention calling her a "hysterical woman" (Drinnon 1970, 44, 54). Inspired by the courage and dedication of the Russian revolutionaries, including women such as Sophia Perovskaya, who had masterminded the assassination of the czar, she had stifled her fear and doubts while Berkman experimented with (failed) attempts to make a bomb. In *Living My Life* she recalled: "I lived in dread every moment for Sasha, for our friends in the flat, the children, and the rest of the tenants. What if anything should go wrong—but then, did not the end justify the means? Our end was the sacred cause of the oppressed and exploited people. It was for them that we were going to give our lives. What if a few should have to perish?—the many would be made free and could live in beauty and comfort. Yes, the end in this case justified the means" (1970a, 88). Fortunately, nothing "went wrong"— even Berkman's failure to kill Frick was perhaps a blessing in disguise. But as we have seen, Goldman was obliged to grapple with the question of ends and means long into the future.

In a perceptive discussion of Goldman's involvement in acts of violence, Richard Drinnon affirms as accurate Goldman's claim, in a letter to Theodore Dreiser in the late 1920s, that "I have never in my life induced anybody to acts of violence" (Drinnon 1970, 78–84). Her support for Berkman's assassination attempt, and her defense of Leon Czolgosz—but not of his act in assassinating President William McKinley—are perhaps best understood, Drinnon suggests, in the context of a formulation by Albert Camus, characterizing such uses of violence as "necessary and inexcusable," or, more in keeping with the views of Goldman and Berkman on the use of violence in revolution, "inevitable and inexcusable" (80, 84). But although this interesting formulation works well for the Russian terrorists, it is not as appropriate for Goldman and Berkman, though for different reasons in each case.

With the outbreak of World War I and the entry of the United States into the war, Goldman found herself committed to a new arena of struggle against violence: antiwar and antidraft agitation. Early in 1917 she co-founded the No-Conscription League and lectured widely against the war and conscription. But her active engagement in the peace movement was cut short by the determination of the government and the courts to silence her. In June 1917 she and Berkman were arrested on charges of "conspiracy to induce persons not to register" for the draft, and she spent most of the remaining eighteen months of her life in the United States in prison, or in unsuccessful legal battles to appeal their imprisonment and deportation orders.

Meanwhile, events in Russia revived the political and theoretical debates and dilemmas concerning war and the use of violence in revolution. For here at last, miraculously and to the astonishment of the world, the first major revolution of the twentieth century had emerged in the most "backward," least economically advanced party to the war in Europe. In the early spring of 1917, Russian soldiers by the hundreds of thousands deserted the front and walked home to their planting, to be met by the revolutionary agitation and massive changes of the February and October revolutions. Of the revolution itself, Goldman wrote, "Rarely has a revolution been fought with as little violence as the Russian Revolution"

(1970b, xlix). But Russia was still at war, and the new revolutionary government was under attack from the "Whites" on many fronts. When Lenin, desperate to reduce the burdens of war on the western front, signed the Treaty of Brest-Litovsk in the spring of 1918, on extremely unfavorable terms, Goldman, who heard of it while still in prison in the United States, was in favor of it. Even though it was a wretched compromise with German imperialism, she "could see no way out of the situation." But when she arrived in Russia she learned that there had been internal dissent among the Communists and other parties about it and widespread anger at the regime for abandoning the Ukrainian peasants, revolutionaries, and resources to the Germans, along with those of Finland, White Russia, and Latvia.[12] Thus those who had greeted the revolution with enthusiasm, Goldman and Berkman among them, were confronted with vexing and fundamental questions, no longer in the realm of theory but rather as urgent issues for action: Should peace be bought at the expense of humiliation and great losses for the revolution? Did the revolution have the right to defend itself? And if so, by what means?

For Goldman and Berkman, these questions were complicated by their anarchist condemnation of government itself as coercive and violent. Support for any revolutionary government would necessarily be a compromise, and support for the Bolsheviks in particular, with their notions of "dictatorship of the proletariat" and the Communist Party as the "advance guard" of the proletariat, demanded a tremendous suspension of disbelief. Berkman was able to sustain this for most of the two years they spent in Russia, but Goldman had seen enough within little more than a year. There were many grounds for her change of heart, but among them, issues concerning the regime's uses of violence and terror to sustain itself were preeminent.

In My Disillusionment in Russia, Goldman argued that the great fallacy of the Bolshevik regime, and indeed of all socialist parties, was the idea of revolution as simply "a violent change of social conditions through which one social class, the working class, becomes dominant over another class, the capitalist class . . . a purely physical change, [which] involves only political scene shifting and institutional rearrangements" (1970b, 258). This idea, she asserted, "is inherently and fatally false":

> Revolution is indeed a violent process. But if it is to result only in a change of dictatorship, in a shifting of names and political

personalities, then it is hardly worth while. It is surely not worth all the struggle and sacrifice, the stupendous loss in human life and cultural values that result from every revolution. If such a revolution were even to bring greater social well being (which has not been the case in Russia) then it would also not be worth the terrific price paid: mere improvement can be brought about without bloody revolution. . . . It is at once the great failure and the great tragedy of the Russian Revolution that it attempted (in the leadership of the ruling party) to change only institutions and conditions while ignoring entirely the human and social values involved in the Revolution. . . . Violence, the tragic inevitability of revolutionary upheavals, became an established custom, a habit, and was presently enthroned as the most powerful and "ideal" institution. (258–59)

In the 1924 preface to *My Further Disillusionment in Russia*, Goldman added some clarifications in response to points raised by readers of the first (truncated) edition. Here she wrote that she did not dispute "that destruction and terror are part of revolution," and she recognized that "in the past every great political and social change necessitated violence. . . . I have never denied that violence is inevitable, nor do I gainsay it now" (1970b, xlviii–xlix).

But she did insist that there must be limits to the forms and magnitude of violence to be in keeping with revolutionary goals: "Yet it is one thing to employ violence in combat, as a means of defence. It is quite another thing to make a principle of terrorism, to institutionalize it, to assign it the most vital place in the social struggle. Such terrorism begets counter-revolution and in turn itself becomes counter-revolutionary" (xlix).

A few years later, Goldman suggested in an interesting letter of November 1925 to Havelock Ellis that she was modifying her conception of the nature, if not the necessity, of "violence" in revolution. She still believed, she wrote, that "great social changes have not and cannot take place without some clash." But she described revolutions as "nothing but the breaking point of accumulated evolutionary forces," which, like a violent storm in nature or in our lives, "creates violent upheavals," such as may take place also "in the social and economic life of the world." However, she had concluded that "the amount of violence in any revolution will depend entirely upon the amount of preparation on the part of the conflicting forces—the amount of INNER preparation." And she explained: "By preparation I mean the growth out of old habits and ideas" (Goldman and Berkman 1975, 69).

She went on to reiterate, as she had argued in My *Disillusionment in Russia*, that "we can neither make nor prevent revolutions. They are as inevitable as hurricanes." But now she declared that "at least we can prevent endless repetition of the mistakes and cruelties of the past." She was frequently told, she wrote Ellis, "that the bolsheviki are merely repeating the methods of the jacobins and that they could not do otherwise." But this now seemed to her "absurd, . . . especially on the part of people who proclaim their faith in progress" (Goldman and Berkman 1975, 69–70): "To me progress means a change not only in ideas but also in method. Here we are, 140 years after the French Revolution, with advancements in every domain of human thought and social affairs, and yet we have developed nothing better than photographic repetition of the methods of the French Revolution" (70).

In a letter to Berkman in 1928, Goldman reflected the struggle going on in her mind on these issues. In connection with his work on the manuscript of *The ABC of Communist Anarchism*, he had posed the question "Has the revolution the right to defend itself?" Goldman's reply was "Certainly, if you believe that no fundamental change can take place without a revolution, you must also believe in its right of defense."

She herself, she wrote, wished she could take the position of Tolstoy and Gandhi that armed defense would be inconsistent with the revolution. "Emotionally I really do. I feel violence in whatever form never has and probably never will bring constructive results." But she could not see that as a realistic position. "My mind and my knowledge of life tell me that changes will always be violent" (87). Her resolution of this internal conflict was to steer away from violence to the extent that might be possible: "At least I want the revolution to eliminate as much as possible the need for violence. I want the revolution to be understood as a process of reconstruction rather than what we believed it to be until now, a process of destruction" (87).

Following up these thoughts a few days later, Goldman wrote: "If we agree that revolution must essentially be a process of reconstruction, destroying as little as possible—nothing at all in fact except such industries that make for war and disease—if we can realize and boldly declare that the only purpose of revolution must be transformation, then terror must go with the rest and prisons and other evil things of today must go with the rest" (89). She recalled that she had once said to Berkman, soon after

they had arrived in Russia: "If revolution cannot solve the need of violence and terror, then . . . I am against revolution." He "flew at her in a
rage," she remembered, "said I had never been a real revolutionist and a
lot more." Now it seemed he had "come to the same conclusion," but
not quite,

> our difference now being that you are loath to let go the thought
> of revolution in terms of destruction and terror. And that I am
> done with for all times. I insist if we can undergo changes in every
> other method of dealing with social issues, we will also learn to
> change in the methods of revolution. I think it can be done. If
> not, I shall relinquish my belief in revolution. That not only be-
> cause of so much waste of human lives, but also because it is all
> so futile, an endless repetition of the same old refrain, "the French
> Revolution Was That Way. All Revolutions Must Be That Way."
> History dictates the course. History has become the new supersti-
> tion like the will of god. I for one no longer believe in that, dear
> Sash. (90)

"The manifold creative energies of the people"

While the issue of violence and its limits was a recurrent theme in Goldman's writings on revolution, she was very clear that violence could never
bring about those fundamental changes in structure and values that she
held to be the true goals of revolution. In discussing revolutionary action,
Goldman sought to go beyond the somewhat static concepts of "mass
psychology" and "revolutionary consciousness" to suggest images of creativity and innovation arising from the people: "It is only when the libertarian spirit pervades the economic organizations of the workers that the
manifold creative energies of the people can manifest themselves, and
the revolution be safeguarded and defended" (1970b, 253). For the Revolution to "advance and broaden" would require "fullest play of personal
initiative and collective effort" (244).

In discussing the readiness of the Russian people to adopt revolutionary slogans and action in 1917, Goldman had attributed this phenomenon to "the passionate yearning for liberty nurtured by a century of
revolutionary agitation among all classes of society" (242). Among "all

classes of society," Goldman included, significantly, the intelligentsia. Despite the counterrevolutionary role she acknowledged was played by many sectors of the intelligentsia, "especially the technical intelligentsia," under Bolshevik rule as before the revolution, there was also, wrote Goldman, "another kind of intelligentsia—one with a glorious revolutionary past of a hundred years." Although "that part of the intelligentsia kept faith with the people," the Bolsheviks initially did not distinguish among different elements of the intellectual classes. They instituted "wholesale terror against the intelligentsia as a class" and undermined constructive work by exacerbating hostility between intellectuals and proletarians. This split, she argued, ran counter to the true interests of the revolution in Russia (1970b, 254–55). "Intellectual and physical labour are as closely related in the social body as brain and hand in the human organism," she wrote, and the revolution required mutual aid and "libertarian cooperation" between workers on the one hand, and professional and cultural classes on the other (256–57).

For Goldman, then, "the development and success of the Revolution depended on the broadest exercise of the creative genius of the people, on the cooperation of the intellectual and manual proletariat" (1970b, 244).

To speak of "the creative genius of the people" was not something that Goldman had always had in mind. In her essay "Minorities Versus Majorities," published in Anarchism and Other Essays in 1910, she had written: "The multitude, the mass spirit, dominates everywhere, destroying quality. . . . Lacking utterly in originality and moral courage, the majority has always placed its destiny in the hands of others" (Goldman 1969, 69, 70). And as to revolutionary spirit, she asserted at that time: "Always, at every period, the few were the banner bearers of a great idea, of liberating effort. Not so the mass, the leaden weight of which does not let it move. . . . [T]he mass itself is responsible for this horrible state of affairs. It clings to its masters, loves the whip, and is the first to cry Crucify! the moment a protesting voice is raised against the sacredness of capitalistic authority or any other decayed institution. . . . In other words, the living vital truth of social and economic well-being will become a reality only through the zeal, courage, the non-compromising determination of intelligent minorities, and not through the mass" (75, 77, 78).

Alice Wexler, in Emma Goldman in Exile, contends that Goldman "never shared Kropotkin's unwavering faith in the revolutionary potential of the masses" (Wexler 1989, 10). But while it is true that Goldman had in earlier years expressed contempt for "the mass," and that she may never have felt "unwavering faith" in "the masses," her analysis of the Russian Revolution was grounded in the view that it was the people, the peasants and workers, who took the initiative in revolutionary action and pressed the revolution forward until it was derailed and brought to a halt by the consummate deceptions and repression practiced by the Bolshevik regime.

In the dark years following Goldman's departure from Russia, there were times when she expressed anger, impatience, or despair at the failure of "the masses" in Russia and elsewhere to bring about and sustain true revolution. Berkman was perhaps even more negative than Goldman, but in a letter of 1927, she wrote him: "I will grant you that [Peter Kropotkin] was very romantic when it comes to his prophecy [of] how the masses will act on the day after the revolution. . . . The entire old school, Kropotkin, Bakunin, and the rest, had a childish faith in what Peter calls 'the creative spirit of the people.' I'll be damned if I can see it. If the people could really create out of themselves, could a thousand Lenins or the rest have put the noose back on the throat of the Russian masses? I don't think so" (Goldman and Berkman 1975, 82). Again in 1931 she wrote him: "I too have come to the conclusion, bitter as it is, that hardly anything has come of our years of effort. And that the mass is really hopeless as far as real progress and freedom are concerned" (49).

Wexler and others have argued that Goldman had lost faith in revolution itself, indeed in "any revolution" (Wexler 1989, 79, 82). Wexler dismissed the distinction Goldman drew in My Disillusionment in Russia between the Revolution and the Bolshevik regime, citing a review of the book by Goldman's friend Henry Alsberg, who, according to Wexler, "interpreted the book, correctly, as 'my disillusionment with revolution'" (Wexler 1989, 82; emphasis added). As it relates to My Disillusionment in Russia, this charge is unpersuasive, given the evidence in the book that Goldman's intellectual analysis was, as she maintained explicitly, based on that distinction, and that she had never intended the title of her book to include the word disillusionment at all.

It is true that in the following years, beset by the insecurity and isolation of her personal and political situation in exile, Goldman expressed gnawing doubts. In April 1922 she could declare, "I am still a revolutionist, though the good catholic communists will deny that" (Goldman and Berkman 1975, 23). But in December she admitted, "I have not the same faith in the masses and in the efficacy of revolution" (Wexler 1989, 79).

And in 1925 she wrote to Berkman, "I can honestly say that I never felt the terrible loneliness and such defeat while I was in America and still fervently believed in the social revolution, which I no longer do" (Goldman and Berkman 1975, 134). However, in the same December 1922 letter noted above, she had suggested a more nuanced position: "So I am not quite sure, as I have been, of the *immediate* results of any fundamental upheaval. And yet I also know that without that upheaval no fundamental change can take place" (Wexler 1989, 79; emphasis added).

Yet as we have seen, the Spanish Revolution brought back her own conviction that, at least in the right circumstances and with the right preparation, "the creative spirit of the people" could not only make the revolution, but even vindicate the "romantic" notions of Peter Kropotkin and other anarchists about what they could achieve "the day after." Shortly after her arrival in Spain in September 1936, Goldman wrote: "I think it is the first time in history that such stress is being laid on the superior importance of running the machinery of economic and social life [during a revolution] as is being done here. And this by the much maligned, chaotic Anarchists, who supposedly have 'no program' and whose philosophy is [believed to be] bent on destruction and ruin. Can you imagine what this means to me to see the attempt made to realize the very ideas I have stressed so passionately since the Russian Revolution?" (1983, 56). A year later, she was deeply impressed that the constructive work by the peasants and workers had, in many instances, grown and improved and "has been perfected so much since last year": "To me, it is miraculous for a people to go on building in the face of war, food shortage and a deadly political regime that has filled the prisons, destroyed some of the collectives and that disposes of all opponents in the dead of the night" (57).

Although Goldman sometimes expressed confidence that the revolution in Spain would prevail, she recognized that it might be overcome by the overwhelming forces against it: "I still cling to my faith in the wonderful spirit of our comrades and . . . their splendid constructive efforts. But the last few weeks have made me anxious and uneasy for the Revolution and the life and marvelous beginning made all over Spain" (28).

She also recognized that the successes in Spain rested on significant differences between the Spanish people and others, and might not be readily transferable to other countries. Writing in 1938 of the "four generations steeped in Libertarian Communism," she remarked: "I am sure it is this that differentiates the Spanish people from the masses elsewhere.

. . . They relied on direct action and not on those in high places. Over and above all was the libertarian principle deeply rooted in the workers and peasants which would have no part of dictatorship" (34). And she concluded: "Never again will anyone dare say Anarchism is not practical or that we have no program. . . . Yes, my dear, I feel it was worth all I have given to the Anarchist movement to see with my own eyes its first buddings. It is my grandest hour" (57). And she asserted: "They may not be permitted to do so for long. But if they should be defeated they will yet have shown the first example in history *how Revolutions should be made*" (1983, 55–56; emphasis in the original).

Conclusion

Although Goldman's ideas on the Russian Revolution and its significance for the theory of revolution have been relatively neglected or even disparaged in the scholarly literature, *My Disillusionment in Russia* has continued to command attention from readers, since the late twentieth and into early twenty-first centuries, as evidenced by several reprint editions that have appeared beginning in 1970, the most recent in 2003.[13] Moreover, the text of Goldman's book has been posted online in the Anarchy Archives at Pitzer College, in two parts: *My Disillusionment in Russia* and *My Further Disillusionment in Russia*. The site reports more than seven thousand visits to the page since the text was posted in March 2000. Although this is a smaller number than the twenty thousand visits to the page containing *Living My Life* at this site, it clearly reflects continuing or renewed interest in this aspect of Goldman's thought.

While Goldman's sustained indictment of the Bolshevik regime in *My Disillusionment in Russia* has led most reviewers and scholars to see the work as merely a partisan polemic, the heart of the book was Goldman's attempt "to outline a general anarchist theory of revolutions" (Drinnon 1961, 246). To summarize the main lines of her theoretical analysis, we may begin with her assertions—highlighted at the beginning of this chapter—that "the complete reversal of all . . . authoritarian principles will alone serve the revolution"; that "to make the Revolution" was not enough, but rather it must advance and broaden into "economic and social reconstruction"; and that "the broadest exercise of the creative genius of the people" must be the foundation for the success of a genuine revolution.

Goldman placed "human values" at the center of the aims and principles of a revolution, with emphasis on values of equity, justice, dignity, and liberty for the individual, closely linked with collective action for social construction. She argued for action to achieve "the complete social, economic, and industrial re-organization of society" and held that this would and must take place through spontaneous mass action of the people, at first to overthrow authoritarian and exploitative institutions, and then to engage cooperatively in projects of collectivization and socialization in the workplace.

Goldman insisted, against the views of even some of her closest anarchist comrades, that revolutionary consciousness was more important than advanced economic development in the course of a revolution, and that revolutionary methods must be consistent with human values. Despite her earlier adventure with Berkman in the attack on Frick, and her initial enthusiasm for the sweep of the revolution in Russia, even with its concomitant uses of violence, she was increasingly persuaded that it would be necessary to "eliminate as much as possible the need for violence" in conducting and building a revolution, and even declared that she would be "against revolution" unless "we can realize and boldly declare that the only purpose of revolution must be transformation, then terror must go with the rest and prisons and other evil things of today must go with the rest." She realized that the Spanish anarchist revolution was imperfect and might succumb to the overwhelming forces of militarism and fascism, but she so admired the dedication of the Spanish revolutionaries and peasantry, with their libertarian and egalitarian collectives and cooperatives, that she declared them the model of "how Revolutions should be made."

Goldman's theory of revolution was not laid out completely in any one of her writings, nor was it fully developed and its problems fully resolved in many particulars. Certainly there are serious gaps in her analysis, such as the failure to recognize women's roles in revolution on a theoretical level. But if it could be said of Nietzsche that he was not a systematic philosopher and that none of his books offers a synthesis of his core philosophy, it seems no derogation of Goldman as a theorist to concede that we may say the same of her. If, then, we are open to a reconstruction of Emma Goldman's theory of revolution along the lines that have been outlined above, it might best be characterized as a set of ideas and principles, evolving over time in her own thought and inviting an ongoing conversation among her readers, in her time and in succeeding generations.[14] This chapter is offered as a contribution to that conversation.

Notes

This is a revised and expanded version of a paper first presented at the annual conference of the National Women's Studies Association, held in Las Vegas, Nevada, June 16, 2002. It is part of a long-term study of women's contributions to political and social theory. I would like to thank Clinton F. Fink for support and discussions over many years in that long-term study and in the preparation of this chapter. I am particularly grateful to Loretta Kensinger and Penny Weiss for inviting me into their conversations on Goldman's political thought on that occasion in 2002 and in this volume. I also wish to thank the Emma Goldman Papers, University of California at Berkeley, and the International Institute of Social History, Amsterdam, the Netherlands, for their assistance in providing research materials.

1. Marian Morton, in *Emma Goldman and the American Left* (1992), devoted a chapter to Goldman's account, as recorded in *My Disillusionment in Russia*, of Goldman's experiences in Russia, but only two paragraphs (at 122–23) to its theoretical content. Richard Drinnon, in *Rebel in Paradise* (1961), gave *My Disillusionment in Russia* fewer than four pages. Alice Wexler, in *Emma Goldman in Exile* (1989) gave as many as twelve pages to the book, devoted mainly to a sustained polemic against Goldman's indictment of the Bolsheviks and their policies. Martha Solomon, in *Emma Goldman* (1987), focused on Goldman "as a writer and rhetorician." Solomon gave *My Disillusionment in Russia* ten pages, of which several are concerned with rhetorical techniques; Solomon takes the position that the book "is a narrative with an implicit argumentative thesis: the Bolsheviks had betrayed the Russian Revolution." The text of *My Disillusionment in Russia* has been posted online (see entry for Goldman 1923 in References).

2. See, for example, Alice Wexler's extended critique in *Emma Goldman in Exile* (1989, 72–85).

3. Wexler wrote that "Goldman condemned Soviet Russia, not because it was too revolutionary, but because it was not revolutionary enough" (1989, 85). But Goldman seldom, if ever, called the Bolshevik regime "Soviet Russia," since she believed that the Bolsheviks had destroyed the Soviets, which she saw as true revolutionary manifestations before the Bolshevik dictatorship subordinated them to its will.

4. See Goldman 1970b, lii–lvi; 1970a, 954–55; Drinnon 1961, 245ff.; Wexler 1989, 81–82.

5. Goldman wrote that she had not taken notes and could therefore give "only the gist of what Kropotkin said," but her report was more than a full printed page in length. In view of Berkman's claim that he had given Goldman full use of the diary he had kept while they were in Russia (Goldman and Berkman 1975, 27), it is surprising to find that in the published version of that diary, titled *The Bolshevik Myth* (1925), Berkman reported much more briefly on the March visit to Kropotkin (74–75), and not at all on the visit in July. Moreover, Berkman's account of what Kropotkin said in March is quite different from that of Goldman. It seems likely, therefore, that Goldman's account was not drawn from Berkman's record, but rather reflects her own recollections, or perhaps even her own views, attributed to Kropotkin in order to lend them authority.

6. Goldman was in Spain from September to December 1936, September to November 1937, and September to November 1838.

7. This was one of the points of difference between Goldman and Berkman. See Berkman to

Emma Goldman, November 25, 1934: "As you know, I have always considered economics the MOST important factor in individual as well as social life, though NOT the ONLY factor" (Goldman and Berkman 1975, 114).

8. Luxemburg, writing on the Russian Revolution of 1905, was referring to the "mass strike," which she wrote was "inseparable from the revolution. The history of the Russian mass strikes is the history of the Russian revolution. . . . [I]t is clear that the mass strike cannot be called at will" (Smith and Carroll 2000, 317, 318; also in Luxemburg 2004, 195, 197).

9. See Woodcock 1962, 356–98, chap. 12, "Anarchism in Spain."

10. Leon Trotsky, in his history of the Russian Revolution, wrote of the soviets: "thanks to the tradition of 1905, the soviets sprang up as though from under the earth, and immediately became incomparably more powerful than all the other organizations which later tried to compete with them (the municipalities, the cooperatives, and in part the trade unions" (1959, 164).

11. Goldman attributed to Kropotkin the analogy between the Bolsheviks and the Jesuits of the Inquisition (1970b, 99). She reiterated the point several times and elaborated it in her "Afterword," concluding: "The historic parallel, almost entirely ignored so far, contains a most important lesson for all coming revolutions and for the whole future of mankind" (260).

12. See the account of Goldman's discussion with Maria Spiridonova on the Brest-Litovsk "peace," in Goldman 1970b, 93–95.

13. For examples of relative neglect or disparagement of Goldman's ideas on revolution, see Goldberg 1975; Kern 1976; Morton 1992; Wexler 1989, 1983; Wenzer 1992. Reprint editions of My Disillusionment in Russia have appeared in 1970 (Apollo), 1983 (Peter Smith), 1991 (Reprint Services Corp.), and 2003 (Dover).

14. On conversation, see Weiss 1998, especially the preface (ix–xi) and chap. 1, "Conversation as a Method" (1–7).

References

Berkman, Alexander. 1922a. "The Russian Revolution and the Communist Party." English translation from the Russian of a 1921 pamphlet by four anonymous Moscow Anarchists. Anarchy Archives, Pitzer College. http://dwardmac.pitzer.edu/anarchist_archives/bright/berkman/.

———. 1922b. "The Russian Tragedy." Anarchy Archives, Pitzer College. http://dwardmac.pitzer.edu/anarchist_archives/bright/berkman/russiantragedy.html.

———. 1925. The Bolshevik Myth (Diary, 1920–1922). London: Hutchinson.

———. 1929. Now and After: The ABC of Communist Anarchism. New York: Vanguard. http://dwardmac.pitzer.edu/anarchist_archives/bright/berkman/comanarchism/whatis_toc.html.

———. 1930. "Diary." Entry for May 22. Alexander Berkman Archive, International Institute for Social History, Amsterdam.

Carroll, Berenice A. 1990. "The Politics of 'Originality': Women and the Class System of the Intellect," Journal of Women's History 2, no. 2: 136–63.

———. 1992. "Originality and Creativity: Rituals of Inclusion and Exclusion." In The Knowledge Explosion: Generations of Feminist Scholarship, edited by Cheris Kramarae and Dale Spender. New York: Teachers College Press.

———. 2000. Introduction to Women's Political and Social Thought: An Anthology, edited by Hilda L. Smith and Berenice A. Carroll. Bloomington: Indiana University Press.

Drinnon, Richard. 1961. *Rebel in Paradise: A Biography of Emma Goldman*. Boston: Beacon Press.

Frankel, Oz. 1996. "Whatever Happened to 'Red Emma'?" *Journal of American History* 83, no. 3: 903–42.

Goldberg, Harold J. 1975. "Goldman and Berkman View the Bolshevik Regime." *Slavonic and East European Review* 53, no. 131:272–76.

Goldman, Emma. 1917. "The Russian Revolution." *Mother Earth Bulletin* 1, no. 3. Reprinted in *Anarchy: An Anthology of Emma Goldman's "Mother Earth,"* edited by Peter Glassgold. Washington, D.C.: Counterpoint, 2001.

———. 1923. *My Disillusionment in Russia*. Incomplete 1st edition; 21 chaps. Garden City, N.Y.: Doubleday, Page. http://dwardmac.pitzer.edu/anarchist_archives/goldman/disillusion/toc.html.

———. 1924. *My Further Disillusionment in Russia*. Remaining 12 chaps. of Emma Goldman, *My Disillusionment in Russia*, omitted from the 1923 edition. Includes publisher's note and 1924 preface by Goldman. Garden City, N.Y.: Doubleday, Page. http://dwardmac.pitzer.edu/anarchist_archives/goldman/further/further_toc.html.

———. 1969. *Anarchism and Other Essays*. New York: Dover. With a new introduction by Richard Drinnon. (Orig. pub. 1910.)

———. 1970a. *Living My Life*. 2 vols. New York: Dover. (Orig. pub. Alfred Knopf, 1931.)

———. 1970b. *My Disillusionment in Russia*. Includes 1922 preface for the first American edition (1923); 1925 preface (revised version of the 1924 preface for *My Further Disillusionment in Russia*); biographical sketch by Frank Harris for the 1923 edition; introduction by Rebecca West for the 1925 edition; 33 chaps. London: C. W. Daniel, 1925. Reprint, New York: Thomas Y. Crowell / Apollo.

———. 1972. *Red Emma Speaks: Selected Writings and Speeches by Emma Goldman*, compiled and edited by Alix Kates Shulman. New York: Random House/Vintage.

———. 1983. *Vision on Fire: Emma Goldman on the Spanish Revolution*. Edited by David Porter. New Paltz, N.Y.: Commonground Press.

Goldman, Emma, and Alexander Berkman. 1975. *Nowhere at Home: Letters from Exile of Emma Goldman and Alexander Berkman*. Edited by Richard Drinnon and Anna Maria Drinnon. New York: Schocken Books.

James, Edward, and Janet James, eds. 1971. *Notable American Women, 1607–1950: A Biographical Dictionary*. 3 vols. Cambridge, Mass.: Belknap Press of Harvard University Press.

Kern, Robert W. 1976. "Anarchist Principles and Spanish Reality: Emma Goldman as a Participant in the Civil War, 1936–1939." *Journal of Contemporary History* 11, nos. 2–3:237–59.

Kropotkin, P[eter]. A. 1971. *The Great French Revolution, 1789–1793*. Translated from the French by N. F. Dryhurst. New York: Schocken Books. (Orig. pub. 1909.)

Levine, Daniel. 1971. *Jane Addams and the Liberal Tradition*. Madison: State Historical Society of Wisconsin.

Luxemburg, Rosa. 1961. *The Russian Revolution and Leninism or Marxism?* Introduction by Bertram D. Wolfe. Ann Arbor: University of Michigan Press. (Orig. pub. 1922.)

———. 2004. "The Mass Strike, the Political Party, and the Trade Unions." In *The Rosa Luxemburg Reader*, edited by Peter Hudis and Kevin B. Anderson. New York: Monthly Review Press. (Orig. pub. 1906.)

Morton, Marian J. 1992. *Emma Goldman and the American Left: "Nowhere at Home."* New York: Twayne.

Smith, Hilda L., and Berenice A. Carroll, eds. 2000. *Women's Political and Social Thought: An Anthology.* Bloomington: Indiana University Press.

Solomon, Martha. 1987. *Emma Goldman.* Boston: Twayne.

Trotsky, Leon. 1959. *The Russian Revolution: The Overthrow of Tzarism and the Triumph of the Soviets.* Selected and edited by F. W. Dupee. Garden City, N.Y.: Doubleday Anchor. (Orig. pub. 1932.)

Weiss, Penny A. 1998. *Conversations with Feminism: Political Theory and Practice.* Lanham, Md.: Rowman and Littlefield.

Wenzer, Kenneth Clarke. 1992. "The Transmigration of Russian Anarcho-Communism." Ph.D. diss., Catholic University. DAI, 53(2): 597-A. DA9219885.

Wexler, Alice. 1989. *Emma Goldman in Exile: From the Russian Revolution to the Spanish Civil War.* Boston: Beacon Press.

Woodcock, George. 1962. *Anarchism: A History of Libertarian Ideas and Movements.* Cleveland: Meridian Books.

6

Who Were Emma Goldman's "Children"?

Anarchist Feminism and Childhood

Penny A. Weiss

"Goldman treats children's lives as relevant to analysis and evaluation of political, economic, military, and familial institutions and practices. She talks about children not only as political subjects but also as political actors; considers them not only as immature adults but individuals in their own right; asks not what the state needs of them when they are grown but what kind of society they need in order to grow; and asks not what rights parents have over children, but what children need from parents."

Weiss begins her essay by recalling images of children and childhood from the traditional canon of political theory. Against this backdrop, Weiss delineates Goldman's approach to the lives of children, one shaped by her distinctive combination of feminism and anarchism. Ultimately, she argues, Goldman's political theory is enriched by the consideration given to the lives of children, and children's lives are enriched by their incorporation into the political.—*The Editors*

Stop me if this sounds familiar. Within a given academic discipline—in this particular case the field of political theory—a large segment of the population is rarely written about in any particular depth, or even at any great length. When they are written about, they are not really the direct or main subject of political inquiry, and are not being treated as primary political actors, but are merely mentioned, often as representatives of some undesirable quality. The words are penned by people who by institutional design and cultural practice have relationships with them that are hierarchical and who exclude them from many practices deemed important or even distinctly human. They appear as a fairly homogeneous group, not receiving the subtle attention required to differentiate them by, say, age, or class. They rarely speak in their own voices.

This sort of pattern is, of course, familiar, because feminist theorists have so thoroughly documented and thoughtfully analyzed the canon's treatment of women.[1] In this chapter I consider another group that fits this unfortunate description: children. The plight of children in political theory's canon indeed resembles that of women, as I will briefly discuss, sometimes for identical reasons. Arguably, the consideration the two groups receive is not only analogous, but also interrelated. But perhaps if we look in some new places—such as Emma Goldman's writings—we can find political theory's more "legitimate" children.[2]

A Bit of History

Let me introduce you to a few of the children who exist in the history of canonical political thought.[3] In Aristotle we meet creatures essentially defined by the fact that "*if* children . . . possess the faculty of delibera-tion," they possess it "only in an immature form" (Barker 1975, 35; em-phasis added). Because of their "youth and immaturity," they are ruled by "the head of the household," and the relation between child and father is "like that of a monarch over subjects" (32). These youthful humans as-sumedly feel affection toward their father-king, for Aristotle asserts both that "the male parent is . . . entitled [to] . . . the[ir] affection" (33), and that youth never resents being governed" (316). Aristotle writes that "the goodness of children . . . makes [a] difference to the goodness of the polis. . . . [I]t must make a difference [since] . . . children grow up to be partners in the government of the state" (37–38). Their education, therefore, "should prepare the way for the occupations of later years" (329).

Thomas Hobbes, too, calls his children "reasonable creatures" only "for the *possibility* apparent of having the use of reason in time to come" (Hobbes 1994, 26; emphasis added). He calls "childish" those adults ig-norant of science (26) and those who confuse custom for justice (61). Hobbes's children "rely principally on helps external" (32), clearly an undesirable, because vulnerable, status to him. Adults lock up their goods because of children (77). Children cause some fundamental but unac-knowledged problems in Hobbes's contractual thinking: he says children are subjects of their parents "from the child's consent, either express or by other sufficient arguments declared" (128), but also that "over . . .

children . . . there is no law . . . because they had never power to make any covenant or to understand the consequences thereof" (77), and yet again that they are subjects by "natural force," because "a man maketh his children to submit themselves and their children to his government, as being able to destroy them if they refuse" (109–10). Regardless, children should be obedient and thankful to parents, for otherwise there would not be "any reason why any man should desire to have children, or take the care to nourish and instruct them, if they were afterwards to have no other benefit from them than from other men" (224). Because of their distinctive and somehow similar situation, "children and madmen are excused from offences against the law natural" (198). Unlike Aristotle's children, Hobbes's are by nature under "the dominion [of] . . . the mother" (129).

These two examples alone reveal some interesting tendencies in political analysis of children. Children are defined by what they lack in comparison to (some) adults, and adults are consequently ridiculed for acting childishly. Various forms of dominion over children (which only sometimes meet the general standards for legitimate political authority) are held to be justified, yet children are expected to respond to their rulers not only with obedience but also with affection and gratitude.

In this chapter, instead of writing more about "what men have said" about children, I write about what women have said, or at least what one particular woman has said. Turning to Emma Goldman for this project may seem surprising. She had no biological children. She did not campaign directly for children, as did other political thinkers and activists of her time, such as Jane Addams, and children were the main subject of relatively few of her essays. But she is, in fact, a very interesting case study. As she works for and writes about numerous other causes, I will ultimately argue, she fully and consistently incorporates children into her thinking. Her analysis of them offers deep challenges to the ideas of Hobbes and Aristotle sketched above. What compels both that attention to children and those challenges, I will also argue, is her anarchist feminism, which makes visible and questionable the authority used against children; the effects of traditional families on them; and the numerous means employed to socialize them into conformity, obedience, and passivity.

Goldman treats children's lives as relevant to analysis and evaluation of political, economic, military and familial institutions and practices. She talks about children not only as political subjects but also as political actors; considers them as not only immature adults but individuals in their own right; asks not what the state needs of them when they are grown but what kind of society they need in order to grow; and focuses not on what rights parents have over children, but on what children need from parents. In the end, her anarchist feminism and her concern about children's lack of liberty are integrated and integral parts of her political theory.

Children in the Landscape

Goldman mentioned children in nearly everything she wrote, which it-self is uncommon—perhaps even unprecedented—in the history of polit-ical thought. Children were always present in her landscape. Whether she was writing about prostitution or patriotism, employment or educa-tion, marriage or morality, syndicalism or the state, the relevance of these topics to children, and of children to these topics, comes through repeat-edly. Critically, the mention that children get is not merely in passing, but actually affects the substance of her argument. For example, in writ-ing about prostitution, Goldman sees child prostitution as an intrinsic part of the institution. Her acknowledgment of that aspect of the practice allows her to connect prostitution not only to economic realities, which is her take on the subject with which we are perhaps most familiar, but also to issues such as sex education, double standards on sexual activity, and child-rearing practices. Because she wrestles with the existence of the child prostitute, her analysis of prostitution ends up being much ful-ler, reckoning with complex relationships between seemingly discrete so-cial practices. The same might be said of her analysis of patriotism, which is richer for its addressing how governments manipulate both children and childish adults into sacrificing for the state and seeing their own as superior to other states. It can also be said—to make clear the pat-tern—of her analysis of the family, which considers, among many other things, the costs to children of overworked parents, of family traditions, and of loveless marriages. Goldman does not just mention children in passing, then. She seems to stop and talk with them, and they affect what she consequently says.

In what follows I am guided by consideration of the following ques-tions: What does Goldman see as the nature of a child? How do her children and their environments interact? How much attention do differences between children get from her? In what ways are and are not her children actual and potential political actors? What might constitute a more ideal childhood to Goldman, and what would be necessary to make it possible? In the end, what does a distinctively feminist anarchist perspective have to teach us about children?

The Nature of the Child

Children are often defined in comparison with adults, much as women get defined in comparison with men, and the comparisons tend, unsurprisingly, to reflect unfavorably on children and women, in ways that are subsequently used to justify excluding them from aspects of the adult/male world. They are not rational enough, or sufficiently morally developed, or experienced enough, it is variously said, to be given voice, choice, control, or power in families, governments, jobs, or schools. Goldman, however, is less concerned with measuring children against the adult to see what the former lack, and more interested in knowing what is distinctive about children so that we meet their needs and allow them to flourish. It is her feminist anarchism that gives her this particular perspective on children: even the most benign nonanarchists are more attentive to what society and the state need children to be shaped into than they are to what individual children are and can become, and most nonfeminists are less attuned than she is to the effects of power in supposedly nonpolitical arenas such as families and schools on what is called one's "nature."

I use two main strategies for getting at what Goldman thinks is the nature of a child. I look, of course, at her writings where children receive the most attention. I also search through her essays to find the kinds of people and things with which children are grouped, the analogies and metaphors Goldman makes that involve children, and the qualities that she calls "childlike."

The analogies Goldman makes involving children contain some revelations about her conceptualization of the young. Starting with a reference to the youngest—babies—she explains people's lack of sustained attention to the evil of prostitution by saying, "Only when human sorrows are turned into a toy with glaring colors will baby people become interested—for a while at least. The people are a very fickle baby that must have new toys every day" (Goldman 1972, 144). Here babies are portrayed as distractible, as interested in amusement and easily entertained, but not for long. She asserts that people and governments know and manipulate this in both adults and children: "The powers that have for centuries been engaged in enslaving the masses . . . know that the people at large are like children. . . . And the more gorgeously the toy is dressed, the louder the colors, the more it will appeal to the million-headed child. . . . An army and navy represent the people's toys" (1969, 135). This appeal explains why governments spend money on military parades, "fireworks, theatre parties, and revelries" (136). Goldman's children are impressionable and manipulable, for better and worse.

Goldman calls Americans "naive . . . crude and immature in matters of international importance" (1972, 64). She considers whether this is "merely a sign of youth," and in doing so reveals two interesting aspects of children. First, she notes that "it is indeed beautiful to possess a young mind, fresh to receive and perceive" (64–65), giving dignity to a youthful stage of life and acknowledging its admirable open-mindedness and perceptiveness. Second, however, she says that "unfortunately the American mind seems never to grow, to mature and crystallize its view" (65). Here she reminds us that youth is a stage, not the end of development, of what people can become, and that it is a stage that can be characterized by an "indefinite, uncertain mind . . . [holding] contradictory ideas . . . a sort of intellectual hash" (65). "Childlike naivety" (1969, 127) apparently has its place and its benefits, but beyond those bounds, which are not merely of age, it is potentially limiting and even dangerous.

Goldman says of the "ignorant mass" that "its reasons are like those of a child," by which she means "it makes no pretense of knowledge or tolerance [and acts] by mere impulse" (48). However, Goldman also refers to something as having "a childlike nature" when it is "sweet and tender, unsophisticated and generous" (148) Positively, again, she admires Santo Caserio, who explains his actions in a childlike manner, whose "reasons for the act are set forth in so simple [and] dignified [a] . . . manner" (1972, 225) She calls savage revenge "child's play" in order to reveal by comparison the horrors of civilized revenge seen in prisons (1969, 119). In these examples, Goldman's children are relatively harmless and straightforward.

Delineating those things and people with which Goldman pairs children reveals yet more of her viewpoint on the young. References to "defenceless women and innocent infants" (104) and to "a drowning child or a crippled woman" (1972, 37) seem to place both women and children in the all-too-familiar position of helpless, endangered dependents. Yet in the first instance cited above Goldman is employing this tactic to condemn political tyranny. King Umberto, she recounts, had ordered the shooting of women and children during a bread riot. In this instance they were not acting helplessly at all, but rebelliously and in concert. In the second instance above she is referencing people's natural sociability. She attributes certain positive acts and characteristics to "intellect or temperament" rather than to government regulations, saying that they "could never have been induced by government any more than the spirit which impels a man to save a drowning child or a crippled woman from a burning building" (37). Pairing "children and cotton slaves" (1969, 129) as illegitimate sources of wealth, Goldman also portrays the child as an economic actor, and an especially exploitable one. Still—like the custom today of speaking about women and children who are injured and killed in wars as being casualties that are somehow essentially different from men who are injured and killed in war—using children, and appealing to common sentiments about children to demonstrate the depths of political corruption, is a practice that always entails the risk of reinforcing those common stereotypes about them even if it also reveals hypocrisy among those claiming to protect children. Goldman's children in these examples are vulnerable to political and economic oppression but, in the absence of corruption, also somehow potentially relatively easy recipients of care.

The images Goldman uses to show the damage done to children are potent, and again speak to the child's nature. A first set of images contains her criticism of those who do not recognize the humanity of the child. She complains that children are "kneaded like dough" and "moulded according to the whims and fancies of those about" them (1972, 107). Too often, a child, capable of so much more, is "treated as a mere machine or as a mere parrot" (107). She compares the fate of a girl being prepared for marriage to "the mute beast fattened for slaughter" (1969, 230). A child is raised as if it were "inanimate matter for parents and guardians, whose authority alone gives it shape and form." Goldman's children are, most emphatically, fully human; in practice, however, they are wrongly silenced and wastefully underestimated.

In a second set of images, plant analogies abound. We erroneously treat the child as a "delicate human plant [kept] in a hothouse atmosphere, where it can neither breathe nor grow freely" (1972, 109). She contrasts the "young delicate tree that is being clipped and cut by the gardener in order to give it an artificial form" with the truly well-reared child who, "allowed to grow in nature and freedom," can reach "majestic height" and "beauty" (112). We should look at a child as a "budding and sprouting personality" (122). Our practices, however, result in "absolute death and decay to the bud in the making" (113). In these plant meta-phors, the nature of the child comes across as hardy, in need of space, and containing within itself much of what it needs to mature, even as it is susceptible to the often-unhealthy manipulations of others. Like a plant that can be "overprotected" to death—overwatered, kept from the sun, and so on—a child's "good" can be wrongly determined to its detri-ment, from a wide assortment of motives.

Looking at what Goldman says about the nature of children when they are the main subject of her essays yields results that are consistent with and further develop the ideas already touched on in the analogies and metaphors. First, Goldman's approach is built on the notion that children can be driven from within to develop, as the plant analogies hinted at. In order to support "the natural growth of the child," we have to allow it "to grow from within" (107) rather than stifling it from without and gradually destroying "its latent qualities and traits" (109). Hence Gold-man characterizes education as properly "a process of drawing out, not of driving in; it aims at the possibility that the child should be left free to develop spontaneously" (120). The "individual tendencies" of a child are revealed "in its play, in its questions, in its association with people and things" (108). Goldman's children may be malleable, but they are not Lockean blank slates. However, while they enter the world with unique sets of tendencies and traits, those do not necessarily unfold entirely on their own or in all social settings.

At times Goldman sounds like Rousseau expounding on negative edu-cation:[4] don't "mold," don't "knead," don't "stifle," don't "cramp," don't "force," and don't "interfere." She brings the same anarchist perspective to bear on schools as on prisons, and in fact finds that against children we routinely use varieties of force that overlap to a frightening degree with those we employ against prisoners (and in neither case, according to Goldman, does this improve the individuals or benefit their communities, however passionately some might contend otherwise). While Goldman sometimes portrays children as helpless in familiar ways, that from which she says they need deliverance is unusual: for example, "unless the young be rescued from that mind and soul-destroying institution, the bourgeois school, social evils will continue to exist" (1969, 148). Her "negative" approach necessarily sees in children a natural desire to learn and develop: "it is reasonable to assume that the child is intensely interested in the things which concern its life" (1972, 121).[5]

Second, Goldman's theory depends on a view of children that says they are not dangerous or destructive. She asserts that belief in the necessity of authority, whether governmental or parental, religious or educational, has "at its base . . . the doctrine that man is evil, vicious, and too incompetent to know what is good for him" (90). She characterizes children in such ways as to make it "safe" to allow them to develop without force and interference. They have "large, wondering, innocent eyes . . . [that wish] to behold the wonders of the world" (108). They have an "original sense of judgment" (111). Importantly, the child "has no traditions to overcome. Its mind is not burdened with set ideas, its heart has not grown cold with class and caste distinctions" (1969, 148). If we are to allow children to flourish, we need to "destroy the cruel, unjust, and criminal stigma imposed on the innocent young" (1972, 149). Even punishment is unnecessary and undesirable, "since the child is thereby led to suppose that punishment is something to be imposed upon him from without, by a person more powerful, instead of being a natural and unavoidable reaction and result of his own acts" (121).[6]

Third, Goldman insists that we recognize the humanity of the child. A child is a person, not a thing, whose thoughts and feelings deserve respect. Her main complaint about schools is that they have "such little regard for [a child's] personal liberty and originality of thought" (118). Like an adult, Goldman's child "is bent on going its own way, since it is composed of the same nerves, muscles and blood, even as those who assume to direct its destiny" (112). Children are more than potentially rational adults, blessed instead with a range of intellectual abilities: they are "ready to receive and assimilate" (120), can know themselves and their relations to others, can express themselves, use judgment and initiative, and work from both experience and imagination (121). They even have some advantages over adults. Not only, put negatively, are they "very vivid . . . not yet having been pounded into uniformity," but, put positively, "their experience will inevitably contain much more originality, as well as beauty" (121). Above all, then, "the child [is] to be considered as an individuality," rather than "as an object to be moulded according to the whims and fancies of those about it" (107).

Differences Between Children

While I have been talking about the nature of the child in general, I do not want to overlook the fact that Goldman makes some distinctions between children of different ages, of various classes, and on the basis of sex. Such distinctions are consistent with what she says about the nature of childhood and also again reveal a more than passing interest in children. In this greater attention to them, Goldman's analysis is increasingly political, an idea that is the subject of the following section of this chapter. Looking briefly at differences between children serves here as a useful bridge between the two main parts of the chapter.

Before regarding the stages of childhood, Goldman studies the familial environment into which children are born. In terms of cultural norms, we are unfortunately born to those who see "the child [as] merely part of themselves" (111). So-called sexual morality leads many to become "incessant breeder[s] of hapless children" (129). She acknowledges that a woman, rather than wanting "the indiscriminate breeding of children," "desires fewer and better children, begotten and reared in love and through free choice" (166). We have lost the fact that it could be "her most glorious privilege, the right to give birth to a child" (140). What we would wish for is that "love begets life [and] no child is deserted, or hungry, or famished for the want of affection" (166). Sexual norms, economics, and family traditions conspire to create a setting in which children are not always wanted, loved, able to be cared for, or treated as fully human. Fascinatingly, insightfully, Goldman acknowledges the desirability of parents "grow[ing] with the child" (167)[7] and of children needing "the love and devotion of each human about him, man as well as woman" (138).

Tragically, from "earliest infancy," Goldman asserts, "every effort is being made to cramp human emotion and originality of thought in the individual into a strait-jacket" (108). The lessons can, from the outset, sometimes differ by sex. "From infancy, almost, the average girl is told that marriage is her ultimate goal" (161). Seeming to address boys, she says that "from early infancy, the mind of the child is poisoned with blood-curdling stories about the Germans, the French, the Italians, etc. When the child has reached manhood, he is thoroughly saturated with the belief that he is chosen by the Lord himself to defend *his* country" (1969, 129). It makes a certain sense to Goldman that "the method of breaking man's will must begin at a very early age; that is, with the child, because at that time the human mind is most pliable" (1972, 116). It is probably not going too far to say that for all children—though in a variety of ways and toward some different ends—this "breaking" is currently the defining element of childhood.

The middle ages of childhood get attention on economic grounds. She refers to "middle-class girls . . . thrust into life's jungle at an early age" (129). It is obvious in reading Goldman that she has seen "mere children, work[ing] in crowded, overheated rooms ten to twelve hours daily" (150), as well as many of those "thousands of women and girls [driven] into prostitution (144), and mourns the "numberless little children ground into gold dust" (132). Of those aspiring to be professionals, she says, "The years of their youth are swallowed up in the acquisition of a profession" (179). Sex-differentiated lessons also persist into adolescence, especially on matters related to sexuality. It is true that in general "the young [are kept] in absolute ignorance on sex matters," but at the point of adolescence we teach that "the boy may follow the call of the wild; that is to say, that the boy may, as soon as his sex nature asserts itself, satisfy that nature; but our moralists are scandalized at the very thought that the nature of a girl should assert itself" (149).

What Goldman's attention to differences between children shows is that they are reared to become particular kinds of adults, prepared to participate in certain kinds of institutions. What children want or can do hardly matters. Their differential treatment by class and sex shows fates to be predetermined.

"Politicizing" Children

In some ways Goldman provides a model for the kinds of questions political theorists should be asking about children. For a political thinker to ask such questions requires that children be deemed relevant to politics, and that they be deemed relevant not only because they will one day become adults, but also because even as children they are fully human. When Goldman "politicizes" children she understands them to be affected deeply by politics, to have social awareness, to be gauges of the legitimacy of social practices, to have claims to liberty, and to be ones whose needs should help to shape their environments. Her understanding of the nature of the child supports her ideas about their place in the social and political world.

Goldman's children are far from politically oblivious. Reflecting back on her own childhood, she says, "Since my earliest recollection of my youth in Russia I have rebelled against orthodoxy in every form." And look how many forms of orthodoxy the young Goldman recognized: "I could never bear to witness harshness whether on the part of our parents to us or in their dealings with the servants. I was outraged over the official brutality practised on the peasants in our neighborhood. I wept bitter tears when the young men were conscripted into the army and torn from homes and hearths. . . . I was indignant when I discovered that love between young people of Jewish and Gentile origin was considered the crime of crimes, and the birth of an illegitimate child the most depraved immorality" (1972, 386–87). Speaking again to children's consciousness, Goldman declares that prostitution is "an institution, known almost to every child" (143). A thinking being, even the impressionable child, can see when "the lives of their parents are in contradiction to the ideas they represent" (114). Goldman's children are aware of and sensitive to injustice. They are not so unthinking as to be oblivious to hypocrisy, or so self-centered as to be blind to inequality, or so impressionable as to accept proffered explanations for abuses heaped on others or themselves without question.

Like adults, Goldman's children are dramatically affected by their environments. Economically, because parents are overworked and underpaid, "the home has been left to the care of the little ones" (1969, 89). Politically, patriotism requires parents to "sacrific[e] their own children" (133). Economics thrust "middle-class girls . . . into life's jungle at an early age" (1972, 129). Moral codes " [condemn] woman to the position of a celibate, a prostitute, or a reckless, incessant breeder of hapless children" (129). Because laws do not solve problems, child labor laws prevail in states where child exploitation flourishes (1969, 64). Familial norms mean that parents "make their children pay for the outrage perpetrated upon them by their parents . . . by traditions and habits" (1972, 124). As these examples show, children's lives are deeply affected by all their surroundings—economic, governmental, educational, familial, and cultural—both directly and through the effects on their parents.

It is in part because of their consequences for children that Goldman criticizes certain institutions. For example, her condemnation of marriage is based in part on its effects on children, and on this subject her writing becomes quite passionate: "The sham, the hypocrisy of it! Marriage protecting the child, yet thousands of children destitute and homeless. Marriage protecting the child, yet orphan asylums and reformatories overcrowded, the spcc [Society for the Prevention of Cruelty to Children] keeping busy in rescuing the little victims from 'loving' parent. . . . Oh, the mockery of it!" (164). Similarly, her criticism of schools is based on what they do to children. What she opposes is the "legal trickery, spiritual debasement and systematic indoctrination of the servile spirit, which process is known as 'education'" (89). And these various institutions do not operate in isolation but conspire against the development of the free individual: "the majority for centuries [have been] drilled in State worship, trained in discipline and obedience and subdued by the awe of authority in the home, the school, the church and the press" (93).

We saw earlier that both Aristotle and Hobbes, despite their dramatically different political and philosophical perspectives, easily justify authority over children and demand obedience from them. Yet when Goldman talks about the pain and loss of constant external interference in one's life, she looks in part to children, who are most obviously subject to widely accepted constraints. It is in writing on education, on children, that she says: "Discipline and restraint—are they not back of all the evils in the world? Slavery, submission, poverty, all misery, all social iniquities result from discipline and restraint." Children, like adults, have claims to liberty. Failure to respect those claims has a number of sources, including a misunderstanding of the abilities and nature of the child and lack of liberty in the lives of adults. Goldman's analysis of the effects of obedience and discipline lead her to question the structure of the family and the school. This is a tremendously important point: Goldman understands children to be affected by politics, broadly understood, but also, and consequently, to be a critical gauge by which to measure the legitimacy of various institutions. Their needs ultimately help her envision anarchist alternatives.

Finally, then, these sensitive and aware youngsters with claims to liberty, who are being deeply and negatively affected by certain practices, should help shape alternatives to the status quo. Goldman is not averse to education, only to certain forms of it. Like other political theorists, she stresses its importance: "It is through the channel of the child that the development of the mature man must go" (1972, 107). Unfortunately, what we create through great and lifelong effort is "a patient work slave, professional automaton, tax-paying citizen, or righteous moralist" (108).

A different education is needed to create "a well-rounded individual-ity" (108). What Goldman endorses is an education whose "scope . . . is truly phenomenal, including sex hygiene, the care of women during pregnancy and confinement, the care of home and children . . . every branch of human knowledge" (75). She applauds Faure's approach: "He took the children out into the open . . . showed them the splendor of the sunset, the brilliancy of the starry heavens, the awe-inspiring wonder of the mountains and seas . . . explained to them in his simple, direct way the law of growth, of development, of the interrelation of all life . . . he prepared them to succor the poor . . . taught them the humiliation, the degradation, the awfulness of poverty . . . the dignity and importance of all creative efforts, which alone sustain life and build character" (1969, 162). She is absolutely insistent that a child can and should be "directing his own efforts and choosing the branches of knowledge which he desires to study" (1972, 120), because children are fit to use their own judgment and initiative (121). The authority over children exercised in schools is criticized on exactly the same grounds as adult obedience to government and religion; more, they are necessary to each other. In Goldman's anar-chist schools, there would be "no coercion" (120) of children, just as there would be none of adults where anarchism prevails.

It is, of course, not enough to change schooling—in fact, one could not truly change schools to align them with an anarchist spirit and *not* change the world outside the school with which it is connected. In a more ideal childhood, the various environments in which a child grows up would work together: "Only when the material needs, the hygiene of the home, and intellectual environment are harmonious, can the child grow into a healthy, free being" (1969, 151). The familial environment would change: "A child born in freedom needs the love and devotion of each human being about him, man as well as woman" (1972, 138). Like teachers, parents would nurture the individuality of the child. Sex would be a topic of "intelligent discussion" (125). We would learn about and tend to a child's soul as we do now their physical well-being (112).

Concluding Thoughts

Those of us who have spent a good deal of time in the company of chil-dren may look at childhood as anarchic in the negative sense of the word, for children certainly bring in their wake all kinds of disorder, as well as in the positive sense, for children have an endless capacity for experimentation. But we also know that those anarchic possibilities are not looked upon kindly, and much of adult interaction with children seems bent on stamping them out. I think it is precisely that aspect of childhood that brings Goldman back to the subject in so much of what she wrote.

Turning children into neither angels nor devils, Emma Goldman reveals to us a unique anarchist feminist perspective on children. While recognizing that there are different stages of childhood, and that children do differ in some ways from adults, her political philosophy nonetheless applies with equal force to adults and youngsters. She makes crimes against children visible in her essays; one might even say that her political ideas are as shaped by the injustices done to children as they are by those perpetrated against adults. Her positive ideas about freedom and individuality have concrete consequences for the lives of children, as they do for adults, and they demand the reshaping of educational, political, and economic practices. Goldman truly integrated children into her political theory, no small or common accomplishment.

Goldman has much to teach us about children, and about how to incorporate children's lives into political thought. She uses the same principles to reveal and to judge what children do and what is done to children as she uses with adults. She examines the environments in which children spend their time with the same critical eye she casts upon those that influence the lives of adults, but without losing the child's-eye view of them, and without losing sight of the special vulnerabilities or gifts of childhood. Goldman's study of children gives her a deeper understanding of adults, of what they have endured and might regain. It gives her a more complete picture of the social environment.

Children whose liberty and individuality are respected have knowledge and experiences that enable them to be free and unique adults, and to see and resist infringements on their freedom or their personality. Treated with respect; nurtured; freed from oppressive schools, families, and workplaces, Goldman's children get to be children without being condescended to. Her challenges to us might be that we respect and learn from the natural anarchy that is childhood, that we adapt to the needs of the young, help develop their potential, and be willing to learn from their distinct perspective.

These are Emma Goldman's children. In comparison with them, Hobbes and Aristotle's children look like victims of neglect in theory and of abuse in practice. Goldman's consideration of children is not always presented with enough detail—her discussion of curriculum changes, for example, makes questionably easy distinctions between the teaching of facts and interpretations of theory—or with enough attention to the needs of very different children, those, as she puts it, with "weak natures" (1972, 115), for instance. But her ideas are invaluable and surpass those of most of her male predecessors. She should be commended for wrestling with the whole child—a being with emotional, sexual, social, and intellectual needs and desires. We should find, as she does, reason to be hopeful about the possibilities for change; and interestingly, some of that hope is to be found in the "very refreshing and encouraging psychological forces" (115) that are evident in children.

We live in a world that thinks that Emma Goldman is wrong about children. Many abuses of children get understood as such fairly easily: for example, we are saddened by young children who are put to work or made to bear arms and by those who are sexually exploited or denied an education. But if Goldman is right, then our mistreatment of them includes not only child labor, but also the way we train children for labor. If Goldman is right, our problems include not only sexual abuse, but also denial of sex education, of sexual freedom, and of sexual choice. If Goldman is correct, we need to address not only lack of access to education, but also education that takes from children much of what makes life worth living—creativity, individuality, and experimentation. If Goldman has captured things rightly, we are wrong not only for sending children to war, but also for training them in the nationalism and patriotism that will justify and garner their support for future wars.

In the United States today there are a few educational experiments that give tremendous choice to children about what and how they learn, just as there are alternate families in which children are heard and are not reared to prove their parents' worth. If we take Goldman's political theory more seriously, greater attention should be paid to such schools and such families. But I fear that trends are taking us further from Goldman's ideals. Standardized testing is all the rage, and it is incompatible with individualized education; "alternative education" has come to mean ever more rigid classrooms for "problem" students; and our public high schools are required to allow the military to set up recruitment tables.

If Emma Goldman is right, we are committing great injustices against our youth. For the world to treat them with the dignity they deserve will require revolutionary changes. Informed by Goldman, among others, we can make moves in that direction with a deeper sense of them as actors, thinkers, and innovators, and with an understanding of them as fully human rather than potentially complete. We can view and interact with children as determining factors of our societies, rather than adapters to it, and as individuals, not undifferentiated members of a homogeneous group. I think she *is* essentially right about children.

Notes

1. Distinctly feminist analyses have been offered on every canonical male theorist, reflecting to some extent the facts that most academics are still trained exclusively via their writings, and that it remains one of the most accessible ways to bring feminist theory into the literature. Valuable as the work is, such critiques are not the sum and substance of feminist contribution to the history of political thought. In fact, in a forthcoming book, *Canon Fodder: Historical Women Political Thinkers*, I argue that we should turn to different philosophers and projects.

2. I believe that it is of critical importance that we not generalize about "what political philosophers have said" about any topic, from women and children to peace and social contracts, when what we mean is a particular subset of them. Too often we define women thinkers out of the group through this familiar practice.

3. I choose Aristotle and Hobbes simply to show two very different and common ways in which political theorists think about children, and two that contrast well with Goldman. There are other models, more and less troubling.

4. See Rousseau's *Emile* (1979). The extent to which his educational scheme is in fact "negative" is often exaggerated, for there is quite a "positive" program endorsed.

5. This is a view that even such "brave" liberals as John Stuart Mill are willing to apply only to adults. See Mill 1978, 9.

6. This is a viewpoint similar to that found in Charlotte Perkins Gilman's 1900 *Concerning Children*, especially in chap. 2, "The Effect of Minding on the Mind" (Gilman 2003).

7. This feature is one developed by Sara Ruddick many decades later in "Maternal Thinking" (1980).

References

Barker, Ernest. 1975 *The Politics of Aristotle*. London: Oxford University Press.

Goldman, Emma. 1969. *Anarchism and Other Essays*. New York: Dover.

———. 1972. *Red Emma Speaks: Selected Writings and Speeches*. Compiled and edited by Alix Kates Shulman. New York: Vintage Books.

Gilman, Charlotte Perkins. 2003. *Concerning Children*. Lanham, Md.: AltaMira Press.

Hobbes, Thomas. 1994. *Leviathan*. Indianapolis: Hackett.

Mill, John Stuart. 1978. *On Liberty*. Indianapolis: Hackett.

Rousseau, Jean-Jacques. 1979. *Emile, or On Education*. New York: Basic Books.

Ruddick, Sara. 1980. "Maternal Thinking." *Feminist Studies* 6:342–67.

Part Two

Historical Roots and Current Connections

7

Manufacturing Consensus

Goldman, Kropotkin, and the Order of an Anarchist Canon

Jonathan McKenzie and Craig Stalbaum

"We synthesize their anarchic writings with dominant receptions in order to contribute to a new way of envisioning a "sovereign" Goldman who is not dependent on Kropotkin for legitimation."

The relationship between Kropotkin and Goldman is frequently characterized as one of mentor and follower. McKenzie and Stalbaum compare the two authors' conceptions of anarchy itself to challenge the accuracy of such a description. They suggest an important connection between that misrepresentation and the recognition of Kropotkin alone of the two as a theorist.—*The Editors*

Before the world experienced the rise of fascist ideologies and totalitarian regimes, revolutionary turmoil threatened to shatter the power structure of the social elite. The late 1800s and 1900s saw massive political changes across Europe and Asia, and here the forces of an anarchist ideal began to take shape. Building on the precepts of communist and existentialist thought, anarchist theorists thought to provide the struggling peoples of the world a window of opportunity into a better world. At the vanguard of these voices for change were Peter Kropotkin and Emma Goldman.

This chapter is concerned with the theoretical ties between Goldman and Kropotkin and how gender may shape their differences (both real and imagined). Within the literature on Goldman and Kropotkin, we have located two patterns of receptivity: those who mention Goldman as a devoted follower of Kropotkin and those who emphasize Goldman's contributions only as far as gender is concerned. The first section of our chapter will provide a brief historical reference of each theorist. In the second section, we closely evaluate the theoretical reception of Goldman and Kropotkin. We then examine, in the third section, Goldman and Kropotkin's theories of anarchy; in the final section, we synthesize their anarchic writings with dominant receptions in order to contribute to a new way of envisioning a "sovereign" Goldman who is not dependent on Kropotkin for legitimation.

We are drawn to this project by a modern wave of political theorists who ask us to question the tenets of the discipline's theoretical canon. This is a particularly popular strategy among feminists who see the paradigm dominated by male figures and their proclaimed universal objectivity (Ring 1987). In order to frame a canon in the first place, we need to have criteria for what (and who) makes a political theorist. This question is directly relevant to our analysis of Goldman and Kropotkin. Are the popular representations of Goldman and Kropotkin within the canon legitimate? We argue that a new mode of reception is necessary, one that values Goldman's stylistic and substantive contributions to anarchist theory.

History

Emma Goldman was born in Kovno, a Russian province, in June 1869. She grew up with her parents until the age of seven, when she was sent to Konigsberg to live with her grandmother. When she was thirteen, Goldman returned to live with her parents, this time in St. Petersburg, where the Russian Revolution was in full swing. Goldman's revolutionary leanings were inspired by the models of Russian nihilists and the fervor of insurgency, which led her to adopt the spirit of the wider revolutionary movement. At seventeen, Goldman immigrated to the United States with her sister Helene. She worked in an American factory, exposing herself firsthand to the harsh conditions of American industrial life, both at work and at home: "the puritan spirit suppresses the slightest manifestation of joy; a deadly dullness beclouds the soul; no intellectual inspiration, no thought exchange between congenial spirits is possible" (Goldman 1969, 11). Shortly following her emigration, Goldman married a young man, one of the few she met who spoke Russian; the marriage, though short, allowed her to explore the mechanisms of traditional social bias.

Goldman found her bearings in the anarchist movement following the Chicago Martyrdom and the Haymarket riots of 1887. The general sociopolitical ignorance of the situation coupled with the deaths of five anarchists stoked the revolutionary fire for many, including Goldman, who responded to the acts with a lifelong struggle against power regimes in all manifestations (13). Engaged by her interest in humanism and the advance of liberty, Goldman moved to New York City in 1889 and quickly immersed herself in the writings, speeches, and companionships of the New York anarchists. In the following years, she spoke frequently anywhere she could find an audience; though her economic conditions and standing within the larger anarchist movement would ebb and flow, her commitment to engaging in political dialogue remained for the duration of her life (Wexler 1989). In 1893 she was imprisoned for ten months, during which time she studied as a nurse, contributing to her stance on birth control for women and allowing her to manage a meager living over the following few years (Falk 1995). Around the turn of the twentieth century, Goldman managed to establish a common dialogue with, among others, Peter Kropotkin, whom she credits highly with her intellectual development.

In cooperation with others, Goldman began a magazine called *Mother Earth* in 1906. The journal flourished, and Goldman continued to enjoy the fruits of her hard work. Between 1906 and her death in 1940, she spoke frequently and published articles and opinion pages on any number of topics, including marriage, political violence, children, drama, patriotism, Christianity, and jealousy.

Peter Kropotkin was born in Moscow in 1842 and educated at elite Russian schools from an early age. He served as an assistant to Czar Alexander II and was an astute scientist as a young man. His scientific endeavors won him acclaim, but his anarchic leanings were his real passion. As a result of an internal commitment to social justice, Kropotkin left his promising career and embarked on a journey to find the heart of social justice, which culminated in his communist leanings and anarchic feeling. His commitment to anarchism and communism resulted in a great many short works, among them the volume *The Conquest of Bread*, which argues for a synthesis between anarchist politics and communist social gathering. In the period between 1886 and World War I, Kropotkin worked tirelessly to promote anarchist communism through works such as *Bread*; books on geography, history, and literature; and the journal *Freedom* (Kropotkin 1972, 12). With these works, as well as public appearances and the informal apprenticeship of several anarchists-to-be, Paul Avrich argues, "more than any other individual, Kropotkin was responsible for spreading the ideas of anarchism and, in the face of serious obstacles, keeping the anarchist movement alive throughout the world" (Kropotkin 1972, 12). Kropotkin remains an admired cornerstone of anarchist thought, often being mentioned as the single most important anarchist theorist of the modern period.

Theoretical Reception

The question that originally brought us to this project was relatively straightforward: did the canon of political theory receive Goldman and Kropotkin differently on the basis of their gender? As we stated at the outset, our early research pointed us toward two possibilities: one, that Goldman was herself characterized by the canon in gendered terms; and two, that Goldman's primary contributions to anarchist thought was the incorporation of gender and gender issues. We have decided to address each of these points in two ways. First, we need to look at how the canon addresses these two; put simply, what others have written about them. Second, we will actually analyze their theories a bit ourselves, using their definitions and conceptions of anarchy as a basis for making our own judgments about their theoretical contributions and to evaluate whether the canonical descriptions of them are accurate.

That Goldman has been treated differently because of her gender is difficult to refute; the difficultly lies in determining exactly how, or if those differences matter. Early waves of political thinkers, writing not long after Goldman, marginalized her ideas. Francis Coker, for example, described Goldman and other "devoted followers" of Kropotkin as having "added no essentially new ideas" to his anarchism (Coker 1934, 217). Any type of inference that this marginalization was the result of sex, however, is essentially impossible to prove; the only valid recourse is to refute the claim by examining their theories side by side. Other gendered characterizations are easier to work through.

We can easily consider how the canon addresses the thinkers with something as simple as names. Goldman is often referred to as "Emma"; Kropotkin is never referred to as "Peter." The first name, the "familiar," is reserved for the woman, while the more professional, masculine name is reserved for the man (Howe 2000; Wexler 1989; Woodcock and Avakumovic 1970).[1] Others try to circumvent this awkwardness by consistently using the full name "Emma Goldman," as if somehow saying "Goldman" is anathema (Reichert 1967). The labels and titles given to the two exhibit similar patterns. For example, consider how Kropotkin is portrayed in his biography by George Woodcock and Ivan Avakumovic. His labels are many: "the anarchist prince," the "White Jesus," "The Prophet," and "The Neglected Sage" (Woodcock and Avakumovic 1970). All labels given to Kropotkin denote wisdom or heroism. This from a man who may have written brilliantly but whose activism in the movement was limited. Goldman was dangerous, but Kropotkin was well liked as a weapon against autocracy (Haaland 1994). Consider, then, Goldman's nicknames: "Red Emma," "Queen of the Anarchists," "the most dangerous woman in America," and so on (Wexler 1989; Schulman 1983). Goldman's titles denote menace and activism, while Kropotkin's announce wisdom and authority.

Whether they use gendered terminology or not, most theorists, it seems (particularly contemporary ones), are content to describe Goldman's contributions through the lens of gender and little else. Alice Wexler, a noted Goldman biographer, commented on Goldman's integration of gender: "Goldman's outspokenness on sexual issues and her own unconventional love life shocked many of her own comrades as well as those outside the movement. If these reservations reflected the conservatism even of many anarchists, there were other, more serious criticisms as well" (quoted in Haaland 1994, 15).

To Wexler, Goldman's originality comes in her commitment to gender issues, which Kropotkin speaks of only sparsely. Wexler characterizes their relationship as that of a student and a teacher (hinting at the "follower" idea). Their connection is "rather formal," but she claims that Goldman "had always taken a certain pride in challenging Kropotkin's thinking, especially his conventional views about women and sex" (Wexler 1989, 32). At a meeting in 1895, however, "she went to him almost as a disciple"; Wexler further suggests that when Kropotkin died shortly thereafter, the Russian anarchist revolution might have died with him (32–33). In this picture we see Goldman in the role of an activist student, one wanting to implement the ideas of the movement without necessarily creating any of her own—unless the ideas revolve around gender.

Wexler does later categorize Goldman as placing "special emphasis on the role of intellectuals in any future revolution" (78–79). Leslie Howe further explains this point. She links Goldman's emphasis on the individual to existential thought, particularly Stirner and Nietzsche, the latter of whom she was particularly fond (Howe 2000, 33–34).

Bonnie Haaland analyzes the philosophical underpinnings of Goldman's work and likewise stresses the importance of gender in Goldman's writings. Most anarchists of the time "presupposed the seemingly permanent and immoveable institution of the patriarchal family" (Haaland 1994, 1). These thinkers used the issue of the public and private spheres, which feminists argued adamantly created a "veil of invisibility" under which questions about sexuality and reproduction were kept out of sight and out of consciousness (Haaland 1994, 1). Haaland claims that Goldman's "inclusion of these issues marked a paradigm shift in anarchist theory—a shift away from androcentric public theory to what contemporary feminists refer to as an 'integrative' form of theory construction" (5). Yet despite this, Haaland classifies Goldman as a Kropotkin follower, as a woman who added gender and some complexities of individualism but still was primarily a product of the anarchist revolution (5–6). These modern commentators note some originality in Goldman's work, though see it as mostly derived from her gender and commentary on it.

Kropotkin, by contrast, typically found Goldman's focus on gender unimportant, or perhaps even counterproductive, since "he contended that feminine equality was an intellectual rather than a biological question" (Woodcock and Avakumovic 1970, 257–58). Only when Goldman commented to him that his age was blinding him to what was an important question for millions of young people did he contend that she might be right (258).

This chapter focuses particularly on Kropotkin and Goldman's anarchist theories in an attempt to unearth a source of critique for each and differences between their respective stances. After a critique of each theorist's anarchist philosophy, we will move toward a synthesis of theory and reception, hoping to contribute to a new understanding of Goldman independent of Kropotkin's shadow.

Peter Kropotkin's rendering of anarchism relies heavily on Marxist studies of economic repression and the relationship of communities to impersonal spheres of production. Kropotkin's anarchist communism responds to the inability of any state to eschew coercive standards in favor of harmonious interaction between free beings. In order to understand what Kropotkin means by *anarchy*, it is necessary to consider his ties with historical materialism and the advent of new social order. In the essay "Objections," Kropotkin writes, "It is of an Anarchist-Communist society we are about to speak, a society that recognizes the absolute liberty of the individual, that does not admit of any authority, and makes use of no compulsion to drive men to work" (Kropotkin 1972, 159). Anarchist-communist positions, then, rely heavily on the choice of individuals to place themselves inside or outside the work force. The basis of criticism of social worth has hitherto been realized on a wage-level analysis; a citizen, in order to properly discern his or her political, social, and ethical worth, must invoke a sliding income scale. This is the essential reconstruction of meaning that Kropotkin seeks through his marriage of anarchism and communism. Communism supplies detachment from wage labor as psychological and social meaning; when combined with anarchism, communist societies begin a new mode of collective meaning. In short, anarchism is the perfect harmony of individuals in a collective setting, devoid of man-made laws (formal or informal) that serve to adjudicate meaning devoid of precept.

In the short essay "Well-Being for All" Kropotkin notes that "well-being for all is not a dream. It is possible, realizable, owing to all that our ancestors have done to increase our powers of production" (1972, 51). Kropotkin theorizes the universal possibilities of production and sustenance of the human race through a response to Malthusian economics that lauds the productive ability of the masses and disparages the owners of production for disallowing collective securities.[2] The history of dearth and abundance in the world is grounded in the reduction of output by the forced restraint of production (52). Kropotkin concentrates on the exploitation of labor, on the manner in which capitalists put it toward ineffective or useless ends that cloud the notion of well-being for all. Kropotkin proposes, as a solution, a return to communism through expropriation, accomplished through practical means: "We have all been bent on studying the dramatic side of revolutions so much, and the practical work of revolutions so little, that we are apt to see only the stage effects, so to speak, of these great movements; the fight of the first days; the barricades. But this fight, this first skirmish, is soon ended, and it is only after a breakdown of the old system that the real work of revolution can be said to begin" (55–56). There is ample evidence of the practicality of Kropotkin's theory of anarchist utopias. Less a dreamer than an historical opportunist, Kropotkin finds the empirical bases of anarchism in everyday life, searching for the fruits of anarchist traditions in public works, communal living, and even government programs. Like the advent of communism through public works and the adoption of a collective spirit, anarchist tendencies are implicit in the course of modern history: "if we observe the present development of civilized nations we see, most unmistakably, a movement ever more and more marked tending to limit the sphere of action of the Government, and allow more and more liberty to the individual" (66).

Kropotkin's Anarchy

Peter Kropotkin's anarchist communism is deeply rooted in deterministic philosophies of historical materialism and the advent of a new, proletarian order. In "Anarchist Communism," Kropotkin characterizes anarchist communism as historically determined by the fall of material individualism as a legitimate source of autonomy (1972, 63). In a sense, Kropotkin's feelings toward the ability of a state to engage a capitalist class with the units of production, in this sense the worker who dies for capitalist hubris, anticipate Habermas's "legitimation crisis," even upholding the possibility of communicative action, although the parameters are almost certainly not equal (Habermas 1974). This legitimation crisis, in Kropotkin's viewpoint, solves itself through the development of public works that respond to wage slavery with communistic engagements for universal public consumption. The examples of libraries and parks demonstrate the idea that communism as an outsource of collective autonomy is alive even within states based on the primacy of capital. From this, Kropotkin surmises that the material progress of collectivities points toward a completely communistic arrangement (1972, 65). The crisis of legitimation reaches its apex with the pure inability of a governmental structure to recognize the autonomy of the individual and provide an affirmation of collective safety. Kropotkin's faith in anarchism is not the operative elimination of contracts, but an affirmation of the ability of individuals and collectivities to police contractual relationships of their own accord. Kropotkin finds that the purposes of government, supported by news media and apologists within and without, become muddled when one considers the actual effect of state-centered programs on "real life": "as soon as we pass from printed matter to life itself, as soon as we throw a glance at society, we are struck by the infinitesimal part played by the government. . . . [A]nother striking fact . . . is the continual extension of the field of enterprise due to private initiative, and the prodigious development of free organizations of all kinds" (67–68).

The amalgamation of communism and anarchism finds its most centered critique through an examination of *homo economicus*. Kropotkin's "practical anarchism" effectively juxtaposes the right to live as a human being with the right to work as a wage slave; he notes, "The right to well-being is the social revolution, the right to work means nothing but the Treadmill of commercialism" (60). Anarchism depends on communism, first and foremost, for the destruction of the division of labor, which only serves to exploit workers and provide material avenues for continued blissful ignorance of the owners of production. The economic basis of oppression is a standpoint that Kropotkin will follow throughout his thought; in fact, his return to the reverence of nature suggests that political economy is the beginning and the end of exploitative states and abrasive interpersonal relationships.

The only characteristics missing from an effective communist regime are the rules of production, for which they stubbornly continue to support capitalist exclusionary policies. Kropotkin writes, "How can we doubt, then that when the instruments of production are placed at the service of all, when business is conducted on Communist principles, when labour, having recovered its place of honour in society, produces much more than is necessary to all—how can we doubt that this force (already so powerful) will enlarge its sphere of action till it becomes the ruling principle of social life?" (65). The importance of Kropotkin's anarchist communism lies in its contempt of the instruments of production as currently organized, which take on a life of their own and distort human nature. For Kropotkin, the problem of capital and exclusion is not necessarily dependent on those who uphold it, but rather, on the system as an organism of the oppression of all, including the capitalists themselves. Anarchist communism would not be possible without the assumption that human nature is distorted by the historical process of capital accumulation. Capital cannot be a proxy of human selfishness, but is a source in itself; the assumptions of anarchist communism support the notion that, at bottom, the removal of capitalism results in the prompt return to an egalitarian nature, realized in total equality and universal autonomy.[3]

In order to replace the primacy of the state, Kropotkin follows Stirner's reverence for nature as the arbiter of social justice (Fowler 1972, 742). Kropotkin notes that the great error of collectivists prior to himself has been the maintenance of the wage system and representative government, which actually seize the ability of a unit to govern itself and enjoy the full fruits of happiness (Kropotkin 1972, 189).[4] At this point, Kropotkin seems to be effacing the sources of inequality themselves, rather than the symptoms. As an anarchist communist, Kropotkin's sense of the economic bases of injustice and the reverence for a human nature that has no taste for servitude and domination without economic pretenses upholds the "goodness" of nature spoiled by an economic system that supplants agency with the all-important goal of "surplus value." Kropotkin is, of course, optimistic that the course of human history will determine that humanity is tired of servitude and will unloose the shackles of subjugation.

Anarchist communism is not the free-for-all that popular opinion would suggest; Kropotkin finds its genesis in works that highlight the needless inactivity of governmental regimes. Instead of allowing total freedom to the individual, Kropotkin's anarchism is entrenched in the nobility of social obligation: "Mikhail Bakunin and Peter Kropotkin in particular vigorously protested that full autonomy for people literally made no sense. . . . Men and women were always interdependent with their fellows, since they were all inescapably social beings. . . . Thus, the celebrated division in the history of nineteenth-century European anarchism between the collectivist/communitarian and the individualist anarchists, may be misleading" (Fowler 1972, 742). As we will see, the delineation between the call to collectivity and the individual spirit is alive in a comparison between Goldman and Kropotkin; Kropotkin's distaste for individual autonomy is refuted in Goldman's individualist thought, and Goldman's approach to the bifurcation of the individual and the collective (or its submission in Kropotkin's thought) provides a compelling theory of anarchism unseen in Kropotkin, or any of the nineteenth-century European anarchists (Fowler 1972).

It appears that Kropotkin's anarchism arises out of a historical study of social tides and concentrates on the stifling effect of the accumulation of capital on what was once a proud egalitarian human nature. For Kropotkin, the essence of anarchy is return, not revolution; the origin of critique is a belief in the ability of humans to subsume associations created by capitalist diversions and assume their spot in a classless world based on mutual aid and dependency. Kropotkin's analysis is purely economic, and any corollary social ills are either created or sustained by the extant industrial order. Anarchy overcomes the present demand through historical analysis of communist and anarchic leanings in human associations through an increasingly limited government. Anarchist communism serves as an optimal outcome for individuals precisely because it is *natural*; that is, distorted images of human nature brought about by the accumulation of capital and social subservience represent a distorted human picture that must be overcome in order to return to harmony.

Goldman's Anarchy

In Goldman's writings and speeches she attacks a great number of social and political institutions, from religion to democracy to marriage. These criticisms are all filtered through her general conception of anarchy, however, and what possibilities it promises for the future. Goldman's best definition of anarchy is found in the essay "Anarchy: What It Really Stands For."

History, Goldman tells us, is the struggle between New and Old ideas (Shulman 1983, 61–62). This new idea, anarchism, meets with heavy criticism from the old. It is considered impractical, violent, and dangerous, but through these criticisms she believes anarchism can be explained to its fullest extent (62).

Using the concepts of Oscar Wilde, Goldman frames practicality as a method of the Old—obviously something can only be practical if it fits in the existing system, which is also, in her eyes, what renders it illegitimate. Practicality should be measured in usefulness, and anarchism is the only solution to "do away with the wrong and the foolish" (63). Similarly, anarchism can hardly be labeled as "destructive" and "violent" when all it seeks to destroy is the "parasitic growths that feed on the life's essence of society," and since the real violence is committed by the state (63). She sees the condemnation of anarchism as merely a product of ignorance; people generally either dismiss new ideas or cling on to superficial definitions of them rather than investigate them fully.

Goldman defines anarchy as a social order free from man-made laws, since by design all governments and authorities rest on the power of violence and are therefore illegitimate. She sees the economy as a vicious evil, but does not restrict herself to a purely economic analysis, for economics is still only part of a larger problem. Anarchism conceptually frames the conflict within humans as one between the individual and social instincts (64). Religion and the state share a similar goal of repressing the discovery of being within individuals; they are both designed to keep man from "becoming conscious of himself" (65). In other words, within these frameworks an individual cannot discover self-meaning or self-expression, or realize that he or she is alive and that his or her own life is sacred, not merely a shadow of the afterlife. Anarchism, she claims, is "the great liberator of man from the phantoms that have held him captive" (65).

Goldman sees humanity withering away under the system of private property. Property has replaced kingship as the despot of her time (67). Rather than relying on coercive mechanisms, anarchism employs "voluntary productive and distributive associations, gradually developing into free communism, as the best means of producing the least waste of human energy" (68). The goal of anarchism is to combat the triple attack on humanity: the mind (religion), needs (property), and the spirit (the state) (68). Goldman does not believe in any type of subordination of the individual, and she disagrees with any human laws, for they are, in William Blackstone's words, "invalid, because they are contrary to the laws of nature" (Blackstone, quoted in Shulman 1983, 70). Goldman contends that the state cannot possibly legitimately enforce law when it is the greatest criminal, stealing (taxes) and killing (capital punishment, war) to achieve its ends (Shulman 1983, 71).

Similarly, consider the treatment of those who turn against the system: criminals. Goldman insists they are simply the product of the corrupt status quo: "Crime is naught but misdirected energy" (71). She frowns on conventional definitions of "human nature" as uniformly and authoritatively corrupt; rather, once humans are liberated from religion, property, and the state, their true human nature will be revealed.

Goldman concludes her essay with an interesting discussion of the merits (or lack thereof) of democracy. She compares voting to gaming (along with Thoreau) and suggests that the anarchist movement cannot survive or achieve through democracy, since that would be putting it in the hands of random chance and the majority. She looks dubiously on the achievements of democracy up to her time, considering that no policy has really relieved the people of their burdens. Instead, democracies protect labor. Even given a significant voice, the forces of labor would not achieve in democracy, for it is still an expanded arena of politics full of "flattering, lying, cheating" that would hardly produce significant results (74). Instead, anarchism must come from a revolution, since no lasting social change has ever come about without one. To Goldman, anarchy is not an inevitable transition in the sense that it will happen automatically given time; it will need to be the product of a dedicated movement.

Using these general ideas and conceptions, Goldman criticizes other cultural and social institutions. She critiques democracy, religion, and marriage, all as means to continue the propagation of the state and the status quo power structure (the exact opposite goals of her anarchist revolution).

Despite championing the rights of the people, Goldman was not a fan of the so-called masses. Her distrust of this group is a large factor in her criticism of democracy. She sees "quantity" as the driving force of her time, both economically, in terms of production maximization, and politically, in terms of quantity of deceit and manipulation. To her, "the majority cannot reason; it has no judgment" (79). She believes that individuality is at an all-time low, for governments and social structures are built on obedience and supplication. She uses Wendell Phillips's notion that public opinion, as a representation of the masses, is the ultimate form of tyranny and ultimately makes individuals fearful of one another because of common dependency (Phillips, quoted in Shulman 1983, 81–82).

This problem with public opinion, along with what she believes to be hypocrisy in democratic systems, is behind Goldman's opposition to the parliamentary idea. Fascism is clear in its hatred of the individual; democracies, by contrast, use false claims of it as a tool for garnering support. She is highly critical of the "rugged individualism" model in American society, since all it has meant is freedom for the masters at the expense of those beneath them (Shulman 1983, 112). Democracies, like other states, are founded on the ideals of authority and consent. People are trained to believe that authority can be legitimate and that "man is evil, vicious, and too incompetent to know what is good for him" (113). Goldman takes what are considered the positive qualities of democracies and presents them as manipulative tools—rather than being free, people are simply more willing to accept their slavery. The very idea of the state conflicts with her ideal of individuals: "every government whatever its form, character, or color—be it absolute or constitutional, monarchy or republic, Fascist, Nazi or Bolshevik—is by its very nature conservative, static, intolerant of change and opposed to it" (115). Government, Goldman believes, is essentially the bane of the individual. Governments emerge from authority, and authority emerges from uniformity. This criticism of government rings similarly to Erich Fromm's "wholesale mechanization of modern life" (116).[5]

Goldman also contends that suffrage (a brimming issue in her day) is simply a means of control and propagation of the system. "Life, happiness, joy, freedom, independence—all that, and more, is to spring from suffrage. In her blind devotion woman does not see what people of intellect perceived fifty years ago: that suffrage is an evil, that it has only helped to enslave people, that it has but closed their eyes that they may not see how craftily they were made to submit" (192). She refutes the idea that somehow women will improve the state and government, that somehow by their intervention a number of problems will be fixed. She does not contend that women should not vote because of some inequality (she agrees that they are perfectly capable of handling the responsibility), but rather that by participating in a corrupt system one only ensures its lasting success. She provides examples of states in which women are allowed to vote or participate highly in government that have not escaped the evils she sees inherent in it. Democracy and suffrage merely help to quell the masses even more easily because such gains provide them with the important illusion of freedom while they still toil away for scraps at the table.

Goldman also targets religion, and specifically Christianity, as being one of the most important elements in the maintenance of the status quo. Christianity, in her view, is "most adapted to the training of slaves, to the perpetuation of a slave society" (233). She takes on the "ethical and social Christ," the institutionalization of Christianity and its inherent mechanisms. She believes that religion flourishes so well because it contains nothing destructive or threatening to the existing order—quite the opposite, in fact. Governments can wield the church easily as a weapon of submission, since it, like any means of persuasion, is far more effective than force over the long term. Through religion's presenting an image of the hereafter that is "indifferent to the horrors of earth," it becomes easier to accept the pain and misery of the modern world (235). The happenings of the now mean little when faced off against eternity, so there is no incentive to push beyond the boundaries of what is, to something that could be. Christianity (and religion generally) is an enemy of change, and anything that is against change tends to be for the state.

Goldman confronts the myth of "blessed are the meek, for they shall inherit the earth" as being an easy doctrine for the advancement of slavery (237). The Christian symbol Christ did nothing for this earth because he had no interest in it, since all that matters is the hereafter. All aspects of this religion are merely tools of authority to Goldman, who, while she detests all religions, make a special point against Christianity: "I feel that no other religion has done as much harm or has helped so much in the enslavement of man as the religion of Christ" (239). Freedom from the chains of the hereafter and the ideology of always looking to the future (rather than the present) comes from atheism, which is the "strongest affirmation of man, and through man, the eternal yea to life, purpose, and beauty" (248).

Goldman's anarchism rests on attacking fundamental institutions and practices that instill gender roles in women and men. Just as she is unafraid to attack widely held conceptions of the "goodness" inherent in democracy and religion, she plunges headlong into an assault on the institution of marriage. She argues that love and marriage have nothing in common; those who married and then loved each other essentially represent an accident. Marriage is "an economic arrangement, an insurance pact" (205). To attain this security, the woman parts with her name and with it her very identity. Marriage, like religion, is an institution to sustain the state and therefore erase individuality. It creates specific roles for those involved and all but subsumes one of them into the identity of the other. The woman receives a man's paycheck, while in return for this security she offers a delicate appearance and sexual favors. The condition of womanhood is a lifelong process—marriage is the ultimate goal, and a woman moves towards it like a "mute beast fattened for slaughter" (206).

Motherhood and wifedom are means of imprisoning a woman and containing her individuality. Again, this follows a similar theme: women who are conditioned to marry, to have their identities dissolved, are very easy to control, both by the husband and by the state. The role of mothers provides a steady stream of supporters to the state in breeding and indoctrinating new young: "The defenders of authority dread the advent of a free motherhood, lest it will rob them of their prey. Who would fight wars? Who would create wealth? Who would make the policemen, the jailer, if the women were to refuse the indiscriminate breeding of children? . . . The race, the race! Shouts the king, president, the capitalist, and the priest. The race must be preserved, though woman must be degraded to a mere machine—and marriage intuition is our only safety valve against the pernicious sex-awakening of the woman" (212). The woman's body has been turned into a machine for the system, a vehicle for reproducing authority and control. Goldman envisions instead women who do not wish to produce "sickly" children who are spiritually and morally corrupt, but rather ones who understand the integral concepts of freedom and individuality.

Anarchy is the only solution to the deeply embedded problems she illustrates. It shatters the barriers of oppression (economic and social) that restrain individuals, both men and women, from achieving their true potential. Rather than hiding behind existing systems that promote false individuality (such as democracies), Goldman wishes to push through these boundaries to a utopia of freedom and enlightenment.

Synthesis

This chapter started with a question: why are Goldman and Kropotkin portrayed differently in their biographies and in the canon of political theory? Kropotkin tends to be a more revered thinker—is this because his writing or ideas are superior? Is there something particularly powerful or convincing about his definition of anarchy as opposed to hers? Is Goldman merely the "devotee" and Kropotkin the "theorist?" An easy answer could just be gender, but this is not very satisfying in and of itself. We wanted to take a deeper look at their writings and draw connections between them.

Clearly the two have vastly different styles of writing. Goldman is fluid, dynamic, passionate, and aggressive—she writes with an obvious purpose and attacks the positions of her adversaries. She cites frequently from a variety of sources. Her arguments generally progress logically and remain captivating. Goldman is writing to an audience—specifically, a street audience: nearly all her compiled essays were once given as speeches.[6] Through circumstance and personal principle, her writings needed to be different from Kropotkin's.

Kropotkin, by contrast, is a systematic and analytical writer. He explores and manipulates economic and social variables toward what he sees as the quintessential anarchist communism. He writes "like a theorist," so to speak, which probably wins him accolades. Kropotkin also rarely existed in the same social strata as Goldman—his work was usually popular (even if in foreign lands) and he could find sponsorship with some regularity (Woodcock and Avakumovic 1970). Kropotkin was not a speaker; he was a writer and an analyst standing in a different position in the world. His emphasis on the practicality of anarchism through its shadows in governmental works and social tides suggests that he is firmly within the corpus of social-scientific investigation. Instead of advocating the promulgation of anarchism through suggestive cries to revolution, he carefully studies the ability of a society to adapt to (or progress toward) revolutionary causes. His deliberate concentration on social realities and detachment from his object of inquiry helps one understand his inclusion in the canon.

One can also point to the different sources of inquiry for Goldman and Kropotkin's respective theories of anarchism. As mentioned earlier, Goldman relied not only on Kropotkin but also on Nietzsche, Stirner, Ibsen, and other contemporaries who provided her with intellectual energies. Kropotkin, meanwhile, concentrated most formally on contemporary anarchists and an historical materialism that defied "theory" and pushed toward verification through empirical observation of social tendencies. Goldman's reliance on a wide array of sources, each of which provides her with a unique sociopolitical voice, connects her to a revolutionary spirit that is missing in Kropotkin's more formal work. Of course Goldman's free employment of ideas, often taken out of the contexts intended by the author, could certainly account for her lukewarm reception as a theorist.[7]

These points suggest that gender certainly played a part in how they wrote and thought. It is more difficult to determine how it affected what others write *about* them. Did Goldman merely add gender to Kropotkin? This is certainly debatable. Clearly she spoke about it at length, while he barely considered it. But consider the full spectrum of their work on anarchy. Kropotkin is willing to devalue the individual for the common good—especially women.[8] To Goldman the individual is the one lasting sovereign. Kropotkin sees anarchist communism as the inevitable future; Goldman certainly sees revolution on the horizon, but she is under no false pretenses that it will come easily. Her life was spent laboring toward fostering this revolution.

Certainly these are theoretical distinctions that separate the thought and ideas of Goldman and Kropotkin, but let us consider typical gendered notions for a moment. What is the ideal masculine theorist, then or now? What qualities does he have? He would need to be scientific, analytical, and detached. He often looks at abstract concepts and deals with unavoidable outcomes. A "feminized" writer, however, values her life experiences and day-to-day utility. To this theorist, her words need to have practical ability. The most abstract concepts must eventually be tied down to the reality of daily living.

What we have here is a stark contrast between Goldman's and Kropotkin's writings. If the canon values the "masculine" version of theory, then Peter Kropotkin is a snug fit. Goldman deals with uncomfortable daily issues inside the "private" sphere of the home—marriage, sex, children, and so on. Kropotkin works primarily with economic and political abstractions. Kropotkin's attention to the manageable, conceptual nature of anarchism and communism provides a focus quite different from Goldman's (Woodcock and Avakumovic 1970). Further, Kropotkin's "responsible" employment of political thinkers, with careful deliberation on the context, contrasts with Goldman's free employment, a more creative means of conversing with political theorists.[9]

One can envision a world in which creative political thinking and passionate, empowered discourse are valuable political tools. Unfortunately, the corpus of political theory does not inhabit such a world. The value of detached, historical social analysis is evident in the canon; Goldman's fervent rhetoric and unorthodox educational background do not provide the proper credentials one would need in order to be well received within the discipline. As we mentioned at the outset, responses to Goldman as a political thinker are lukewarm at best. Most people pay more attention to Goldman the personality than to Goldman the thinker, which is a serious disservice of the field. Goldman's anarchy stands on its own when compared with Kropotkin's thought, something most intellectuals have not thought possible. We do not dare to classify either writer's work as "better," but we discovered ground on which to differentiate the two. Her concentration on the sovereignty of the individual, the employment of drama, and a concentration on the unity between self and other provide solid foundations for a utopian theory of anarchy. The similarities between Goldman and Kropotkin are numerous, but one in particular warrants attention as we close this chapter: both theorists believed most strongly in the reverence of nature and the ability of humans, whether alone or in voluntary collective arrangements, to make harmonious living an objective. The belief in an essentially egalitarian nature, ruined by economic or sociopolitical forces, provides the basis through which a faith in anarchism can be oriented. The importance of these theorists to the canon cannot be separated on this matter.

Notes

1. Howe, Wexler, and Woodcock and Avakumovic all refer to Goldman as "Emma" numerous times in their work. Others, such as Reichert, always use her full name, as if "Goldman" is too

awkward alone. At no point do they do the same with Kropotkin. Is this a significant gendered construct denoting familiarity and comfort (the feminine) versus professionalism and distance (masculine)? If so, does this influence the way we characterize political theorists in general?

2. Kropotkin responds to Malthus indirectly by positing the collective determination of the value of production as a possible avenue out of destruction.

3. Kropotkin writes about the "power upholding the present system" but does not explicitly state that this is a process devoid of active human contemplation. In light of his assumptions concerning the swift adoption of communist principles after the destruction of the instruments of production, however, it is a safe assumption.

4. The last paragraph to "The Collectivist Wages System" in *Conquest of Bread* reads: "For the day on which old institutions will fall under the proletarian axe, voices will cry out: 'Bread, shelter, ease for all!' And those voices will be listened to; the people will say: 'Let us begin by allaying our thirst for life, for happiness, for liberty, that we have never quenched. And when we shall have tasted of this joy, we will set to work to demolish the last vestiges of middle-class rule: its morality drawn from account-books, its 'debit and credit' philosophy, its 'mine and yours' institutions. 'In demolishing we shall build,' as Proudhon said; and we shall build in the name of Communism and Anarchy" (Kropotkin 1972, 189).

5. Erich Fromm similarly argues that within democracies, individuals are destroyed by automaton conformity. In order to gain comfort and security, individuals simply behave and dress like everyone else. See Fromm 1941.

6. Goldman's speaking schedule varied by year and opportunity, of course. Speeches provided funds and an opportunity to spread the word. When one considers her disdain for the masses, it is an interesting choice of tactics. A chronology of Goldman's speaking schedule can be found at the Berkeley Digital Library, http://sunsite.berkeley.edu/Goldman/Guide/chronology6900.html.

7. Free employment of ideas is certainly not a charge unique to Goldman. One can decide for oneself whether it is legitimate grounds to discount her political thought.

8. In *Conquest of Bread* Kropotkin wonders why so many women are made to cook meals for their families when relatively few could simply combine their efforts and produce a communal food supply. This would be far more efficient, of course, but he does not question the fact that *women* are still doing this work.

9. Consider Kropotkin's treatments of *Das Kapital*, in which he debates the historical value of Marx's wage system on the basis of Marx's writings and intentions. Compare this with Goldman's employment of Nietzschean ideas in a free manner, with little concern for Nietzsche's own intention.

References

Baldwin, Roger N., ed. 1970. *Kropotkin's Revolutionary Pamphlets*. New York: Dover Press.

Capouya, Emile, and Keitha Tompkins, ed. 1975. *The Essential Kropotkin*. New York: Liveright Books.

Coker, Francis W. 1934. *Recent Political Thought*. New York: D. Appleton-Century.

Falk, Candace, ed. *Emma Goldman: A Guide to Her Life and Documentary Sources*. The Emma Goldman Papers. Berkeley Digital Library. http://sunsite.berkeley.edu/Goldman/Guide/chronology6900.html.

Fowler, R. B. 1972. "The Anarchist Tradition of Political Thought." *Western Political Quarterly* 25, no. 4:738–52.

Fromm, Erich. 1941. *Escape from Freedom*. New York: Ferris Printing.

Goldman, Emma. 1969. *Anarchism and Other Essays*. New York: Dover.

Haaland, Bonnie. 1994. *Emma Goldman: Sexuality and the Impurity of the State*. Montreal: Black Rose Books.

Habermas, Jürgen. 1974. *Legitimation Crisis*. Translated by Thomas McCarthy. Boston: Beacon Press.

Howe, Leslie A. 2000. *On Goldman*. Belmont, Calif.: Wadsworth.

Kropotkin, Peter. 1899. *Memoirs of a Revolutionist*. New York: Houghton Mifflin.

———. 1972. *The Conquest of Bread*. Edited by Paul Avrich. New York: New York University Press.

Nietzsche, Friedrich. 1968. *The Will to Power*. Translated by Walter Kaufmann and R. J. Hollingdale. New York: Vintage.

Reichert, William O. 1967. "Toward a New Understanding of Anarchism." *Western Political Quarterly* 20, no. 4:856–65.

Ring, Jennifer. 1987. "Toward a Feminist Epistemology." *American Journal of Political Science* 31, no. 4:753–72.

Shulman, Alix Kates, ed. 1983. *Red Emma Speaks: An Emma Goldman Reader*. New York: Schocken Books.

Weiss, Thomas G. 1975. "The Tradition of Philosophical Anarchism and Future Directions in World Policy." *Journal of Peace Research* 12, no. 1:1–17.

Wexler, Alice. 1989. *Emma Goldman in Exile: From the Russian Revolution to the Spanish Civil War*. Boston: Beacon Press.

Woodcock, George, and Ivan Avakumovic. 1970. *The Anarchist Prince: A Biographical Study of Peter Kropotkin*. New York: Klaus Reprint.

8

Emma Goldman and the Spirit of Artful Living

Philosophy and Politics in the Classical American Period

Lynne M. Adrian

"In her drama lectures, in her life itself, and in the art she created in her autobiography, Emma Goldman developed, articulated, and helped popularize the aesthetic concept of "artful living, which is, I believe, crucial to understanding the temper of the classical period of American Philosophy."

Goldman was an avid follower of modern art and particularly of the drama. Influencing and popularizing important modern dramatists such as Eugene O'Neill, and the aesthetic insights of John Dewey, Adrian shows the ways Goldman's aesthetic vision melds European and American traditions to create a new social and artistic vision. Goldman's ideas emerge from this essay as vital in shifting perceptions of art from a focus on product to a focus on process, a shift that allows life itself to emerge as a site of artistic endeavor.—*The Editors*

Emma Goldman is an important, though neglected, figure of the classical period of American philosophy. Though she was almost entirely self-educated and regarded herself as an anarchist agitator, her impact on the thought of American intellectuals was wide ranging and profound. Goldman's thinking covered a multitude of subjects; this essay will focus on a singular area that may be among the most ignored but most important aspects of her thought-aesthetics. Unique historical conditions during this modernizing era allowed Goldman to construct an aesthetic that shifted the concept of art from a *product* to a *process*. Because of this shift all creative human endeavors, and indeed life itself, could be regarded as artful. Moreover, the concept of artful living is a necessary insight into much of the intellectual activity of the period, and through her writing and speaking Emma Goldman did much to vitalize this concept in the intellectual and artistic world. During the years from 1906 to 1916 Goldman lectured from 120 to 320 times a year. She "later estimated that she had spoken to between 50,000 and 75,000 people every year."[1] Many of her contemporaries credited her with introducing them to the moderm drama, particularly in its connection to developing industrial society and not merely as an isolated aesthetic variance, and her drama lectures often inspired the formation of drama study groups. "According to one observer, as Goldman spoke she burned 'with the flaming ardor of an apocalytic vision' that she found expressed so eloquently in Whitman, Neitzsche, Gorky and Hauptmann."[2] She also provided both the funds and the sustaining vision for her magazine *Mother Earth* (circulation three to five thousand), which was one of the first important pre–World War I "little magazines" with readers ranging "from Italian immigrant silkworkers and Philadelphia pharmacists to Alfred Stieglitz, Eugene O'Neill, and the painter Robert Henri."[3]

During the fin-de-siecle years, the conception of art was changed radically. Previously art had been defined in terms of the beautiful—a product only of those human endeavors directed into certain traditionally approved channels, such as classical music, drama, poetry, novels, painting, sculpture, and ballet. Between 1890 and 1915 American intellectuals and artists began to regard other forms as artistic. For these Americans, art had ceased to be a *product* and had become instead a *process* through which something whole and richly satisfying was produced. With this shift one could now think of living life not only in a beautiful way, but *artfully* as well, making life itself part of one's artwork. These beliefs opened for the first time the prospect that anyone engaging fully in a human occupation might be an artist. If the painting was merely the trace left by the artistic process of living, as Henri maintained, then it could be regarded as no more inherently a work of art than a well-made table, a freely educated child, or a labor union improving the ability of many to live wholly.

Artful living became the process of living all of one's life in an artful manner, of creating a unity and meaning out of all the experiences of life. It was in part derived from a central anarchist principle that "the goal of the ethical life was to live in harmony with one's principles and to reduce inconsistency so that one could be an inspiration to others."[4] It differed from "beautiful living" in that it did not consist of merely appreciating the beautiful things around oneself. It was rather an active, synthetic principle involving the process of conscious human creation. As a process it was a rich, wholistic concept, which could never be reduced to a set of first principles offering a pattern to be followed; instead it was an idea or direction that must be individually synthesized.

Artful living, then, with its view of art as a process, seems perfectly suited to someone like Goldman, whose life and thought were almost one. One of the most striking features of Emma Goldman's writing is the extent of her knowledge. She quoted diverse sources, from the Bible to Marx, Whitman to Goethe, Kropotkin to Jefferson, and all with equal fluency. Such literacy is particularly amazing when one pauses to remember that Goldman completed only one year of education in a German *Realschule* and some technical training in nursing. Though grounded in European philosophical anarchism, Goldman's use of organism and creativity in her aesthetics related more directly to the American tradition, particularly that of the Transcendentalists. In addition to the European sources of anarchism (Bakunin, Proudhon, Kropotkin, and Nietzsche— and, for Goldman, Freud as well), she was also versed in the American philosophical tradition of Jefferson and the Transcendentalists.[5]

Shortly after Goldman's arrival in New York City and her active entrance into the anarchist movement, she became acquainted with Justus Schwab, an anarchist and the owner of an inn where east side radicals often met. He introduced her to the writings of Whitman, Emerson, Thoreau, Hawthorne, Spencer, Mill, Jefferson, and other English and American authors, all of which she eagerly absorbed. She noted in her autobiography the importance of her intellectual affinity to these figures, stating that simultaneous attempts to interest her in spiritualism failed completely.[6] After a brief period of intense review of thinkers such as Jefferson, she turned increasingly to the Transcendentalists. She was influenced by these thinkers, and they were incorporated into both Goldman's concept of anarchism and her political activism. "As time went on she drew rather on other figures in the American background, on Emerson, Whitman, and especially, Thoreau. Contrary to uncritical thinking on this subject, there was in America a native radical tradition that meshed nicely with anarchist theory. . . . Thus while the content and form of her dream came primarily from Russian sources, this dream could put down roots in the hospitable soil of a native tradition."[7]

The clarity with which this synthesis of thought occurred was remarkable. American and European traditions are no longer differentiated, and concepts are not drawn from one or the other. Instead, Goldman blended the two into her own use of the terms. A key instance of this blending is her use of the concept of "organicism." Use of organic metaphors to explain both individual persons and social constructs are common in both European anarchist thought and American Transcendentalism. Organic metaphors occur throughout Goldman's writing as well, often in crucial places in her discussion of aesthetics and education. In fact, Goldman used organic metaphors to bridge the two key contradictions within anarchist theory. One of these perennially problematic contradictions is the question of whether the intellectuals or the workers will be the guiding force in developing anarchism. Goldman followed both European anarchist theory and the example of Thoreau in advocating a unity between intellectual and manual labor, noticing that "intellectual and physical labour are as closely related in the social body as brain and hand in the human organism. One cannot function without the other."[8] The other tension within anarchism is between individual and the mass as the locus of social changes and regeneration. This tension is expressed in the problematic relationship between individual and communistic anarchism. Here also, Goldman was dependent on an organic metaphor to demonstrate that in her anarchist theory individualism could be blended with working-class consciousness and commitment and eventually be revolutionarily enacted through syndicalist economic practices. "Anarchism is therefore the teacher of the unity of life; not merely in nature, but in man. There is no conflict between the individual and the social instincts, any more than there is between the heart and the lungs; the one the receptacle of the precious life essence, the other the repository of the element that keeps the essence pure and strong. The individual is the heart of society, conserving the essence of social life; society is the lungs which are disturbing the element to keep the life essence—that is, the individual—pure and strong."[9]

Despite Goldman's frequent references to the Emerson-Whitman tradition, it is important to note several critical differences in her use of terms such as "organicism." For Emerson and Thoreau, organic unity was given by a deistic Oversoul. For these men the world was a wholistic, unified "garden" in which problems of discord were caused by human unwillingness to assume the proper place in nature and to perceive the overriding organic unities of the universe. For Goldman, however, this organic unity in the individual and society as a whole was created through growth in consciousness and in greater freedom of individual expression. As she wrote in *Anarchism and Other Essays*, "I begin with an admission: Regardless of all political and economic theories treating of the fundamental differences between various groups within the human race, regardless of class and race distinctions, regardless of all artificial boundary lines between woman's rights and man's rights, I hold that there is a point where these differentiations may meet and *grow* into one perfect whole."[10] Thus, social unity and harmony mimic nature, but they were arrived at not from imitation of a preexisting pattern in nature, but through conscious human growth and free choice.

Because of Goldman's atheism, this rooting of both creativity and good and evil in humankind is especially emphatic. Creativity is internal and thus artful, rather than being a derivative of the Oversoul as it is for Emerson. One creates art through an active process rather than from becoming Emerson's transparent eyeball, seeing nature whole. While Emerson emphasizes process in art (the vision over the picture produced), it is still a process *towards* a fixed ideal which both the philosopher and the artist seek. Since Transcendentalism often drew on Hegelian idealism, such an emphasis is not surprising. For Goldman, however, any preexisting categories are deadening and process is ongoing—not fixed by being a process *towards* an ideal, but rather one that is an end in and of itself. Thus, living can be considered *artful* rather than *beautiful* because it is a creative process, the artistry residing in the individual's own efforts toward unity and growth rather than in living in harmony with a universal plan of God or Nature. The Transcendentalists, in this view, have only the potential for *beautiful* living in harmony with nature, rather than *artful* living.

This different attribution of the source of unity also creates very different interpretations of good and evil. For Emerson evil is not really terribly "bad," because once it is thoroughly understood evil can be seen as united with good in the Oversoul. For Goldman, however, evil is situated within the province of humanity. Either it is the result of present conditions (as she maintains is 90 percent of all crime), or it is inherent in the individual, in which case no amount of legislation would eradicate it. Thus, evil is real and not merely human failure to understand the ultimate order of the universe. Goldman would further credit much of the Transcendentalists' desire to explain evil as the lack of understanding of the underlying order of the universe to Nietzsche's concept of transvaluation, whereby people turn a vice that cannot be overcome into a virtue, rather than admit their impotence. Emerson unified evil with good in the glorified Oversoul because of an inability to eradicate it; if evil cannot be eliminated it must instead be converted into a part of the good. Goldman herself uses a similar process when she locates organicism in human creativity; since she no longer finds human beings impotent, bound to follow unknown, greater powers, she reverses the previous transvaluation. The resulting end of human impotence renders possible *artful* rather than merely *beautiful* living.

Emma Goldman's artful living is lucidly demonstrated by her concern for the artist's position in society. Though she tended to focus her attention upon drama, she was familiar with many artists, and other art forms, and always believed that a large part of her success in the United States was due to her refusal to limit herself solely to subjects in political economy.[11] Even during tense political situations, she deemed the modern drama an appropriate subject, for example, choosing to lecture on Ibsen's *Enemy of the People* during a particularly violent free-speech fight.[12] For her, "the modern artist is, in the words of August Strindberg, 'a lay preacher popularizing the pressing questions of his time.'"[13] The work of such artists was essential, for Goldman believed that political harangues alone could never reach sufficiently large audiences to revolutionize social conditions. "An adequate appreciation of the tremendous spread of the modern, conscious social unrest cannot be gained from merely propagandistic literature. Rather must we become conversant with the larger phases of human expression manifest in art, literature, and, above all, the modern drama—the strongest and most far-reaching interpreter of our deep-felt dissatisfaction."[14]

Having accepted such a vital role for the artist in the regeneration of society, Goldman was nonetheless unstinting in her criticism of those who failed to speak honestly of daily life and instead chose material success. In an article entitled "Intellectual Proletarians" she referred to the artists who chose to become successful in contemporary social terms as "dead souls upon the intellectual horizon. The uncompromising and daring spirits never 'arrive.' Their life represents an endless battle with the stupidity and the dullness of their time. They must remain what Neitzsche calls 'untimely,' because everything that strives for new form, new expression or new values is always doomed to be untimely."[15] For Goldman, many members of the bohemian art community fit into the same category. In an address to them in 1909 she clearly outlined her position on artful living and its importance in her aesthetic.

> The majority of the (artist) Guilders impressed me as people to whom "bohemianism" was a sort of narcotic to help them endure

the boredom of their lives. Of course there were others, those who knew the struggle that is the lot of every sincere and free person, whether he aspires to an ideal in life or in art. To them I addressed my talk on "Art in Life," pointing out . . . that *life in all its variety and fullness is art, the highest art.* The man who is not part of the stream of life is not an artist, no matter how well he paints sunsets or composes nocturnes. It certainly does not mean that the artist must hold a definite creed, join an anarchist group or a socialist local. It does signify, however, that he must be able to feel the tragedy of the millions condemned to a lack of joy and beauty.[16]

Alfred Stieglitz, whose "291" art gallery and *Camera Work* magazine introduced both art photography and abstract art to the United States, considered himself an anarchist and helped support *Mother Earth,* as did the noted photography critic Sadakichi Hartmann.[17] However, the most influential convert Goldman made to her aesthetics was probably the painter Robert Henri, who defined himself as an anarchist from the 1890s until his death in 1929. He became one of Goldman's personal friends who regularly attended her art and drama lectures and held long discussions on aesthetics with her while he painted her portrait. Henri is particularly significant because he influenced an entire generation of artists through the art classes Goldman persuaded him to offer at the Modern School of the Francisco Ferrer Center in New York City. Henri trained not only the so-called Ashcan painters, but also Arthur B. Davies, the organizer of the Armory Show in 1913, and other important figures in the American abstract art movement, including Stuart Davis and Man Ray.[18] Rockwell Kent referred to Henri as "possibly the most important figure in our cultural history."[19]

Henri is perhaps the clearest example of this shift from product to process and from beautiful life to artful living in the thought of the artistic community. In *The Art Spirit,* a compilation of notes, articles, fragments of letters, and talks to students, he opens by stating: "Art when really understood is the province of every human being. It is simply a question of doing things, anything, well. It is not an outside, extra thing."[20] Thus, art is no longer a separate enterprise, but has become a part of all life. It is no longer the province of a select few who can paint or sculpt, but includes the doing of anything well, by anyone. This position leads Henri to state later in his work that "I am not interested in art as a means of making a living, but I am interested in art as a means of living a life. It is the most important of all studies, and all studies are tributary to it."[21] Still later in the work, he states that "to be an artist is to construct, and to whatever degree one shows the genius for construction in work of any sort, he is that much an artist. The *artist* life is therefore the desirable life, and it is possible to all."[22]

Goldman's links to new movements in art were not restricted to the visual arts. If anything, her impact was clearer in the drama, which was her particular forte as a critic and popularizer. The Free Theater at the Ferrer Center "held a pioneering place in the 'little theater' movement which emerged in New York during the war. Links between the Free Theatre and drama groups in Greenwich Village were numerous. . . . The Provincetown Players, launched in 1916, emerged from the same circles, with Floyd Dell, Hutchins Hapgood, Eugene O'Neill, William Zorach, and Stella Balantine (Emma Goldman's niece) among the founders. Harry Weinberger, a close friend of Emma and Berkman, became the group's attorney, and M. Eleanor Fitzgerald, Berkman's companion, its manager and most vital figure. Among its first productions were works by Mike Gold and John Reed, as well as Dell and O'Neill, all of whom attended the Ferrer Center."[23] In turn, in her role as drama critic, Goldman was "one of the first to recognize [O'Neill's] importance as a modern dramatist, and she afterwards lectured on him in England."[24]

While her magazine *Mother Earth* is not noted for its innovative aesthetic choices, it seems possible that other related magazines reaped the artistic benefits *Mother Earth* missed because Goldman personally tended to prefer realistic writers. *The Masses* opened its pages to many of the anarchists connected with the Ferrer Center and Goldman; her friend Theodore Dreiser wrote an article for *Revolt* (published by fellow *Mother Earth* editor Hippolyte Havel); and the Ferrer Center's in-house magazine *The Modern School* regularly published works by innovative artists such as Hart Crane, Wallace Stevens, and Mike Gold.[25]

I would further maintain that Emma Goldman's concept of artful living had an impact on the aesthetics Dewey develops in *Art as Experience*. "Emma Goldman . . . was a friend of John Dewey's and 'had a high regard for his ideas.'"[26] In turn, Dewey was publicly defending her as early as 1901, when he responded to the press attacks that followed McKinley's assassination by insisting "that Emma Goldman's 'reputation as a dangerous woman was built up entirely by a conjunction of yellow journalism and ill-advised police raids. She is a romantically idealistic person with a highly attractive personality.'"[27] Throughout her lifetime, Dewey continued to be a personal friend and correspondent of Goldman's; he was one of the sponsors of her 1934 visa request, and gave one of the addresses at a welcoming dinner in New York City.[28] Given their friendship, it does not surprise me that Dewey's assertion in the opening chapter of *Art as Experience* that "the intelligent mechanic engaged in his job, interested in doing well and finding satisfaction in his handiwork, caring for his materials and tools with genuine affection is artistically engaged"[29] echoes Goldman's comparison of making a table to an artist painting. Dewey begins with the strong belief that art is not separate from life, and that "*theories* which isolate art and its appreciation by placing them in a realm of their own, disconnected from other modes of experiencing, are not inherent in the subject-matter but arise because of specifiable extraneous conditions."[30] In fact, as George Axtelle observed, "Dewey greatly expanded the common usage of the term 'art': any activity carried on with loving care for its outcome is by definition art."[31] While more systematically developed as philosophy, Dewey's aesthetics seem to echo Goldman's concept of artful living.

It is certainly suggestive to see Emma Goldman as a key connection between "artful living" as an aesthetic concept, innovative arts, art educators, and philosophers of aesthetics. In her drama lectures, in her life itself, and in the art she created in her autobiography *Living My Life*, Emma Goldman developed, articulated, and helped popularize the aesthetic concept of "artful living," which is, I believe, crucial to understanding the temper of the classical period of American philosophy.

Notes

1. Alice Wexler, *Emma Goldman: An Intimate Life* (New York: Pantheon Books, 1984), 166.

2. Martin Solomon, *Emma Goldman* (Boston: Twayne, 1987), 26.

3. Wexler, *Emma Goldman*, 124.

4. Blaine McKinley, "'The Quagmires of Necessity,' American Anarchists and Dilemmas of Vocation," *American Quarterly* 34 (1982): 504. See also David DeLeon, *The American as Anarchist: Reflections on Indigenous Radicalism* (Baltimore: Johns Hopkins University Press, 1978).

5. In regard to the influences of American thinkers, it is important to note that Emma Goldman considered herself to be more an American than of any other nationality. After having established deep roots in the United States, her deportation in 1919 was a personal tragedy mitigated only by her belief that in Russia she could help in building the revolution. After leaving Russia in 1921, she became virtually a woman without a country, and to the end of her life Goldman felt a deep bond with the United States. As she noted in her autobiography, "There still was a large place in my heart for my erstwhile country, regardless of her shabby treatment. My love for all that is

ideal, creative, and humane in her would not die. But I should rather never see America again if I could do so only by compromising my ideas." Emma Goldman, *Living My Life*, 2 vols. (1931; New York: Dover, 1970), vol. 2, 988.

6. Goldman, *Living My Life*, vol. 1, 145.

7. Richard Drinnon, *Rebel in Paradise: A Biography of Emma Goldman* (New York: Bantam, 1973), 41–42n.

8. Emma Goldman, *My Further Disillusionment in Russia* (Garden City, N.J.: Doubleday, 1924), 166.

9. Emma Goldman, *Anarchism and Other Essays* (Port Washington, N.Y.: Kennikat Press, 1910), 52.

10. Ibid., 213.

11. Goldman, *Living My Life*, vol. 2, 527.

12. Goldman, *Living My Life*, vol. 1, 495.

13. Emma Goldman, *The Social Significance of Modern Drama* (Boston: Richard G. Badger, 1914), 3.

14. Goldman, *Anarchism and Other Essays*, 241.

15. Emma Goldman, "Intellectual Proletarians," in *Red Emma Speaks: Selected Writings and Speeches by Emma Goldman*, ed. Alix Kates Shulman (New York: Vintage Books, 1972), 177–78.

16. Goldman, *Living My Life*, vol. 1, 463–64; emphasis added.

17. Paul Avrich, *The Modern School Movement: Anarchism and Education in the United States* (Princeton: Princeton University Press, 1980), 153, 125–26.

18. Donald Dew Egbert, *Socialism and American Art: In the Light of European Utopianism, Marxism, and Anarchism* (Princeton: Princeton University Press, 1967), 96; Avrich, *The Modern School Movement*, 157; Diane Kelder, ed., *Stuart Davis: Documentary Monographs in Modern Art* (New York: Praeger, 1971), 3–4.

19. Avrich, *The Modern School Movement*, 150.

20. Robert Henri, *The Art Spirit*, comp. Margery Ryerson (Philadelphia: J. B. Lippincott, 1923), 15.

21. Ibid., 158.

22. Ibid., 221.

23. Avrich, *The Modern School Movement*, 143.

24. Ibid., 145.

25. Ibid., 130, 141, 164.

26. Ibid., 38.

27. Drinnon, *Rebel in Paradise*, 106.

28. Ibid., 344.

29. John Dewey, *Art as Experience* (New York: G. P. Putnam's Sons, 1934), 5.

30. Ibid., 10. See also Max Eastman, "John Dewey," *The Atlantic Monthly* (December 1941), 671–85.

31. George Axtelle, "John Dewey and the Genius of American Civilization," in *John Dewey and the World View*, ed. Douglas E. Lawson and Arthur E. Lean (Carbondale: Southern Illinois University Press, 1964), 55.

9

Emma Goldman on Mary Wollstonecraft

Alice Wexler

"Goldman really presented two conflicting images of Wollstonecraft: the "pioneer of modern womanhood" and the tragic romantic heroine. . . . These two images, the positive and the tragic, reflect a contradiction that informs the entire essay, and that corresponds to a conflict in Goldman's thought."

Wexler's angle is a fascinating one—she not only explains what Goldman had to say about Wollstonecraft, but also explores what that portrayal of Wollstonecraft says about Goldman herself. Delving into similarities, contrasts, and parallels between the two great figures, Wexler offers significant insights into both.—*The Editors*

Introduction

In the November 1911 issue of the anarchist magazine *Mother Earth*, there appeared an announcement of a forthcoming lecture by Emma Goldman entitled "Mary Wollstonecraft, the Pioneer of Modern Womanhood." This lecture is significant in suggesting the uses which a twentieth-century anarchist feminist was able to make of the eighteenth-century author of *A Vindication of the Rights of Woman*. Goldman's lecture expresses the struggle of one woman to both appropriate and dissociate herself from a heroine she found inspiring and terrifying at the same time. The lecture suggests both the possibilities and the limitations of the past

I would like to thank Kay Trimberger and David Schickele who read earlier versions of this paper. Permission for the use of quotations from Emma Goldman's letters and papers has been granted by Ian Ballantine, Miss Goldman's literary executor, who controls all rights in the property of Miss Goldman. The text of the lecture on Mary Wollstonecraft has been transcribed from a microfilm copy of the original typewritten manuscript in the Emma Goldman Papers, Manuscript and Archives Division, The New York Public Library, Astor, Lenox and Tilden Foundations. I am also grateful to Charles H. Hapgood for permission to quote from a letter to Hutchins Hapgood. Emma Goldman's erratic spelling and punctuation have been regularized, and most abbreviations eliminated. Her characteristically Germanic style of capitalization has been retained.

as a source of strength for the present. It also illuminates the process by which the present may simultaneously reveal and distort the past.

More specifically, Goldman's portrait of Wollstonecraft is significant as the most revealing short self-portrait she ever wrote. Writing about her precursor, Goldman expressed some of her most characteristic and contradictory attitudes: a blend of idealism and elitism; equal respect for intellect and for passion; deep concern for the welfare of the masses, but contempt for "the mass" and "the majority"; commitment to freedom, but a tendency to appeal to "fate"; scorn for wealth and power, but an admiration for heroes. Goldman's anarchism was founded less on an iden-tification with the masses than on a sense of identity with the great rebels and martyrs of the past. Mary Wollstonecraft was one of those great re-bels. In describing her vision of Wollstonecraft, Goldman also described her vision of herself.

Afterword

"The most notable fact that culture imprints on women," writes Adri-enne Rich, "is the sense of our limits. The most important thing one woman can do for another is to illuminate and expand her sense of actual possibilities."[1] Although Rich was writing about biological mothers and daughters, her insight also applies to their historical counterparts. For early nineteenth-century feminists such as Frances Wright, Lucretia Mott, and Elizabeth Cady Stanton, Mary Wollstonecraft's *Vindication of the Rights of Woman* was an important source of inspiration. The revival of Wollstonecraft's personal reputation in the late nineteenth century stimulated renewed interest in her life, as well as her ideas. By the early twentieth century, a number of rebellious women were finding in that life a major statement of female potentiality. Despite, or perhaps because of, her complex and ambivalent legacy, the attempt to assess that legacy was for some women, at least, a way of clarifying their own identities and options. To confront Mary Wollstonecraft was also a way of confronting oneself.

That Emma Goldman should identify with Mary Wollstonecraft is not surprising. As a leading figure in the international anarchist movement between 1889 and 1940, Goldman looked to Wollstonecraft as a precur-sor of her own revolt against the constraints of authority, particularly against the economic, intellectual, and social restrictions on women. Like Wollstonecraft, Goldman also called for a transformation of consciousness, the overcoming of inhibitions and fears that would make it more possible for women "to be human in the truest sense."[2] Both stressed inner freedom, independence of mind and judgment, as essential elements of liberation. "Independence," wrote Wollstonecraft, "I have long considered as the grand blessing of life, the basis of every virtue."[3] "Until woman has learned . . . to stand firmly on her own ground and to insist upon her own unrestricted freedom . . . she cannot call herself emancipated," echoed Goldman.[4]

Parallels between the lives of Wollstonecraft and Goldman are also striking, despite the fact that one grew up in eighteenth-century England, the other in nineteenth-century Russia, Germany, and America. Both came from middle-class families of declining fortunes. Both women perceived their mothers as downtrodden, but rejecting. Both recalled childhoods dominated by fathers who were harsh, authoritarian, and unloving, but at the same time somewhat ineffective in their dealings with the world outside the family. Both Wollstonecraft and Goldman had been rebellious from an early age, intense in their desires for education and independence, as well as love. They both directly confronted the enormous gap between their own soaring ambitions and the few alternatives available to young women who sought economic independence. Both women were angry, energetic, passionate, and intellectual, yet also subject to periods of depression. Unlike Wollstonecraft, who was primarily a writer, Goldman was predominantly an activist, whose multiple talents made her one of the most respected figures in the anarchist movement during her lifetime. Yet while Goldman often described herself as an agitator and propagandist (as well as publisher of *Mother Earth*), she ultimately came to think of herself as an educator, like Wollstonecraft.

Goldman evidently became interested in Wollstonecraft in 1911, when she first presented this lecture. She indicated that she had read about Wollstonecraft before that year and had also attended a lecture in 1893 given by another anarchist, Voltairine de Cleyre, on the eighteenth-century feminist. Yet Goldman's own comments and the fact that neither Wollstonecraft nor the *Vindication of the Rights of Woman* are mentioned in any of her feminist essays (most of which were written prior to 1911) suggest that her disapproval of Wollstonecraft's love life had blocked her appreciations for any strengths or insights to be gained, either from the life or the work. If Wollstonecraft did influence Goldman's thinking about women, that influence was unacknowledged.[5]

By 1911, changes in Goldman's life, and the publication of a new biography, revived her interest. That same year, G. R. Stirling Taylor published *Mary Wollstonecraft: A Study in Economics and Romance*. The similarities in content, emphasis, and quotations between this study and Goldman's essay indicates that it was almost certainly Goldman's main source of information. Yet it is not Goldman's reading of Taylor, but rather her "misreading," her modification of Taylor's interpretation, that provides the most revealing glimpse, not only of Goldman's understanding of Wollstonecraft, but also of herself.

For Taylor, Wollstonecraft's blend of powerful intellect and passionate temperament was indicative of her greatness. Goldman agreed. For Taylor, Wollstonecraft's intellectual and sexual struggles culminated in a successful resolution. If her life and ideas shocked the sensibilities of most of her contemporaries and earned her a scandalous reputation, she also earned the admiration and respect, during her lifetime, of some of the most brilliant radical minds in London. Despite the agony of her affair with Imlay—which drove her twice to attempt suicide—she ultimately recovered from this affair. Her capacity to form a more mutual, less obsessive, and more satisfying relationship with William Godwin was evidence of her ability to learn from experience, and to really live in accordance with her ideal of combining intimacy and independence. As Taylor described it: "She had in her famous book taught what she held to be the true theory of the sex relation. She now had an opportunity of putting her theories into practice in at least a partially complete form. For a year she lived a life of comparative quiet and content. She saw enough of Godwin to soothe her restless desire for personal affection; she had the freedom which satisfied her great sense of independence; and together they gave her peace."[6]

Goldman's interpretation was quite different. While admitting that Wollstonecraft had been admired by many brilliant London intellectuals, Goldman emphasized the rejection and repudiation by the general public which attended such daring nonconformity. Yet this "lack of understanding" was not the deepest "tragedy" of her life, in Goldman's view. Rather, it was her own inner conflict, "the fact that having seen new possibilities for human advancement, the pioneers can not take root in the old, and with the new still far off they become outcast roamers of the earth, restless seekers for the things they will never find."

In Goldman's interpretation, Wollstonecraft's unhappy passion for Gilbert Imlay was the great turning point and tragic climax of her life, and one from which she never really recovered. Goldman observed elsewhere that she thought Wollstonecraft's life had been "wrecked through that one great passion." The subsequent relationship with Godwin, from Goldman's perspective, was pallid by comparison, "a sweet and tender comaraderie, not of the wild primitive kind but the quiet mature warm sort, that soothes one like a cold hand upon a burning forehead." Goldman suggested that her death may have come at an appropriate moment. "For he who has ever tasted the madness of life can never again adjust himself to an even tenor." She came close to suggesting that Wollstonecraft's early death in childbirth was somehow just retribution for her daring intellectual and social revolt, as well as being the inevitable price of wisdom. "Mary Wollstonecraft aimed for the highest summit of human possibilities," Goldman wrote. And like the falcon "who soared through space in order to behold the sun and then paid for it with his life, Mary drained the cup of tragedy, for such is the price of wisdom."

Taylor, however, had not intimated that Wollstonecraft's life was tragic. In his interpretation, she had triumphed. He had mentioned "the tragedy of the prophet crying in the wilderness" only in passing, in relation to the *Vindication*.[7] Goldman made this idea a central theme. Indeed, Taylor had suggested a final integration between her love life and her intellectual life in the relationship with Godwin. Goldman emphasized instead "the discrepancy between her world of ideals and her world of love" which caused her to attempt suicide. Instead of growth and achievement, Goldman emphasized anguish and pain. Instead of respect, she emphasized repudiation. Given the evidence in Taylor's biography, why did Goldman see Wollstonecraft's life as somehow doomed and unsuccessful? Why, in short, did she see it as "tragic"?

In fact, Goldman really presented two conflicting images of Wollstonecraft: the "pioneer of modern womanhood" and the tragic romantic heroine. The positive Wollstonecraft was a woman who triumphed over her circumstances by virtue of her intelligence and determination. She was a "daring fighter," a "pathfinder," a "pioneer" who would "not tread the beaten tracks," would not compromise, who "aimed for the highest summit of human possibilities." The tragic Wollstonecraft was a "born" rebel whose life seemed continually bound by the exigencies of "fate," "destiny," and "inevitability." So, for example, it was "inevitable" that the advance guards should be "isolated, shunned, and repudiated by the nearest and dearest of kin." Wollstonecraft was "destined by her very nature" to become a great rebel. She was "doomed to suffering by the very wealth of her being." She was also "doomed" to become the helpless prey of love, but "so strange is fate" that she had to "pay with her life" for the life of her child.

These two images, the positive and the tragic, reflect a contradiction that informs the entire essay, and that corresponds to a conflict in Goldman's thought. On the one hand, she believed in free will, the human power to make choices and to act, the possibility of freedom. On the other hand, she seemed also to believe, perhaps at a less conscious level, that many aspects of human behavior were determined by heredity, by destiny, by conditions beyond human control. Rather than attempting to assess the weight of specific factors in any given situation, Goldman tended to alternate between determinist and voluntarist modes of explanation, without any real attempt at integration.

Thus, Goldman's anarchism was based on a belief in the power of the individual to act, the power of "the ideal" to motivate economic and social revolt. "I do not believe in this theory 'what has to be must be.' It is an excuse for cowards and weaklings," she once wrote.[8] And in her own life, Goldman translated this belief into action. Her tremendous energy as an agitator, propagandist, nurse, publisher, author, organizer, theatrical manager, and drama critic testifies to her success in shaping her life according to her own will.

Yet in her private correspondence, Goldman often alluded to fate, heredity, destiny, and inevitability, particularly in describing or explaining her own behavior. She once described her psyche as that of a gambler, "driven by an irresistible force, until he had lost his last shirt."[9] She "could no more help crying out [against injustice] than I could if I were drowning. I am an anarchist of the Topsy variety—I was just born so."[10] Thus, her ambivalent portrait of Wollstonecraft—as both architect and victim of her own life—suggests Goldman's similarly conflicting images of herself.

Goldman's tendency to appeal to "fate" also suggests a certain self-dramatizing quality characteristic of her personality. The inflated, sentimental, grandiose tone of the Wollstonecraft essay, particularly at the beginning, conveys Goldman's tendency to imagine herself, like Wollstonecraft, as a great prophet whose vision placed her far beyond the capacity of her contemporaries to appreciate or understand her. There was, of course, considerable truth in this idea. Still, Goldman's narcissism often led her to downplay the efforts of other radicals who shared her struggle and at times to regard the very people she was trying to reach with a kind of Nietzschean contempt. Her observation that Wollstonecraft was "pretty much alone as every great soul must be alone—no doubt, that is the penalty for greatness" suggests the way Goldman often thought about herself.[11]

Goldman may have emphasized the negative or "tragic" aspect of Wollstonecraft's life because she was feeling depressed about her own life around the time she wrote the essay. Early in 1911, in a particularly low mood, Goldman wrote a poignant letter to her friend, Hutchins Hapgood, describing feelings of sadness and resignation that contrast dramatically with her determined and optimistic public persona:

> I must be getting old, Hutchie dear. I see nothing but clouds most times, or is it my own fancy? I can not tell. I only know I have grown so damnably sensitive to all kinds of impressions, as if my soul were covered with tissue paper. Fate or the devil must have entered into some sort of a conspiracy when I was thrust into the public arena. I realize more and more how deficient I am for that. And yet I am not much fit for a private life. Truth is, I am pretty much of an abortion, Hutchie boy. I find life hard to endure under all circumstances. You see, I am not as lucky as you. I too do not like myself, still less do I like life, or that which we call life. . . . Contrary to my reputation, I never could enter into a momentary relationship. Every experience meant more to me than the birth of a child. I have always paid much more than I got out, which is no one's fault but my own, possibly I am too insatiable, I don't know. . . . I am a queer specimen, Hutchie darling. It's only fortunate my friends do not know me, or I would be lonelier than I am now.[12]

The mood evoked in this letter may well have led Goldman to emphasize the anguish, the loneliness, the feelings of inner conflict and unsatisfied longing in Wollstonecraft's life, because these feelings seem to have characterized her own life while she was thinking and writing about Wollstonecraft. There was an additional reason for Goldman to emphasize at this moment in her life both the "tragic" and the "inevitable" in the life of Wollstonecraft. At the time she wrote the essay, Goldman had been involved for three years in a love affair which she regarded as similar in certain ways to Wollstonecraft's passionate involvement with Imlay. Goldman's lover was Ben Reitman, a flamboyant and irascible doctor from Chicago, ten years younger than she. Like Imlay, Reitman was an American who symbolized for the immigrant Goldman the brashness, exuberance, and "primitive" quality of American life. Just as Imlay was always leaving Wollstonecraft on "business," Reitman too was a restless wanderer (and former hobo) who could not stay peacefully with Goldman for long. Reitman left his medical practice in Chicago in 1908 and for nearly ten years traveled with Goldman for several months each year as manager during her lecture tours. He was very effective in this role, being a talented publicist and promoter (although not an anarchist). Yet their times together were stormy and full of conflict. Although their sexual relationship was intense and satisfying, Goldman felt tormented, not only by Reitman's long absences (he continued to maintain a home in Chicago), but also by his continual infidelities, which he seemed unable or unwilling to control. Despite her perception of him as shallow, narcissistic, and callous, she was obsessed by him with an intensity she occasionally described as "not a healthy thing by any means."[13]

Committed to freedom and independence in love as well as in politics, Goldman found herself feeling bound and enslaved by her passion for Reitman. Unable to explain this obsession with a man of whom her reason disapproved, she generally attributed it to "destiny" or to "ironies of fate." Her erotic dependence on Reitman, and consequent unhappiness, was "inevitable."[14]

Emphasizing the element of fate and destiny in Wollstonecraft's life, Goldman was also describing her own feelings of helplessness before emotional forces she could neither understand nor control. Emphasizing Wollstonecraft's need for love, and the importance of sexuality in her life, Goldman also described her own intense hunger for love, and the pervasive feelings of unsatisfied longing that persisted throughout her life. Her vision of Wollstonecraft's life as "tragic" suggests her sense of her own relationship with Reitman as "a great painful tragedy," but one which she felt powerless to change.

In a larger context, Goldman's emphasis on the "tragic" in Wollstonecraft's life reflects her conception of the "tragedy" of the "emancipated" or "modern" woman which she retained throughout her life. In her essay, "The Tragedy of Woman's Emancipation," first published in 1906, Goldman had criticized the American feminist movement for focusing too narrowly on the "external tyrants" while neglecting the power of the "internal tyrannies" which "seem to get along as beautifully in the heads and hearts of the most active exponents of woman's emancipation, as in the heads and hearts of our grandmothers."[15] Goldman wrote that the narrowness of the modern ideal of emancipation induced women "to make a dignified, proper appearance, while the inner life is growing empty and dead." It had made of her "a compulsory vestal," fearful of love and sexual intimacy. "The tragedy of the self-supporting or econom- ically free woman does not lie in too many, but in too few experiences." Only by "emancipating herself from emancipation," that is, by beginning with her "inner regeneration," and cutting loose "from the weight of prejudices, traditions and customs" that stifled her sexual and emotional life, would she really liberate herself from the chains of the past.

Later in her life, Goldman described this conflict somewhat differ- ently. "The tragedy of all emancipated women, myself included," she wrote in 1925 to her comrade, Alexander Berkman, is that "we are still rooted in the old soil, though our visions are of the future and our desire is to be free and independent."[16] Most of Goldman's activist and radical women contemporaries would probably have rejected her implied assess- ment of their lives as tragic. For the autobiographies and correspondence of women such as Charlotte Perkins Gilman, Elizabeth Gurley Flynn, Jane Addams, Crystal Eastman, and Lillian Wald convey their authors' sense of purpose and deep satisfaction with their lives. Nevertheless, it is Goldman's awareness, not only of the external, objective barriers to emancipation, but also the internal, subjective ones—the power of irra- tional emotions to persist even in the face of clear intellectual awareness of their irrationality—that gives her feminism its significance today. If her sensitivity to the power of sexuality and emotion in her own life caused her to exaggerate—at times—its power in other lives, that same sensitivity also formed the basis of her most compelling feminist insights.

In this light, it is instructive to compare Goldman's portrait of Woll- stonecraft with that of Ruth Benedict, written only a few years later, between 1914 and 1917.[17] For Benedict, Wollstonecraft's story was "that most precious of human documents: the story of a life that achieved an idea." The idea, however, was not an abstraction learned in a study. It was grasped from experience. "She attained to her idea by the rich pro- cesses of living; and the faith which she had laid hold on, she brought again stoutly to its testing in her own experience." Her life was a series of passionate experiments, lived "with all the alertness of her brain fo- cused upon the abrupt experiences of her life." For Wollstonecraft, "life had no axioms; its geometry was all experimental. She was forever testing, probing; forever dominated by an utter unwillingness to accept the pretense, the convention in place of the reality. She reasoned because she must; because a passionately intellectual attitude toward living was her essential tool."

Benedict regarded the *Vindication of the Rights of Woman* as "the main statement of her life idea," an idea which "has become one of the great forces that is shaping our modern world." Yet despite Wollstonecraft's "startling way of 'raising all the questions at once'—religious, economic, sexual and philosophic," Benedict also emphasized the limits of her challenge: her love of domesticity, her approval of marriage, her affection for family life. She "never feared that she was upsetting the balance of society by asking a little elbowroom for women; those unheard-of changes she demanded . . . promised no terrors for her. She knew the world was not so insecurely poised."

In the *Vindication of the Rights of Woman*, Wollstonecraft had regarded love as an "unwelcome intruder." Yet her own life had been profoundly shaped by its vicissitudes. Unlike Goldman, Benedict saw the relationship with Godwin as the culmination of her search for happiness. Wollstonecraft died "in the prime of her maturity, a woman with whom life had gone hard, upon whom fate had loved to play the full gamut of its ironies, but—let us say it in all honor—one who had come to her last resting bed, 'weary and content and undishonored.'"

In the conclusion of her essay, Benedict spelled out the personal meaning of Wollstonecraft to her own life. The contrast between this conclusion and Emma Goldman's reflects more than the difference between the two individual sensibilities. It also illuminates the distance between women of Goldman's generation, culture, and class background, and those of Benedict's. The pessimism of Goldman's essay reflects the constraints imposed upon the female imagination by the conservatism of East European Jewish culture, anti-Semitism, the shock of immigration to America, and the descent from petit-bourgeois to proletarian class status.

"'Girls do not have to learn much!'" Goldman recalled her father telling her as a child. "'All a Jewish daughter needs to know is how to prepare gefüllte fish, cut noodles fine, and give the man plenty of children!'"[18] From her father's perspective, her wishes "to study, to know life, to travel," to marry only for love (or to love and not marry) were simply expressions of disobedience. In his eyes, she became "a loose character" and a "disgrace" to the family. In the context of this world, the revolt of a woman like Wollstonecraft, even to a rebellious daughter like Goldman, appeared an ambivalent challenge: to freedom, intellectual growth, and self-expression, on the one hand; to rejection, inner conflict, and anguish on the other.

Goldman, like Wollstonecraft, was successful in escaping the claustrophobic world represented to her by her parents. She even managed eventually to win their respect and admiration. Still, one senses that she never wholly forgot (or forgave) those early paternal curses, which represented the judgment not simply of one father, but of an entire class and culture. Her ironic sense of herself as the devil's "own child," as someone whose head was "made for a rope, not for a hat," was one legacy of that familial conflict.[19] Her portrayal of Wollstonecraft reflects her confidence that her own revolt had been necessary and legitimate, but also her fear that such audacity and ambition must inevitably be accompanied by tragedy.

The greater optimism of Benedict's essay reflects the expanded sense of possibilities available to women born seventeen years later into the educated American middle class. Benedict's widowed mother was a teacher and librarian who encouraged her daughter's intellectual interests. Benedict attended college and worked as a teacher and social worker, both before and after her marriage, prior to beginning a career as an anthropologist when she was in her thirties. At the time she wrote on Wollstonecraft, Benedict was struggling with the question of how, as a woman married to a man she loved, she could also engage in challenging work. (Neither teaching nor social work satisfied her.) Struggling with the problem of vocation, she wrote in her diary of 1914 of her plan "to steep myself in the lives of restless and highly enslaved women of past generations and write a series of biographical papers from the standpoint of the 'new woman.' My conclusion so far as I see it now is that there is nothing 'new' about the whole thing except the phraseology and the more independent economic standing of recent times—that the restlessness and groping are inherent in the nature of women and this generation can outdo the others long since past only in the frankness with which it acts upon these."[20] Three years later, in 1917, she wrote that she longed "to speak out the intense inspiration that comes to me from the lives of strong women. They have made of their lives a great adventure; they have proved that out of much bewilderment of soul, steadfast aims may . . . [emerge]."[21]

The world in which Benedict had grown up was one in which the lessons of the *Vindication of the Rights of Woman* had begun to be felt, in the form of increased educational and professional opportunities for at least some women. Hopes such as those cherished by Goldman as a child no longer appeared as outrageous assaults on parental authority. The normality of female sexual desire was more openly asserted, as was the legitimacy of women's intellectual and political aspirations.

Within the context of this world, Mary Wollstonecraft was neither as heroic nor as tragic as she had appeared to Goldman. Neither, however, was she as radical. If Goldman had romanticized Wollstonecraft, she nevertheless grasped the radicalism of Wollstonecraft's project, both in life and in thought. In presenting a less heroic, less romantic Wollstonecraft, Benedict also domesticated her. Her goals were more possible because they were more limited. In contrast to Goldman's contradictory portrait, Benedict's more integrated portrayal suggests both the narrowing of vision and the widening of actual possibilities available to her generation and class. To Goldman, Wollstonecraft's challenge had been both personal and political. To Benedict, her challenge was almost entirely personal. Reacting against the conservatism of the middle-class American suffrage movement in the years before World War I, Goldman saw Wollstonecraft as a great historical heroine whose vision was far more radical than that of the suffragists. Identifying herself with that same movement, Benedict saw Wollstonecraft as a contemporary. Goldman's feminism was one aspect of a total ideology of anarchist revolution. The liberation of women involved the transformation of all aspects of society.

For Benedict, feminism seemed to mean liberalizing the structures of marriage, family life, and work. Her comments on Wollstonecraft suggest the boundaries of her own beliefs: "She had more faith in the love of husband and home and children than those have had since then who have feared to shift an ornament or open a window in the house of love, lest it should tumble in ruins." Goldman's feminism was romantic, radical, and revolutionary. Benedict's feminism was practical, liberal, and reformist. Goldman projected into her portrait of Wollstonecraft both her greatest hopes and her worst fears about the possibilities of love and freedom. Benedict saw her hopes confirmed. Her Wollstonecraft was less tormented, in part because Benedict's world was closer to accepting the life of such a woman, but also because the feminist expectations shaped by that world were more limited:

> In the National Portrait Gallery hangs a picture of Mary Wollstonecraft, a picture of her as she was a few scant months before

her death. I remember the child I was when I saw it first, haunted by the terror of youth before experience. I wanted so desperately to know how other women had saved their souls alive. And the woman in the little frame arrested me, this woman with the auburn hair, and the sad, steady, light-brown eyes, and the gallant poise of the head. She *had* saved her soul alive; it looked out from her steady eyes unafraid. The price, too, that life had demanded of her was written ineradicably there. But to me, then, standing before her picture, even that costly payment was a guarantee, a promise. For I knew that in those days when she sat for that picture, she was content. And in the light of that content, I still spell out her life.[22]

That two women as different as Emma Goldman and Ruth Benedict could both look to Mary Wollstonecraft for inspiration suggests, not only the richness of Wollstonecraft's legacy, but also the process by which each generation both discovers and creates its own predecessors. In recreating Wollstonecraft, Goldman inadvertently drew the outlines of her own idealized self-image. Similarly, Benedict portrayed a Wollstonecraft with striking similarities to herself, or to what she hoped to become. It is difficult to know whether or not Benedict or Goldman recognized themselves in these portraits, or whether they were changed by the encounter with Wollstonecraft. In any case, in the attempt to delineate Wollstonecraft for themselves, both women revealed some of their own deepest values, hopes, and fears. In reinventing Wollstonecraft, both Goldman and Benedict were also inventing themselves.

Notes

1. Adrienne Rich, *Of Woman Born* (New York: Norton, 1976), 246.

2. Emma Goldman, "The Tragedy of Woman's Emancipation," *Mother Earth* 1 (March 1906): 10.

3. Mary Wollstonecraft, *A Vindication of the Rights of Woman* (1792; reprint ed., New York: Norton, 1967), n.p.

4. Goldman, "Tragedy," p. 3.

5. Goldman to Ben Reitman, 26 July 1911. Ben Reitman Papers, University of Illinois, Chicago Circle, Library, Chicago, Ill. I am grateful to Candace Falk for first calling my attention to this reference.

6. G. R. Stirling Taylor, *Mary Wollstonecraft: A Study in Economics and Romance* (1911; reprint ed., New York: Haskell House, 1969), 193.

7. Ibid., 110.

8. Goldman to Ben Reitman, June 22, no year, Ben Reitman Papers.

9. Goldman to "friend," 20 February 1909, Ben Reitman Papers.

10. Quoted in Richard Drinnon, *Rebel in Paradise* (1961; reprint ed., New York: Bantam, 1973), 22.

11. See Emma Goldman, *Living My Life* (1931; reprint ed., New York: Dover, 1970), 343.

12. Goldman to Hutchins Hapgood, 23 February 1911. Hutchins Hapgood Papers, Beinecke Rare Book and Manuscript Library, Yale University, New Haven, Conn.

13. Goldman to Ben Reitman, 9 July 1912 and 26 September 1912. Ben Reitman Papers.

14. Goldman to Ben Reitman, 30 December 1909, Ben Reitman Papers.

15. Goldman, "Tragedy," 9–18.

16. Goldman to Alexander Berkman, September 4, 1925, in *Nowhere at Home: Letters from Exile of Emma Goldman and Alexander Berkman*, ed. Richard Drinnon and Anna Maria Drinnon (New York: Schocken, 1975), 128.

17. Ruth Benedict, "Mary Wollstonecraft," in *An Anthropologist at Work: Writings of Ruth Benedict*, ed., Margaret Mead (Boston: Houghton Mifflin, 1959), 491–519.

18. Goldman, *Living My Life*, 12.

19. See Frank Harris, "A Biographical Sketch of Emma Goldman," in *Contemporary Portraits*, 4th ser. (New York: Brentano's, 1923); reprinted in Emma Goldman, *My Disillusionment in Russia* (New York: Thomas Y. Crowell, 1970), xi; and Goldman to Lillian Mendelsohn, 9 September 1938, William Mendelsohn Papers, Laguna Hills, California.

20. Ruth Bennett, "Journals," *An Anthropologist at Work*, 132.

21. Benedict, "Journals," 140.

22. Benedict, "Mary Wollstonecraft," in *An Anthropologist at Work*, 519.

10

Dancing in the Revolution

Emma Goldman's Feminism

Alix Kates Shulman

"In speech after speech, essay after essay, she made clear that woman's oppression was distinct from general economic or political oppression, that some of the restrictions on women's liberty had different causes and consequences than the restrictions on men's liberty, that, in other words, women, because of the institutions of the patriarchal family and puritan morality, were oppressed precisely as women—on top of whatever they suffered as citizens, workers, or being poor. This to me is the heart of a feminist analysis."

Perhaps in our hunger for feminist heroines, we label some figures as "feminist" without sufficient thought about exactly what the title means in different times and varying contexts. Shulman, a feminist figure herself to whom we owe much, especially for her efforts to bring Goldman into political conversation, lays out precisely what she thinks constitutes Goldman's feminism. She differentiates it from feminism today and from other strands of feminism in Goldman's time. It emerges as a complex, well-developed, demanding theory and practice, fully intertwined with anarchism.—*The Editors*

Red Emma Goldman. By the time she was deported to Russia along with 248 others in the shameful Red Scare of 1919, Emma Goldman's name was a household word. In the first decades of this century, the notorious revolutionary was known as the Queen of the Anarchists and the Most Dangerous Woman in the World. During her thirty years as an anarchist agitator, union organizer, free speech activist, and birth control advocate, the notorious Red Emma was feared as a promoter of violence, free love, and anarchy. This outspoken enemy of capitalism, the state, and the family was arrested so often that she never spoke in public without taking along a book to read in jail. The radical journal she founded and edited

This article has benefited greatly from talks with Rosalyn Baxandall, Judith Walkowitz, Meredith Tax, Ann Snitow, and John Ehrenreich.—A.K.S.

for more than a decade, *Mother Earth*, was once suppressed by the government because of an article she wrote on prostitution. A brilliant and fearless speaker, during her career she was arrested uncounted times and three times imprisoned: once for allegedly inciting to riot at a workers' rally, once for instructing a large audience in the use of contraceptives, and once for conspiring, on the eve of World War I, to obstruct the draft. And even after she was deported, she managed to make a comeback to public consciousness in the thirties through her sensational autobiography, *Living My Life*.

Nevertheless, by the time I decided to write about EG a dozen years ago, her books had all long since gone out of print and few people I knew had ever heard her name. But in those same dozen years—years which have seen the rise of the women's liberation movement from a tiny handful of radical feminists to a sprawling, diverse, embattled mass movement—Emma Goldman's name has re-emerged from obscurity to become a veritable password of radical feminism. Her works rose from the limbo of being out of print to the heaven of being available in paperback. EG's face adorns T-shirts, her name headlines posters, her words are repeated on banners. There is an Emma Goldman Clinic for Women in Iowa City, an Emma Goldman Brigade in Chicago, an Emmatroupe in New York City; screenplays have been written and stage plays produced about EG's life in cities from Indianapolis to Denver to Hollywood. Feminists from as far away as Japan and Sweden have come to me searching for material on Emma. EG is now clearly one of the heroes of the women's movement, enshrined as a militant feminist foremother.

To some who have studied the period, this new elevation may seem ironic, for this same Red Emma opposed the women's suffrage campaign, she fought bitterly the social purity doctrines which motivated many feminist reformers; by her own admission she was frequently denounced by other feminists as "an enemy of women's freedom" and "a man's woman," and the movement to which she devoted her life was not the woman's movement at all, but the anarchist movement, a movement which not only paid no special heed to women but was self riddled with the usual sexism.

Re-examining EG's views on women and society after a decade of my own hard-won political education through the women's liberation movement, reflecting on the whole complicated mix of EG's ideas and actions, life and times, I am convinced anew that not only was she a feminist, but in some ways she was one of the most radical feminists of her era.

Of course, like all of us, she was many other things besides. No one will dispute that she was foremost an anarchist. Politically, she was a communist-anarchist. Personally, she was an individualist, a superwoman of sorts. She was a woman who chose not to have children, she was passionate, she was romantic, a woman who placed great personal importance on sexual love with men. Like all of us, she was impatient with certain sorts of behavior and generous in her understanding of other sorts. And all of these factors had their consequences in her particular brand of feminism, and even affected the kinds of mistakes she made. Although it is tempting to declare one or another position not "truly" feminist if it is at odds with one's own position, feminism is not a monolith; there are many different, even at times contradictory, positions which may spring from good feminist motives. Given the best feminist intentions, it is still not always clear which position will most benefit women at a given time. Feminists may even sometimes be wrong. For better or worse, any large political or social movement, powered by passion, must eventually sustain internal debates, divisions, factions, and splits. And although the terms of the debate over what constitutes feminism and who qualifies as a "true" feminist are different now from what they were in the early decades of this century, in many ways they are similar and in some ways even the same. There are and have always been several different important strands of feminist politics. Economic issues, issues of sex and the family, legal and constitutional issues, woman-centeredness; and these strands aggregate in different patterns of overlap and exclusion, depending on the time, the place, and the individuals who embrace them.

Most of us, for example, recognize that the current feminist movement has among its components what some have called bourgeois feminism (embodied in the organization NOW and the publication Ms.), socialist feminism (fairly represented, I think, in such journals as *Feminist Studies*), conservative feminism (surfacing most strongly in the recent anti-pornography movement), radical feminism (evident in many of the small, unnamed consciousness-raising groups of the late sixties and early seventies, though perhaps less visible now), as well as lesbian-separatism, the feminism of women's culture (called in France "neo-femininity"), the woman's studies movement, the woman's health movement, the reproductive rights movement, and many more. And all these different strands unite and split in many different ways over particular issues like ERA, abortion, pornography, protective labor legislation, divorce reform, child custody, etc.

Similarly, in EG's time, the sprawling woman's movement included a myriad of tendencies, including bourgeois feminism, comprising great numbers of mostly middle-class suffragists; the women's trade union movement in which EG was an early organizer; reform feminism (a tendency that historian William O'Neill calls, perhaps misleadingly, social feminism), which embraced the settlement house movement, the woman's club movement, the child labor reform movement, among others. There was also an important strain of conservative feminism, centered around issues of what was called social purity: these feminists were against drink (many of them belonged to the militant WCTU), against pornography, against prostitution, against male lust, and against sex other than for procreation. There was also what I would call radical feminism, a tendency surviving from an earlier time which based its analysis of gender divisions on a radical critique of the family, and often embraced the sexual radicalism of the birth control and Free Motherhood movements.

It would be a mistake to view any of these positions, rooted in the circumstances and political struggles of their day, as either timeless or absolute. They were constantly changing under pressure of new circumstances and alliances. (By the end of the suffrage fight, for example, which had been launched in the nineteenth century by genuinely radical feminists like Elizabeth Cady Stanton and Susan B. Anthony, inglorious compromises had been made with deeply conservative constituencies.) If we are to *understand* any particular group's or individual's politics, instead of simply labeling them, we must try to get underneath their positions on any given issue and probe the principles and motives that lay behind them.

What, then, of Emma Goldman's motives? Where did her thought fit into this messy picture? What was the particular configuration of factors in her position on women? First and most important, she was a sexual radical when it came to women. She rocognized issues of sexuality and the family as absolutely basic to woman's oppression. She honored the importance of not only economic factors, but also socio-sexual issues, like the effect of sexual repression (which she called puritan morality), enforced childbearing, marriage, and the nature of the patriarchal family. "It is Morality," she wrote with a capital M, "which condemns woman to the position of a celibate, a prostitute, or a reckless, incessant breeder of hapless children . . . Religion and morality are a much better whip to keep people in submission than even the club and the gun."[1] And again: "Nowhere is woman treated according to the merit of her work, but rather as a sex. It is therefore almost inevitable that she should pay for her right to exist, to keep a position in whatever line, with sex favors. Thus it is merely a question of degree whether she sells herself to one man, in or out of marriage, or to many men."[2] And of marriage itself, she wrote: "The institution of marriage makes a parasite of woman, an absolute dependent. It incapacitates her for life's struggle, annihilates her social consciousness, paralyses her imagination, and then imposes its gracious protection, which is in reality a snare, a travesty on human character . . . Marriage prepares the woman for the life of . . . a dependent, helpless servant, while it furnishes the man the right of a chattel mortgage over another human life."[3] Clearly, there is something deeper here than a purely libertarian view of sexual freedom or anti-government attack on marriage, though these motives are basic. While her contemporaries were stressing the legal and economic barriers to women's freedom, EG was denouncing what she called the "internal tyrants" that thwart and cripple women. Throughout her two-volume autobiography runs the steady narrative of the injuries dealt her as a woman, by anarchists and others alike. She felt that almost every man she lived with tried in some way to inhibit her activities as unsuitable to her sex; they treated her— even her—as, in her words, a "mere female." In speech after speech, essay after essay, she made clear that woman's oppression was distinct from general economic or political oppression, that some of the restrictions on women's liberty had different causes and consequences than the restrictions on men's liberty, that, in other words, women, because of the institutions of the patriarchal family and puritan morality, were oppressed precisely as *women*—on top of whatever they suffered as citizens, workers, or being poor. This to me is the heart of a feminist analysis. Even professional women and so-called "emancipated" women were in Goldman's view victims of these forces, as were the lowly prostitutes. In her suppressed essay "The Traffic in Women," she wrote: "It would be one-sided and extremely superficial to maintain that the economic factor is the only cause of prostitution. There are others no less important and vital . . . I refer to the sex question, the very mention of which causes most people moral spasms."[4] Of course, she identified the state with its laws and the church with its morality as agents of women's oppression, but she never doubted that sexual and reproductive matters were at the very heart of women's inferior position in society. To my mind, this uncompromising sexual radicalism, on which EG acted repeatedly throughout her life, makes her an indisputable radical feminist, worthy of the recognition she is now widely accorded, though it is hardly the whole of her position on women. Further, it went beyond the sexual radicalism of the bohemian women of her day who practiced free love in Greenwich Village, for, unlike them, EG was always political, fighting to change the social structures that restricted women instead of simply changing her own life.

Ellen Willis, a contemporary radical feminist writer, a founder of Redstockings in the late 1960s, writes in her new collection of essays, *Beginning to See the Light*: "The essence of women's oppression is the denial of our autonomy, particularly in regard to our sexual and reproductive functions; though restrictions on women's access to economic resources have been a major means of keeping us in our place, the object has been less to create a class of specially exploited workers than to ensure our dependence on marriage and subordination to men."[5] It seems to me that this is not far from EG's analysis; on the basis of such an analysis, EG walked out of an international Anarchist Conference in Paris when she was forbidden to deliver a paper on female sexuality, and repeatedly courted arrest by lecturing on birth control and even homosexuality. As Margaret Anderson, editor of the famous *Little Review*, put it, "Emma Goldman was sent to prison for advocating that women need not always keep their mouths shut and their wombs open."

Emma Goldman's major anti-feminist stance, her opponents charged, was her opposition to woman's suffrage. How shall we understand this? In her time, the suffrage movement was predominantly a middle-class movement, at least one great branch of which was deeply conservative, puritanical, and even racist, going so far as to propose literacy tests to keep immigrants and other poor disenfranchised. For EG, whose life had been spent in the struggle of workers and the poor, such a movement would have to be suspect. She once described the English suffrage bill as "a wretched little bill which will benefit a handful of propertied ladies, with absolutely no provision for the vast mass of working women."[6] Even the Socialist Party and certain women labor leaders supported the suffrage only with many misgivings, fearing that the immediate vote for women would in effect increase conservative votes. EG shared such misgivings. Further, as an anarchist who opposed government in all its forms, whether elected or not, who considered all government corrupt and the state the major agent of oppression, she thought the struggle for the vote a diversion from women's real struggle and opposed it. "I am not opposed to Woman Suffrage on the conventional ground that woman is not equal to it. I see neither physical, psychological, nor mental reasons why women should not have the equal right to vote with man. But that cannot possibly blind me to the absurd notion that women will accomplish that wherein man has failed."[7]

It was not only for class reasons or on purely anarchist grounds that she opposed suffrage; arguing from expediency, she also opposed it on the grounds of women's interest. She saw the whole social purity movement, from the Temperance Unions and Prohibition Party to the deeply anti-sexual Purity Leagues, most of which were allied to the suffrage movement, as profoundly inimical to woman's freedom. One of the major arguments advanced in support of suffrage was that women would purify politics if granted the vote. But, wrote Goldman in her essay on Woman Suffrage, "To assume that [woman] would succeed in purifying something which is not susceptible of purification is to credit her with supernatural powers."[8] At best, the vote would be irrelevant for women.

> [Woman's] development, her freedom, her independence, must come from and through herself. First, by asserting herself as a personality, and not as a sex commodity. Second by refusing the right to anyone over her body; by refusing to bear children, unless she wants them; by refusing to be a servant to God, the State, society, the husband, the family, etc., by making her life simpler, but deeper and richer. That is by trying to learn the meaning of substance of life in all its complexities, by freeing herself from the fear of public opinion and public condemnation. Only that, and not the ballot, will set women free.[9]

Goldman acknowledged that some women wanted the vote *in order to* free their sex from bondage to Church, state, and home, and that a few women in the trade union movement supported suffrage as well. But, she argued, the majority of suffragists wanted the vote in order to "make her a better Christian and homemaker and citizen of the State—the very Gods that woman has served from time immemorial."[10] The struggle for the vote, then, seemed to Goldman a diversion, a cooptation of woman's hopes, and a corruption, by way of the enemy, (i.e., government). Her estimate of the practical consequences of the vote, and her hostility to government, unfortunately blinded her to the natural rights arguments in favor of suffrage. But while her active opposition to suffrage was wrong, it was not anti-feminist or anti-woman, for it was based on her desire to see women free. And indeed, her prediction of how little the vote would actually benefit women has turned out to be correct, to this day.

As a role model and exemplar, as a stunning speaker, a star, as an anarchist leader of immense energy and integrity, always willing to go to jail for her principles, Emma Goldman did not escape the problems frequently associated with the superwoman. The impact of the superwoman on women of lesser accomplishment is always ambiguous, double-edged. While she stands as an important example to others of what it is possible to achieve, for ordinary women mired in the structures of daily life, the model of the superwoman may also serve as a rebuke, making her ask herself, what's wrong with me? An anarchist like EG, an individualist concerned not only to change social structures but to live out her principles as well, was sometimes impatient with women who were unable to follow her example. Goldman frequently exhorted people not only to *organize* to resist authority but to change their ways as individuals. One of the main problems with the individualism associated with anarchism is its emphasis on will, so that a failure to change is seen as a failure of the individual will. Thus, sometimes EG seems to blame women, the victims, for their own oppression (as she sometimes seems to blame men, and even workers, for theirs). In her speech on Jealousy, for example, which she insists can be rooted out by will, she says:

> It is only too true that we all smart under the burdens of iniquitous social arrangements, under coercion and moral blindness. But are we not conscious individuals, whose aim it is to bring truth and justice into human affairs? The theory that man is a product of conditions has led only to indifference and to a sluggish acquiescence in these conditions. Yet everyone knows that adaptation to an unhealthy and unjust mode of life only strengthens both, while man, the so-called crown of all creation, equipped with a capacity to think and see and above all to employ his powers of initiative, grows ever weaker, more passive, more fatalistic.[11]

This attitude may seem disingenuous when tempered by some of the facts of EG's personal life. Candace Falk, who has been studying EG's vast correspondence and whose biography of EG will be published next year,[12] has discovered that many of EG's strongest public statements against monogamy, jealousy, etc., were forged in the midst of her own painful battles against the very feelings she denounced. Her speech against jealousy, for example, was composed, reports Falk, during the most jealous phase of one of EG's most important love affairs. This knowledge is hardly shocking, however, given that writers frequently focus on matters of special personal significance; indeed, it helps to humanize the superwoman. But the disparity between EG's statements of her ideals in her writings (which necessarily comprise my main sources here) and her personal struggles to live up to them, however, understandable, could hardly reassure the women she lectured.

It is true that EG does not always identify with women in their struggle, especially middle-class women, and given her great hostility to marriage, especially wives. In her writings, as in her life, there is a peculiar mix of understanding and blame, as in the following passage from her essay "Marriage and Love":

> It is not important whether the husband is a brute or a darling . . . marriage guarantees woman a home only by the grace of her husband. There she moves about in *his* home, year after year, until her aspect of life and human affairs becomes as flat, narrow, and drab as her surroundings. Small wonder if she becomes a nag, petty, quarrelsome, gossipy, unbearable, thus driving the man from the house . . . Married life, complete surrender of all faculties, absolutely incapacitates the average woman for the outside world. She becomes reckless in appearance, clumsy in her movements, dependent in her decisions, cowardly in her judgment, a weight and a bore, which most men grow to hate and despise.[13]

And what, according to EG, is the solution to this state? Defiance and rebellion. Free love and free motherhood, without the sanction of church or state, as she herself has lived. At times she does seem to sympathize with the unfortunate plight of wives and emancipated women alike—as, for example, when she writes with understanding: "It has been conclusively proved that the old matrimonial relation restricted woman to the function of man's servant and the bearer of his children. And yet we find many emancipated women who prefer marriage, with all its deficiencies, to the narrowness of an unmarried life: narrow and unendurable because of the chains of moral and social prejudice that cramp and bind her nature."[14] But at other times she seemed almost to be saying, if you suffer in marriage, it's your own fault for getting married. Leave your husband and be free. If you suffer jealousy, stop seeing your spouse as property. If you suffer loneliness as an emancipated professional woman, go out and practice free love. It was this unfeeling attitude, as well as her position on suffrage, that must have both shocked and angered many feminists.

Here, for example, is the angry response to such a view by another anarchist-feminist, Voltairine de Cleyre, Emma's comrade, also unmarried:

> It has often been said to me, by women with decent masters, who had no idea of the outrages practiced on their less fortunate sisters, "Why don't the wives leave?" Why don't you run, when your feet are chained together? Why don't you raise your hands above your head when they are pinned fast to your sides? Why don't you spend thousands of dollars when you haven't a cent in your pocket? Why don't you go to the seashore or the mountains, you fools scorching with city heat? If there is one thing more than another in this whole accursed tissue of false society which makes me angry, it is the asinine stupidity which with the true phlegm of impenetrable dullness says, "Why don't the women leave!" Will you tell me where they will go and what they shall do? When the State, the legislators, has given to itself, the politicians, the utter and absolute control of the opportunity to live; when through this precious monopoly, already the market of labor is so overstocked that workmen and workwomen are cutting each others' throats for the dear privilege of serving their lords; when . . . seeing and hearing these things reported every day, the proper prudes exclaim, "Why don't the women leave," they simply beggar the language of contempt. . . . There is no society for the prevention of cruelty to women.[15]

You can see, then, that neither sympathy nor hostility to the plight of married women was implicit in anarchist doctrine.

If EG was impatient with middle-class and married women, she nevertheless did identify strongly with the needs and desires of the working-class women she helped to organize. As a trade union organizer in the tradition of bread and roses, she insisted that women ought to earn enough money so that they might be more than mere drudges and have some pleasures in life—roses, books, occasional tickers to the theater, and of course, romantic love. "A so-called independence," she wrote, "which leads only to earning the merest subsistance is not so enticing, not so ideal that one could expect women to sacrifice everything for it."[16] Even as a young revolutionary, she identified with ordinary women's feelings and desires, demanding pleasure in life. When her comrades disapproved of her love of dancing as a frivolity unworthy of a true revolutionary, she grew incensed, retorting that a revolution without dancing, without "beautiful radiant things,"[17] was not worth fighting for.

She had little trouble identifying with working-class women, with the women she met in prison, with the ghetto women she counseled on birth control as a midwife, or with the despised prostitutes. Indeed, she even tried to become a prostitute briefly herself, though without success, and saw the condition of the prostitutes as a paradigm of woman's subordinate position in society, the perfect example of society's blaming the victim. "Society [she wrote" has not a word of condemnation for the man, while no law is too monstrous to be set in motion against the helpless victim. She is not only preyed upon by those who use her, but she is also absolutely at the mercy of every policeman and miserable detective on the beat . . . the authorities in every prison."[18] EG was no more in favor of prostitution than she was in favor of marriage; still, you don't hear her exhorting prostitutes to leave the Life and become file clerks, say, as I heard some middle-class feminists do at a conference on prostitution in 1970. Far from blaming these victims, EG's understanding of their plight was large, her sympathy generous. She identified with prostitutes because of their class and because they defied the sexual hypocrisy of puritanism, as she did herself. That she could not easily identify with middle-class wives, especially those who felt personally threatened by her views, was, I think, less a failure of her feminism or even a function of her anarchism than it was a function of her own desires and an ordinary human failure of imagination.

But even though at times Goldman's anarchism led her to seek solutions in *will* rather than in new social structures, for the most part her anarchism worked *for* her feminism rather than against it. There are certain ways in which anarchism and feminism—at least insofar as feminism is more than simply a movement to help women under capitalism get ahead—seem to me to have a certain affinity. Though the two movements have quite different histories, arriving at their positions through different routes, certain basic analogies between them hold up. Anarchism by definition, and radical feminism as it has evolved, are both fundamentally and deeply anti-hierarchical and anti-authoritarian. Both operate through loose, voluntary social organization from the bottom up, relying on collective activity by small groups, forming, for example, day care centers, battered-women shelters, anti-rape squads, consciousness-raising groups, rather than, say, large political parties; and both favor direct action to promote change. As the anarcho-feminist Lynn Farrow wrote a few years ago, "Feminism practices what Anarchism preaches."

To what parts of our own women's movement does EG's feminism chiefly appeal? EG was an anarchist. Her vision was of a world in which *everyone* would be free of the tyrannies of capitalism, patriarchy, church, and state. Though she understood the pressures and conditions under which women uniquely suffered, and repeatedly fought anarchist men who refused to acknowledge the importance of the sex question (including the great international anarchist leader Peter Kropotkin himself), she saw all those tyrannies as mutually supporting, and none really the kingpin. In this way she differs from those feminists who see woman's oppression as somehow prior to every other sort. Goldman fought them all. The fight itself was central to her politics; she was ever militant. Indeed, it may be as much for her own militancy as for her views that she is admired by radical feminists today;—especially today, when feminism seems to be growing softer, safer, less political. Just as EG herself admired the militant English suffragists the Pankhursts, who put themselves in chains, went on hunger strikes, and endured forced feeding for their cause, though she thought their efforts misguided, so we admire Goldman. As for our own contemporary cultural feminists whose vision of woman-as-flower is more marked by retreat than struggle, EG would probably be impatient with them—even though she herself sometimes invoked the concept of "women's nature."

Her main quarrel with her own women contemporaries was that she steadfastly refused to see women as inherently either better or worse than men. If male egotism, vanity, and strength operated to enslave women, it was partly, she argued, because women themselves idolized those qualities in men, creating a self-perpetuating system. When women changed their consciousness, broke that circle, and freed themselves from such ill-suited ideals, they might then "incidentally" also help men to become free, she wrote.[19] But it was up to women to make their revolution. The line here between blaming the victim and recognizing the necessity for a new consciousness is thin but crucial. In one of her most frequently quoted remarks, one that has been invoked in the name of consciousness-raising and even of the women's liberation movement itself, Goldman insists on complexity and struggle: "True emancipation begins neither at the polls nor in courts. It begins in woman's soul. History tells us that every oppressed class gained true liberation from its masters through its own efforts. It is necessary that woman learn from that lesson, that she realize that her freedom will reach as far as her power to achieve her freedom reaches."[20] Women should start taking responsibility for their own lives, instead of trying to improve or purify men. That women were no worse than men meant that with struggle they could become self-determining. "Since woman's great misfortune has been that she was looked upon as either angel or devil, her true salvation lies in being placed on earth; namely in being considered human."[21] This is the essence of Emma Goldman's feminist vision as it must be of ours.

Notes

1. "Victims of Morality" in Alix Kates Shulman, ed., *Red Emma Speaks: Selected Writings and Speeches of Emma Goldman* (New York: Random House, 1972), 128–129.

2. "Traffic in Women," in ibid., 145.

3. "Marriage and Love," in ibid., 164–165.

4. Ibid., 149.

5. Elln Willis, *Beginning to See the Light* (New York: Alfred A. Knopf, 1981), xviii.

6. "Woman Suffrage," in Emma Goldman, *Anarchism and Other Essays* (New York: Dover Books, 1969), 206.

7. *Anarchism*, p. 198.

8. Ibid.

9. Ibid., 211.

10. Ibid., p. 197.

11. *Red Emma Speaks*, 174.

12. Candace Falk, *Love, Anarchy, and Emma Goldman* (New York: Holt, Rinehart & Winston, forthcoming, 1983).

13. *Red Emma Speaks*, 163–64.

14. "The Tragedy of Women's Emancipation," in ibid., 139.

15. Voltairine de Cleyre, *Selected Works* (New York: Mother Earth, 1914), 351–52.

16. "Tragedy," 136.

17. Emma Goldman, *Living My Life* (New York: Alfred A. Knopf, 1931), 56.

18. "Traffic in Women," 152.

19. *Living My Life*, 556–57.

20. "Tragedy," 142.

21. "Woman Suffrage," 189–99.

11

Speaking with Red Emma:

The Feminist Theory of Emma Goldman

Loretta Kensinger

"She challenges us by always keeping the individual and individual freedom in the center of any ethical vision of community. . . . Goldman's work provides us with a unique bridge between the past, present, and future of feminism's most radical visions."

Building on Shulman's analysis, Kensinger expands our understanding of Goldman's feminism by viewing it through lenses provided by more contemporary scholars. In the first section, Charlotte Bunch's four-part model of feminist theory allows us to zoom in on four simple questions: What is the world Goldman describes, particularly for women? What is her analysis of how this world comes to be? What is her vision of what women's lives could be? And what strategies does Goldman provide for getting to that vision? Lest we risk "heroification" of this vital woman's ideas, the second section explores the tensions and complexities that emerge in Goldman's feminist vision and practice. In the final section, bell hooks's notion of liberatory practice is employed to once more reframe Goldman's feminist ideas. Using hooks, Kensinger shows that Goldman's feminism is both grounded in the conditions and concerns of her own historical era and capable of still speaking to us in powerful and healing ways.—*The Editors*

Bridging the Gap in Time and Place

I encountered Emma Goldman as a young adult woman, in my early graduate career, just as I was discovering feminist theory. I was thrilled. Here was a woman who gave voice to my post-hippy-inspired desire for free and open love, a woman who had no illusions that the effort to implement ideology was easy, and a woman who was willing to expose her own personal struggle against the "internal tyrants" of past experi-

This essay would not have been possible without the support provided by a California State University, Fresno, Affirmative Action Faculty Development Program Award 2001/2002. Thanks are also due to the Wonder Women Writers, particularly Mary Coomes and Theresia Rogerson, for encouragement and feedback, and to Lynn Jacobsson for writing space.

ence—jealousy, anger, a desire for recognition—to bring these ideals to life. I drew courage from her as I worked to integrate and implement my growing feminist consciousness. As I turned a turbulent forty, on the heels of a cynically stolen presidential election, facing terrifying renewed international and nationalistic crises, accompanied by multiple losses in my own personal life, I returned to study this inspiration of my youth. As before, Goldman's life seemed to have something personal to say relevant to today. I admired how she kept moving forward in the face of incredible adversity and of great changes in the social world, changes that left her a spokesperson for a once vibrant international movement whose salience with progressives was in decline. As I entered my seventh year working in various capacities to implement feminism within higher education, I found myself moved by the depth of her effort to retain her "beautiful ideal," by her ability to avoid cynicism, and by her perseverance. But I also became aware that for myself, and for others, Emma Goldman for too long had remained a predominately symbolic figure. In the midst of this new postmodern century, carrying all the unresolved burdens of the past two centuries of modernity, in this middle age of life, it was time to take her seriously as a thinker. Here I want to explore her rich and complex contributions to feminist thought.

There are at least four challenges confronting me as I attempt to lay out the feminism of Emma Goldman. First, there is the problem of idolizing the life of this remarkable woman in a way that erases her humanity and complexity. As I move to engage her work with the serious reflection it so richly deserves, I struggle with how to come to terms with my own admiration while embracing the complex life and ideas of such a personally and socially important, yet iconic, figure. Second, there is the challenge of looking back from today, presenting the danger of erasing the sheer radical foundations of her ideas. Third, there is the commonly held judgment of her ideas that she is an unoriginal thinker, an unsystematic or emotional thinker, or a thinker who failed to address the means of moving toward her goals. Fourth, I am confronted with the dilemmas inherent in attempting to consolidate a definition of such a complex and disparate idea as "feminism." What, after all, is feminism either for the anarchist Goldman or for us? Staying cognizant of these challenges, in this chapter, I introduce a few of the central, as well as unique, elements of Goldman's feminism; explore some of its tensions; and use bell hooks's notion of liberatory theory to reexamine ways that Goldman's feminism remains healing. Goldman can in many ways serve as an important link between the radical politics and realities between the turn of two centuries. Accused of being the "most dangerous women in America," she was among the first people deported from the United States for political reasons. She challenges us by always keeping the individual and individual freedom in the center of any ethical vision of community. For Goldman the communal individual is both a material corporal reality (namely, Goldman as embodied person; revolutionists as they live; current constructions of life options) and an idealized form (the person after the revolution; the potential person). Spanning the individual and the community, the material and the ideal, Goldman's work provides us with a unique bridge between the past, present, and future of feminisms' most radical visions.

Red Feminist Emma

The project of outlining a basis of anyone's feminism is one fraught with limitations, since the concerns of most feminists—including Goldman—extend well beyond any narrow reduction to what some might call "women's issues." Further, feminism and feminist theory are complex entities and no solitary or single definition of either can capture their diversity. I cannot hope in a short chapter to contextualize adequately the work of a feminist within her time or explain fully our desire to understand her within our time. After noting that feminism, both in Goldman's time and ours, is multivaried and multifaceted, Shulman rejects "simply labeling" Goldman's politics, in order to "try to get underneath [her] positions on any given issue and probe" what "lay behind them" (1998, 7). Like Shulman I do not want to get trapped in the process of defining feminism in advance of letting feminism emerge from Goldman's work, nor do I want to hold her accountable to standards not reflective of her own period. However, I do think some grounding is helpful, serving as a tool to guide our analysis of Goldman's ideas. Charlotte Bunch, in her essay "Not by Degrees: Feminist Theory and Education" (2000), develops a four-part model for exploring feminist theory. Bunch asserts that all feminist theory, to be most useful, should allow us to describe reality, analyze its causes, develop a vision, and lay out strategies for achieving that vision (13–14). Her model provides a useful set of questions to ground this analysis. How does Goldman describe the world of women and men? What is her analysis of the reality she sees for women? What vision of a changed world did she carry? What strategy did she propose to use to get to that vision?

The literature on Goldman often simply asserts that she is a feminist. For example, the back cover of Theresa and Albert Moritz's *The World's Most Dangerous Woman: A New Biography of Emma Goldman* (2001) includes the description of the book as a biography on the "the feminist and anarchist Emma Goldman." The back cover of Candace Falk's *Love, Anarchy, and Emma Goldman* (1990) describes Goldman "as a social and labor reformer, revolutionary, anarchist, feminist, agitator for free love and free speech, and advocate of birth control." Further, in his article "Whatever Happened to 'Red Emma'? Emma Goldman, from Alien Rebel to American Icon" (1996), Oz Frankel discusses Emma Goldman as an icon, noting her appeal to various audiences and pointing to her reclamation as a "a precursor of modern feminism."[1] While Frankel might find that Shulman's 1982 analysis "problematizes not just Goldman's status among feminist heroines but implicitly the function and even the possibility of any 'role model' in a post radical era" (Frankel 1996, 929), in 1998 Shulman leaves no doubt that she views Goldman as a feminist and role model. Shulman states that in "re-examining Goldman's views on women and society . . . I am convinced anew that not only was she a feminist, but in some ways she was one of the most radical feminist of her era" (4–5). Additionally, the Web site for the Emma Goldman Papers Project asserts that Goldman "stands as a major figure in the history of American radicalism and feminism." There is, apparently, little doubt that Goldman is a feminist. Why people would come to the conclusion that Goldman is a feminist seems to be firmly grounded in her work. A quick glance at her writing shows she addressed issues at the heart of twentieth-century feminism. For example, among her speeches and essays published in *Anarchism and Other Essays* (Goldman 1969) are titles such as "The Tragedy of Woman's Emancipation" (212–25), "The Traffic in Women" (177–94), and "Marriage and Love" (226–39). Further, Goldman was a pioneering advocate of reproductive rights and was arrested for violating the Comstock Act by distributing birth control information. She was a mentor in the early work of Margaret Sanger, though Sanger did not espouse anarchism in her later work (Glassgold 2001). While this discussion shows us that Goldman is often considered a feminist, and provides grounding for why she is so labeled, we still must dig deeper to understand the content of her feminism.

Goldman hammers out the complex, sometimes critical, link between gender and radical revolutionary politics. Her feminism is intricately entwined within her anarchist thought and she consistently recognizes the unique position and challenges women face in relation to questions of liberty and freedom. While other anarchists and radicals certainly considered "the woman question," Goldman pushed this analysis further, by critically linking the radical and labor movements, and the women in these movements, with the more radical elements of the women's movement. It is no small wonder, then, that Rebecca West, journalist, socialist, and feminist, was among her supporters during Goldman's exiled stay in England. While Goldman finds that women's work in both productive and reproductive labor is often devalued in the radical movements, she also continually emphasizes women's agency in her critiques of the women's movement, indeed often celebrating women's unique roles in human community. Women are certainly not merely victims within her assessment of the world. And a central element of Goldman's contributions is her emphasis on gender as an experience grounded in material realities of life. As a materialist, Goldman recognizes the diversity in women's experiences. She consistently describes a world where some women (as well as men) benefit at the expense of the majority of others.

It is her firm recognition of the class differences between women that brings Goldman to a complex analysis of the failures of the politics of the mainstream women's movement of her day. She is scathing in her assessment of this movement's shortcomings. In both "Woman Suffrage" and the "Tragedy of Women's Emancipation," she argues against the popular view that the extension of the vote to women would moralize politics (1969). The extension of the vote to anyone, she asserts, had never moralized politics. Women, divided by class interest as much as men, would not have similar interests when employing the vote any more than men had. Women would vote with their class/economic and religious/moral interests. Goldman relies on evidence from places where women had the vote to show that class interests still dominated politics. She brings to this socialist analysis her anarchist observation that women's traditional link to a conservative sense of morality has meant that women's vote led to harsh attacks on civil liberties. In her autobiography, Goldman asserts that the women's movement leaders of her day did not see her as an ally; she reports that in response to some of her talks women's movement supporters "would rise up against me and cry" 'you're a man's woman and not one of us" (1970, vol. 2, 557). But careful analysis of her criticisms shows that they are grounded not in a rejection of the movement, but in a rejection of what she considered to be its bourgeois tendencies: tendencies antithetical to her commitment to socialist anarchy, tendencies that she consistently asserted would not free women.

That she was, in fact, committed to an alternative feminist politics that diverged from mainstream radical and women's movements of the period is evident in a number of places. For Shulman (1988), Goldman is first and foremost a feminist because "she was a sexual radical when it came to women. She recognized issues of sexuality and the family as absolutely basic to women's oppression. She honored the importance of not only economic factors, but also socio-sexual issues" (7). We can see on a deep and personal level both the radical basis of Goldman's critique of the women's movement and her support of the need for women to be free in her sympathetic analysis of the work of Mary Wollstonecraft. Goldman remarks:

> The woman's movement of today and especially the suffrage movement will find in the life and struggle of Mary Wollstonecraft much that would show them the inadequacy of mere external gains as means of freeing their sex. No doubt much has been accomplished since Mary thundered against women's economic and political enslavement, but has that made her free? Has it added to the depth of her being? Has it brought joy and cheer in her life? Mary's own tragic life proves that economic and social rights for women alone are not enough to fill her life, nor yet enough to fill any deep life, man or woman. She understood only too well that mere political changes are not enough and do not strike deep into the evils of Society. (1988, 253)

Additionally, near the end of her essay "Woman Suffrage," we find Goldman celebrating the anniversary of the Seneca Falls Convention: "What wonderful accomplishments, what wonderful triumphs!" After noting the changes in the sixty some years since Seneca Falls, Goldman adds, "All that without suffrage, without the right to make laws, without the "privilege" of becoming a judge, a jailer, or an executioner" (1969, 210).

A pattern emerges from this analysis. While sexuality and family are the central concerns in her analysis of women's position, Goldman believes that legal changes, and tinkering with economics, while not unimportant to women, would not free them. In her celebration of the achievement at Seneca Falls, we see that Goldman finds that women's organizing is important, and in calling attention to the progress since that convention she tacitly supports the legal changes that undergird women's newfound professional and economic freedom. But while she celebrates such changes, she seeks deeper, more meaningful changes in women's lives. Both her analysis of Wollstonecraft and that in "Woman Suffrage" reveal that Goldman, as an anarchist, takes issue with women's attempts to claim power through laws and courts. She recognizes that equality is not liberty and that equality in a corrupt system, while certainly possible, will not lead to liberty. She uses anarchist and socialist ideas to push the mainstream women's movement to expand its scope by recognizing both the power of class as well as the flaws in overemphasizing political reforms as a means to bring long-lasting change to women's lives.

Further, anticipating later feminist analysis of consciousness and consciousness-raising, we see in her analysis of Wollstonecraft that a central principle in her notion of freedom for women is grounded in psychological change. In assessing the family and sexuality, Goldman's feminist theory includes a concrete analysis of power and social structures, but moves beyond social structures to provide a critique of what we might today call the process of internalization, what Goldman called the "internal tyrants." Her critique of these internal constraints on women, and women's collusion in those constraints, presents another major component of Goldman's critique of women's emancipation in her day. In "Woman Suffrage" Goldman states that women would gain freedom not by the vote but "by trying to learn the meaning and substance of life in all its complexities, by freeing herself from the fear of public opinion and public condemnation" (1969, 211). Thus, for Goldman, a major aspect of feminism must be providing women with the strength to stand against social conventions, conventions that she sees as a linchpin in the foundations of social structures that determine women's fate by constricting their life choices and options.

At the heart of Goldman's feminism is women's struggle to be independent, authentic individuals. Thus the struggle for women is, at heart, an anarchist struggle. But, as Shulman reminds us, Goldman's anarchist struggle is not merely some rugged individualism devoid of community. Goldman is, after all, a socialist anarchist. She believes that freeing individuals of the constraints of structures and ideologies not of their own determination leads to creation of a society built on communal and participatory praxis. Wexler notes the ways in which this attitude is revealed within Goldman's biography: "Despite her insistent emphasis on the individual, Emma Goldman was concerned, above all, with individuality, not individualism. She was opposed to conformity, not to collectivity, and she sought all her life to create a community hospitable to the dissenter and the rebel" (1989, 153). In a 1926 piece article for the *Rochester Times-Union* these elements of Goldman's thought are further exposed. Goldman starts by noting that many of her early ideas had been borne out by time, particularly her assertions of the shallowness of the belief that the women's vote would lead to a purifying of politics, and she remarks that mainstream feminists no longer made claims about women's moralizing influence on the political world. However, in this article Goldman tempers her earlier analysis by noting that the broader women's movement was not in "vain": "Many factors have contributed to create the modern type of woman, the most vital factor being sex solidarity among women. Necessity taught them at an early stage in their struggle that the slave has never been freed by his master that his emancipation could only be brought about by the spirit of solidarity between his fellow slaves. So, too, the solidarity of sex among women has, I think been a tremendous impetus and encouragement in their struggle to assert themselves in their right to their place in the world—their right to be themselves" (Goldman, 1926, col. 3).

In the end, Goldman found the struggle for emancipation, while sometimes misguided, still worthwhile, because of the solidarity it generated among women, a point underemphasized in accounts of Goldman's feminism. When Goldman praises women for coming to a sense of similarity of experiences as a sex, we see the emphasis on collectivity noted by Wexler. Further, Goldman's recognition of the need for "solidarity of sex" contradicts a rigidly individualistic interpretation of Goldman's anarchism. In Goldman's view the process of emancipation was flawed when it did not take into account both individual freedom and internal tyrants. She, however, also saw that emancipation required group identification.

Another important element, also underplayed in most accounts of Goldman's anarchism, and by extension her feminism, is its deeply internationalist and multicultural nature. The depth of her transnational concerns with diversity is seen in the examples she draws on in speeches and essays; in the breadth of her organizing activities; in the range of contributions reflected in the articles found in the magazine put out by Goldman and Alexander Berkman, *Mother Earth*; and in the topics as well as addressees of her vast correspondence (Drinnon and Drinnon

1975; Falk, Pateman, and Moran, 2003; Glassgold 2001; Goldman 1969). A few of the more unique examples of this overlooked aspect of her thinking again reveal the complexity, depth, and range of both her transnational and multicultural analyses.

For example, antinationalism is a central concern to Goldman's ideas of anarchism. Her views are reiterated in a letter written from Paris to Ben Capes, dated February 16, 1927, which opens with a discussion of the idea of striving to create a Jewish state in response to anti-Semitism. Goldman writes, "And more than ever the last years have convinced me that there is no hope for mankind so long as they are divided through boundaries and blinded by their nationalistic view" (Drinnon and Drinnon, 1975, 71). "It is certain," continues Goldman, "that the moment the Jews will have their own state, they will become as reactionary and centralistic as all other nations" (71). She reiterates this belief to Berkman in a letter from Montreal of February 12, 1935, in which she critically, if briefly, assesses the rise in anti-Semitism as well as the nationalist aims of Zionism. Having sent an article clipping that links anti-Jewish feeling to economics, she notes, "But there is so much more to anti-Semitism, tradition of centuries, ingrained antipathies, and what not. I don't see how that is going to be done away with even in a free society. Witness Russia. One thing is certain, Palestine won't. There is already as much disagreement and antagonism in Palestine among the Jews as outside of it" (114–15). We see here that she recognizes the psychological depths ingrained within human intolerance, as well as the limits of structural change for extracting such prejudice, even as she reinforces her transnational and antinationalist philosophy. In this discussion we see both her intense antinationalism and her complex respect for transnational movements of liberation. Both are revealed further in her statements on Gandhi's struggles, on which she commented in a June 29, 1928, letter to Berkman from St. Tropez (87), and in a letter to Henry Alsberg from Nice dated March 24, 1931 (99). Goldman's feminism is not only linked to transnational, global, anti-imperialist movements; her vision also recognizes the importance of both cultural and sexual diversity as central questions of human freedom. She sees a connection between liberation and sexual freedom not only for women: her analysis of Walt Whitman and her discussion of responses to her lectures on homosexuality confirm the seriousness with which she treated the issue of sexual freedom for all people. Writing to Evelyn Scott from Toronto on November 21, 1927, Goldman positively accredits Whitman's literary originality to his gayness: "The fools do not seem to realize that Walt Whitman's greatness as a rebel and poet may have been conditioned in his sexual differentiation, and that he could not be otherwise than what he was" (141). She lectured on homosexuality and defended Oscar Wilde (1970, 2:555–56, 1:269). We see in each of these examples that while our places within a culture and the history of our different cultures need to be historically accounted for, Goldman recognized great dangers in the process of coming to such group identity when the individual was not accounted for. What she called "mob think" could lead to blind prejudice and nationalism, both antithetical to her belief in anarchy.

A complex vision of a better world emerges from Goldman's understanding and analysis. Shulman concludes that ultimately anarchism "worked for" Goldman's feminism, noting the affinity in the two movements (1998, 16–17). For Goldman feminism could not be divorced from anarchism; the struggle was one in the same; it was not just for women, but for a better and different society. Shulman finds that Goldman's appeal to contemporary feminists is located in Goldman's broader vision that "*everyone* would be free" and in Goldman's militancy in putting forward this vision (17). Shulman suggests that while "the line . . . between blaming the victim and recognizing the necessity for a new consciousness is thin," it is still "crucial" because it points to Goldman's insistence on both "complexity and struggle" (18). In the end, she quotes Goldman's statement "Since woman's great misfortune has been that she was looked upon as either angel or devil, her true salvation lies in being placed on earth: Namely in being considered human" (18–19). Again, this statement revels the complexity of Goldman's analysis in that it hints at the problem that dichotomies have posed for women, an area of critique that would occupy much of feminism's theoretical space after the women's liberation struggles in the later half of the twentieth century. Shulman ends her discussion by noting, "This is the essence of Emma Goldman's feminist vision as it must be ours" (19). While feminism, anarchism, and economic socialism are central components in her thinking, Goldman continually and critically reassesses the meaning of these concepts throughout her lifetime.

Interestingly, Goldman prioritizes vision over strategy in her theory. As an anarchist, she is reluctant to lay out a grand strategic scheme, partly because of her belief that each individual and community will need to find its own strengths and means of contributing to society. Further, believing in the power of the moment, she also believes in the need for flexibility regarding localized needs and communities. While she is reluctant to lay out a precise strategy for getting to the feminist and anarchic ideal world, she clearly and quite consistently does promote certain types of action. For example, while critical of organized labor, she consistently supports labor movements and strikes. And she speaks throughout her career to the power of freeing education from the confines of arbitrary rules (Goldman 1969, 145–66). In all her activities, a strategy that emerges as central to her theoretical ideals is seen in her firm commitment to direct action.

Goldman's view of direct action includes a varied response to the use of violence. She was a Russian immigrant who, according to her autobiography, was attracted to Russia's strong tradition of *attentat*, radical individual acts of political courage. In Russian revolutionary thinking, these acts were performed to inspire courage in the masses by demonstrating the power of one individual to rise up against formidable odds. In assessing any act of revolutionary violence, regardless of whether it is judged strategically useful or a failure, Goldman insists, we must seek to understand the context of state and economic violence that motivates such action. This complex view is particularly evident in the controversy that erupted in the anarchist community over Leon Czolgosz's assassination of President William McKinley. Despite a brutal public and government attack on anarchists, forcing Goldman to live underground for a period, she consistently refused to condemn Czolgosz for his action, seeking instead to reveal its motivation in the context of an unjust world (1970, 1:295–334).

Over time a subtle shift emerges in Goldman's thinking about violence (Shulman 1998, 251–54). A unique and instructive example of this shift is provided in a letter to Berkman from St. Tropez dated June 29, 1928 in which she attempts to help him address the question of whether the revolution has a "right to defend itself":

> Certainly, if you believe that no fundamental change can take place without a revolution you must also believe in its right of defense. It is only Tolstoy's or Gandhi's position which would make it inconsistent to take up arms in defense of the revolution. I wish I could take their positions. Emotionally, I really do. I feel violence in whatever form never has and probably never will bring constructive results. But my mind and my knowledge of life tell me that changes will always be violent. At least I want to elimi-

nate as much as possible the need for violence. I want the revolution to be understood as a process of reconstruction rather than
what we believed it to be until now, a process of destruction. But
no matter how much we will try, the change is bound to be violent and [we] will need to be ready for defense. (Drinnon and
Drinnon 1975, 87)

For Goldman, direct action moves well beyond the *attentat* and includes
an insistence that we embody the revolution within lived experience,
bringing one's life into accord with one's analysis. This moves the revolution from a distant goal to a quotidian series of actions and resistance.
For Goldman, the end of the revolution cannot be known, it can only be
lived. She embodied this ideal by using the most public and personal of
means to communicate her ideas to her audiences, discussed in more
detail below. In Goldman's hands, speaking itself became an important
strategic component, a strategy similar to the notion of "speaking truth
to power" that was popularized in later radical movements.

The preceding points provide us with resources with which to create
a broad understanding of Goldman's feminism. Her feminism embraces
women's sexuality and bodies, women's individual will, and women's
need to engage in active resistance. Her feminism involves reflection on
our personal life choices at the same time as it accounts for the social
world. It is a feminism that recognizes women's own position as a part of
current power relations, does not excuse women's actions that perpetuate
the positions of power in society, and expects women to alter their lives
to bring them in line with their demands for equality. For Goldman,
women will not be freed through asking for freedom. Women will become
free through their own power. Revolution for women means first and
foremost freeing our minds by moving now to assert our own desires and
wills. But revolution would occur not only within our minds. An important factor in women's struggle for revolution is women's recognition of
the need to join in common cause. Goldman's theoretical outlook is internationalist, linking social struggles across the globe, particularly those
against the power of the state, capitalism, and religion. She sees multiple
strategies as necessary for moving toward her revolutionary vision; involving living one's life in line with the vision one seeks; endeavoring to
bring change forward through education; seizing key moments of contradiction through direct action; and recognizing political violence as a necessary, indeed likely, component of change.

Tensions, Complexities, and Contradictions

James Loewen, in Lies My Teachers Told Me (1995), describes the process of heroification, whereby real-life flesh-and-blood individuals are transformed into flat heroes—divorced from shortcomings, internal conflict, doubts, mistakes, and unpopular opinion. Beyond historical inaccuracy, and boredom, Loewen draws out at least two other dangers in heroification. First, the process deprives us of role models as we face contemporary struggles; humans cannot emulate idols. Second, the messy ideals these "heroes" advocated within their life become sanitized, decontextualized, or disappeared, making it impossible to discuss critically notions of human agency and responsibility. Adding insights specifically related to Goldman, Oz Frankel, in "Whatever Happened to 'Red Emma'? Emma Goldman, from Alien Rebel to American Idol" (1996), discusses the danger of deradicalizing the ideas and lives of historical figures as they are reclaimed by later generations. For Frankel, "Goldman's posthumous career presents not merely another example of the malleability of memory, collective or other, but also a clear trajectory: An incredible journey from the militant fringes of the extreme Left, from exile, to a safer place approaching the political center or, if you wish, the Americanization of the un-American" (904). Frankel does not argue that the journey of "Americanization" is necessarily conservative, or that the "guises under which she has been remembered are an affront" (941). However, Frankel does believe that "in the effort to win her a place in the national pantheon there has been little discussion of the more controversial elements of her legacy" (941). This fits well with Loewen, who in ending his discussion of heroification notes that we need heroes, but we need them with all their flaws and fullness, including the context, richness, change, and justifications of their ideas. In this way, heroes help us learn how to cope with our own limitations as we see how they struggled to cope with their own. Only attention to the details and openness to the problems and contradictions of Goldman's thought will be fair to her, a woman who was so critical of others and demanded so much from humans in the name of ideology. Only then will her struggles be useful to us as lessons in the ability of human beings to grapple with ideals in the messy world of their real lives. When read today, Goldman's ideas, as Frankel warns, are rife with controversial challenges and tensions. I will touch on only a few here, but enough to show the need for context in understanding the complexity of Goldman's ideas.

As we look at Goldman from our own understandings of feminism, her work is often jarring in its immersion in the highly troubling language that was then prevalent in academic and activist discourse. There is a deep tendency in Goldman to use language that appears to naturalize women's roles. When she talks about women's nature she seems to include a variety of meanings, often among them sexuality and passion. While she does celebrate women's moves to embrace some attributes she perceives as male, she also celebrates women's roles as mothers and as situated within the home in ways we might now read as essentializing, even as she works against this tendency by claiming women's rights to control the conditions of motherhood. Indeed, in a very conflicted section of "Woman Suffrage," Goldman laments women's attempts to compete with men in traditionally male roles: "Oh I know some have succeeded, but at what cost, at what terrific cost! The import is not the kind of work woman does, but rather the quality of the work she furnishes"(1969, 210). But she concludes this essay by also noting that woman's "development, her freedom, her independence, must come from and through herself. First by asserting herself as a personality, and not as a sex commodity. Second, by refusing the right to anyone over her body; by refusing to bear children, unless she wants them; by refusing to be a servant to God, the State, Society, the husband, the family, etc, by making her life simpler, but deeper and richer" (211). In some sense, we see reflected in Goldman's writing the tensions between a maternal and materialist analyses of women's position in society that is found in much feminist analysis of the day, and a tension also reflected in now-current conflicts between cultural and poststructuralist feminisms (among others, see Alcoff 1988).

Goldman's rhetorical choices, while imbuing her work alternately with romanticism and humor, often undercut her vision. For example, Goldman at times relies on praise or condemnation rather than argumentation to build her case, describing ideas that are useful in promoting individual and collective liberation as "progressive" or "advanced," while concepts not meeting her often quite rigid standards are dismissed as "backward" and "primitive." Martha Solomon in her 1988 "Ideology as Rhetorical Constraint: The Anarchist Agitation of 'Red Emma'" has developed perhaps the most sustained critique of the rhetorical limits of Goldman's theory. In an insight that is not too surprising to anyone who has read Goldman's work, Solomon finds that "to reinforce her arguments which developed perspective by incongruity, Goldman regularly used rhetorical techniques that heightened her assessments. Hyperbole, or overstatement is a recurrent characteristic of her attacks on social institutions" (189). Solomon notes, for example, Goldman's tendency to make "no distinctions among varieties of religions" in Goldman's critiques of the power of these institutions (189). Regarding Goldman's rhetoric, Solomon also mentions how "in the same way, Goldman's ideological commitment led her to adopt a caustic sarcasm in discussing issues" (189).

While Goldman provides a deep and profound analysis of the way women's life choices are constricted by economic realities and social and religious mores, and celebrates some of the movement made by women toward coming to understand their communal interests, in her analysis of the women's movement of her day she often overemphasized women's ability to control situations in which they found themselves. For Shulman, many of the problems within Goldman's understandings of feminism stemmed from Goldman's emphasis on "free will," which led sometimes to victim-blaming postures. Particularly troubling in this regard is Goldman's tendency to exaggerate women's responsibility for the construction of men's power in women's lives. In her autobiography Goldman recalls one speech on the topic of "feminism" in which she referred to man as the "under dog" (1970, 2:556). She relates that she "resented her sex's placing every evil at the door of the male" and argues that who men are is in no small part a result of their mothers' influence. In concluding this section of the autobiography, she remembers arguing that "woman is naturally perverse . . . ; from the very birth of her male child until he reaches a ripe age, the mother leaves nothing undone to keep him tied to her." She continues, "It is really woman's inhumanity to man that makes him what he is. When she has learned to be as self-centered and as determined as he, when she gains the courage to delve into life as he does and pay the price for it, she will achieve her liberation, and incidentally also help him become free" (557). Troubling sentiments indeed.

But is she really to be interpreted as saying that it is women—not capitalism, not religion—that are the heart of men's status in society? Is she really asserting that women must become men to be free? If we look to her essays for guidance, a more complex understanding of these statements emerges. In "The Tragedy of Women's Emancipation," for example, Goldman recognizes man's own role in the creation of the dilemma in which women exist: "The average man with his self-sufficiency, his ridiculously superior airs of patronage towards the female sex, is an impossibility for woman. . . . . Equally impossible for her is the man who can see in her nothing more than her mentality and her genius, and who fails to awaken her woman nature" (1969, 220). Men, it seems, do hold some accountability for the situation in which women exist. Still, Goldman's statement about women's contributions to the construction of males is disturbing. The power of individuals, moved by their own free will, to overcome larger realities that construct their lives is overdetermined in Goldman's analysis. While she provides a strong analysis of the economic and social forces that shape people's lives, when directing her sharp wit to the issue of changing women's status or men's roles Goldman appears to loose sight of the intensity and depth of these vital structural realities.

Perhaps Goldman held others to high standards because she demanded so much of herself: "As a role model and exemplar, as a stunning speaker, a star, as an anarchist leader of immense energy and integrity always willing to go to jail for her principles, Emma Goldman did not escape the problems frequently associated with the superwoman" (Shulman 1998, 11–12). This image of Goldman as superwoman is one of the more obvious shifts in Shulman's analysis of Goldman. Comparing the different introductions to Shulman's anthologies, Frankel points out that "Shulman no longer described Goldman as a 'superwitch' but as a model of the 'superwoman" (1996, 929). But, in using her own life as metaphor for the lived revolution, Goldman understands that the demands she makes on women are not easy. Indeed in her autobiography she exposes the difficulties of building a life in line with revolutionary ideals. She notes that she left Russia to avoid the threat of an arranged marriage and her father's abuse. She left Rochester, New York, not only to embrace the revolution but also to escape the social judgment of a conservative Jewish community upon her leaving her marriage. She walked away from an operation she claimed would make her able to bear children in order to live the revolution. Goldman was not asking women to do what she had not already done. Further, her high expectations are held not only of women. Friends, workers, revolutionists—are all held to an exacting standard of personal behavior. Holding herself, or her friends, to these rigid revolutionary standards, however, is often difficult for Goldman to sustain. In the tumult that frequently emerges in her complex, often needy personal relationships with Ben Reitman or Berkman, failures to live up to ideals are sometimes excused in ways she seldom leaves open to others in her essays. Jealousies, infidelity, abrasiveness, dependence, attraction to younger women, and differences in ideals are often rationalized as natural by-products of an existence within a culture of ownership, as the result of the pressures imposed by already living lives outside traditional mores, or as the result of the narrow-mindedness of others (Falk 1990; Goldman 1970).

Solomon finds that these tensions in the rhetoric of Goldman's work limit the solutions Goldman provides to the problems women face: "Her individualistic anarchism prevented Goldman from completing the rhetorical process inherent in altering perspectives through incongruity" (Solomon 1988, 191). In other words, while Goldman could push her audiences to see the problem, she left little room for them to act or be motivated to act. According to Solomon, Goldman's method "demanded that her would-be followers reject all aspects of the contemporary social structure in favor of an ill-defined alternative, romantically characterized in Rousseauesque terms as the 'natural' product of the uninhibited human 'spirit.' . . . In the case of women, Goldman castigated not only women who were pursuing traditional roles as wives and mothers but also "liberated" women who were pursing their careers and professional lives. If both alternatives were flawed, on what basis could a female listener erect an alternative?" (192).

While Solomon builds a strong case that Goldman's rhetorical strategies reveal, and perhaps contribute to, deep contradictory impulses within Goldman's feminism, I wonder if this particular critique of Goldman's strategic use of this rhetoric misses the point. After all, while Goldman's rhetoric may not inspire action in everyone, she certainly, even by Solomon's own account, and certainly by the accounts of others, did move many to action. Solomon reports that "Roger Baldwin, founder of the ACLU [American Civil Liberties Union], attested to [Goldman's] impact on his thinking" (191). Further, the only alternatives available to women were not simply the dichotomous choice between their traditional role and a new professional role. Both alternatives, from an anarchist or feminist position, do have limits and constraints. Both tradition and professionalism are imbedded in structures simultaneously imbued and bolstered by patriarchal and capitalist values. Thus, for Goldman, neither, in the end, will prove satisfactory in seeking to create free women.

The model on which Goldman tries to "erect an alternative" to the flat and bankrupt existence of capitalism is exemplified in her life. She draws on her life as source of theoretical example. Living life toward an ideal is complex, messy, and contradictory. Goldman's use of her life reflects all the disappointments, egotism, triumphs, and joys of the human experiences. Her limits should remind us of the problem of self-righteousness, which can too often hold others to standards we ourselves have difficulty achieving. However, contradictions within the practice of her life should not negate Goldman's contributions to feminist theory. Her use of her life as personal example for her theoretical explorations, her nascent connection of sexuality with the experiences of women's oppression, her focus on reproductive freedom, and her analysis of the centrality of women and gender to any understanding of radical liberty remain vital original contributions.

Liberatory Healing and Emma Goldman

In "Theory as Liberatory Practice," bell hooks lays out a unique and powerful approach that helps gauge when theory is acting to help move us toward liberation (1994, 59–75). Relying on the ideas that liberation is primarily an act of healing from injustices and that theorizing is at root a means of making sense of the world around us, hooks forges powerful links between the personal and political and between activism and theory. Starting from her experience, hooks moves from a personal reflection of her own needs for liberation, her own quest to understand and heal, to the larger quest for liberation and healing within the women's movement: "I came to theory because I was hurting—the pain within me was so intense that I could not go on living. I came to theory desperate, wanting to comprehend—to grasp what was happening around and within me. Most importantly, I wanted to make the hurt go away. I saw in theory then a location for healing" (59). Yet hooks continues with caution: "Theory is not inherently healing, liberatory, or revolutionary. It fulfills this function only when we ask that it do so and direct our theorizing towards this end" (61). In her assessment of the women's movement, she examines ways that academic, predominately white feminism has not been directed toward healing because it so often re-creates alienating intellectual structures and ignores diversity. Hooks praises the "critical intervention" of women of color who worked to "challenge and deconstruct the category 'woman'" as well as the "appropriation and/ or devaluation of work that did not 'fit,' that was suddenly deemed not theoretical" (63). She reminds us that while theory is available to all people, we must work to recognize that "there are so many settings in this country where the written word has only slight visual meaning, where individuals who cannot read or write can find no use for a published theory however lucid or opaque. Hence, any theory that cannot be shared in everyday conversation cannot be used to educate the public" (64). While noting the necessity to bridge the theory/practice divide, hooks appreciates the struggle of producing theory, the difficulty of putting ideas onto the page. Her notion of healing also encompasses incidents of anti-intellectualism that impatiently ask organizations to move from naming to action without adequate reflection on root causes or strategizing through to solutions. Simply because ideas are complex or reflective does not mean they are unnecessary. Action requires grounding, and theory provides this opportunity when it is done well. For hooks, the main functions of theory that claims to be liberatory, as feminism does, is critical reflection that provides a means of identifying what we are healing from, as well as some course to bring us toward healing. Such healing theory starts with lived experience and is responsive to the needs of all women. She ends her essay by asserting:

> Mari Matsuda has told us that "we are fed a lie that there is no pain in war," and that patriarchy makes this pain possible. Catharine McKinnon reminds us that "we know things with our lives and we live that knowledge, beyond what any theory has yet theorized." Making this theory is the challenge before us. For in its production lies the hope of our liberation, in its production lies the possibility of naming all our pain—of making all our hurt go away. If we create feminist theory, feminist movements that address this pain, we will have no difficulty building a mass-based feminist resistance struggle. There will be no gap between feminist theory and feminist practice. (75)

Hooks's notion of liberation as healing is a provocative metaphor. Its power as a uniquely feminist approach to liberation emerges both in the progression of her analysis and in the merits of her reasoning. With her opening concentration on her own family history, grounded in gender, class, and race, she demonstrates that the healing that is liberatory is above all personal, requiring a critical and reflective stance on the most intimate and formative moments of our lives. Our first experiences with injustice are encountered in childhood. It is our quest to understand the unsatisfactory explanations given to us that fuel our first attempts to break free of the confines of tradition. But hooks's text quickly moves from this formative experience out to the public world of the academic, political, and ethnic communities she inhabits as an adult. With this shift the metaphor of healing as liberation is also transformed, as she moves from an attempt to understand her life on this very intimate level to a quest to understand the social world. Her personal healing is linked with the healing of these social worlds, and the healing of those worlds is linked to the well-being of each of its members. Thus, when feminist academics write in prose that is inaccessible to others, hooks can both respect the difficulty in expressing complex ideas, while recognizing the alienation such language can cause. She locates the healing not in the degradation of the theoretical enterprise but in the recognition of the need for dialogue between communities. However, these communities must be situated as equals for the liberation to occur.

Here I want to dig more deeply into Goldman by using hooks's notion of liberatory feminist theory. I believe that hooks's idea of what makes theory liberatory is useful because it helps us see Goldman in a new light, sharpening our understanding through new questions, such as, What does Goldman seek to heal? Whom does she seek to heal? How does she allow us to heal? Further, hooks's text reminds us to look beyond stated words, to consider the underlying flow and approach as necessary components in grasping the full depth of healing represented in Goldman's work.

Like hooks, Goldman uses and reflects on her own personal experience as evidence for much of her theoretical work. And like hooks, Goldman finds theory helpful in healing the pain and injustices that are first experienced in the most intimate interiors of family life. Goldman's arguably most famous work, *Living My Life*, is perhaps the clearest example of her attempt at creating a self-reflective, liberatory, healing theory. The text itself was written at the request of friends as Goldman searched for meaningful, and economically viable, occupations in the period following her exile from the United States and escape from Russia. As her correspondence with Berkman and others attests, the act of writing the text was one of personal healing for Goldman. In the autobiography, she courageously examines the abuse in her family, the patriarchal powers that dominated her young life, the difficulty of immigration, and the harsh working conditions endured by the poor. Further, the text was controversial in its day because of the detail with which Goldman approaches issues of sex and sexuality. However, Falk (1990) argues that in order to construct her life as a supreme act of living the revolution, Goldman did not expose all aspects of her personal life to scrutiny. Still, this openness to discussing sexuality is additional evidence of the personal nature of Goldman's work, as well as her desire to heal us as a society from conventions that would leave such a vital part of human experience unexamined.

The healing, and thus liberatory, aspects of Goldman's work go well beyond her personal experience. At the center of her writing is a belief that the pain of others is a primary concern in the life of a revolutionary. She becomes a nurse as a means of finding a useful occupation while dealing with the boredom of prison life. Then through her experiences as a nurse outside prison, she develops a critique of the dangers not only to women's health but also to women's ability to live in a state of liberty, given the lack of access to reproductive knowledge and care. The experiences she gained in observing the lives of women are the cornerstone of her ideas on liberation and freedom. The centrality of this focus on sexual freedom and reproductive choice within her ideas is reflected in her articles, lectures, and arrests. A revolutionary should seek to heal the pain caused to people's lives by societal constraints and attitudes.

In her reliance on the spoken word, biography, writings in the popular press, and personal correspondence as the primary means of communicating her theoretical ideas, Goldman challenges notions of what it is to "do" theory. Not for Goldman the sustained argument of a *Das Capital*—instead, her written ideas come to us in volumes of letters, in the speeches that survive through her essays, in news reports and interviews, and within the pages of her autobiography. Interestingly, for someone who spent months on the road giving speeches, Goldman, in the preface to *Anarchism and Other Essays*, is clear on the limits of lectures as a means of motivating deeper theoretical reflection: "I came to see that oral propaganda is at best but a means of shaking people from their lethargy: It leaves no lasting impression" (1969, 42). Reflecting on the distraction of hearing the spoken word, she points to the intimacy of texts that allow reflection. Despite later expressing a belief in the "importance of written, as against oral expression" (43), she does find that texts are often read only for what people want to see, in that "the pupil will accept only that which his mind craves" (42). The best an activist can do, she believes, is create ground from which thought can grow. It is this desire to create a space for reflection on her ideas that leads her to produce a volume of essays. Thus, in her use of essays, Goldman does engage some very traditional forms of theoretical criticism. She also published a treatise on drama, which was somewhat respected in its day. Yet the primary forms from which her ideas emerge in writing are not the longer treatises or manuscripts traditionally associated with political theory.

Despite the limits she came to see with the spoken word, one of the central methods Goldman used to develop her ideas was the talks and speeches she gave throughout the United States. Her essays reflect the topics and titles of her speeches, and the speeches were the basis of many of her published works. She chose to speak in part because English was not her first language and she was more comfortable speaking it than writing it. Additionally, she communicated her ideas through a massive correspondence, particularly rich examples of which were written to her lifelong comrade Alexander Berkman (for important examples, see Drinnon and Drinnon 1975; Falk, Pateman, and Moran 2003). The Drinnons, in the introduction to *Nowhere at Home: Letters from Exile of Emma Goldman and Alexander Berkman*, write:

> Letters became Emma Goldman's medium primarily because she was an exile and because in them the gap between the written and the spoken word was at its narrowest. A short stride over the gap enabled her to express her great strength as a speaker and conversationalist. It was as though she were responding to an earnest questioner after a lecture or having her say after a fine meal in someone's apartment. She spoke with directness and intensity from the current edge of her thinking, feeling, experiencing—and not incidentally therewith effectively revoked the official edict of separation from all she held dear. This "proclivity to spread myself in letters," for which she was chided by Berkman and others, meant that her distant friends had access to her continuous present and to her self-revelation of different aspects of character to different correspondents. (xv)

In Goldman's use of both correspondence and speeches as a means of communicating ideas and positions, her theoretical methods provide an important bridge between the private and the public, between the personal and the political. The acts of using speeches as the basis for future writing and of choosing the format of letters to communicate ideas are familiar to many recent feminist theorists of and are found in some of the most circulated collections of the second wave (see Lorde 1984; Moraga and Anzaldúa 1983.) For hooks, one of the major functions of liberatory theory is to connect theory and action. Liberatory theory does this, she argues, by speaking about our ideas of the world in a way that is accessible to most people, not only the highly educated. If, as hooks asserts, one of the goals of some liberatory theory is to translate the work of others into more accessible language, then Goldman's primary methods for distributing her ideas present another way of understanding how her theory is liberatory. The liberatory nature of her work comes not only in what is said, but also in her attempt to say it in ways that are accessible to a wide audience.

I believe that one of the reasons Goldman is often discredited as a thinker has to do with the style in which she worked through and publicized her ideas. Because these were not, indeed are not, the major methods of theoretical development common in scholarship, she is often dismissed as being either unoriginal or unsystematic in her thought. Certainly many of us, like Goldman, rely on others for inspiration. Marx certainly borrowed from Hegel. In this sense, as Goldman acknowledges, she owed a great deal to the voices around her—Bakunin, Kropotkin, and Berkman. But Goldman did more than mimic the ideas of these thinkers; she analyzed them, reflected on them, and altered their meanings to better understand the realities in which she lived. For example, she comes to a different stand from that of Berkman on the efficacy of violence, hope in the "masses," and the status of the United States, differences made particularly clear in their correspondence as presented in *Nowhere at Home*. Further, while discussions on women's emancipation and free love circulated within a number of different radical circles of the period, Goldman's concise insights into both the structural and social impacts of marriage, love, and women's emancipation are certainly unique to her, as was the central role she gave these questions in her analysis of what revolution must come to mean.

Additionally, if we look closely at her talks and speeches we see an analysis that moves and deepens with each topic covered. For example, in "Woman Suffrage," and "The Tragedy of Women's Emancipation" she not only works through similar themes, she also expands her ideas (1969, 195–211, 212–25). Between these pieces Goldman moves from deconstructing the claims of suffrage supporters to analyzing the roots of women's larger oppression. She notes that the problems for women are both structural and internal and cannot be addressed separately. This recognition of both internal and external "tyrants" that hamper women's emancipation finds its echo in the later feminist motto "The personal is political." While the focus of "The Tragedy of Woman's Emancipation" is on the social customs and mores that women internalize as conditions of survival, "Marriage and Love" explores the economic and psychological costs of one of the major forces constructing women's reality (1969, 226–39). And in "Marriage and Love" we see Goldman's notions of revolution linked to her understanding of issues affecting women's lives; she uses the difference between love and marriage as an opportunity to explore a view of revolution not simply as a deconstructive enterprise but as a reconstructive one. While attacking notions of marriage, she leaves the reader with a clear sense of what she means by love itself. The problems of living up to this ideal of love are then worked out more fully in "Jealousy: Its Causes and Cures" (Goldman 1998, 215–21). We could trace similar depth in her discussion of revolution, prostitution, crime, and even rape, and add to the breadth of our understanding of her ideas by taking seriously her autobiography and letters as parts of this theoretical legacy.

Although Goldman's faith in, and relationship to, the "masses" was certainly not blind romanticism, and is often ambivalent, although her work is sometimes elitist, and often contradictory, her use of the speech, the letter, the popular essay, and the autobiography as her preferred space to transmit her ideas does reflect her desire for both individual and communal space. In her method she assumes that publics can know. And in this sense her methodology heals the rift in the divides of knowledge areas; she acts as translator of ideas, expanding the space and area where theory is done. In hooks's sense, her work is liberatory because it actively seeks to expose the wounds of Goldman's personal past, to consider deeply the causes of injustice she sees in the world around her, and to build from theory a means of reflective action, seeing in action a cite of theoretical reflection.

Continuing Discussions

At a friend's birthday party I asked the women gathered—historians, philosophers, women's and ethnic studies scholars, social workers, and feminists—if they thought that Emma Goldman was a feminist. The responses were telling. Alluding to ideas I had developed in my dissertation, one said that the answer was mixed; feminism was multifaceted and the conception of feminism would matter to the response. Another wondered if perhaps the question was, Why does it matter today if she was a feminist? I talked about my attraction to her work and noted how others were drawn to her. Another friend reminded me that as " everywoman," fitting all things at all times, Goldman must be problematized. Quite practical and supportive, a final friend suggested that laying out a few aspects of feminism itself might be necessary to answer this question. My friends where correct: what feminism looks like today, what feminism looked like to Goldman, why feminism matters to us today, and the complexity of Goldman's thought and life are indeed central to answering the question. In this chapter I have tried to continue this accounting, providing insight into her feminism, its strengths and weaknesses, its ability to still speak to us today, indeed its liberatory nature.

While this chapter does give insight into Goldman's feminism, including its troubling tendencies and healing potential, the chapter is not without its limits. One of the major challenges in researching Goldman's ideas is what I find to be its most unique strengths. To discover Goldman's theory, one cannot simply go to conveniently written volumes, making it a challenge to read her work for consistency and coherency. Further, her immigrant background and internationalist commitments mean that her written work is not always available in English. She was often more comfortable, particularly in her early years in the United States, writing for non-English-language publications aimed at Russian, German, and Jewish immigrant populations. Thus, a weakness of this analysis is its necessary overreliance on English-language materials.

I have concentrated here on giving a sense of the breadth and originality of Goldman's feminism. Our understanding of her feminism would be greatly enhanced by exploring particular themes that run through her writing. For example, if we are to truly understand the nuances of her contributions as a feminist theorist future research should include comprehensive examinations of her complex views on reproductive choice, sexuality, suffrage, and the women's movement. The focus on breadth also raises the need for a more particularized understanding of the links she forged between feminism and other radical ideas. Here one vital area ripe for further analysis is her problematic and shifting notion of free will, and how this notion influenced her views on women. Additionally, in this chapter I have only touched on Goldman's somewhat shifting and ambiguous relationship to political violence. In the wake of 9/11, her responses and stands on the use of violence in pursuit of revolutionary goals, as well as her understanding of state-sponsored terror, seem particularly vital to flesh out if we are to gain a fuller understanding of ideas central to her theory. The implications for her views on feminism of her stands on violence should be a central focus of such analysis.

Despite the contradictions and tensions in her theoretical ideas, Goldman's ability to speak across time continues to be powerful and important. In researching this chapter I had the pleasure of going to the Emma Goldman Papers Project at the University of California at Berkeley. A wonderful place to walk into, it is a place reflective of both the difficulties and promise of taking seriously the ideas reflected in Goldman's often iconic life. In this small, quiet building Goldman continues to inspire new generations. In gaining entrance to the research center, located off campus in a low-lying, unassuming brick building, one has to duck under an unkempt and untamed tree to go through the door. The front room is a hub of activity as young volunteers, students, and interns work diligently at projects alongside dissertating and longer-term scholars, associated both with academic and nonacademic knowledge production. Chaos seems to reign at first, for the tight space overflows with filing cabinets, boxes, and donated furniture. But with the help of a knowledgeable staff, order begins to appear. I cannot help but continue to think about the implications of Goldman's ideas as I leave the archive and walk past a Starbuck's filled with customers and then stores advertising low-priced deals on shoes produced in third world sweatshops. Considering Goldman today reminds us that these contradictions are not new, recommitting us to revolutionary ideals and action. In ending her sweeping history of Western feminisms, LeGates writes, "Ultimately, what makes activism worthwhile is not the chance of success but the process of struggle. It is the self-determination individuals achieve over their own lives and the supportive culture they create in league with other women or with men in a common fight. It is empowering, therefore, to recognize the efforts of activists over so many centuries while appreciating the obstacles that still exist" (374–75). Reassessing Goldman's feminist ideals from within our own age can help us as we attempt to bring revolution into our daily lives, struggling with the inevitable contradictions and tensions inherent in this task of empowerment. This chapter has shown that we still have much to learn about the feminism of Red Emma. Goldman remains a complex and powerful voice, capable of providing thoughtful and jarring analysis useful to understanding the complexities of our world.

Note

1. As we begin to look at the feminism of Goldman, Frankel reminds us that contemporary discussions of Goldman's feminism often reflect as much about the feminism of the period in which they are written in as they do Goldman's own ideas. For Frankel, in the 1980s, two approaches arose within feminist assessments of Goldman: "a great personal identification and empathy with a multifaceted, human, and troubled historical figure or a more judgmental verdict and a degree of distancing" (1996, 929). Among others, Frankel uses a number of Alix Kates Shulman's essays and Alice Wexler's biographies of Emma Goldman as examples of these two approaches. These approaches lead to a primarily biographical focus on Goldman, or to a deemphasizising of the more controversial parts of her vision. Keeping Frankel's critical concerns in mind, I still find that Shulman's essays provide a useful starting point from which to outline the basic tenants and tensions at the heart of Goldman's feminism. Particularly useful is Shulman's "reappraisal" of Goldman's feminism, located in her 1998 edition of *Red Emma Speaks* (a work not discussed in Frankel).

References

Alcoff, Linda. 1988. "Cultural Feminism Versus Post-structuralism: The Identity Crisis in Feminist Theory." *Signs* 13 (Spring): 405–36.

Bunch, Charlotte. 2005. "Not by Degrees: Feminist Theory and Education." In *Feminist Theory: A Reader*, edited by Wendy Komar and Frances Barkowski. 2d ed. Mountain View, Calif.: Mayfield. (Orig. pub. in *Quest: A Feminist Quarterly* 5 (1979): 7–18.)

Drinnon, Richard, and Anna Maria Drinnon, eds. 1975. *Nowhere at Home: Letters from Exile of Emma Goldman and Alexander Berkman*. New York: Schocken Books.

The Emma Goldman Papers Project. http://sunsite.berkeley.edu/Goldman.

Goldman, Emma. 1926. "Feminism's Fight Not Vain, Emma Goldman's Conclusion." *Rochester Times-Union*, November 16. NEA Service. Reprint edition. The Emma Goldman Papers Project Archives. Document no. 23347.

———. 1969. *Anarchism and Other Essays*. With a new introduction by Richard Drinnon. New York: Dover. (Orig. pub. 1917.)

———. 1970. *Living My Life: Emma Goldman in Two Volumes*. 2 Vols. New York: New American Library. (Orig. pub. 1931.)

———. 1988. "Mary Wollstonecraft: Her Tragic Life and Her Passionate Struggle for Freedom." In *A Vindication of the Rights of Woman: An Authoritative Text, Backgrounds, the Wollstonecraft Debate, Criticism*, edited by Carol H. Poston. New York: W. W. Norton. Reprinted from *Feminist Studies* 7, no. 1 (1981): 114–21. (Orig. pub. 1911.)

———. 1998. "Jealousy: Its Causes and Cures." In *Red Emma Speaks: Selected Writings and Speeches by Emma Goldman*. 3d ed. Edited by Alix Kates Shulman. Reprint, New York: Vintage Books. (Orig. pub. 1915.)

Falk, Candace. 1990. *Love, Anarchy, and Emma Goldman*. New Brunswick: Rutgers University Press. (Orig. pub. 1984.)

Falk, Candace, Barry Pateman, and Jessica Moran, eds. 2003. *Emma Goldman: A Docu-*

mentary History of the American Years. Vol. 1, Made for America, 1890–1901. Berkeley and Los Angeles: University of California Press.

Frankel, Oz. 1996. "Whatever Happened to 'Red Emma'? Emma Goldman, from Alien Rebel to American Icon." Journal of American History 83, no. 3:903–52.

Glassgold, Peter. 2001. Anarchy! An Anthology of Emma Goldman's Mother Earth (1906–1918). Washington, D.C.: Counterpoint.

hooks, bell. 1994. "Theory as Liberatory Practice." Teaching to Transgress: Education as the Practice of Freedom. New York: Routledge.

LeGates, Marlene. 2001. In Their Time: A History of Feminism in Western Society. New York: Routledge.

Loewen, James. 1995. Lies My Teacher Told Me : Everything Your American History Textbook Got Wrong. New York: New Press.

Lorde, Audre. 1984. Sister Outsider: Essays and Speeches. Freedom, Calif.: Crossing Press.

Moraga, Cherríe, and Gloria Anzaldúa, eds. 1983. This Bridge Called My Back: Writings by Radical Women of Color. Forward by Toni Cade Bambara. New York: Kitchen Table: Women of Color Press. (Orig. pub. 1982.)

Moritz, Theresa, and Albert Moritz. 2001. The World's Most Dangerous Woman: A New Biography of Emma Goldman. Vancouver: Subway Books.

Shulman, Alix Kates. 1982. "Dancing in the Revolution: Emma Goldman's Feminism." Socialist Review 12 (March–April): 3–44.

———. 1998. "Emma Goldman's Feminism: A Reappraisal." Red Emma Speaks: Selected Writings and Speeches by Emma Goldman. 3d ed. Edited by Alix Kates Shulman. Reprint, New York: Vintage Books.

Solomon, Martha. 1988. "Ideology as Rhetorical Constraint: The Anarchist Agitation of 'Red Emma' Goldman." Quarterly Journal of Speech 74:184–200.

Wexler, Alice. 1989. Emma Goldman in Exile: From the Russian Revolution to the Spanish Civil War. Boston: Beacon Press.

Part Three

Political Change: Theory and Practice

12

Anarchist Alternatives to Competition

Martha A. Ackelsberg and Kathryn Pyne Addelson

"The contrast is not simply between competition and cooperation, but between different understandings of equality, justice, knowledge, and—importantly—the nature of social reality."

Ackelsberg and Addelson show that anarchism in general, and anarchist feminism in particular, enjoy what many most deny it possesses: a distinctive ability to effect social change. Consistent with Goldman's political ideas, revolutionary anarchist practice as discussed here is based on the compatibility of freedom with community, structure, and cooperation.—*The Editors*

In the women's movement of the 1970s, many feminists came to see competition as one means by which male dominance, and class and racial dominance, were created and maintained. They saw competition for positions according to "merit" and competition for power or influence within pluralist political structures to be ways of organizing institutions so as to preserve a social order in which some gained a lion's share of communal-social resources and others, only crumbs. When these feminists organized the women's unions, women's clinics, abortion referral and rape crisis centers, bookstores, magazines, and early women's studies courses, they attempted to put into practice collective, nonhierarchical, noncompetitive ways of organizing their work. Many of these feminists called themselves anarchist and consciously drew on anarchist principles.[1] Anarchists, decentralist socialists, and others who value worker control and participatory democracy have offered alternatives to competition which challenge the necessity of hierarchical work orders and question the rules by which pluralist political structures reward the few at the expense of the many.

As feminists examined the competitive structures and practices prevalent in U.S. society, they came to understand competition as a mechanism for justifying and legitimating an unequal distribution of social resources. Just as Plato conceived of a "myth of the metals," the so-called Noble Lie that, he believed, would explain to people the unequal distribution of roles and responsibilities in his ideal society (and, importantly, lead them to accept their places in it), so the prevailing political and social ideology in the United States insists that the existing distribution of resources is a result of "competition," or "the free market."

To explain social relationships in this way is, effectively, to treat them as the consequences of a game, with its rules more or less set. Such an approach masks relationships of power and powerlessness, and the particular ways in which existing rules benefit some at the expense of others. Many feminists recognized this in the early stages of the second wave of the U.S. feminist movement.

In this paper we argue, first, that this conceptualization of politics and social relationships is seriously misleading; and, second, that anarchism (and, in particular, anarchist-feminism) offers an alternative conceptualization which can incorporate a more complete vision of social reality and the process of social change. To show this, we consider two alternatives to competition as it is understood in the contemporary United States. One is drawn from feminist activism in Canada and the other from U.S. labor history. The Vancouver Women's Health Collective, a self-managed workplace, offered an alternative to hierarchically organized, management-run enterprise. In the Lawrence (Massachusetts) Textile Strike of 1912, anarchist methods of direct action worked as an alternative to competing interest groups in the pluralist political arena. In both cases, the contrast is not simply between competition and cooperation, but between different understandings of equality, justice, knowledge, and—importantly—the nature of social reality.

The dominant tradition in the United States is political liberalism—liberalism of a sort that insists upon liberty and "free" competition, both in the marketplace and among the citizens. Competition is intrinsic to liberalism in several ways. There is competition in the political sphere—often conceived as pluralist competition in which conflicting interest groups try to influence voters or their elected representatives. This kind of political competition appears as a fact of life in the United States, and many "liberal feminist" groups have tended to become interest-group organizations, trying to gain influence in this competitive struggle, using more or less established structures to attempt to win offices or influence policy.[2]

Other ways competition is intrinsic to liberalism in the United States have to do with the workplace and the economic marketplace. The capitalist "free enterprise" economy requires that businesses compete for a share of the market and that workers compete for jobs. This economic competition is overlaid with ideas about "survival of the fittest" and getting one's due for excellence and hard work under a meritocracy.

Many writers in the liberal tradition view hierarchy as a necessary condition of social life. They argue that coordination is necessary, and that the most efficient form of coordination is hierarchical organization. According to this liberal view, "competition"—based on skills, intelligence, or other "relevant" criteria, depending on the particular institution in question—is the most efficient, and the fairest, way to assign people to their places in hierarchical organizations. When the competition is held fairly (that is, when the rules are known to all, and when all appropriate competitors have an equal chance at playing the game), the result is a "meritocracy," in which positions go to the "most qualified."[3]

When liberals turn a critical eye toward U.S. society and see that the most highly rewarded jobs tend to be held by white, upper-class males, and that many highly qualified women and people of color never make it to the tops of the hierarchies, their explanation is that something has gone wrong with the competition. They attribute this "unfair" sorting to various kinds of discrimination on the part of those hiring, or those making up qualifying exams, and so on. Their proposed solution: end discrimination; adopt, as a goal, equal opportunity. Then, those few women and people of color who excel can join the few men who rise to the top and become vice presidents of banks, account executives, department managers, or full professors. (The numbers are few, of course, because the positions are few.)

Many writers and activists in the Marxist and other socialist traditions have criticized liberal individualism. They have seen pluralist political competition, and hierarchy and privilege, as problematic in themselves. They have invited us to look behind the story liberals tell, and to recognize that it is capitalism—a set of relationships of power and authority in the economic realm—that generates economic classes, the privileges (and relationships of domination and subordination) that go with them, and the need for claims about "competition" and "meritocracy" to justify these inequalities.

These Socialists treat class and economic factors as the most crucial, deriving all other relationships of domination and subordination in society from those fundamental ones. They hold that people committed to social change must work together to overcome the economic structures of capitalism. Through such a struggle, they will make clear what claims about competition and meritocracy cover up, and will contribute to the undermining of all hierarchies, social, political, or sexual. Socialist feminists—noting the sexism of socialist movements and the fact that power based on gender and race often continues to be exercised even in socialist settings—have, in turn, challenged the classic socialist view and insisted that an analysis that locates the source of all oppression in economic relationships is incomplete.[4] While we agree with socialist feminists that the Marxist analysis, too, is inadequate, we believe that the Marxist framework itself is so flawed that it cannot be corrected through the simple addition of gender concerns.

While each of these approaches provides us with a particular "handle" on competition and hierarchies (particularly within the United States), each also leaves some important questions unanswered. We wish to argue here that instead of trying to modify these traditions, feminists would do better to turn to another—the anarchist tradition—which offers a different story about the nature and consequences of competition and the possibilities of cooperation.[5]

When we say *anarchist*, we mean to locate ourselves in the communalist-anarchist tradition of Bakunin, Kropotkin, Goldman, the Spanish anarchists, and grass-roots women's liberation groups in Europe and North America. The analyses of competition and hierarchy these groups have offered have varied, but all share a number of common perspectives: (1) a criticism of existing societies' focus on relationships of power and domination; (2) a vision of an alternate, egalitarian, nonauthoritarian society, along with claims about how it could be organized; and (3) a strategy for moving toward this alternate society. We shall see that the Vancouver Women's Health Collective and the Lawrence Textile Strike embody these perspectives in their organization and in their action.

What do anarchist theorists have to say about the nature and possibilities of cooperative, rather than competitive, social organizations? Perhaps the most important point is that anarchism does not mean *lack* of but, rather, *different* structure. Human freedom is a social product: Freedom and community are compatible, but communities need to be structured in particular ways to support that freedom. In particular, they must be egalitarian: Society (including structures of work) should be arranged to foster relationships of reciprocity and cooperation (what anarchists have traditionally termed *mutualism*). Thus, there would be no need for economic inequalities or differential work incentives. The institutions in and through which people interact should encourage them to cooperate with one another, not to compete. Finally, people will come to recognize that the fulfillment of the self need not be achieved at the expense of others.

Freely organized groups, set up by people to meet their own needs, should replace centralized, hierarchical means of coordination. Leaders may well arise in some situations, but the right or authority to "command" a situation should not inhere in roles or offices to which some people have privileged access. Finally, instead of competing with nature—or even attempting to conquer it—people should orient themselves to finding new ways to live in harmony with our physical surroundings.

While this vision may not seem very different from one offered by Marxists and other socialists, anarchists have some important things to say about the process of social change. They insist that means be consistent with ends: that the process of revolution take place in and through structures that reflect the sorts of relationships in which people aim to live. Anarchism implies a concept of revolutionary practice which consists in creating new forms of communal-social existence, new ways to meet people's needs, forms through which people can struggle to overcome their own subordination. In the contemporary European and North American context, one of the most common manifestations of such new forms are collective workplaces (of which the Vancouver collective serves as an example). In 1912, this revolutionary practice guided the Lawrence Textile Strike. Not simply an action for higher wages or shorter hours, that strike was part of the anarchist process of social revolution.

Competition in a Hierarchy Versus Cooperation in a Collective

The hierarchical work structures that many of us take for granted are quite recent creations. The reorganization of work in the Industrial Revolution involved changes in social arrangements as well as in technology— the division of manufacturing jobs into small tasks, bringing workers together under one roof in a factory, and separating the planning of work from its execution. These changes often had the effect of denying workers effective control over their work and of removing satisfaction from it.[6] In the twentieth century, the social revolution continued, and hierarchy extended, with managerial as well as manual work increasingly specialized. Over time, the deficiencies of rigid hierarchies have been widely recognized[7] and new models and practices have been developed which modify them to varying degrees. Nevertheless, the basic hierarchical structure, the assumptions it rests upon about the inferior intellectual and creative capacities of those farther down in the hierarchy, and its function as a mechanism of social control remain characteristic of most industries and many offices.

It is precisely such assignment of roles and rewards by competition that is problematic in the view of feminists, anarchists, and others. Hierarchical and collective methods of organizing work are not simply different ways of doing the same thing. They are based on different conceptions of knowledge, understanding, and rationality—and of right and justice.[8]

The Vancouver Women's Health Collective was established early in 1973 when women from a variety of local feminist health services (abortion referral and self-help among them) joined together.[9] The collective offered abortion counseling, contraceptive advice and diaphragm fitting, a health information phone line, and drop-in service. The members engaged in community education—for the public as well as for medical and nursing students—part of which took place through collective women's study groups. They also ran a self-help clinic, which aimed to empower women so that they could take responsibility for their own health.[10] Out of their roots in the women's movement, the members were determined to use feminist principles in a collective workplace structure.[11]

The collective operated on the premise that the more information one has in a given situation, the more power she has and the more responsibility she can take for her own actions. To withhold information is to keep people powerless. As a result, the collective was structured so that information, power, and responsibility were distributed as equally and as widely as possible. Instead of vesting authority in particular individuals who held managerial positions and controlled information, the collective rotated all coordinating and administrative positions among its members. Decisions concerning matters that touched on policy, whether large or small, were made by consensus at weekly meetings. Members rotated through all jobs, and taught one another the information they needed to perform them. The sharing of coordinating positions and consensus decision making were also major methods of information exchange. The group engaged in self-criticism at their weekly meetings, avoiding the situation where "the boss" is the only one with authority to criticize workers or the workplace. In theory at least, all members of the collective were equal participants in running the organization and in making and carrying out decisions. In practice, as in any collective, some members had more time to contribute, some had been around longer and knew more, some were newcomers who needed to learn more before they could fully take part.[12]

This collective had a "rational" structure, in the sense that positions and procedures were clearly set out.[13] However, the decision procedure in this collective reflected an understanding of rationality different from that characteristic of hierarchical work situations. Rationality derived from firsthand knowledge of the situation. Those making policy decisions knew every aspect of the work because they had done it. Because of the way work was organized, they could bring their own experience, rather than the expertise of managers, to the decision process.

Finally, while hierarchically organized workplaces assume that inequalities in both power and material rewards are necessary to provide incentives for workers, this collective was based on the assumption that people do their best not when they feel they must compete with others, but rather when they can work cooperatively with them.[14] Linda Light and Nancy Klieber, for examle, distinguish between what they term "social power" or the power to dominate or control others, and what they refer to as "personal power" or "autonomy." Personal power is associated with independence, self-reliance, self-actualization, and confidence.[15] They state that hierarchically organized groups differentially distribute the two kinds of power so that there is competition among individuals for both sorts. By contrast, they argue collectively organized workplaces *increase* personal power for all involved. The *sharing* of social power seems to generate personal power. People feel better about themselves, and they act more creatively and responsibly, when they work with others toward a common end. In collectives, workers' freedom and autonomy on the job is greater than it is in hierarchical work organizations. There is some evidence that benefits carry over to the nonwork lives of the participants. Carole Pateman, for example, has argued that increased opportunities for taking responsibility in the workplace affect people's sense of self-confidence and what is termed "political efficacy" *outside* the workplace.[16]

However, increased feelings of efficacy are not by themselves sufficient to assure that workers will have more autonomy and personal freedom in their lives. Collective workplaces as we know them exist in a larger society that is characterized by competition and hierarchy. Members of collectives often try to change those larger competitive structures, but they are not always successful—certainly not to the degree that their members are assured of achieving full autonomy or experiencing their full personhood in their nonwork lives. Members of the Vancouver Collective did try to work for broader political change by taking a self-help orientation and by working to educate the women who used their services. Yet, like any collective in contemporary North America, the group had to operate within larger competitive structures. Neither the collective as a unit nor its members as individuals had much social, economic, or political power within that larger context—power either to change it or to stave off its impacts on them.

The Vancouver collective operated in the context of a mass political movement in which many groups were working for more democratic workplace structures. There were also major efforts to change the nature of the health care system and a free clinic movement. Those groups denied the appropriateness of "competition" as a method of distributing goods and services. But this is where many collectives confront and have confronted their most difficult challenges. Food co-ops offer alternatives to supermarkets that must attract members/shoppers if they are to survive. Health care collectives offer alternatives to medical practices that must attract patients. Paradoxically, collectives committed to cooperative, noncompetitive modes of working must engage in competition even to survive. This struggle is particularly difficult when there is no strong mass movement to support their efforts.

Pluralist Political Competition Versus Direct Action

Anarchists provide alternatives not only to competition in the workplace but also to "political competition" and struggles for "power" as ways of organizing the distribution of resources and control over policy making in political communities, large and small.

"Interest-group liberalism," which views political life as a series of competitions for power among groups of people representing different interests, provides the dominant understanding of politics in the United States. The assumptions underlying it are that most people know what their interests are, and are more or less capable of articulating and organizing around them. Politics is the competitive battle for preeminence among groups: The group with the most clout has its preferences enacted into policy. The system can be called democratic because it is formally open to the formation of new groups, because no one group wins every time, because there is apparent consensus on the "rules of the game," and because it seems that anyone who cares enough has a chance to influence policy. The role of politicians, and of laws, is to keep the competition fair—that is, played according to the rules.[17]

Although many women's organizations have learned to organize to be "effective" within this system, the shortcomings of the pluralist perspective ought to be evident. Most simply, those who already have access to power because of money, class, race, sex, age, or the like are able not only to keep it but to enhance it. More specifically, in treating interests as characteristics of individuals, the pluralist perspective masks the power of corporate groups to define the agenda of politics. Furthermore, it denies people the opportunity to think about or act upon our goals as members of communities. It encourages us to think about politics as a game in which there are winners and losers, rather than as an activity in and through which we can discuss and act on issues of common concern. More generally, the particular ways in which interests, groups, and competition play in this story virtually guarantee the continuing disadvantage, if not exclusion, of significant numbers of people from the competitive process, and the continuing advantage of those who, by virtue of corporate or other economic power, effectively "play" by very different rules.[18]

There are other modes of thinking about politics and engaging in political activity that avoid some of these pitfalls and challenge the notion of politics as a competitive game. Anarchists have developed other approaches quite self-consciously; feminists have as well—although not always so self-consciously. The theory and practice of direct action provide one such alternative.

Direct action methods have been used in many different movements in the United States to bring about social change. Freedom schools, sit-ins, health collectives, food co-ops, and industrial strikes are all examples of direct action methods to effect change by *creating new realities*, on however small a scale, rather than by attempting to influence decision makers through a pluralist bargaining process. Anarchists have argued explicitly that direct action can empower people by providing opportunities for them to learn about the realities of power in their societies and to recognize their own abilities to effect change. Through direct action, that is, people can come to understand their own interests and to learn how to create a society that better suits them.

Historically, in the United States, Canada, and western Europe, women have tended to be more centrally involved in direct action struggles than in more traditional "political" movements.[19] Many contemporary feminists have also adopted direct action methods, although often without any theoretical self-consciousness.

Early in this century, the anarcho-syndicalist Industrial Workers of the World (the IWW, or "Wobblies") used direct action methods in two major strikes: the Lawrence Textile Workers' Strike and the Paterson Silk Workers' Strike. Syndicalists were dedicated to revolution not by violent overthrow of the government but by nonviolent "industrial warfare." They believed that workers, if united, could effectively shut down the capitalist system, and replace it with a form of social coordination structured by worker syndicates rather than by a political state with its elected officials, courts, police, and armies.

The Wobblies were activists, and their theorizing was done through their practice.[20] The perspective they developed about human knowledge, individual interests, and rational decision making was very different from the pluralist one. Specifically, they argued that people's social positions affect what their interests are, their awareness of those interests, and their ability to forward them. Political/social action must be a continuous process of changing reality: both to educate workers and to empower them, enabling them to recognize their own powers, their own ability to create new realities.

According to their anarcho-syndicalist perspective, when workers reach the point of striking, they have come to recognize, at least to some extent, that their interests as workers are not being served. A more complete understanding of their interests, however, requires an analysis of the social, economic, and political system in which they live and work. This, according to the Wobblies, was not a matter of studying Marx but of acting—and then learning from the action and from other people's reactions. The Wobblies' best-known success was in the Lawrence Textile Strike.

The Lawrence strike began in January 1912, when workers walked out after a wage cut. It was an unusual strike. First, it began spontaneously, and only later was it shaped by IWW leaders. Second, it broke down the traditional divisions between workers and community members, men and women, and united all in a remarkable display of unity. As one participant summarized, "It was a new kind of strike. There had never been any kind of mass picketing in a New England town. Ten thousand workers picketed. It was the spirit of the workers that seemed dangerous. They were confident, gay, released, and they sang. They were always marching and singing."[21]

One of the ways this strike was "new" was the degree to which it involved women and children, who constituted over half the textile workers at the Lawrence plant. The mass picketing involved men, women, and children in an endless parade around the strike zone. There were women delegates elected to the strike committee, and one of the Wobblies' star organizers, Elizabeth Gurley Flynn, helped to guide the strike. But to place the Lawrence strike solely within labor movements history is to misunderstand both the place of women in it and the nature of anarchist politics. For the Lawrence strike was *not* simply a workers' strike; it was a revolutionary community effort that engaged the women and children at home as well as those who worked. It was a community move toward anarchist revolution, and it was quite different from the strikes led by unions such as the American Federation of Labor, in which women were, with few exceptions, supports for their men's efforts at getting higher wages within the capitalist workplace.[22]

The Wobblies used strikes as a means to gain advantages in wages or work conditions, but also as direct actions through which workers and their families and communities educated themselves about the nature of capitalism and the state and transformed themselves into a working class capable of changing the economic and political structure of the society in which they lived. As Melvyn Dubofsky has summarized,

> Wobblies hoped that simple ideas would lead to action, and that action in turn would transform the strikers' originally simple concepts into more complicated revolutionary principles. In other words, the simple concept that employers mistreated workers would result in a strike, the nature of which would teach the strikers about the realities of class, the viciousness of employers, and the depravity of the capitalist state, and from this, the strikers would derive a sense of class consciousness and revolutionary principle.[23]

This view of education and injustice contrasts sharply with that of competitive, meritocratic perspectives. *Injustice* refers, here, not to discrimination or bias in applying the rules but to unfairness in the rules themselves and in the basic social and economic arrangements.

Once the Lawrence strike began, workers and members of the community took action on their own initiative.

> The strike committee organized an elaborate system directed by a relief committee composed of representatives of all nationalities caught up in the struggle. Each ethnic group also had its own special relief committee. These committees investigated the needs of applicants, provided soup kitchen for single men, and furnished food or store orders for families. The committees provided for fuel, shoes, medical assistance and, in some cases, even rent. Although loosely organized and administered by uneducated immigrants, the committees operated with remarkable efficiency.[24]

The underlying assumption here is that personal power and knowledge come from acting on one's beliefs, and testing and changing them through action. The result is knowledge of the existing society and its injustices, as well as knowledge of how to change it. For the period of the strike, at least, direct action methods enabled women, men, and children to experience their own power and to exercise some influence over others in the absence of formal "social power."

Conclusion

While this article can provide only a brief overview of some of the anarchist alternatives to the competitive structures so many of us take for granted in the contemporary United States, we hope we have demonstrated that alternatives do exist. Even though the prevailing belief system in the United States insists that competition is the one best way to understand the process of sorting people into jobs and of distributing scarce resources, anarchist alternatives make clear that there is more than one way to tell the story.

From the anarchist perspective, competition serves to justify vast differentials of power, authority, resources, and even human dignity in society. The ideological dominance of the competitive model leads most people to believe both that hierarchy is fair (because it is efficient and necessary) and that their own place in it is, somehow, deserved. Such understandings both contribute to individual and communal disempowerment and discourage any efforts at social change in the direction of a more cooperative, less competitive society.

To the extent that feminists accept the liberal/competitive story and challenge existing practices only on the grounds of discrimination (or meritocratic fairness), we contribute to the perpetuation of social hierarchies and to the disempowerment of all people who find themselves disadvantaged by those structures. Conversely, to the degree that we recognize the empowering potential of cooperatively structured institutions and practices, name them, validate them, and support them, we can participate both in enabling people to recognize their own abilities and in creating institutions and practices that are, in themselves, the building blocks of a new society. Feminists of the women's liberation movement in the 1970s acted out of such an understanding. We must not lose that understanding.

This perspective takes on particular urgency when we consider it in the light of recent works on moral decision making that suggest that meritocratic orientations are compatible with (white, middle-class) male modes of operation in the United States.[25] However problematic those studies may be in other respects, they do raise the possibility that women and members of minority and working-class groups may be disadvantaged from the start in any competitive structure, no matter how "fair" its rules or how fairly they are applied. In addition, they suggest that members of nondominant groups (whether women, working-class people, or people of color) are more attuned to cooperative orientations and may even perform better in situations of cooperation than of competition. From this perspective, too, maintenance of competitive structures disadvantages those already disadvantaged, and severely limits the range of human experience reflected in social institutions.

All this is not to say that the process of creating a society based on cooperative, rather than competitive, principles would be a simple one: The experiences of both the Vancouver Women's Health Collective and of the Wobblies should make clear that the opposition to such alternatives is severe.[26] It is to say, however, that such alternatives have existed historically and continue to be developed in our own day. We must recognize that competition is not the only way to play, and more important, that competitive structures need to be opposed not only by cooperative structures but in cooperative ways.

Notes

1. See, for example, the journals *Quest*, *The Second Wave*, and, more recently, *Social Anarchism*. For an overview of women's liberation see Sara Evans, *Personal Politics* (New York: Vintage, 1979), also Kathryn Pyne Addelson, "Moral Revolution," in *Women and Value*, ed., M. Pearsall (San Diego: Wadsworth, 1986).

2. NOW, for example, has come to adopt such strategies, although in the late 1960s and early 1970s it participated in the more broad-based collectivist movement.

3. See, for example, Max Weber, "Bureaucracy," in *From Max Weber: Essays in Sociology*, ed. H. H. Gerth and C. W. Mills (New York: Oxford University Press, 1958), 196–244 and John Rawls, *A Theory of Justice* (Cambridge: Harvard University Press, 1971).

4. See, for example, Zillah Eisenstein, ed., *Capitalist Patriarchy and the Case for Socialist Feminism* (New York: Monthly Review Press, 1975); and Kate Young, Carol Wolkowitz, and Roslyn McCullagh, eds., *Of Marriage and the Market* (London: CSE Books, 1981).

5. Alison Jaggar omits anarchist feminism and "black feminism" from her typology of feminisms in her recent book, asserting that they do no constitute positions separable from other feminist theories (see *Feminist Politics and Human Nature* [Totowa, NJ: Rowman and Allanheld, 1983]). As we shall argue, this belief constitutes a serious misunderstanding of anarchism and a mistaken view of "theory." It may result from an overemphasis on the work of academic feminists. We hope that this article will serve to challenge her claims.

6. See S. Marglin, "What Do Bosses Do?" *Review of Radical Political Economics* 6, no. 2 (Summer 1974): 33–60.

7. See, for example, Michael Crozier, *The Bureaucratic Phenomenon* (Chicago: University of Chicago Press, 1964).

8. As we noted earlier, liberal social theory analyzes this hierarchical division of labor as both necessary and rational—necessary in that it guarantees efficiency, and rational in the special sense that officeholders secure the right to command under a legally established, impersonal order which clearly defines their authority in terms of the offices they hold. Formal rules define relations among workers and regulate both competition and cooperation. To the extent that the hierarchy is characterized as a "meritocracy," competitors are said to win out on grounds of their qualifications, defined by their job descriptions and judged in part by standardized tests. According to the liberal story, the fair and impartial application of these procedures defines justice and efficiency, in the operation of both the workplace and the economy.

9. Information on the Vancouver Women's Health Collective was taken from Nancy Klieber and Linda Light, *Caring for Ourselves: An Alternative Structure for Health Care* (Vancouver, B.C.: School of Nursing, University of British Columaia, 1978).

10. Women's self-help groups differed from some others, for example, Al-Anon, because members consciously shared a relation to a sexist society and health care system. Their goal was not simply to provide services (or even to help women help themselves) but to change the way the women related to the health care system and society as a whole, so as to challenge that sexism. *Our Bodies, Ourselves*, by the Boston Women's Health Collective (New York: Simon & Schuster, 1971), is probably the best-known product of the women's health movement.

11. Their place in the women's health movement led them to be concerned with health care delivery, and they made efforts to treat their patients with respect and to give them power over their

own health—for example, through their self-help clinic. In this article, we limit ourselves to discussing the workplace structure.

12. Initially, the Vancouver collective was staffed entirely by volunteers. Over time, however, there was a marked increase in funding, so that many workers could be paid. Being staffed by paid workers is rarely a problem for collectives, but being staffed by a combination of paid and volunteer members often is. See Klieber and Light, *Caring for Ourselves,* chap. 15.

13. We should note that clearly stated rules and procedures are not necessarily present in all collectives—and that their absence is often problematic. See, for example, Joreen, "The Tyranny of Structurelessness," *The Second Wave* 2, no. 1, and Jane Mansbridge, "Town Meeting Democracy," *Working Papers* 1, no. 1 (Spring 1973): 5–15.

14. See, for example, Georgia Sassen, "Success Anxiety in Women: A Constructive Interpretation of Its Sources and Significance," *Harvard Educational Review* 50, no. 1 (February 1980); 13–24; also Carol Gilligan, *In a Different Voice* (Cambridge: Harvard University Press, 1982), especially chap. 3. Anarchist writers and activists have also addressed these issues directly. See, for example, Peter Kropotkin, *Mutual Aid;* Colin Ward, *Anarchy in Action* (New York: Harper and Row, 1974); and Martha Ackelsberg, "Revolution and Community: Mobilization, De-politicization, and Perceptions of Change in Civil War Spain," in *Women Living Change,* ed. Susan C. Bourque and Donna Robinson Divine (Philadelphia: Temple University Press, 1985), especially 94–99.

15. Klieber and Light, *Caring for Ourselves,* 18.

16. Carole Pateman, *Participation and Democratic Theory* (Cambridge: Cambridge University Press, 1970), especially chaps. 4 and 5.

17. For a particularly clear presentation of this perspective, see Edward C. Banfield, *Political Influence* (New York: Free Press, 1960); and Joseph Schumpeter, *Capitalism, Socialism, and Democracy* (New York: Harper & Row, 1974), especially chaps. 19–23.

18. See, in particular, Michael Parenti, "Power and Pluralism: The View From the Bottom," *Journal of Politics* 32 (1970): 501–30; Lewis Lipsitz, "The Grievances of the Poor," in *Power and Community,* ed. Philip Green and Sanford Levinson, (New York: Pantheon, 1970): 142–72; and, on the issue of community, Michael Sandel, *Liberalism and the Limits of Justice* (Cambridge: Cambridge University Press, 1983); and Michael Taylor, *Community, Anarchy, and Liberty* (Cambridge: Cambridge University Press, 1982).

19. Temma Kaplan was one of the first to notice this relationship, though she adopts a somewhat different terminology and analytical framework. See, for example, "Female Consciousness and Collective Action," *Signs* 7, no. 3 (1982); 545–67. See also Paula Hyman, "Immigrant Women and Consumer Protest: The New York City Kosher Meat Boycott of 1902," *American Jewish History* 60 (1980): 91–105; and Dana Frank, "Housewives, Socialists, and the Politics of Food: The 1917 New York Cost-of-Living Protests," *Feminist Studies* 11, no. 2 (Summer 1985): 255–85.

20. It is characteristic of anarchist theory that the theorizing be done through practice, rather than in abstract writings by "intellectuals" or political leaders. If Marxist or liberal theory is taken as a paradigm, then anarchists appear to have no theory (or to be simplistic or naive theoretically). But to apply that paradigm is seriously to misunderstand anarchist theory and practice.

21. Mary Heaton Vorse, cited in R. D. Boyer and Herbert M. Morais, *Labor's Untold Story* (New York: Radio and Machine Workers, 1972), 175. Melvyn Dubofsky's discussion of the strike is thorough and helpful; see *We Shall Be All: A History of the Industrial Workers of the World* (Chicago: Quadrangle Books, 1969). See also Elizabeth Gurley Flynn, *The Rebel Girl: An Autobiography, My Life (1906–1926)* (New York: International Publishers, 1973).

22. Important exceptions to this generalization are those women who organized women workers in what was to become the International Ladies Garment Workers' Union. See, for example, Alice Kessler-Harris, "Organizing the Unorganizable: Three Jewish Women and Their Union," *Labor History* 17 (Winter 1976): 5–23. But even this exception is partial: The union was fighting for better wages and hours, not for a reorganization of the economic and social system. For another view of

the *community* nature of the strike, see also Ardis Cameron, "Bread and Roses Revisited: Women's Culture and Working Class Activism in the Lawrence Strike of 1912," in *Women, Work, and Protest: A Century of United States Women's Labor History*, ed. Ruth Milkman (Boston: Routledge and Kegan Paul, 1985).

23. Dubofsky, *We Shall Be All*, 284, reporting Elizabeth Gurley Flynn's analysis.

24. Ibid., 250. Participants reported very similar experiences with anarchist-sponsored committees to organize the distribution of basic necessities in Republican Spain during the Spanish Civil War. See, for example, Ackelsberg, "Revolution and Community," 85–115.

25. See, for example, Georgia Sassen, "Success Anxiety in Women"; Carol Gilligan, *In a Different Voice;* and Sue J. M. Freeman, "Women's Moral Dilemmas: In Pursuit of Integrity," in *Women Living Change*, ed. Bourque and Divine.

26. The Syndicalists and Anarchists faced persecution and imprisonment in the wave of patriotic fervor that carried the nation into World War I. After the war, there were deportations and the severe repression of the 1920s "Red Scare" that saw the notorious executions of Sacco and Vanzetti. When the unions finally came to the textile industry they came through the AFL-CIO and labor and capital became competing interest groups under a liberal ideology.

13

In Defense of Emma Goldman

Voltairine de Cleyre

Delivered in New York, Dec. 16, 1894

"But whether she or I be right, or both of us be wrong, of one thing I am sure; the spirit which animates Emma Goldman is the only one which will emancipate the slave from his slavery, the tyrant from his tyranny—the spirit which is willing to dare and suffer."

Voltairine de Cleyre's speech "In Defense of Emma Goldman" provides fascinating insight into the similarities and differences between her anarchism and that of Emma Goldman, as seen by de Cleyre. This is a piece on political change, and especially about what can make it effective. Her enemies are the same as Goldman's, de Cleyre makes clear, but the means they advocate sometimes differ, for reasons she explains here.—*The Editors*

The light is pleasant, is it not my friends? It is good to look into each other's faces, to see the hands that clasp our own, to read the eyes that search our thoughts, to know what manner of lips give utterance to our pleasant greetings. It is good to be able to wink defiance at the Night, the cold, unseeing Night. How weird, how gruesome, how chilly it would be if I stood here in blackness, a shadow addressing shadows, in a house of blindness! Yet each would know that he was not alone; yet might we stretch hands and touch each other, and feel the warmth of human presence near. Yet might a sympathetic voice ring thro' the darkness, quickening the dragging moments.—The lonely prisoners in the cells of Blackwell's Island have neither light nor sound! The short day hurries across the sky, the short day still more shortened in the gloomy walls. The long chill night creeps up so early, weaving its sombre curtain before the imprisoned eyes. And thro' the curtain comes no sympathizing voice, beyond the curtain lies the prison silence, beyond that the cheerless, uncommunicating land, and still beyond the icy, fretting river, black and menacing, ready to drown. A wall of night, a wall of stone, a wall of water! Thus has the great State of New York answered EMMA GOLDMANN; thus have the classes replied to the masses; thus do the rich respond to the poor; thus does the Institution of Property give its ultimatum to Hunger!

"Give us work" said EMMA GOLDMANN; "if you do not give us work, then give us bread; if you do not give us either work or bread then we shall take bread."—It wasn't a very wise remark to make to the State of New York, that is—Wealth and its watch-dogs, the Police. But I fear me much that the apostles of liberty, the fore-runners of revolt, have never been very wise. There is a record of a seditious person, who once upon a time went about with a few despised followers in Palestine, taking corn out of other people's corn-fields; (on the Sabbath day, too). That same person, when he wished to ride into Jerusalem told his disciples to go forward to where they would find a young colt tied, to unloose it and bring it to him, and if any one interfered or said anything to them, were to say: "My master hath need of it." That same person said: "Give to him that asketh of thee, and from him that taketh away thy goods ask them not back again." That same person once stood before the hungry multitudes of Galilee and taught them, saying: "The Scribes and the Pharisees sit in Moses' seat; therefore whatever they bid you observe, that observe and do. But do not ye after their works, for they say, and do not. For they bind heavy burdens, and grievous to be borne, and lay them on men's shoulders; but they themselves will not move them with one of their fingers. But all their works they do to be seen of men; they make broad their phylacteries, and enlarge the borders of their garments: and love the uppermost rooms at feasts, and the chief seats in the synagogues, and greetings in the markets, and to be called of men, Rabbi, Rabbi.'" And turning to the scribes and the pharisees, he continued: "Woe unto you, Scribes and Pharisees, hypocrites! for ye devour widows' houses, and for a presence make long prayers: therefore shall ye receive the greater damnation. Woe unto you, Scribes and Pharisees, hypocrites! for ye pay tithe of mint, and anise, and cummin, and have omitted the weightier matters of the law, judgment, and mercy, and faith: these ought ye to have done and not left the other undone. Ye blind guides, that strain at a gnat and swallow a camel! Woe unto you, Scribes and Pharisees, hypocrites! for ye make clean the outside of the cup end plaster, but within they are full of extortion and excess. Woe unto you, Scribes and Pharisees, hypocrites! For ye are like unto whited sepulchres, which indeed appear beautiful outward, but within are full of dead men's bones and all uncleanness.

Even so ye outwardly appear righteous unto men, but within ye are full of hypocrisy and iniquity. Woe unto you, Scribes and Pharisees, hypocrites! Because ye build the tombs of the prophets and garnish the sepulchres of the righteous; and say, 'if we had been in the days of our fathers we would not have been partakers with them in the blood of the prophets.' Wherefore ye be witnesses unto yourselves that ye are the children of them which killed the prophets. Fill ye up then the measure of your fathers! Ye serpents! Ye generations of vipers! How can ye escape the damnation of hell!"

Yes; these are the words of the outlaw who is alleged to form the foundation stone of modern civilization, to the authorities of his day. Hypocrites, extortionists, doers of iniquity, robbers of the poor, blood-partakers, serpents, vipers, fit for hell!

It wasn't a very wise speech, from beginning to end. Perhaps he knew it when he stood before Pilate to receive his sentence, when he bore his heavy crucifix up Calvary, when nailed upon it, stretched in agony, he cried: "My God, my God, why hast thou forsaken me!"

No, it wasn't wise—but it was very grand.

This grand, foolish person, this beggar-tramp, this thief who justified the action of hunger, this man who set the right of Property beneath his foot, this Individual who defied the State, do you know why he was so feared and hated, and punished? Because, as it is said in the record, "the common people heard him gladly"; and the accusation before Pontius Pilate was, "we found this fellow perverting the whole nation. He stirreth up the people, teaching throughout all Jewry."

Ah, the dreaded "common people"!

When Cardinal Manning wrote: "Necessity knows no law, and a starving man has a natural right to his neighbor's bread," who thought of arresting Cardinal Manning? His was a carefully written article in the FORTNIGHTLY REVIEW. Who read it? Not the people who needed bread. Without food in their stomachs, they had no fifty cents to spend for a magazine. It was not the voice of the people themselves asserting rights. No one for one instant imagined that Cardinal Manning put himself at the head of ten thousand hungry men to loot the bakeries of London. It was a piece of ethical hair-splitting to be discussed in after-dinner speeches by the wine-muddled gentlemen who think themselves most competent to consider such subjects when their dress-coats are spoiled by the vomit of gluttony and drunkenness. But when EMMA GOLDMANN stood in Union Square and said, "if they do not give you work or bread then take bread," the common people heard her gladly and as of old the wandering carpenter of Nazareth addressed his own class, teaching throughout all Jewry, stirring up the people against the authorities, so the dressmaker of New York addressing the unemployed working-people of New York, was the menace of the depths of society, crying in its own tongue. The authorities heard and were afraid: therefore the triple wall.

It is the old, old story. When Thomas Paine, one hundred years ago, published the first part of "The Rights of Man," the part in which he discusses principles only, the edition was a high-priced one, reaching comparatively few readers. It created only a literary furore. When the second part appeared, the part in which he treats of the application of principles, in which he declares that "men should not petition rights but take them," it came out in a cheap form, so that one hundred thousand copies were sold in a few weeks. That brought down the prosecution of the government. It had reached the people that might act, and prosecution followed prosecution till Botany Bay was full of the best men of England. Thus were the limitations of speech and press declared, and thus will they ever be declared so long as there are antagonistic interests in human society.

Understand me clearly. I believe that the term "constitutional right of free speech" is a meaningless phrase, for this reason: the constitution of the United States, and the Declaration of Independence, and particularly the latter, were, in their day, progressive expressions of progressive ideals. But they are, throughout, characterized by the metaphysical philosophy which dominated the thought of the last century. They speak of "inherent rights," "inalienable rights," "natural rights," etc: They declare that men are equal because of a supposed, mysterious wetness, existing somehow apart from matter. I do not say this to disparage those grand men who dared to put themselves against the authorities of the monarchy, and to conceive a better ideal of society, one which they certainly thought would secure equal rights to men; because I realize fully that no one can live very far in advance of the time-spirit, and I am positive in my own mind that, unless some cataclysm destroys the human race before the end of the twentieth century the experience of the next hundred years will explode many of our own theories. But the experience of this age has proven that metaphysical quantities do not exist apart from materials, and hence humanity can not be made equal by declarations on paper. Unless the material conditions for equality exist, it is worse than mockery to pronounce men equal. And unless there is equality (and by equality I mean equal chances for every one to make the most of himself) unless, I say, these equal chances exist, freedom, either of thought, speech, or action, is equally a mockery.

I once read that one million angels could dance at the same time on the point of a needle; possibly one million angels might be able to get a decent night's lodging by virtue of their constitutional rights; one single tramp couldn't. And whenever the tongues of the non-possessing class threaten the possessors, whenever the disinherited menace the privileged, that moment you will find that the constitution isn't made for you. Therefore I think anarchists make a mistake when they contend for their constitutional rights. As a prominent lawyer, Mr. Thomas Earle White of Phila., himself an anarchist, said to me not long since: "What are you going to do about it? Go into the courts, and fight for your legal rights? Anarchists haven't got any." "Well," says the governmentalist, "you can't consistently claim any. You don't believe in constitutions and laws." Exactly so; and if any one will right my constitutional wrongs I will willingly make him a present of my constitutional rights. At the same time I am perfectly sure no one will ever make this exchange; nor will any help ever come to the wronged class from the outside. Salvation on the vicarious plan isn't worth despising. Redress of wrongs will not come by petitioning "the powers that be." "He has rights who dare maintain them." "The Lord helps them who help themselves." (And when one is able to help himself, I don't think he is apt to trouble the Lord much for his assistance.) As long as the working-people fold hands and pray the gods in Washington to give them work, so long they will not get it. So long as they tramp the streets, whose stones they lay, whose filth they clean, whose sewers they dig, yet upon which they must not stand too long lest the policeman bid them "move on"; as long as they go from factory to factory, begging for the opportunity to be a slave, receiving the insults of bosses and foremen, getting the old "no," the old shake of the head, in these factories they built, whose machines they wrought; so long as they consent to herd like cattle, in the cities, driven year after year, more and more, off the mortgaged land, the land they cleared, fertilized, cultivated, rendered of value; so long as they stand shivering, gazing thro' plate glass windows at overcoats, which they made, but cannot buy, starving in the midst of food they produced but cannot have; so long as they continue to do these things vaguely relying upon some power outside themselves, be it god, or priest, or politician, or employer, or charitable society, to remedy matters, so long deliverance will be delayed. When they conceive the possibility of a complete international federation of labor, whose constituent groups shall take possession of land, mines, factories, all the instruments of production, issue their own certificates of exchange, and, in short, conduct their own industry without regulative interference from law-makers or employers, then we may hope for the only help which counts for aught—Self-Help; the only condition which can guarantee free speech, (and no paper guarantee needed).

But meanwhile, while we are waiting, for there is yet much grist of the middle class to be ground between the upper and nether millwheels of economic evolution; while we await the formation of the international labor trust; while we watch for the day when there are enough of people with nothing in their stomachs and desperation in their heads, to go about the work of expropriation; what shall those do who are starving now?

That is the question which EMMA GOLDMANN had to face; and she answered it by saying: "Ask, and if you do not receive, take,—take bread."

I do not give you that advice. Not because I do not think that bread belongs to you; not because I do not think you would be morally right in taking it; not that I am not more shocked and horrified and embittered by the report of one human being starving in the heart of plenty than by all the Pittsburgs, and Chicagoes, and Homesteads, and Tennessees, and Coeur d'Alenes, and Buffaloes, and Barcelonas, and Parises; not that I do not think one little bit of sensitive human flesh is worth all the property rights in N. Y. city; not that I think the world will ever be saved by the sheep's virtue of going patiently to the shambles; not that I do not believe the expropriation of the possessing classes inevitable, and that that expropriation will begin by just such acts' EMMA GOLDMANN advised, viz: the taking possession of wealth already produced; not that I think you owe any consideration to the conspirators of Wall Street, or those who profit by their operations, as such nor ever will till they are reduced to the level of human beings having equal chances with you to earn their share of social wealth, and no more, not that I would have you forget the consideration they have shown to you; that they have advised lead for strikers, strychnine for tramps, bread and water as good enough for working people; not that I cannot hear yet in my ears the words of one who said to me of the Studebaker Wagon Works' strikers, "if I had my way I'd mow them down with gatling guns"; not that I would have you forget the electric wire of Ft. Frick, nor the Pinkertons, nor the militia, nor the prosecutions for murder and treason; not that I would have you forget the

4th of May, when your constitutional right of free speech was vindicated, nor the 11th of Nov. when it was assassinated; not that I would have you forget the single dinner at Delmonico's which Ward Mc.Allister tells us cost ten thousand dollars! Would I have you forget that the wine in the glasses was your children's blood? It must be a rare drink—children blood! I have read of the wonderful sparkle on costly champagne;—I have never seen it. If I did I think it would look to me like mother tears over the little, white, wasted forms of dead babies;—dead—because—there was no milk in their breasts! Yes, I want you to remember that these rich are blood-drinkers, tearers of human flesh, gnawers of human bones! Yes, if I had the power I would burn your wrongs upon your hearts in characters that should glow like live coals in the night!

I have not a tongue of fire as EMMA GOLDMANN has; I cannot "stir the people"; I must speak in my own cold, calculated way. (Perhaps that is the reason I am let to speak at all.) But if I had the power my will is good enough. You know how Shakespeare's Marc Antony addressed the populace of Rome:

> "I am no orator, as Brutus is,
> But as you know me all, a plain blunt man
> That love my friend. And that they know full well
> That gave me public leave to speak of him.
> For I have neither wit, nor words, nor worth,
> Action, nor utterance, nor the power of speech
> To stir men's blood. I only speak right on.
> I tell you that which you yourselves do know,
> Show you sweet Caesar's wounds, poor, poor dumb mouths,
> And bid them speak for me. But were I Brutus
> And Brutus Antony, there were an Antony
> Would ruffle up your spirits, and put a tongue
> In every wound of Caesar's, that should move
> The stones of Rome to rise and mutiny."

If, therefore, I do not give you the advice which EMMA GOLDMANN gave, let not the authorities suppose it is because I have any more respect for their constitution and their law than she has, or that I regard them as having any rights in the matter.

No. My reasons for not giving that advice are two. First, if I were giving advice at all, I would say: "My friends, that bread belongs to you. It is you who toiled and sweat in the sun to sow and reap the wheat; it is you who stood by the thresher, and breathed the chaff-filled atmosphere in the mills, while it was ground to flour; it is you who went into the eternal night of the mine and risked drowning, fire-damp, explosion, and cave-in, to get the fuel for the fire that baked it; it is you who stood in the hell-like heat, and struck the blows that forged the iron for the ovens wherein it is baked; it is you who stand all night in the terrible cellar shops, and tend the machines that knead the flour into dough; it is you, you, you, farmer, miner, mechanic, who make the bread; but you haven't the power to take it. At every transformation wrought by toil some one who didn't toil has taken part from you; and now he has it all, and you haven't the power to take it back! You are told you have the power be-cause you have the numbers. Never make so silly a blunder as to suppose that power resides in numbers. One good, level-headed policeman with a club, is worth ten excited, unarmed men; one detachment of well-drilled militia has a power equal to that of the greatest mob that could be raised in New York City. Do you know I admire compact, concentrated power. Let me give you an illustration. Out in a little town in Illinois there is a certain capitalist, and if ever a human creature sweat and ground the grist of gold from the muscle of man, it is he. Well, once upon a time, his workmen, (not his slaves, his workmen,) were on strike; and fifteen hun-dred muscular Polacks armed with stones, brickbats, red hot pokers, and other such crude weapons as a mob generally collects, went up to his house for the purpose of smashing the windows, and so forth; possibly to do as those people in Italy did the other day with the sheriff who at-tempted to collect the milk tax. He alone, one man, met them on the steps of his porch, and for two mortal hours, by threats, promises, cajoler-ies, held those fifteen hundred Poles at bay. And finally they went away, without smashing a pane of glass or harming a hair of his head. Now that was power! And you can't help but admire it, no matter if it was your enemy who displayed it; and you must admit that so long as numbers can be overcome by such relative quantity, power does not reside in numbers. Therefore, if I were giving advice, I would not say, "take bread," but take counsel with yourselves how to get the power to take bread.

There is no doubt but that power is latently in you; there is little doubt it can be developed; there is no doubt the authorities know this, and fear it, and are ready to exert as much force as is necessary to repress any signs of its development. And this is the explanation of EMMA GOLDMANN'S imprisonment. The authorities do not fear you as you are, they only fear what you may become. The dangerous thing was "the voice crying in the wilderness" foretelling the power which was to come after it. You should have seen how they feared it in Phila. They got out a whole platoon of police and detectives, and executed a military maneuver to catch the little woman who had been running around under their noses for three days. And when she walked up to them, why then, they surrounded and captured her, and guarded the city hall where they kept her over night, and put a detective in the next cell to make notes. Why so much fear? Did they shrink from the stab of the dressmaker's needle? Or did they dread some stronger weapon?

Ah!—the accusation before the New York Pontius Pilate was: "she stirreth up the people." And Pilate sentenced her to the full limit of the law, because, he said, "you are more than ordinarily intelligent." Why is intelligence dealt thus hardly with? Because it is the beginning of power. Strive, then, for power.

My second reason for not repeating EMMA GOLDMANN's words is, that I, as an anarchist, have no right to advise another to do anything involving a risk to himself; nor would I give a fillip for an action done by the advice of some one else, unless it is accompanied by a well-argued, well-settled conviction on the part of the person acting, that it really is the best thing to do. Anarchism, to me, means not only the denial of authority, not only a new economy, but a revision of the principles of morality. It means the development of the individual as well as the assertion of the individual. It means self-responsibility, and not leader worship. I say it is your business to decide whether you will starve and freeze in sight of food and clothing, outside of jail, or commit some overt act against the institution of property and take your place beside TIMMERMANN and GOLDMANN. And in saying this I mean to cast no reflection whatever upon Miss Goldmann for doing otherwise. She and I hold many differing views on both Economy and Morals; and that she is honest in hers she has proven better than I have proven mine. Miss Goldmann is a communist; I am an individualist. She wishes to destroy the right of property, I wish to assert it. I make my war upon privilege and authority, whereby the right of property, the true right in that which is proper to the individual, is annihilated. She believes that co-operation would entirely supplant competition; I hold that competition in one form or another will always exist, and that it is highly desirable it should. But whether she or I be right, or both of us be wrong, of one thing I am sure; the spirit which animates EMMA GOLDMAN is the only one which will emancipate the slave from his slavery, the tyrant from his tyranny—the spirit which is willing to dare and suffer.

That which dwells in the frail body in the prison-room to-night is not the New York dressmaker alone. Transport yourselves there in thought a moment; look steadily into those fair, blue eyes, upon the sun-brown hair, the sea-shell face, the restless hands, the woman's figure, look steadily till these fade from sight, as things will fade when gazed long upon, look steadily till in place of the person, the individual of time and place, you see that which transcends time and place, and flits from house to house of Life, mocking at Death. Swinburne in his magnificent "Before a Crucifix" says:

> "With iron for thy linen bands,
> And unclean cloths for winding-sheet,
> They bind the people's nail-pierced hands,
> They hide the people's nail-pierced feet:
> And what man, or what angel known
> Shall roll back the sepulchral stone?"

Perhaps in the presence of this untrammeled spirit we shall feel that something has rolled back the sepulchral stone; and up from the cold wind of the grave is borne the breath that animated ANAXAGORAS, SOCRATES, CHRIST, HYPATIA, JOHN HUSS, BRUNO, ROBERT EMMET, JOHN BROWN, SOPHIA PEROVSKAYA, PARSONS, FISCHER, ENGEL, SPIES, LINGG, BERKMANN, PALLAS; and all those, known and unknown, who have died by tree, and axe, and fagot, or dragged out forgotten lives in dungeons, derided, hated, tortured by men. Perhaps we shall know ourselves face to face with that which leaps from the throat of the strangled when the rope chokes, which smokes up from the blood of the murdered when the axe falls; that which has been forever hunted, fettered, imprisoned, exiled, executed, and never conquered. Lo, from its many incarnations it comes forth again, the immortal Race-Christ of the Ages! The gloomy walls are glorified thereby, the prisoner is transfigured: And we say, reverently we say:

> "O sacred Head, O desecrate,
> O labor-wounded feet and hands,
> O blood poured forth in pledge to fate
> Of nameless lives in divers lands!
> O slain, and spent, and sacrificed
> People! The gray-grown, speechless Christ."

14

Emma Goldman

The Case for Anarcho-Feminism

Marsha Hewitt

"Goldman's feminist insights deepened and enriched anarchist thought because she tried to show interdependence of collective social transformation and the inner psychological, mental, and spiritual liberation of individuals. It is this legacy that anarcho-feminists must develop further and build upon."

In her essay Hewitt considers the consequences of linking anarchism and feminism. She argues that separating the two is a mistake both theoretically and politically, a position she attributes to Goldman as well.—*The Editors*

Feminists are still divided on the question of separation, which, simply put, is the dilemma of whether to forge links with other emancipatory movements for social change.

Many feminists insist that the struggle for the liberation of women will be compromised if women participate in organizations and movements in which men are involved. As one libertarian feminist of my acquaintance recently put it: "Feminists have little to gain directly from the anarchists . . . in fact . . . anarchism has much to learn from the feminist movement . . . it is crucial that women work together alone and that men form their own all-men's groups."

This is a point of view with which I have some sympathy. My own experience in working with men on various political projects has been that no matter how understanding of feminist issues and arguments they may be, most men do harbour some degree of sexism. Not even women can entirely escape a sexist culture. Women, like men, are socialized by the same historical and cultural process, although women experience a specific form and sometimes a greater degree of social injustice. It would be both foolish and erroneous to say that women have not themselves internalized various sexist attitudes toward both other women and men. There is a strain in feminist thinking, for example, that tends to identify the male with nature and thus sees the world in terms of the false dichotomies of 'phallocentricity' as opposeed to 'gynocentricity.'

We must recognize that women are and always have been active participants in history, whether or not this fact has been acknowledged; women have been *at the centre* of the historical process and culture. Our consciousness has been shaped in ways similar to that of males, so that we too live and experience alienation; we too think in terms of antagonistic duality. This does not mean to say, however, that women or men are devoid of the capacity for critical self-consciousness or the ability to recognize alienation and oppression, and that they cannot attempt to overcome this existential situation.

It is not a pleasant experience to run up against sexism in the attitudes and behaviour of one's comrades. The frustration and disappointment that result can well lead women to the conclusion that their only option is to get out of groups which include men and form their own separatist organizations. But although it is tempting as a short-term solution to anger and frustration, the separatist option is a mistake, on the level of both theory and praxis. A sectarian politics based on gender, or on *anything else*, can too easily become a politics of paranoia, and as such stands in danger of being marginalized and irrelevant. Instead, I must agree with the point of view expressed in the Anarcho-Feminist Manifesto of ANORG (the Anarchist Federation of Norway) which reads, in part: "A serious anarchism must also be feminist, otherwise it is a question of patriarchal half-anarchism, and not real anarchism. It is the task of the anarcho-feminists to secure the feminist feature in anarchism. There will be no anarchism without feminism."

I would add to this statement by asserting that there will be no real, effective feminism without anarchism. Emma Goldman would agree. It was her conviction that feminism could not develop an adequate theory and praxis of liberation in isolation from the larger struggle for human liberation. Alice Wexler, in her biography, *Emma Goldman: An Intimate Life*, quotes Goldman: "My quarrel with the feminists . . . was that most of them see their slavery apart from the rest of the human family."[1] Goldman believed that "regardless of all artificial boundary lines between woman's rights and man's rights . . . there is a point where these differentiations may meet and grow into one perfect whole."[2] The danger of feminism as a single-issue politics oriented strictly to the emancipation of women, is, of course, social and political reformism; as Goldman herself saw in her critique of the women's suffrage movement, women achieving the vote does nothing to challenge the prevailing political system—it merely strengthens it. Liberation presupposes the radical transformation of the entire political, economic, and social order. And while this ultimate goal may be impossible, we must think and act according to this *necessarily* utopian ideal. It is a question of living creatively, of creative fictions, necessary fictions that are not divorced from the realm of rational possibility.

According to Alice Wexler, Goldman "gave a feminist dimension to anarchism and a libertarian dimension to the concept of women's emancipation."[3] She did so by insisting that anarchists acknowledge the political nature of sex, by recognizing that women's complete sexual and reproductive freedom is absolutely central to women's emancipation. This is an insight which cannot be over-emphasized in any discussion of feminism *or* anarchism, because an analysis of the politics of sexuality will further reveal the interconnected complexity of human experience, in terms of thought, feeling and action: we are now required to think feelingly. This forces us to re-think the nature of revolution as *process*, as transformative praxis of thought, feeling and collective social activity.

In making the link between sexual liberation and human liberation, Goldman saw power through hierarchy and domination as extending beyond economic structures and social institutions. It is the task of contemporary anarcho-feminists to develop this analysis. An awareness of domination as an internal, mental construct that reflects the structures of consciousness is crucial to contemporary anarchist thought. According to Murray Bookchin, "Hierarchy is not merely a social condition; it is also a state of consciousness, a sensibility toward phenomena at every level of personal and social experience."[4] Anarchism is and must be much more than a critical analysis of social structures and organizations of domination; its challenge goes far beyond opposition to the State. Anarchist theory recognizes the power of ideas to change material conditions, and the "primacy of consciousness in shaping the conditions of life."[5] As such, thought and language—the means by which we interpret and communicate our experience of the world—is praxis as much as it is social activity. Goldman rejected the determinant nature of the role of economics in social structures and personal relations. According to Wexler, she went even farther than her anarchist contemporaries in her insistence that "The key to the anarchist revolution was a revolution in morality,

314 Political Change: Theory and Practice

the 'transvaluation of all values,' a conquest of the 'phantoms' that have held people captive."[6] This, of course, explains Goldman's interest in culture, art, and literature, as well as her regard for the power and influence of the individual, however problematic at times her views on this latter point may have been.

What Goldman understood as well was the necessity of transforming the very manner in which we think, although she confined herself mostly to discussions of social mores and attitudes. But her insistence on the centrality of sexuality, and its potentially creative energy as a positive force in the process of individual and social transformation, helped break new ground for later developments in anarchism and feminism which have in turn helped foster a deeper understanding of the relationship between theory and praxis. This is an area which is in need of further exploration: that theory (by which I mean critical thinking) *is* praxis, and praxis *is* theory. Thus the revolutionary process must by necessity take place within the mind as well as in society, or no liberatory, transformative change is possible. It cannot be overemphasized that I am not referring simply to 'correct' ideas or 'right' ideology, because a fixed ideology is a closed system, and is thus inherently authoritarian. Critical thinking must always be open and changing within the historical process. At this point I want to make it perfectly clear that feminism is as much a critical theory, a theory of knowledge—a rationality critique, but *not* an alternative rationality, as some feminists would argue—as it is a practical, social movement.

If we restrict our theory/praxis dialectic to the social and economic sphere, we fall into the trap of reification, where 'the revolution' is understood to take place at a specific point in history, after which heaven is established on earth in the form of concrete/concretized bureaucracies and institutions of the post-revolutionary order. This results in an 'October Revolution' that produces reified socialism; a process is replaced with dead institutional forms and new hierarchies of domination. Critical self-consciousness disappears, it becomes anathema, and thus with it comes the obliteration of the historical subject—human beings. The locus of change, of praxis, of the dialectic itself* which is human beings as historical agents, dissolves into new (old) mechanisms of control and authoritarianism, inevitably.

This is Emma Goldman's most important contribution to anarcho-feminism, which contemporary anarcho-feminists must further develop, and that is the importance of the transformative power of ideas, and the necessity to live the revolution in our daily lives, including our most intimate personal relationships. What I wish to explore a little further here is the concept of thought as revolutionary praxis. Here it is appropriate to quote Gajo Petrović, a Yugoslav Marxist who was a member of the journal *Praxis*: "An interpretation of the world that does not change the world is both logically and empirically impossible. When man [*sic*] interprets the world, by this very fact he changes at least his conception of the world. In changing his conception of the world he cannot help changing his relationship to the world as well. And in changing his conception and his behaviour, he influences the conception and actions of other people with whom he is in different relationships . . . Is he . . . outside the world when he thinks and interprets the world?"[7]

Thought is not just passive reflection on completed action; what Petrović says about thought as praxis and the relationship between consciousness and action is important to both feminism and anarchism, because in challenging the rigid dislocations of private and public, subject and object, thought and action, male and female, humanity and nature, this critique attempts to address the nature of epistemological alienation. How we live and experience our most intimate relationships with others, how we live out our daily lives and how we *think* our lives and about our lives is in itself part of the ongoing revolutionary process.

To return to the theme of sexual liberation and its role in the revolutionary process, Goldman very clearly saw the destructive and oppressive impact of the institutionalization of female sexuality in the structure of marriage, and its implications for the social restriction of women: "As always, [Goldman] especially stressed the repressiveness of marriage, both as an 'economic arrangement, an insurance pact,' and as 'a safety valve against the pernicious sex-awakening of woman.' Was anything more outrageous, she would ask, 'than the idea that the healthy, grown woman, full of life and passion, must deny nature's demand, must subdue her most intense craving, undermine her health and break her spirit, must stunt her vision, abstain from the depth and glory of sex experience until a 'good' man comes along to take her unto himself as a wife? This is precisely what marriage means."[8]

Here I want to say a brief word on the question of marriage and monogamy. I do not wish to argue that marriage and monogamy are synonymous, although they are often so identified. The left must rethink the values which it used to denounce as 'traditional'—values of family, monogamy, and committed relationships. The sexual revolution did its share to reduce sexuality to technical experimentation for its own sake, and so contributed to the concept of sexuality not as a shared, meaningful experience between people, but as a commodity exchange. And women suffered a great deal of exploitation during the 'sexual revolution' of the 1960s and early '70s, partly because they, too, bought into this particular ideology. The left must begin to see that 'traditional' values such as monogamy can be oppressive or be emancipatory. It is vital that a new analysis be constructed of sexual ethics and values, because today the 'New Right' has stepped into the breach and is dominating the discourse on 'traditional' values with a popular positive response. Certainly, Emma Goldman understood very well the contradictions of interpersonal relationships, the contradiction and tension between the principle of 'varietism' and the agonizing experience of sexual jealousy and the deep desire to form exclusive sexual relationships, as her correspondence with Ben Reitman clearly shows. However, we cannot afford to dismiss these contradictions. We must begin to analyze them with dignity and humanity.

In the traditional marriage arrangement, with all its legal and social sanctions and its sexual division of labour, women are deprived of autonomy and the opportunity for growth. But the most insidious form of oppression of women was the internalization of those restrictions imposed by society and marriage which undermined women's capacity to think about real alternatives to their condition. Goldman saw, and rightly so, that women's liberation was not to be realized in external, material improvements, although these are obviously important; the key to the liberation of women must begin with their 'inner regeneration,' with their willingness to "cut loose from the weight of prejudices, traditions and customs. True emancipation, [Goldman] argued, began not at the polls or in court, but in woman's soul."[9]

Goldman's feminist insights deepened and enriched anarchist thought because she tried to show interdependence of collective social transformation and the inner psychological, mental, and spiritual liberation of individuals. It is this legacy that anarcho-feminists must develop further and build upon.

The feminist vision *is* a libertarian vision, as Peggy Kornegger has written: "Feminists have been unconscious anarchists in both theory and practice for years."[10] The most important link between feminism and anarchism is a common recognition of the need to transform the power structures and social relations of hierarchy and domination. Anarchism helps feminism to address the problem of power, to understand its destructive dynamics, and to pose alternative forms of organization. The feminist practice of 'networking,' for example, has much in common with anarchist forms of organization, particularly affinity groups and federated organizations. Perhaps eco-feminist thinking has begun to develop an-archo-feminism in ways that attempt to show the integral connections between ecology and feminism. The eco-feminist perspective views life "on earth as an interconnected web, not a hierarchy. There *is* no natural hierarchy; human hierarchy is projected onto nature and then used to justify social domination."[11] The abuse of power through hierarchy and domination is a human construct which we are socialized to accept and reproduce in all aspects of social life, from personal relations to social institutions. Anarcho-feminism understands very well the interconnect-edness of oppressive social institutions and personal relations, as is re-flected in the paradigm of traditional marriage. Goldman saw the relationship between *enforced* monogamy and the "domestication and ownership" of women, which created a male monopoly of women's sexu-ality.

It seems to me that insights such as those which I have mentioned reveal the natural (in terms of inherent logical necessity) affinity between anarchism and feminism, on the level of both theory and practice. Femi-nists cannot operate in isolation either from men or from other emanci-patory social movements; we simply cannot afford to do so. "A feminist movement which is confined to the specific oppression of women cannot, in isolation, end exploitation. We have to keep struggling to go beyond our own situation."[12] It is also the special task of anarcho-feminism to draw out and reflect upon the interrelatedness of all forms of oppression, whose common root is domination. There is no liberation for anyone without the liberation of all. An anarcho-feminist analysis is able to show the interconnected roots of misogyny, imperialism, militarism, the arms race, and the attempt to obliterate nature, and therefore insists that the revolutionary project/process is a comprehensive, multidimensional proj-ect/process that is taking place now, in all areas of human experience. Domination is the source, focus and rationale of all hierarchy, be it rank, class, family, the State, or sex/gender.

Thus whatever our negative experiences may be in working with men in a common movement for a better society, it is important not only that we remain in that movement, but that we confront sexist behaviour and attitudes in our comrades at each point of encounter. As women, we are specially placed to do it, since our life experience as women has taught us an intimate lesson about the dynamics of power. In confronting our male comrades with this knowledge, we can only strengthen the movement, and with it, hopefully, but more problematically, our personal relationships.

Notes

1. Alice Wexler, *Emma Goldman: An Intimate Life* (New York: Pantheon Books, 1984), 197.

2. Emma Goldman, *Anarchism and Other Essays* (New York: Dover, 1969), 213.

3. Wexler, *Emma Goldman*, p. 277.

4. Murray Bookchin, *The Ecology of Freedom* (Palo Alto, Calif.: Cheshire Books, 1982), 4.

5. Wexler, *Emma Goldman*.

6. Ibid., 98.

*. What I mean here by 'dialectic' is the dialectic of negativity; that is, negation and transcendence in which we engage as beings of praxis. The structure of praxis is that of human negativity and creativity, or alienation and its transcendence. This is the essential nature of a critical and revolutionary dialectic, the locus of which is the human being.

7. Gerson S. Sher, *Praxis: Marxist Criticism and Dissent in Socialist Yugoslavia* (Bloomington: Indiana University Press, 1977), 104.

8. Wexler, *Emma Goldman*, 193.

9. Ibid., p. 195.

10. Carol Ehrlich, "The Unhappy Marriage of Marxism and Feminism: Can It Be Saved?" in *Women and Revolution*, ed. Lydia Sargent (Montréal: Black Rose Books, 1981), 114.

11. Ynestra King, "The Ecology of Feminism and the Feminism of Ecology," *Harbinger* 1, no. 2 (Fall 1983), 17.

12. Sheila Rowbotham, *Woman's Consciousness, Man's World* (Harmondsworth: Penguin, 1973), 123–24.

15

The Emma Goldman Clinic
Mission Statement

About Us:
The Emma Goldman Clinic

"She saw the misery that too many unplanned children brought to the poor. She dared to change the social situation of her day by giving lectures on available birth control methods and their use. By doing so she broke the law of that time and was arrested and jailed. She challenged the social values of her day and urged that people be given the knowledge and ability to plan births and space the arrival of children. In recognition of her challenging spirit, the clinic was named in her honor."

The Emma Goldman Clinic finds in Goldman's life and principles direct inspiration and clear direction. The programs of one are as wide ranging yet coherently connected as the political commitments of the other. The clinic is among the oldest organizations in a long list of institutions named for Goldman.—*The Editors*

> Woman's development, her freedom, her independence,
> must come from and through herself.

About Us

The Women's Health Project, Incorporated, is a not-for-profit organization whose purpose is to provide health services and education. The Women's Health Project, Incorporated, opened the Emma Goldman Clinic in September 1973, eight months after the U.S. Supreme Court declared that the right to choose an abortion is constitutionally guaranteed.

The Emma Goldman Clinic was the first outpatient abortion clinic in Iowa and the first women-owned and -operated health center in the Midwest. The clinic is staffed by women with a variety of educational and work experiences who receive extensive training when they join the staff. Along with other duties, clinic staff assist the physicians who perform the abortions.

In addition to her skills, each worker was hired because she holds both a pro-choice and a client-centered philosophy. We believe that every woman has a right to determine the outcome of her pregnancy regardless of her age, marital status, race, or income. You do not need parental or spousal consent to come to our clinic. However, the state of Iowa has imposed parental-notification restrictions for women under the age of eighteen seeking abortion services. Please call the clinic for additional information.

The Emma Goldman Clinic, the first women-owned and -operated health care center in the Midwest and the first outpatient abortion clinic in Iowa, was founded in September 1973 by a group of dedicated community women. Today it is one of the most highly regarded nonprofit health care facilities in the country.

As an early leader in the women's health movement, the Emma Goldman Clinic is pleased to see many traditional health care providers adjusting their health care services to address the multifaceted health care needs of women. We believe we played a critical role in bringing the awareness of these needs into more institutional medical settings. We also believe there is still work to be done. Women's health needs are expanding and evolving as our awareness increases. At Emma, rather than issue prepackaged chronologically dictated care for women, we listen to the knowledge each woman carries about her health, and work with her to support her own well-being.

Namesake

The clinic was named for Emma Goldman, a nurse, anarchist, and cultural lecturer. As a nurse she saw the misery that too many unplanned children brought to the poor. She dared to change the social situation of her day by giving lectures on available birth control methods and their use. By doing so she broke the law of that time and was arrested and jailed. She challenged the social values of her day and urged that people be given the knowledge and ability to plan births and space the arrival of children. In recognition of her challenging spirit, the clinic was named in her honor.

Mission Statement

The Emma Goldman Clinic is a not-for-profit organization founded and operated by women. We exist to empower women in all life stages through the provision of quality reproductive health care, active education, and the promotion of women's voices in public policy. We believe that controlling our bodies and health is integral to establishing the quality of our lives. We promote participatory health care, informed decision making, client rights, advocacy for women, and expansion and support of women's choices.

We acknowledge that oppression can be perpetuated on both the individual and institutional level. The Emma Goldman Clinic is committed to participating in the struggle to end all forms of oppression based on

- ableism
- ageism
- body size
- classism
- ethnic origin
- racism
- religion
- sexism
- sexual identity
- national origin

Institutionally, we strive to increase economic, geographic, structural, and language accessibility for the women we serve. We are actively committed to staff diversity in employment policies and practices. We strive to provide an atmosphere in which diversity is acknowledged and celebrated.

We offer nonjudgmental quality health care services to all women. Our goals are inspired by our belief in the larger ideals of feminist philosophy: political, economic, and social equality.

Promoting Self-Health

Setting Standards for Care

We offer women comprehensive information about health issues and treatments, empowering them to make decisions for their own health care. Once a woman has experienced this type of care, we believe she will expect the same standard of care from all health care providers for herself, her friends, and her family. In this way, we help make all health care providers more responsive to the needs of their clients, and therefore elevate universal standards of care.

Self-Cervical and Self–Breast Exams

We promote regular self-exams as a tool for learning and monitoring what is normal and healthy. While this does not replace the need for routine exams from a health care provider, it is another way women can take responsibility for their own health.

Patient Rights

In our abortion and gynecology services we promote patient rights. This includes being totally informed of medical diagnosis, procedures, possible complications, and aftercare; medications and their side effects; the right to read and copy all medical records; the right to confidentiality; the right to have a patient advocate; the right, in short, to become an intelligent participant in your own health care by having all questions answered in a language you can understand.

Emma Goldman Clinic's position as a leader in the women's health movement is a legacy we strive to carry forward. This means advocating for women's health care needs from the exam room to Capitol Hill.

We acknowledge that women are capable of understanding and evaluating information about their own bodies and health. Women belong at the center of decision making for their health care. For this reason, we strive to promote clients rights through all our services. These rights include

- complete and accurate information about diagnosis, procedures, and possible complications
- information about medications and side effects
- access to all medical records
- confidentiality
- a patient advocate or support person
- nonjudgmental health care

Every woman has the right to become an informed participant in her own health care. We want women to be empowered by the information they gain and through the choices they make.

Challenging Medical Practices

Breast Implants

The clinic assisted a client through the maze of medical transport regulations so her biomedical tissue could be entered as evidence in a class-action lawsuit against breast implant manufacturers.

Norplant

When Norplant was released as the latest and greatest method of birth control, the clinic made the decision not to offer Norplant to our clients. The reason for this decision was twofold. First, enough research had not been done on its side effects and removal. Second, some legislators and law enforcement officials proposed uses of Norplant that had the potential of mandating birth control in a way that would disproportionately affect young women, low-income women, and women of color. The clinic is opposed to legislated birth control and was unwilling to participate in oppression through coercive birth control tactics.

Lobbying

Legislators and Regulatory Boards

We work with elected officials and regulatory board representatives at every governmental level to ensure the fair and equitable treatment of women in health care policy.

Affiliations

The Emma Goldman Clinic works very closely with other health care providers throughout the region. We are also affiliated with a number of national public policy organizations, including the National Abortion Federation (NAF), National Abortion Rights Action League (NARAL), and National Coalition of Abortion Providers (NCAP). Our work with these organizations helps us stay informed and to effectively direct our advocacy efforts.

Access

The clinic seeks to improve the ability of women to make choices for themselves. Beyond the right to legal abortion, choice depends on access and affordability of services. Every day we provide services for women from all over Iowa and neighboring states. For many women, finding the funds for services is a tremendous obstacle. A woman's ability to pay is often limited by low income, no credit, a dangerous home situation, or the inability to use family insurance.

The Emma Goldman Clinic Access Project includes

- half-price gynecology services for teens
- discounted services for students
- free pregnancy testing and options counseling
- reduced-fee abortion services for women living on lower incomes
- additionally reduced fee abortion services for women on Title XIX
- services for victims of rape or incest

Bibliography

Goldman's Writings

Anarchism and Other Essays. 1969. Introduction by Richard Drinnon. New York: Dover.

Living My Life. 1970. 2 Vols. New York: Dover.

My Disillusionment in Russia. 1923. New York: Doubleday.

Nowhere at Home: Letters from Exile of Emma Goldman and Alexander Berkman. 1975. Edited by Richard Drinnon and Anna Maria Drinnon. New York: Schocken Books.

Red Emma Speaks. 1983. Edited by Alix Kates Shulman. New York: Schocken Books.

The Social Significance of the Modern Drama. 1914. Boston: Richard G. Badger.

Vision on Fire. 1983. Edited and with introductions by David Porter. New Paltz, N.Y.: Commonground Press.

Additional Books

Brown, L. Susan. 2003. *The Politics of Individualism: Liberalism, Liberal Feminism, and Anarchism*. Montreal: Black Rose Books.

Dark Star Collective, ed. 2002. *Quiet Rumours: An Anarcha-Feminist Reader*. Introduction by Roxanne Dunbar-Ortiz. Edinburgh: AK Press.

Farrow, Lynne. 1988. *Feminism as Anarchism*. Montreal: BOA.

Haaland, Bonnie. *Emma Goldman: Sexuality and the Impurity of the State*. Montreal: Black Rose Books.

Roussopoulos, Dimitrios I. 2000. *The Anarchist Papers*. Montreal: Black Rose Books.

Additional Articles

Cook, Blanche Wiesen. 1977. "Female Support Networks and Political Activism: Lillian Wald, Crystal Eastman, Emma Goldman." *Chrysalis* 3:43–61.

Goldberg, Harold J. 1975. "Goldman and Berkman View the Bolshevik Regime." *Slavonic and East European Review* 34 (April): 272–76.

Poirier, Suzanne. 1988. "Emma Goldman, Ben Reitman, and Reitman's Wives: A Study in Relationships." *Women's Studies* 14 (Summer): 227–98.

Wexler, Alice. 1982. "Emma Goldman in Love." *Raritan: A Quarterly Review* 1 (Summer): 116–45.

Miscellaneous

Barko, Naomi. 1982. "The Emma Goldman You'll Never See in the Movies." *Ms.*, March.

Canadian Broadcasting Corporation. 1983. "Emma Goldman: A Life of Anarchy." Toronto.

Contributors

MARTHA A. ACKELSBERG is professor of government and women's studies at Smith College. Her research and teaching focus on feminist theory, democratic theory, urban politics, and social movements. She has published numerous articles on aspects of women in/and Spanish anarchism, on contemporary women's community-based activism, and on feminist/democratic theory. A revised version of *Free Women of Spain: Anarchism and the Struggle for the Liberation of Women* is forthcoming. She is currently at work on a book that looks at the programs of the National Congress of Neighborhood Women that deal with difference and diversity. The study will explore the ways they provide interesting models for us to think anew both about leadership in democratic communities and organizations and about how to acknowledge ethnic, racial, and class differences without reimposing inequalities.

KATHRYN PYNE ADDELSON is Mary Huggins Gamble Professor of Philosophy at Smith College and teaches in the Program in the History of the Sciences. She is the author of *Impure Thoughts: Essays on Philosophy, Feminism, and Ethics* and *Moral Passages: Toward a Collectivist Moral Theory*. She is also co-founder of the Center for Mutual Learning at Smith.

LYNNE M. ADRIAN is an associate professor of American studies at the University of Alabama in Tuscaloosa. She holds a B.A. from DePaul University, Chicago, in social sciences; her M.A. from the University of Minnesota and Ph.D. from the University of Iowa are both in American studies. Her research interests are late nineteenth- to early twentieth-century social and intellectual history, American women, and the scholarship of teaching and learning in interdisciplinary studies.

BERENICE A. CARROLL is professor of political science and women's studies at Purdue University and professor emerita at the University of Illinois at Urbana-Champaign. Her books and articles include *Design for Total War: Arms and Economics in the Third Reich*; *Liberating Women's History: Theoretical and Critical Essays*; *Women's Political and Social Thought: An Anthology* (coedited with Hilda L. Smith); "The Politics of 'Originality': Women and the Class System of the Intellect"; and "Christine de Pizan and the Origins of Peace Theory." She has served in numerous professional and activist capacities, including as past president of the National Women's Studies Association. Carroll has received numerous awards, among them, in 1997, the lifetime Service Award from the Consortium on Peace Research.

JANET E. DAY is an assistant professor at the State University of New York, Oneonta. Her research interests include analyzing the linkage between how a given theorist understands the individual, the individual's relations with others, and social and political organization. She received her B.A. from Kalamazoo College and her Ph.D. in political science from Purdue University, where she wrote her dissertation on Ayn Rand and Emma Goldman.

VOLTAIRINE DE CLEYRE (1866–1912) was described by Goldman as "the most gifted and brilliant anarchist woman America ever produced." Among the writings of this freethinker, pacifist, anarchist, and feminist, are "Anarchism and American Traditions," "Direct Action," "The Economic Tendency of Freethought," "Selected Poems," and "The Gods and the People." *Selected Works of Voltairine de Cleyre* was printed in 1914 by Mother Earth; *Selected Works of Voltairine de Cleyre, Pioneer of Women's Liberation* was published by Revisionist Press in 1972; and *Exquisite Rebel: The Essays of Voltairine de Cleyre*, edited by Sharon Presley and Crispin Sartwell, was published by the State University of New York Press in 2004.

THE EMMA GOLDMAN CLINIC is a feminist nonprofit health care facility located in Iowa City, Iowa. Services include abortion, gynecology, a donation-based walk-in clinic, massage therapy, reproductive health care education, and advocacy. Services are offered from a client-centered, nonjudgmental, respectful approach. The clinic collaborates extensively with national, state, and local sister organizations to work toward eliminating oppression and to ensure that people have a voice in the public policy surrounding reproductive health care issues. These goals are inspired by the belief in the larger ideals of feminist philosophy: political, economic, and social equality. The clinic can be contacted via its Web site at www.emmagoldman.com. A booklet of their history, *The Emma Goldman Clinic: Celebrating Thirty Years*, is available.

CANDACE FALK received her Ph.D. in political theory from the History of Consciousness at University of California, Santa Cruz. She initiated the Emma Goldman Papers and has served as its editor/director since 1980. Her book *Love, Anarchy, and Emma Goldman* was cited by the *New York Times* as among the Notable Biographies of 1984. In collaboration with editors at the Emma Goldman Papers, she has published a twenty-thousand-document microfilm edition of Goldman's letters and manuscripts and government documents, trial transcripts, and selected newspaper reportage on Goldman and her circle. The companion guide, *Emma Goldman: A Guide to Her Life and Documentary Sources*, won the 1995 Kanner Prize for the Best Bibliographic Work in Women and/or Gender History. In 1998, she received a Guggenheim Fellowship for a work, still in progress, of reflections on more than twenty-five years of concentrated editorial engagement with Emma Goldman. Falk is working with her colleagues at the project on a four-volume edition of selected papers, *Emma Goldman: A Documentary History of the American Years, 1890–1919*. Volume 1, *Made for America, 1890–1901* (2003), and volume 2, *Making Speech Free* (2005) have been released.

KATHY E. FERGUSON is director of women's studies and professor of political science at the University of Hawai'i. She is the author of numerous books and essays, including

Oh, Say, Can You See? The Semiotics of the Military in Hawai'i (with Phyllis Turnbull); *Kibbutz Journal: Reflections on Gender, Race, and Militarism in Israel*; *The Man Question: Visions of Subjectivity in Feminist Theory*; and *The Feminist Case Against Bureaucracy*. She was honored with a Fulbright appointment at Ben Gurion University and has taught in Austria and Sweden. She is currently writing a book on Emma Goldman as a political thinker.

MARSHA HEWITT is professor of social ethics and religion at Trinity College at the University of Toronto. Her areas of teaching, research, and writing include critical theory, feminist theory, psychoanalysis, and religion. She is the author of a number of articles and books, including *Critical Theory of Religion: A Feminist Analysis*. Her current research interests are in the areas of religion and violence and critical theory and in psychoanalysis and democracy. In addition to teaching and writing, Professor Hewitt is a psychoanalyst in private practice in Toronto.

LORETTA KENSINGER is associate professor and coordinator of women's studies at California State University, Fresno. She first fell in love with Emma Goldman after reading "Marriage and Love" in her first feminist theory course (taught by Penny Weiss). Along with a reconsideration of Goldman's ideas, Kensinger's research interests and publications have included work on U.S. feminist analysis of Afghanistan, exclusions in traditional categories of feminist thought, and feminist pedagogy. She is committed to linking activism and theory and participates regularly in efforts to advance feminism, peace, labor, and diversity.

LORI JO MARSO is director of women's and gender studies and associate professor of political science at Union College in Schenectady, New York. She is author of *(Un)-Manly Citizens: Jean-Jacques Rousseau's and Germaine de Staël's Subversive Women* and coeditor of *Simone de Beauvoir's Political Thinking*. Her current book project, *Feminist Thinkers and the Demands of Femininity*, examines the lives and work of exemplary feminist thinkers (Mary Wollstonecraft, Germaine de Staël, Emma Goldman, and Simone de Beauvoir) to discuss the dilemmas of living and transforming norms of femininity.

JONATHAN MCKENZIE is a Ph.D. student in the Political Science department at Purdue University. His primary areas of interest are contemporary political thought and environmental politics.

ALIX KATES SHULMAN left her native Cleveland, Ohio, at twenty for New York's Greenwich Village, seeking a freer place to spend the 1950s. Along with *Red Emma Speaks: An Emma Goldman Reader*, she has written eleven books, including novels, memoirs, books for children, and numerous short stories and essays. Her debut novel, *Memoirs of an Ex-Prom Queen*, was called by the *Oxford Companion to Women's Writing* "the first important novel to emerge from the Women's Liberation Movement." Among her other awards, Shulman has received a National Endowment for the Arts Fellowship in fiction and was visiting artist at the American Academy in Rome. She spends part of the year in New York City with her partner of eighteen years and part alone on an island off the coast of Maine, writing on a solar-powered laptop and foraging for food.

CRAIG STALBAUM is a Ph.D. student at Purdue University. He is interested in the intersections of international politics and gender, as well as the evolving (or devolving) pop culture consciousness of both.

JASON WEHLING is a freelance Internet writer. Among his essays that attract much attention are "Netwars: Activists Power the Internet," "Zapatismo: What the EZLN is Fighting For," and "Anarchism and the History of the Black Flag."

PENNY A. WEISS is associate professor of political science at Purdue University. She is author of *Gendered Community: Rousseau, Sex and Politics* and *Conversations with Feminism: Political Theory and Practice* and coeditor (with Marilyn Friedman) of *Feminism and Community*. The end is in sight for her next book, *Canon Fodder: Historical Women Political Thinkers*, which includes work on Christine de Pizan, Mary Wollstonecraft, Sei Shonagon, Anna Julia Cooper, Virginia Woolf, and Mary Astell, among others. She is considering whether or how to bring her work with children (biological and foster, in the classroom and on the soccer field) into more conversation with the academic world.

ALICE WEXLER received a Ph.D. in Latin American history from Indiana University and gradually became interested in U.S. women's history, a field that was just developing in the 1970s. She taught for ten years at Sonoma State University before deciding to become a full-time writer. She continues to teach part time at various universities and serves as a research scholar at the University of California, Los Angeles, Center for the Study of Women. Since the early 1980s Wexler has been actively involved with the Huntington's disease community, primarily as a trustee of the Hereditary Disease Foundation. Her books include *Mapping Fate: A Memoir of Family, Risk, and Genetic Research* and *Emma Goldman in Exile*. She was a former Fulbright Fellow in Venezuela and has been awarded fellowships from the National Endowment for the Humanities and the American Council of Learned Societies.

Index

Lightning Source UK Ltd.
Milton Keynes UK
UKHW011853150320
360352UK00011B/60